THE LION, THE FOX & THE EAGLE

THE LION, THE FOX & THE EAGLE

A Story of Generals and Justice
in Yugoslavia and Rwanda

Carol Off

Random House Canada

Canadian Cataloguing in Publication Data

Off, Carol
    The lion, the fox and the eagle : a story of generals and justice in Rwanda and Yugoslavia

Includes index.
ISBN 0-679-31049-5

1. MacKenzie, Lewis, 1940- . 2. Dallaire, Romeo A. 3. Arbour, Louise, 1947- .
4. United Nations – Peacekeeping forces – Rwanda. 5. United Nations –
Peacekeeping forces – Bosnia and Herzegovina. 6. Rwanda – History – Civil War,
1994 – Atrocities. 7. Yugoslav War, 1991-1995 – Atrocities. 8. War crime trials –
Rwanda. 9. War crime trials – Yugoslavia. I. Title.

JZ6374.O33 2000   341.5′84′094974209049   C00-931170-X

Jacket and text design: James Ireland Design Inc.

Visit Random House of Canada Limited's Web site: www.randomhouse.ca

Printed and bound in Canada

10 9 8 7 6 5 4 3 2 1

This book is dedicated to the memory of Yvan Patrie

February 22, 1948 to October 14, 1999

"The United Nations was created
to prevent you from going to hell;
not to take you to heaven."
— *Henry Cabot Lodge, Jr.*

"You can safely appeal to the United Nations
in the comfortable certainty that it will let you down."
— *Conor Cruise O'Brien*

CONTENTS

INTRODUCTION

This is a story about right and wrong, and about people who can, and cannot, tell the difference between the two. The villain is not a person so much as a giant bureaucracy, the United Nations, which was founded to create a more civilized world but has instead created a sophisticated system of reasons why we cannot be more civilized.

The lion, the fox and the eagle symbolize three Canadians who played critical parts in the drama of the final decade of the twentieth century. All three were employed by the United Nations. They were not necessarily chosen for their missions because they are Canadians, but their nationality was a determining factor—the United Nations has come to depend on Canada for people the world believes it can trust. The three were required to rely on their personal moral compasses, since the UN had lost its own. They did so with varying degrees of success.

These characters—two generals and a judge—made decisions that affected the lives of millions. Unlike so many others at the UN, they did not act behind the scenes or in the diplomatic shadows, but were front and centre, openly stating their objectives and publicly influencing events. They became celebrities around the world, and all were decorated or honoured by their country for their perceived accomplishments. As a journalist, I was fascinated by all three; as a Canadian, I followed the events in which they were involved, and covered many of them with feelings of pride and admiration. But in this book, the characters that emerge are different from the ones we witnessed on the international stage. In some instances, their real acts of heroism have been obscured; in others, the heroism was never really there. I have come to see these stories as a Greek drama in three acts, each a test of human character in an impossibly difficult situation.

As Communist Europe collapsed in 1989, the world order went topsy-turvy. Nation-states braced themselves for the fallout, Canada not least among them. Canada likes to play an international role out of proportion to its place in the scheme of things, and it hoped to have a suitable part in the New World Order. As our neighbour to the south became the single superpower on the globe, Canada feared the immense influence it would wield. Our government has always supported global organizations as a counterweight to the influence of the United States, and in the 1990s that had never seemed more crucial.

The United Nations is the most important of all the institutions Canada uses as a conduit to the larger world. Lacking sway at the Security Council—the UN's powerful inner cabinet—Canada turns to other functions of the organization to find its sphere of influence. Chief among them is peacekeeping. Canadians are the world's pre-eminent peacekeepers, and Canada is the only country that has sent soldiers to every important mission since the UN first defined its peacekeeping role.

As the history books tell us, Canada invented peacekeeping. It was Lester B. Pearson, as secretary of state for foreign affairs, who stood in the United Nations in 1956 and proposed a solution to the tense standoff between France and Great Britain—our two colonial founders—over the Suez Canal: "While the political climate of the Middle East is maturing towards the time when conditions will be more appropriate for a comprehensive settlement, it is essential, I think, for the countries of the region, and indeed for us all, that there should be no return to the former state of strife and tension and conflict on the borders.... And this...might well require the continuing presence of a United Nations Force...."

The idea of a United Nations force became the prototype for all such missions in the future, and Pearson won a Nobel Peace Prize for his suggestion. The image of Canadians as international do-gooders is a part not just of the national mythology, but of Canadian foreign policy. Canada is one of only a handful of nations that include peacekeeping as a permanent part of their national defence, and no other country gives peacekeeping such a defining role in its international politics. It is in our genetic code as a nation.

The United Nations drew up the blueprint for how the world should react to future conflict through its defining charter of 1945 and more definitively through the Universal Declaration of Human Rights, drafted for the UN by McGill University Dean John Humphrey and passed three years later. The two documents between them are a proclamation that all people—from every nation—deserve the same security of person and fundamental rights. It's unlikely such a consensus on first principles would have been reached without the horrors of the Second World War and the Nazi Holocaust to prick the world's conscience. The overwhelming response to those catastrophes was "never again."

Pearson's call for a lightly armed force to intervene, peacefully, in global conflict is drawn from the imperatives of the UN charter. But peacekeeping is really an ad hoc, unofficial outcropping of the code—a way to physically step into the breach in a country's affairs to ensure the idea of "never again." As a term, peacekeeping is never mentioned, but Pearson derived the idea from the international responsibilities outlined in chapter six of the charter, entitled "Pacific Settlement of Disputes." Chapter six calls for the UN to intervene at the behest of "the parties to any dispute" and attempt to mediate a solution. The charter's chapter seven suggests flexing more muscle: "Action with respect to threats to the peace, breaches of the peace, and acts of aggression" calls upon signatories of the UN charter to get tough with countries that are destabilizing a region, or the world, through their acts of aggression. Increasingly, peacekeeping has become chapter seven material.

People who have been caught up in horrible conflicts generally feel a sense of relief when they see the Canadian peacekeepers arrive. That's certainly how they saw things in Rwanda when international soldiers landed in the capital, Kigali, under the leadership of Brigadier General Roméo Dallaire. The appearance of this confident Canadian, who was in complete control (it seemed) of the United Nations Assistance Mission in Rwanda (UNAMIR), dispelled the rumours of impending mass murder. A Rwandan woman named Odette Nyiramilimo told an American reporter, Philip Gourevitch, "Really, it was UNAMIR that tricked us into staying. We saw all those blue helmets, and we talked with Dallaire. We thought even if Hutus start to attack us, the three thousand men of UNAMIR should be enough. Dallaire gave us his phone number and his radio number and said: 'If anything happens, you call immediately.' So we trusted him."

It may seem naive to trust that much, but such is the power of the blue helmet around the world—a piece of apparel with the symbolic power of a halo. Despite incidents of soldiers running seriously amok, the reputation of the peacekeeper is as intact as it was in the days of Lester Pearson.

The lion in this narrative is Roméo Dallaire. He was an experienced officer at the peak of his career in the Canadian Department of National Defence when, in the summer of 1993, he was sent on what should have been a routine peacekeeping mission. Within ten months of Dallaire's arrival in Rwanda, 800,000 people were dead. These were not soldiers who fell in armed conflict, but civilians who were hacked to death and cut into pieces by fellow Rwandans. If people had known that the general could not resist the slaughter, they say they would have fled. And as testimony to that, families of murdered Rwandans have since attempted to sue Roméo Dallaire for failing to protect them.

The story, as it emerges, is complex. Dallaire sent a series of memos to UN peacekeeping command in New York City, warning his superiors of what was about to happen. The dire messages in those memos went unheeded. Some were not even passed on to the Security Council. As far as the UN Department of Peacekeeping Operations was concerned, it was enough for Dallaire to fulfil his role of monitoring a ceasefire. That was his mission. But Dallaire saw the horror coming down the rails like a speeding train, and he tried to recruit the UN in a bid to stop it. The fact that he created a workable plan that could have disarmed the aggressors and prevented one of the great tragedies of the past century is now only a movie that plays over and over in his head. His failure to do so, and the hell of watching the genocide of Tutsi and of Hutu moderates over a period of just one hundred days, has left him a broken man, haunted by his memories and nightmares.

The mythical image of the lion is also one of isolation and independence. Dallaire was eight thousand kilometres away from the UN and the people who made the choices that affected the lives of everyone in Rwanda. Undone by the moral vacuum of the Security Council, Dallaire took matters into his own hands as best he could. He was able to protect a group of about thirty thousand people who were targeted in the massacres. It took a lion's courage to personally face down genocidal killers, but Dallaire is also the lion because of the isolation in which he now lives for having failed to prevent the deaths of so many others.

I have attempted to put all the elements of Dallaire's extraordinary story together for the first time, and to describe his personal quest for the truth about the international failure in Rwanda. What emerges is a picture of a man who is in many ways the author of his fate: he made his own decisions, relying on his own moral core, and he now suffers the consequences.

The fox in this account is Major General Lewis MacKenzie, a man who had nearly thirty years of peacekeeping experience before he landed the job as sector commander in Sarajevo for the first months of the Bosnian war. MacKenzie ran a humanitarian mission whose task was to take over the city's airport and keep it open to relief workers and aid. In a few short weeks he became our most famous peacekeeper, celebrated as the embodiment of everything Canadians aspire to be on the international stage.

MacKenzie was a hero to me as much as to any other Canadian, in a country starved for heroes. He prided himself on telling it like it is, and the whole world listened to him because he was not an American speaking for the Pentagon but an independent voice. Only later, when I learned that the word "MacKenzie" had entered the Bosnian vocabulary as a pejorative term for peacekeeper, did it occur to me that there might be more to the story.

MacKenzie saw it as his responsibility to tell the world that it should not intervene militarily in what was—like Rwanda—a premeditated and extended act of terrorism on a civilian population. In Bosnia's case, the horror was crafted and executed by the regime of Slobodan Milosevic. Instead of demanding a mandate to stop the acts of ethnic cleansing by a rogue state calling itself the Republika Srpska, MacKenzie encouraged the UN to do what it was already disposed to do: nothing.

After he was forced to leave Bosnia, fearing for his life, MacKenzie toured the Western world, warning governments not to get involved in an ugly ethnic war unworthy of the death of peacekeepers. He urged foreign governments not to use force or air strikes to stop the conflict in the Balkans. He insisted that the people he had been sent to help were simply members of clans bent on killing each other in a blood feud that went back centuries. His punchline? "Dealing with Bosnia is a bit like dealing with three serial killers: one has killed fifteen, the other ten and the other five. Do you help the one who has killed five?"

Opening the Sarajevo airport was a brave and dramatic accomplishment: peacekeepers, pilots and aid workers risked their lives daily to bring food and medicine into Bosnia. But it also became an excuse for not intervening to stop the slaughter. The people of Sarajevo were considered ungrateful for not recognizing the superhuman effort of foreign aid workers, and for insisting instead on NATO air strikes. Looking back, it is now clear that such air strikes were needed to end the war—which they did—three years later, after 200,000 people had died.

Two Canadian generals witnessed genocide and ethnic cleansing in two countries. One general attempted to stop the slaughter in Rwanda by warning the United Nations that the horrors were about to begin. The other general told the UN, and the international community, that there was little anyone could do to deter the violent people of Bosnia from killing each other. These were two generals from the same country and the same peacekeeping tradition, but with wholly different attitudes; for both, the results were the same — the United Nations did not act, and innocent people perished.

The failure of these crucial peacekeeping missions in Bosnia and Rwanda left a blight on the United Nations and its Department of Peacekeeping Operations, and seriously put in question just what on earth this institution was good for. The UN struggled to save its reputation and prove that the slogan "Never Again" was not just a bumper sticker but a real commitment. And so, in the fall of 1993, it established the International War Crimes Tribunal for the Former Yugoslavia in The Hague, Holland. A year later, the horrors of Rwanda were handed over to the same body, which created a parallel process, the International Criminal Tribunal for Rwanda.

Justice Louise Arbour became the chief prosecutor for war crimes in Rwanda and the former Yugoslavia in the early spring of 1996. She is the eagle in this narrative. When the forty-nine-year-old Ontario appeals court judge touched down in The Hague, she believed she was on an adventure that would break the culture of impunity that had existed in the two countries since the wars began. She quickly learned that she was expected to clean up the mess left from the two botched UN peacekeeping missions, and to assuage the international conscience.

Arbour believed the international tribunals reflected an age of enlightenment at the UN. Instead of blaming everyone, collectively, for clan warfare, the tribunal mandate stated that *individuals* are responsible for war crimes and must be brought to justice. As this book will argue, this is exactly the right response to the wars in Rwanda and Yugoslavia. It reiterates the principle that the Nuremberg trials established — that groups or nations of people do not hold collective responsibility for crimes. Instead, charges should be laid against the individuals who issue — or carry out — the orders for those crimes. But from the moment Arbour arrived, she suspected that the UN was not interested in war crimes trials at all. It was interested in the *appearance* of war crimes trials.

I met Arbour and interviewed her for the first time when she had only recently discovered this. In the course of that first conversation, I found that her face betrayed her disappointment even when her answers didn't. Underfunded, understaffed, confused in their mission, the tribunals were careering around without focus, rife with corruption and incompetence, and unable to effect a single arrest while the world sleeved a brow, content that the first such criminal tribunals since the Nuremberg trials would soon bring the bad guys to justice.

When I met her again a year later in The Hague, Arbour had persuaded the UN and the NATO generals to see things her way. She had kept her eagle eye on the prize and helped to save the tribunals from an untimely demise. Hers is the success story in this book. Arbour believes that the UN, for all its failures, still has the potential to lead the world into a new and better era of human rights.

Canada could play an important role in reinventing the UN if it has the courage to follow its own moral convictions. The departments of National Defence and Foreign Affairs and International Trade are strenuously lobbying for changes to the United Nations and the way it conducts the business of peacekeeping. It's fitting that the country that came up with the concept in the first place should have some idea of how to improve it. National Defence has offered plans for an international rapid-reaction force that would be ready to drop into the world's hot spots with robust rules of engagement. The foreign affairs department is a leader in efforts to create a permanent international criminal court that would try those guilty of crimes against humanity. And Canada is arguing for an expanded and more effective Security Council, one that is not controlled and manipulated by the biggest and most powerful members of the United Nations.

But in its focus on UN reform, Canada has failed to look at its own role in peacekeeping, preferring to sweep those problems under the carpet. The federal government's only public review of recent peacekeeping failures was the Somalia inquiry, convened to investigate the behaviour of Canadian soldiers in Somalia, and in particular the violent death of a Somali boy at the hands of Canadian peacekeepers. The government prematurely shut down the inquiry in 1997 when Jean Chrétien decided to call an early election. There has been no other opportunity for a national debate on Canada's role in peacekeeping.

Canadians led two peacekeeping missions that were, by the UN's own admission, failures, and yet we have had no national review of those events.

There is no public record of why Lewis MacKenzie came home prematurely. There is no national review of why Roméo Dallaire's warnings went unheeded, especially considering the fact that he sent his crucial memos to Maurice Baril, another Canadian general serving at peacekeeping headquarters in New York City. Canada has never publicly asked why NATO denied Louise Arbour the support she needed to make crucial arrests in Yugoslavia.

One United Nations critic, David Rieff, says Lester Pearson would roll over in his grave if he saw what peacekeeping has become. But it may be that Canada is on the cusp of a new era of international relations, an era that will be successful only if we have the courage to examine our own mythologies and iconography in the light of hard and tragic facts. This book is intended to be part of that examination.

BOOK ONE
The Lion

1

SLOUCHING TOWARDS THE MILLENNIUM

God is my light and my salvation.
—Psalm 27, chosen by
Father Georges-Henri Lévesque as the motto for the
National University of Rwanda

ON October 16, 1999, Rwandan radio announced, amidst other news of the day, that leaders of a religious sect in the capital city of Kigali had been arrested. The four women were not terrorists or fanatics but members of a group calling itself Croyants du Christ, and they were incarcerated for failing to show identity cards. The Croyants du Christ had received a message from God that the end of the world was approaching. They were to refrain from eating anything but boiled beans and from washing with soap, and they were commanded by God to no longer carry any documents or papers. They could not explain why they had received these particular orders, just that they were going to obey them.

In the final months of the twentieth century, there was nothing exceptional about millennialists and doomsday cults. But the Croyants du Christ are worthy of note because there are so few people in the world who can so credibly claim to know what the end of the world may be like. Of all nations on earth, how many have seen the devil walk or heard the pounding hoofs of the Four Horsemen of the Apocalypse as distinctly as the tiny African republic of Rwanda?

Rwanda is extraordinarily beautiful. The centre of the country is covered by lush green hills, heavily cultivated for growing bananas, coffee and tea.

This rolling expanse is so consistent over such a vast area that Rwanda is often described as the land of a thousand hills (*mille collines*). European colonizers called it the Switzerland of Africa. In the east, the undulations end in a series of mountains and volcanoes (some still active); in the west, the country is bordered by the African Great Lakes system of Kivu and Tanganyika, a part of the Nile River delta. The tropical climate, the fortress-like natural protection of mountains and lakes, the good soil and abundant water —all have allowed Rwanda to prosper over the centuries, but the same conditions have also created the most populated country in Africa, with every inch of arable soil cultivated and every banana tree accounted for.

The mountains and lakes have also made Rwanda difficult to reach. When travel and exploration in Africa became fashionable in the nineteenth century, only the most ambitious ventured that far. In recent times, even before its tragedy, Rwanda was rarely listed in guidebooks as a place to visit. Few would have heard of the country if not for Dian Fossey, who thrust Rwanda into the international spotlight during the 1970s and 1980s with her campaign to save its mountain gorillas from extinction. A movie about her work, based on her book *Gorillas in the Mist*, captured the world's imagination and touched a sentimental chord in Western society. Fossey was found murdered in her cabin in Rwanda, on December 26, 1985. (Though she had numerous enemies in the lucrative gorilla poaching industry, her death is still considered a mystery).

Rwanda is just south of the equator, but its elevation—over one thousand metres—moderates the African sun and creates a climate with average temperatures of 20°C, heavy rains and perpetual humidity. The red earth is terraced high into the hills and covered in lush vegetation. A steamy mist often swirls around the blue-green landscape, creating an otherworldly quality. Spiritualism is deep in the fibre of the country: some legends suggest that the area was the original Garden of Eden, and that the first humans walked its hills.

What little historic record exists indicates that the region that is now called Rwanda was settled two thousand years ago by ancestors of the Hutu and Tutsi peoples; another people, the Twa (named pygmies by the white colonizers), are believed to be its original inhabitants. These groups lived together for centuries in loosely associated principalities; some cultivated crops, others cattle, and a handful of the most prosperous did both. Eventually, they all came to speak a common language, Kinyarwandan, and to share the same customs and culture. They began to consolidate under one *mwami*, or king, during the Middle Ages, and by the end of the eighteenth century Rwanda was a strong, even aggressive state, often looking to expand its tiny, land-locked territory. Local community leaders exerted a great deal of influence over the population, but they all reported to the king, who enjoyed an absolute, almost god-like, power.

The distinctions among Hutu, Tutsi and Twa were principally occupational. Those who owned cattle (and tended to have more wealth because of it) were called Tutsi, while land cultivators were Hutu. Twa were more disadvantaged and formed a sub-class of servants and workers. The monarchy and members of the ruling elite and their entourages were Tutsi, and the sceptre of power was passed down through their generations, reinforcing their social advantages. Rwandans themselves saw their differences as matters of wealth and class, not ethnicity. Ethnic distinction would come with the Europeans.

The political and social machinery of Rwandan society became highly evolved and complex over hundreds of years, and proved utterly fascinating to white explorers of the nineteenth century. Leading the pack was John Hanning Speke, an Englishman who wrote about Rwanda in his *Journal of the Discovery of the Source of the Nile*. Nineteenth-century Europe was abuzz with exploration and adventure, but unfortunately for Africans, men like Speke were also entranced by the pseudo-sciences of eugenics and race. Europeans were told by their academics that white men were superior and natural world leaders. The theory that black and coloured people were of a lesser order, perhaps even subhuman, fitted neatly with Europe's commercial exploitation of Africa and Asia at the time, providing the colonizers with a "reasoned" argument to excuse the abuse of natives during their ruthless extraction of natural resources.

When white men explored Rwanda, they were intrigued by their discernment of ethnic differences between the Hutu and the Tutsi, and fascinated particularly with the physical look of the Tutsi, who are often tall and thin, with more aquiline noses and thinner lips than their Hutu neighbours. John Speke described the Tutsi as men "who were as unlike as they could be from the common order of natives." Europeans needed little more than this to celebrate the elegant Tutsi as a kind of African Caucasian; they assumed that their look implied higher intelligence than that of the squat, broad-nosed Hutu. Speke and others soon declared the Tutsi to be natural leaders.

Some Europeans began to speculate that the Tutsi might be descendants of the original inhabitants of the Garden of Eden, or even survivors of the lost continent of Atlantis, picking up on variations of the story of original man that is part of Rwanda's own folklore. All of this mythology and bad science might have just ended up in the same dustbin as the theory that the world is flat, except that Speke introduced one enduring idea: he claimed that the Tutsi looked different because they were actually descendants of Christians from Ethiopia who had migrated with their handsome long-horned cattle down to this part of the Nile basin. Their superior culture and brainpower, according to Speke, meant they could easily have conquered the inferior people of the region. In the next century, this theory would have devastating consequences, first for the Hutu and then for the so-called superior race.

The Germans were the first to colonize Rwanda, at the turn of the twentieth century. The Belgians usurped them after the First World War. Typical of colonizers, Belgium wanted to extract the wealth of Rwanda efficiently and with little administrative cost. The European-created ethnic separation of Hutu, Tutsi and Twa proved extremely convenient. The Belgians decided that the superior Tutsi would hold positions of authority and, of course, be in their service. Hutu were shut out of opportunities for advancement within the white-dominated hierarchy, and even denied rights to higher education.

The Belgian-imposed caste system meant that being a Tutsi mattered more than ever before. In the 1930s, the Belgians launched a registration system that required everyone to be documented as Tutsi, Hutu or Twa, and they subsequently required Rwandans to carry identity papers with them at all times, indicating their so-called race. To ensure that everyone was registered correctly, the Belgians took to measuring craniums and nose lengths to determine "racial" class.

The Hutu now found themselves locked into an inferior social position for life. Tutsi people took full advantage of the system, enjoying the absolute lifetime status and prestige awarded by the Belgians. The French social scientist Gérard Prunier (one of the most important scholars on African societies in general and Rwanda in particular) concludes that the Tutsi probably did migrate from somewhere north and are of a different ancestry than the Hutu. But he says it was Europe's impermeable caste system that created an apartheid for which both peoples would pay dearly.

Following the Second World War, there was an international sea change of ideas regarding the use and abuse of colonies. The nascent United Nations began to pressure European powers to loosen up. In Rwanda, Belgian authorities reluctantly allowed Hutu access to higher education. White priests, including Canadian-born missionaries, had been converting the Africans to Catholicism for decades, and they played a pivotal role in schooling the population. The Canadian clergy spoke French (Belgium had made French the official language of Rwanda) but carried none of the colonialists' baggage.

The colonial empires of Africa began to crumble in the 1950s. By the early 1960s, Belgian rule in the Congo region had all but come to an end. The Belgians failed to reinforce Tutsi domination before withdrawing their own administration, supporting instead the idea of Rwandan majority rule.

In 1960, the Hutu took power, and a year later, declared Rwanda a republic. Discrimination and political repression by the Belgian colonists and their willing partners, the Tutsi, came to an end as Belgium pulled out completely. The imposed ethnic distinctions that had benefited the Tutsi during Belgian rule now got turned against them. If the Tutsi were in fact members of an old invading force that the colonists had endorsed, they had no place in the new Rwanda.

Identity cards that had once been gold passes for Tutsi became death warrants. In the first decade of Hutu-dominated government, twenty thousand Tutsi were killed. Another 300,000 fled the country into neighbouring Uganda and Burundi, where many of the men inevitably regrouped into a rebel movement. These rebels made frequent forays into Rwandan territory throughout the 1960s; the attacks were quickly suppressed by the Hutu government, and were followed by a heavy retaliatory crackdown on the Tutsi still at home.

Despite the brutality of the regime, the foreigners who stayed on after the Belgians left supported it. Quebec priests took up key positions of influence within Rwandan society as the Belgian priests withdrew. French Canadian Dominicans founded the National University of Rwanda on November 3, 1963 — the first institution of its kind in Rwanda and, over the next decade, the government of Canada invested more than $50 million in the institution, in addition to supplying key personnel. Lester Pearson, then prime minister, became a chief supporter.

The Quebec priests, many with their own strong nationalist sentiments, supported the Hutu revolt against the smaller Tutsi elite. A phenomenon, later called Hutu Power, spread through Rwandan society and found fertile ground at the National University. Its Canadian founder, Father Georges-Henri Lévesque, perhaps unwittingly, referred to the Tutsi rebels as *inyenzi*, the Rwandan word for cockroach. It was the pejorative used first by the Hutu to describe the rebels and later by the genocidal death squads to describe their targets. Father Lévesque was clearly in an optimistic frame of mind when he unveiled the university's motto — "God is my light and my salvation." Rwanda would see little light or salvation in the coming decades.

Within the Hutu leadership itself there was friction, particularly between those from the south, who tended to be more moderate and accommodating of their Tutsi neighbours, and the extreme Hutu nationalist members from northern Rwanda. In 1973, a northern Hutu, General Juvénal Habyarimana took control of the country in a *coup d'état* and subsequently claimed that he would unite Rwanda in a more homogeneous whole. The general was out of the classic African-dictator mould: every citizen of Rwanda was required to belong to his political organization, and no other party was legal.

Habyarimana immediately recognized the strategic value of the National University and began to use it as a power base. Key positions were taken over by the president's extended family, particularly relatives on his wife's side. These new staffers established a "crisis committee" on campus whose job it was to draw up lists of Tutsi who were to be expelled. Among the crisis committee members was a young activist named Léon Mugesera, who continued his education at Laval University in Quebec and later became a key Hutu Power agitator in Rwanda.

Throughout Africa, a new form of colonization was replacing the old. The Cold War created a need for Western governments to establish spheres of influence in African countries, and that meant any number of despots could find, and cultivate, foreign patrons who would help them hold onto power. France took a shine to French-speaking Rwanda, and provided General Habyarimana with substantial weapons and military support to help defend himself against the Tutsi rebels, who by the 1970s had become the Rwandan Patriotic Front (RPF). The RPF had its base just over the border in Uganda (part of English-speaking Africa, and a country regarded with contempt by France). It made frequent incursions into Rwanda, only to be pushed back by French-trained and -equipped soldiers. Without French assistance, the Rwandan army would have had a tough time resisting the rebels: the RPF was highly disciplined, and became even more so in the late 1980s under the leadership of Paul Kagame, an American-trained Tutsi militant who had grown up in exile.

In the late 1980s, coffee prices collapsed. The international demand for tin also went into a tailspin, leaving Rwanda with only one solid source of income: foreign aid. Agencies ranging from the World Bank to the Canadian International Development Agency (CIDA) were sustaining the country with handouts. But with the exception of France, foreign countries and international aid organizations didn't want to support a regime that was suspected of murdering members of a national minority. To continue to receive foreign aid, Habyarimana had to clean up his act and share power with his republic's Tutsi population. He also had to find a way to allow the refugee Tutsi, a second generation now growing up in exile, to come home. The native Tutsi population was much reduced, from just over 17 per cent before the revolution to 9–12 per cent. Approximately 600,000 Tutsi were refugees.

France continued to supply Rwanda with weapons and, perhaps more important, military training while President Habyarimana pretended to pursue economic and political reforms. The forced exile of Tutsi slowed down in the 1980s, as the country prospered, and the Rwandan minority enjoyed some of its best years since 1961. Tutsi living in Rwanda began to lose much of their organic connection to Tutsi in exile, who were becoming not only bitter but also English-speaking in Uganda. If Habyarimana had developed a base of Tutsi support within the country, he might have been able to resist the forces outside. It was by no means a given that the Tutsi minority in Rwanda wanted to be under the rule of the rebel Paul Kagame. But Habyarimana lost this opportunity, probably because he was heavily influenced by the extremists in his own entourage, especially his wife.

Agathe Habyarimana, the Lady MacBeth of Rwanda, had been building a militant team of supporters of her own throughout her husband's reign. She headed up a small but powerful elite of extremists with close ties to the northern home base of the ruling family. This select group of Hutu Power members came to be called the "Clan de Madame." Prominent among them was madame's brother, Protais Zigiranyirazo — educated at the National University under Father Lévesque and also at Lévesque's own alma mater, Laval University.

Clan members were sent out into the regions of Rwanda to spread the message that Hutu must be prepared to exterminate the *inyenzi*—the cockroaches. One of the conspicuous examples of this recruitment campaign was in November 1992, when Léon Mugesera, who had joined the government's Ministry of Information, travelled into northern Rwanda to deliver a speech at a rally for the president's own political party. Mugesera had written speeches for Habyarimana and also anti-Tutsi pamphlets but the rhetoric in those texts did not come close to the outrageous incitement to hate he presented at the rally. Mugesera told his audience, "We the people must take responsibility for wiping out the scum." And also: "Know that the person whose throat you do not cut now will be the one who will cut yours." His speech was tape-recorded and sent to the minister of justice, a member of the moderate liberal party, who subsequently issued a warrant for Mugesera's arrest. Though the full tape has since been lost, various excerpts still exist from radio reports and eye witnesses. Mugesera told the crowd that the Hutu should send the Tutsi back to where they came from, by way of the Nyaborongo River, which goes to Ethiopia. This was a direct reference to the John Speke theory of Tutsi origins. Mugesera later claimed that he was only speaking metaphorically about the opposition parties and not issuing an incitement to kill. But he didn't stay around to witness the result of his oratorical skills; by the time the bodies of hundreds of thousands of Tutsi were indeed floating downstream towards Ethiopia, he was living with his family once again in Quebec City.

A government-licensed broadcaster—Radio Télévision Libre des Mille Collines (RTLMC)—became the most powerful tool of the Hutu Power leadership. RTLMC disseminated Clan de Madame propaganda in the form of a steady stream of reminders to its mostly young listeners that the Tutsi had once oppressed them. The prime source of information for most Rwandans is radio, and it was easy to monopolize the airwaves with the anti-*inyenzi* message.

Moderate political elites in Rwanda, both Tutsi and Hutu, were deeply alarmed by what they saw as the deliberate development of a culture of violence. Without access to the backrooms of the presidency, they couldn't know the full extent of what was being planned: the organized murder of the Tutsi population and anyone who didn't overtly support President Habyarimana. But they knew that the growing atmosphere of frenzy and fear could easily be turned on them.

Habyarimana kept assuring foreign governments that he would not allow the Hutu Power movement to harass the Tutsi, but it's doubtful that he would have been able to stop the extremists who surrounded his wife even if he had tried. In any case, his main concern was with the militant Tutsi in exile: it was clear that what they really wanted was not a simple homecoming, but to assume power. Paul Kagame and the RPF gave little thought to the effect their war efforts had on the local Tutsi population. Characteristic of liberation armies, they believed people who didn't support them were probably traitors.

In October 1990, the RPF invaded Rwanda with weapons and uniforms supplied by the Ugandan army. Uganda had recruited many Rwandans into its own fighting force, and these soldiers subsequently departed to join the RPF, taking their equipment with them. Uganda encouraged an RPF victory: it wanted the Tutsi refugee population to go home. Meanwhile, Habyarimana was still under enormous pressure from the international community to create a multi-party system and to allow for the return of hundreds of thousands of Tutsi in exile. He was being pushed and pulled in all directions while his wife's powerful brothers and the other extremists within his own party were making it clear that they had absolutely no interest in sharing power with the banished Tutsi, and certainly not with Paul Kagame.

As the war with the RPF accelerated, the Clan de Madame organized groups of young men into death squads while stockpiling weapons and recruiting more members to the cause. These extremists fanned out into the regions to stir up the Hutu peasants, telling them of their "work obligations" and that they should be ready, when they are called upon, to start Operation Extermination against the *inyenzi*. (There was also Operation Zero, a reference to the number of Tutsi who would be left when they finished.)

Following centuries of feudalism under the *mwami*, Rwandan society functioned smoothly through its burgomasters who exerted regional control. An overlay of rigorous paternalism imposed on the citizenry by the Roman Catholic Church reinforced what was already a system of blind obedience to authority. The Clan de Madame and the other extremists knew they had to recruit Rwanda's town and village leaders in order to make their plans work. To reinforce the message perpetrated by *agents provocateurs* (Mugesera and his ilk), RTLMC pumped out a steady stream of popular music mixed with a rap-rant of racist jargon and hatred. When the killing began in earnest, the radio station would even tell death squads where people were hiding and what street they had been seen fleeing along.

Under such circumstances, the president's influence was diminishing. The many little opposition parties he had allowed to flourish—hoping they would cancel each other out—began to consolidate into ever more strident camps. The status quo was unsupportable: with human rights abuses piling up, foreign aid organizations began to pull out. The economy, already hit by the collapse of coffee prices and staggering under the weight of bankrolling a civil war (even with millions in military aid and under-written loans from France), became a worse mess. The president feared a complete economic collapse in Rwanda, something even his enemy at arms wanted to avoid. The RPF wanted to take over a functioning state.

In August 1993, Juvénal Habyarimana and Paul Kagame declared that they were ready to stop the war. On August 4, the two sides met in the capital of neighbouring Tanzania to sign the Arusha Accords—a peace agreement that was supposed to permit the refugees to return, the RPF to set up shop in Rwanda as part of the Rwandan army, and the opposition parties to play a viable role in running the government. The signing was a grand ceremony attended by the major leaders of Africa—none of whom believed the peace agreement would work—and by members of the inter-national community, who breathed a sigh of relief that the worst of the Rwandan crisis was over.

As the Arusha Accords were being signed, Brigadier General Roméo Dallaire was in the midst of preparations for the twenty-fifth-anniversary celebrations of the Fifth Mechanized Brigade of Canada in Valcartier, Quebec. Dallaire, a forty-seven-year-old artillery man, was the brigade's commander, and in the summer of 1993, he was making the best of a slow career. The man his friends described as the life of the party, who also pushed his soldiers as hard as he pushed himself and ended communiqués to those under his command with "*Allons-y!*" ("Let's go!"), was discover-ing what so many ambitious career officers had already learned: in the Canadian Forces in peacetime, you rose quickly through the ranks until there was no place else to go. As commander of the Valcartier brigade, Dallaire was competing with dozens of other generals for the few plum jobs at the top while just a little too far away from National Defence Headquarters in Ottawa.

The Fifth Mechanized had morphed out of another outfit dating back to the First World War. It had fought bravely at Ypres, Vimy Ridge and Passchendaele, and during the Second World War had taken part in the raid on Dieppe. The predominantly French-speaking brigade had become one place in the forces where francophone soldiers found they could build careers as the DND created new French-Canadian regiments at Valcartier. The lack of opportunity for Quebeckers had been a sore point in the armed forces for decades. Dallaire was anything but a Quebec nationalist—his loyalty was firmly federalist—but he was acutely aware of the history of discrimination against francophones and was determined to make something of his years at Valcartier.

Dallaire had known little else but the soldier's life. He was an army brat whose father fought in the Second World War; his wife, Elizabeth, was the daughter of an officer and war veteran. Dallaire loved the precision and discipline of the military: he studied its history and revelled in stories of battles. He lived to visit the famous sites in Europe where his countrymen had fought. He studied in Canadian military colleges at St. Jean, Quebec, and Kingston, Ontario, as well as in England and at the famous Marine Corps Command and Staff College in Quantico, Virginia. Dallaire was as prepared to defend his country as any soldier could be.

Canadian soldiers, even those from Quebec, had known some heady times during the post-war years. As a member of the North Atlantic Treaty Organization (NATO), Canada fancied itself among the front ranks of the cold warriors, and its troops were dedicated to training and preparing for the Third World War. The zenith of any Canadian soldier's career was to serve at the NATO base in Lahr, West Germany, where Dallaire was trained for combat and later instructed others.

Dallaire was what military people call a NATO man, and he was one of the best of them: his defence knowledge was predicated almost exclusively on the needs of the NATO alliance. With the Cold War spurring the government to keep its defence department happy, Dallaire and his colleagues had known the best and most peaceful years Canadian soldiers had ever experienced. In 1989, Canada had five thousand personnel at the base in Lahr.

Then suddenly came the fall of the Berlin Wall and the collapse of the Cold War. By 1993, the base at Lahr was closed. Opportunities for senior officers dried up: members of the top-heavy Canadian armed forces fought each other for the few scraps of promotion that still existed. A kind of rot and stagnation plagued the organization. Many of those who climbed to the top of the military hierarchy were the ones who kept their noses clean and learned how to hide the little (eventually big) stinky messes that various peacekeeping missions began to produce.

A review of the general attitude among the Canadian armed forces, taken in 1995, revealed that 83 per cent of military personnel had lost confidence in their senior leaders. The Phillips Employee Feedback Survey, as it was called, found that people in all the forces saw the brass as "self-interested careerists and empire-builders." The best-selling book *Tarnished Brass*—a scathing review of DND failures by Scott Taylor and Brian Nolan—described the mood: "To understand the enormity of the betrayal of trust by the brass and the widening gulf it has created between themselves and the ... men and women who follow the honourable profession of arms is to know why morale has fallen so low."

Canadian military life was changing rapidly in the 1990s. For decades, those on the inside considered peacekeeping the B Team of the Canadian Forces. Soldiers with nothing better to do could serve some years in places like Cyprus, where the job amounted to little more than watching the green line that had been established years earlier to separate the warring factions. Ordinary Canadians may get a little thrill when they see their countrymen in blue berets, but the military brass and the soldiers themselves—quite logically—saw their most important job as preparing to defend their country against possible enemies.

The New World Order of the 1990s all but terminated that traditional role of the modern military and launched something altogether new and unpredictable. As the prospect of another great war vanished, there was a proliferation of nasty little wars fought without rules and with an ugly predilection for killing civilians. Peacekeepers were dispatched around the world to somehow quell these uprisings and impose order on rogue states. In the 1990s, Canada sent as many soldiers off into the world wearing blue berets as it had had in Lahr when the Berlin Wall came down.

For the Canadian government, peacekeeping was a great public-relations boon. Prime Minister Brian Mulroney (who, after he stepped down in 1993, became President George Bush's first choice for the next secretary-general of the United Nations) took credit for being an international do-gooder even as his government was slashing the heart out of the Canadian Forces through budget cuts. Soldiers received extra money to go on the often devastating missions; they were paid on a sliding scale, depending on the frequency of missions, and the bonus could be as much as one thousand dollars (though it was more often in the hundreds of dollars). A lot of servicemen and women, desperately in need of cash, came back from one hellhole and headed out for another. Such incentives worked to staff the operations, but the rate of mental illness and family breakdown became a scandal. Some marriages couldn't sustain the long separations, and many young people couldn't cope with the horrors they encountered on these excursions, where they often found themselves in the midst of murdered children and gang-raped women. Instead of offering professional help, at first the Department of National Defence (DND) did its best to ignore the effects these missions were having on the overworked soldiers. It wasn't until 1997 that the government did any kind of a forces-wide investigation into the well-being of its military personnel. The Standing Committee on National Defence and Veterans' Affairs crossed the country in that year, conducting hearings with people in uniform and recording horror stories about the military's quality of life. Everything from family violence to abject poverty (soldiers were lining up at food banks to feed their children) had somehow been overlooked by DND.

In the first half of the 1990s, the UN established twenty-four new peace-keeping missions: that's six more than the total for the preceding forty-three years. Canadians served on almost all twenty-four of them, and many were the same overworked personnel. To the Canadian public, these were grand acts of peacekeeping. But those in the forces referred to the missions by a far less romantic name—Operations Other Than War (OOTW). There was often no peace to keep.

In March 1993, Canadians saw the worst that peacekeeping could produce when two paratroopers, members of the Canadian Airborne Regiment, tortured to death a sixteen-year-old Somali youth. The government and the military brass chose to ignore the central decay of a department that had been unable to detect the bad characters and properly train the good. Instead, DND just got rid of the Airborne. But the leadership did start to recognize the strain of involving Canadian soldiers in so many missions, if only because with the scandals the PR value of peacekeeping was beginning to erode.

The UN has no armed forces of its own: it depends entirely on the kindness of donor countries. While Canada considers peacekeeping part of the national heritage, other countries see it as, at best, an opportunity to impose some aspects of their own foreign policy on situations, and at worst as a nuisance. The conflicts of the 1990s required rapid response, but the voluntary nature of the missions—in terms of *matériel*, as well as people— meant that the UN rarely got to the conflict in time, and sometimes didn't get there at all. Canada was one of the few countries the UN could rely on to pull off personnel, *matériel* and timing.

But peacekeeping was no longer a business of guarding the green line between two armies at war. Soldiers sent into these civil conflicts could make little sense of them: paramilitaries roamed the countryside burning homes; warlords ran local governments. Who would want to be peacekeepers in such places? There was too little glory and too much peril. But there was no other tool to counter the social breakdowns of the decade. International diplomacy was failing badly — European statesmen couldn't make sense of the New World Order and the Americans were principally interested in reaping the fiscal rewards of a vastly reduced post–Cold War defence budget. So the UN Security Council was trying to use peacekeeping — a military device that had never really been thought out — as the central instrument of conflict management for the world. At the peak in the 1990s, the UN deployed eighty thousand peacekeepers and needed many more. To make matters worse, there was no money. The United States wouldn't pay its UN dues, and was almost a billion dollars in arrears. The UN was close to bankruptcy: many peacekeeping contingents had to rely heavily on their own countries. The UN reluctantly supplied the minimum to its missions.

Secretary-General Boutros Boutros-Ghali, an Egyptian government bureaucrat whom the State Department loathed, couldn't get much co-operation from anyone. The dues-paying delinquents in Washington wanted a docile UN that was an extension of U.S. foreign policy, and Boutros-Ghali complained that the Americans didn't understand geopolitics. The secretary-general was determined to set some priorities for the United Nations. He had scorned pleas for help from Bosnians facing their second year of ethnic cleansing; he told people in Sarajevo that he could name ten other conflicts more important than theirs. Boutros-Ghali was thinking about Africa, and he believed the world should be more interested in its problems. That wasn't going to happen. Neither the Americans nor the Europeans had much strategic interest there, and no one wanted to see their soldiers come back from Africa in body bags.

The peace negotiators in Arusha had been quite specific about which countries they thought could operate effectively in Rwanda. The government had serious reservations about Belgian soldiers running around the country, while the Rwandan Patriotic Front rejected any plan that called for French peacekeepers to be part of the mission. They would both accept

Canadian military—first, because they spoke French, and second, because Canada's history in Rwanda consisted of founding the university and contributing much financial aid. When Boutros-Ghali came looking for troops to help ensure the success of the Arusha Accords in the late summer of 1993, Canada was among his first stops.

Ottawa resisted strenuously. The government and the Department of National Defence were still reeling from the Somali scandal, not only from the shame of the Airborne soldiers having tortured a boy to death, but also from evidence that the defence department tried to cover it up. Other scandals of a non-lethal nature had come out of Cambodia, where peacekeepers, including Canadians, were caught running a black-market empire. In Bosnia and Croatia, Canada was taking casualties. And now the United Nations was asking for Canadian troops in Rwanda. Ottawa wanted to learn how to say no.

But the UN was desperate. The Rwandan government had finally agreed to allow Belgian soldiers to take part in the mission, but not to lead it. Would Canada at least provide a French-speaking force commander (FC), if there was a battalion of well-trained Belgian para-commandos as part of the mix? The UN made a case to Ottawa that this mission not only was the safest possible, but might even help restore confidence in the whole business of peacekeeping. A Canadian FC would give the Rwandan mission credibility and do much for the tattered reputation of the Canadian Forces. Ottawa capitulated.

Roméo Dallaire was staring down the tunnel of a long, dull finish to his military career when he got the call, two days before his brigade's twenty-fifth-anniversary party, asking him to report to UN Headquarters in New York. Ottawa had picked Dallaire to be force commander for the UN monitoring mission to Rwanda. It would later become the United Nations Assistance Mission in Rwanda (UNAMIR). Dallaire was unwitting enough to be thrilled.

There was a fair bit of jealousy within the leadership ranks of the armed forces. Dallaire had signed up for any mission that might come up. Countless twenty-five-year-olds were into their third overseas adventure in the 1990s, but he had yet to serve on one. The UN wanted a French-Canadian for the job and few were more qualified than Dallaire. But it wasn't exactly a plum position—Dallaire, himself, characterized it as "a benign and low priority mission." Why was he so elated at the opportunity?

"If you train as a firefighter all your life, all you want to do is put out fires," he says. "If there's a small fire in a garbage can you all jump to put it out." Dallaire would get his fire and it would not be small.

Dallaire made his first and only reconnaissance trip to Africa in August 1993, with a group of military and civilian observers. The fact-finding mission was supposed to include professionals who were knowledgeable about all aspects of the region, but the key expert needed eye surgery and backed out just before they were about to leave. The others on the team were about as informed on Rwanda as Dallaire, who by his own admission didn't know much. The only other Canadian on the tour was Major Brent Beardsley, assigned by DND to assist Dallaire in Rwanda. Beardsley was the one other person who would stay with the Rwanda mission after this fact-finding trip — the rest would have nothing more to do with it. A smart, hard-driving officer from the Royal Canadian Regiment, Beardsley would be of endless service to Dallaire and UNAMIR in the coming months. But he and Dallaire agreed that they went into Africa blind.

Even though Dallaire knew little of African culture and politics, after studying the hilly and even mountainous terrain, the potential trouble spots, the borders with other countries, he knew he would need about five thousand troops to implement the UNAMIR mandate. Boutros-Ghali presented this request to the Security Council, but he indicated to Dallaire that it was laughably unrealistic. There was no support among the Permanent Five members of the Security Council (France, China, the United States, Russia and France) for such a big mission. But Dallaire approached the job from the very beginning as a soldier who knew his strategic needs. What no one could prepare him for was that the UN didn't care about such needs. The UN wasn't in the business of doing the job properly; it did it only as well as the powerful Security Council would permit. And in the mission-choked months of 1993, the council wasn't about to permit very much.

The United Nations looked upon the Rwanda mission as a cakewalk, and as a chance for UN peacekeeping to rehabilitate its damaged reputation. Dallaire was to monitor an agreement that both sides claimed they wanted. If there was going to be trouble — and by this point, the Permanent Five countries had their own internal intelligence reports that indicated a potential for big trouble — Rwanda was a poor country of not much strategic value to any world power. A U.S. State Department official later admitted that he had been told by his bosses to remove Rwanda from Washington's list of international hot spots *after* they knew of the potential for major conflict. Boutros-Ghali wasn't going to use his waning clout to push the Security Council, especially the Americans, into a major commitment. The Rwanda mission was going to be cheap and cheerful.

Dallaire believed he could monitor the Arusha Accords with five thousand troops; UN military experts estimated it would take eight thousand. The United States recommended five hundred, and the Security Council finally approved twenty-five hundred soldiers. Boutros-Ghali told Dallaire that it was better to have the smaller force, since it would be easier and faster to get troops together and into the field. The Belgians would be augmented with troops from African and Asian countries (who would be highly motivated, if less well trained); the core of the force would be a battalion of Bangladeshis.

Ever the optimist, Dallaire decided to live with his lot. He could not have imagined in his wildest dreams how incompetent and unprepared the Bangladeshi soldiers would be. Nor could he anticipate that most of the equipment, and even much of the food and many medical supplies, would not arrive in Rwanda until after the killing began.

Dallaire flew into Kigali as force commander of UNAMIR on October 22, 1993. He was in his element: though only three staff officers accompanied him, soon there would be soldiers to lead and real work to accomplish. He was struck by the extraordinary beauty of the landscape — the rolling mist-covered hills, the deep blue-greens of the vegetation, the delicious humid climate with its perpetual breath of spring. He and Beardsley came to the same conclusion: they were in paradise.

Dallaire had no feelings of foreboding. "There was absolutely no perception that there was anything but the very positive vibrations that were coming out of Rwanda from both sides," Dallaire reflected later. "This was going to be a classic peacekeeping mission.... It would be a very positive exercise for the UN, which was reeling under the Somalia implications." And besides, Dallaire was simply supposed to be the military man. The UN would appoint a special representative to lead the mission and provide the diplomatic glue that would make sure the Arusha Accords didn't come unstuck. What would Dallaire have to do? Basic stuff. Prevent soldiers from firing off their AK-47s. Watch for flare-ups. His mood was buoyant.

Dallaire later realized how much it would have helped if he had known the contents of a report filed by a United Nations research team just as he was heading out to Kigali. The report described gross violations of human rights in Rwanda, and had even used a word the UN would still recoil from weeks into the slaughter: *genocide*. It might have made a difference to his planning had Dallaire been told of an International Commission of Inquiry into Human Rights Abuses in Rwanda, which reported in the spring of 1993 that the government of Rwanda was behind a number of recent massacres, and that death squads were preparing for even larger massacres. (The report was filed with the United Nations Human Rights Commission). It might have helped if Dallaire had known even half of what was being cooked up in Mrs. Habyarimana's kitchen in the spring and summer of 1993. But the Canadian general was blithely ignorant. The brass at peacekeeping headquarters in New York City just had too much to do to worry about the little mission to Rwanda.

2

INTO AFRICA

I've seen the devil of violence, and the devil of greed, and the devil of hot desire.... These were strong, lusty, red-eyed devils, that swayed and drove men — men I tell you. But as I stood on the hillside, I foresaw in the blinding sunshine of that land I would become acquainted with a flabby, pretending, weak-eyed devil.
—Joseph Conrad, *Heart of Darkness*

Marlow, the dark and cynical central character of *Heart of Darkness*, is a man who has seen too much of human folly. In the novel, he undertakes the same adventure as his creator, Joseph Conrad. At the end of the Victorian era, as white explorers continued to coin their fantastic theories about black people and ethnicity, Conrad took a job with a Belgian company in the Congo, where he witnessed the "rapacious folly" of colonial rule. In the novel, Marlow becomes overwhelmed by what he encounters in the Congo. Conrad's metaphor for evil is the extraordinary greed of "the company," which is capable of extracting everything of worth from the land while turning its people into slaves and destroying them with European diseases. His character, Marlow, finds himself caught between two strains of the truly sinister. There are the indigenous "lusty red-eyed devils," lurking in the jungle, ready to pounce. But what horrifies him even more are the "flabby weak-eyed devils" — the company men. "I let him run on, this papier-mâché Mephistopheles, and it seemed to me that if I tried I could poke my forefinger through him, and find nothing inside but a little loose dirt, maybe."

The company's preoccupation with ledgers and the bottom line allowed the flabby devils to write off the deaths of many Africans. "I respected the fellow," says Marlow, ironically, about the company man: "Yes, I respected his collars, his vast cuffs, his brushed hair. His appearance was certainly of a hairdresser's dummy; but in the great demoralization of the land he kept up appearances. That's backbone." *Heart of Darkness* is not so much a place as a frame of mind, a journey into the darkness of the soul as it finally arrives at a place where there are no explanations for anything.

Roméo Dallaire entered such a place in the fall of 1993. Unlike Conrad, or the fictional Marlow, he was full of wide-eyed innocence. He would soon learn not only about red-eyed devils but about the papier-mâché ones. The "company" for Dallaire turned out to be the United Nations.

"I confess that my initial view of Rwanda was biased by history and by naive preconceptions," Dallaire wrote in an article years later. "To me, much of Africa was the domain of missionaries and NGOs [non-governmental organizations], and it was the victim of ruthless resource extraction. But as I discovered, the quality of the political leadership was very high." Dallaire is an intense but gregarious man who thrives on human contact. He possesses that unique brand of Québécois bonhomie: an emotional outgoingness that often made anglophone colleagues at DND squirm, but that fit right into the tactile African culture. Africans had learned over the years to accommodate the usual European "reserve." Those who met him found Dallaire a refreshing change from the usual "company men."

A trim, handsome man with a tidy moustache and boundless energy, Dallaire has grey-blue eyes that are one moment cold flint and the next warm with emotion. He never ceases to be amazed by what he's been told or has seen and he often reacts to people's stories with exaggerated disbelief or laughter. His French Catholic education was rigorous on morality, but he learned his code of social justice more from his parents, whose defining experience had been the Second World War.

Upon arriving in Rwanda, he was almost immediately swept up into the society and culture of the country and he inevitably broke the company man's most sterling rule: he "went native." Whether colonizer or peacekeeper, any cynical veteran of such foreign postings would tell you that personal connections can cloud one's judgement when self-interested decision-making suddenly may be required.

But Dallaire was no such veteran, and he couldn't resist becoming involved. He had been expecting an intellectual backwater. But Rwanda's elite had been shipping off its children to the best universities in France, Belgium, even Quebec for many years. And Rwanda's own state university had high-quality teachers trained abroad. Dallaire delighted in the society he found in Kigali. Though it wasn't really his role, he endeavoured to meet with the leaders of Rwanda's political parties and others whose job it was to implement the difficult Arusha Accords. Many of these politicians were slated to hold key positions in the "broadly based transitional government"—representatives of several parties who would run the country until there could be free and fair elections—which was the cornerstone of the peace agreement. While there were certainly a number of extremists in Rwanda's political ranks, Dallaire ferreted out the most progressive and moderate politicians, and even became chummy with some of them, especially Landoald Ndasingwa, one of the leaders of the Rwandan Liberal Party.

Ndasingwa and his Montreal-born wife, Hélène Pinske, a jolly, vibrant woman, had two handsome children and a large extended family. They were part of the enlightened educated class Dallaire hoped would help make his mission a success. He often visited the family at their little Kigali establishment, the Hotel Chez Lando. Dallaire was particularly intrigued with Pinske, a fellow Quebecker who had managed to make a place for herself in Rwandan society. The family was widely regarded as progressive. Ndasingwa would tell visitors, "I am a Tutsi, my wife is a white Canadian, several members of my family are married to Hutu—in fact, we are all tired of this ethnic business."

Dallaire really wanted to believe that his new friend was right—that everyone was getting tired of this ethnic business—as he attempted to pull his mission together. But the problems were immediately obvious. First of all, the Arusha Accords had emphasized that peacekeepers, and other UN personnel, needed to take up their posts with haste since the fragile little deal could easily unravel. The signatories had insisted that UN troops would have to be on the ground within six weeks to ensure success. For the notoriously slow UN, such a deadline was impossible to meet. The Security Council didn't even pass Resolution 872, authorizing the peacekeeping force for Rwanda, until October 5—nearly nine weeks after the accords had been signed. By November 1, forty Tunisian blue berets were all in the way of armed peacekeepers that Dallaire had. The Belgian contingent wouldn't arrive until the end of November. It would be months before Dallaire had substantial numbers of troops on the ground.

Dallaire's problems were not confined to Rwanda. A *coup d'état* in its tiny twin neighbour, Burundi, began to destabilize the region as Dallaire took up his post. More than 300,000 Hutu refugees poured over the border into Rwanda in October after President Melchior Ndadaye, the first Hutu ever to be elected to lead Burundi, was kidnapped by Tutsi extremists and murdered. The Burundi refugees came with the hysterical message that the Tutsi could not be trusted, and that they were out to kill the Hutu. It was a gift to the Hutu Power leaders fomenting fear and paranoia in Rwanda.

Dallaire witnessed the consequences in Rwanda of a crisis that originated in another country, and he was learning what students of the area know all too well: much of Africa is fundamentally unstable. Governments can fall like dominoes, and the consequences can be devastating. Dallaire tried to ignore the crisis in Burundi; he wanted to stay focused on his mission in Rwanda. But he knew it was a major problem—the southern flank of the country was no longer secure, and he had no troops to guard it.

And then there was money, or the lack of it. Dallaire had estimated he would need $200 million for the proposed twenty-two-month mission. The UN decided he would have to do the job with only $54 million. The figure was ludicrous but also completely academic: the budget wasn't approved until March of 1994—two weeks before the genocide began.

The UN had been reeling from a mini-scandal since August 1993, when twelve staff members had been caught tinkering with the UN books. As it turned out, the staffers were just trying to make the institution run more efficiently and no money actually went into their own pockets. But they had failed to tender contracts (the UN requires three bids) or to follow the rigid procedural rules. In reaction, UN bean-counters subjected all subsequent budget requests to draconian review: the already lethargic institution went into near paralysis. Dallaire had to negotiate for everything and spent 70 per cent of his time (even during the war) dickering over any expenditure that exceeded five hundred dollars. A simple requisition for flashlights—for example—took a mountain of paperwork and several letters. The flashlights finally arrived, but the batteries never did.

Never mind the big important items such as armoured personnel carriers (APCs) or weapons and ammunition. If they did arrive, they were often unusable. This was pretty typical for the UN—veteran peacekeepers bought much of what the mission needed in the way of supplies on the black market or arm-twisted their own country into providing it. But

Dallaire was a NATO man with a military sense of how things should be done. He found the system loathsome. His only relief from the absurd bickering over supplies came from his new African friends.

But by November, politicians like Landoald Ndasingwa, and the others who supported the Arusha Accords, were becoming not only disappointed with the UNAMIR mission, but also alarmed. The agreement had called for a force that could ensure the safety of returning refugees, guarantee the overall security of the country and "neutralize" the armed gangs that were spreading throughout the land. Translated into dollars, that scale of operations would put the UNAMIR budget way over the top. Much of what the negotiators at Arusha had agreed on never made it into the final draft of the UN resolution or the mandate of the mission. Words like *assure*, *direct* and *guarantee* were watered down to their cheaper versions: *help*, *contribute* and *supervise*. This little game of semantics may seem unimportant, but it was these words that determined whether Dallaire was allowed to intervene to save lives. In the beginning Dallaire didn't think this mattered much, since he didn't anticipate needing such freedom to act. Nonetheless, he made one prescient move.

In the parlance of UN peacekeeping, UNAMIR was a chapter six mission. Lester Pearson pointed out that chapter six of the charter allows the UN to help a country that desires peace if both sides of a conflict agree to it. As it's been defined over the years, the job is to work with the parties in conflict in a completely neutral fashion. Peacekeepers can never take sides — even, as some force commanders interpret it, to save lives. Intervening to save someone may be interpreted as being partial.

The UN definition of peacekeeping is so short on details that peacekeepers turn to another military tool — the rules of engagement (ROE). In a peacekeeping mission, the force commander writes up the ROE with the help of the countries providing the troops. Dallaire constructed his rules shortly after the coup in Burundi. He knew of a number of murders that had occurred since the Hutu refugees started flooding over the border, and he wanted to give himself the widest possible latitude to deal with perpetrators. Within four weeks of the start of his mission, Dallaire submitted his ROE to the Department of Peacekeeping Operations. The rules were pretty straightforward, except for one. Paragraph seventeen states: "There may also be ethnically or politically motivated criminal acts committed during this mandate which will morally and legally require UNAMIR to use all available means to halt them. Examples are executions, attacks on displaced persons or refugees." If Dallaire's masters back at the UN had been less overwhelmed, they probably would have removed that clause. Using "all available means" would be expensive. But Dallaire never heard back from headquarters. He assumed his ROE had been approved.

Those who worked with the general knew him as inexhaustible, always certain that where there's a will there's a way. Dallaire's work ethic had been shaped by his heritage and upbringing. Dallaire's father had been a non-commissioned officer in the Canadian armed forces during the Second World War. After the war was over, he had stayed behind in Holland for a year, as one of the soldiers responsible for re-deploying the leftover arsenal. Dallaire senior—Roméo Louis—was billeted with a Dutch family and that's where he met his bride, Catherine Johanna Vermaessen. They were married in 1945 and Romualdus Antonius Johannes Loudivicus Roméo (the first four names are Latin versions of his father's and mother's patrimony—an old Dutch tradition) was born in Holland in June 1946. Dallaire senior returned to Canada with his regiment while Roméo junior and his mother arrived in Quebec, six months later, on a Red Cross boat full of war brides.

Dallaire grew up first in a shabby war veterans' housing complex near Quebec City, then he moved with his family to a tough east-end community in Montreal. His mother—a stern and pious woman—sent him to Boy Scouts with the Anglicans to ensure that he got a grounding in the English language. Dallaire spoke English with his Dutch mother and French with his father; with much influence from his parents, his politics became decidedly federalist over the years.

Roméo wanted to join the armed forces as soon as he was old enough, even though his father, who left the service as a career sergeant, warned him there were few opportunities for a French boy, especially in artillery. In fact, Dallaire entered at just the right time, though his father didn't live to see his son become a general.

His was a hard and often deprived upbringing, and it made Dallaire a focused and determined workaholic. But his intensity was leavened by an energetic sense of fun. Friends from his bachelor days remember how Dallaire would spontaneously decide they should all drive to Montreal from Quebec City to catch a hockey game and enjoy late-night steaks and beer. At the NATO base in Germany, Dallaire would get friends to go off on excursions around Europe to visit old battle sites. A military man by day and a party animal by night is how the old crowd remembers him—until he met Elizabeth and became a family man.

Though gregarious with friends, he was uncompromising with those who served under him. Depending on their energy level, they either complained about or admired the way Dallaire would stride into a room, fire off a dozen assignments and continue on to another meeting without a pause. Dallaire bubbled over with ideas: if even a fraction of them stuck, he felt he had accomplished something. He inspired loyalty among some and frustration among others who often wished he would stay in one place long enough to finish a thought.

Within the authority of the UN, an irrepressible dynamo could only be an irritant. From his headquarters in central Kigali, installed in a crumbling old athletes' hostel attached to the Amahoro sports stadium, Dallaire could spend an entire day on the phone to New York, trying to reach someone who would subsequently tell him that what he wanted was impossible. In Rwanda, Dallaire's positive nature wore thin.

He was frustrated not only by the UN but by his own lack of understanding of the country he was in. New York had provided little information; his reconnaissance mission had lacked the necessary experts; and he felt that he didn't have the required aptitude for complex political manoeuvrings. Only once had he waded into political waters back home; in 1990, he'd encouraged a group of fellow officers to join him in an intervention critical of Quebec separation. They produced a carefully constructed discussion paper pointing out the exorbitant costs an independent Quebec might incur if it attempted to set up its own armed forces, and they submitted the brief to the Quebec government's Bélanger-Campeau Commission on the viability of Quebec independence. With a great deal of help from some savvy friends, Dallaire avoided getting himself into any real trouble. The intervention was politely received by the commission but its members were already preparing to write a positive report on the "affordability" of sovereignty. Dallaire got a powerful lesson as to what a quagmire the public arena can be.

In Rwanda, he was confronted with a quagmire of epic proportions. Habyarimana was claiming that he was trying to put the transitional government into place, but in truth his circle was doing everything possible to avoid it. What else could the UN expect? The Arusha Accords, if implemented, would mean the end of Habyarimana's absolute power. What dictator would willingly give up such privilege? It would take tremendous political leverage, in addition to impeccable diplomatic skills, to push Habyarimana out.

Those who served with Dallaire in Rwanda describe November 1993 as the time they first sensed the darkness closing in. The small group of officers couldn't say exactly what it was, only that there was a tension, a feeling. Belgium had sent a few experienced intelligence personnel to be part of the mission, even though it was strictly verboten for peacekeepers to conduct any form of espionage (it would create the impression that the UN didn't trust the people it was supposed to be helping). The Belgian military intelligence officers were quickly able to learn that the death squads of the Habyarimana government, and of the Clan de Madame, were in an advanced state of war preparation. The Presidential Guard was distributing weapons. There had been a number of significant political assassinations. No one could figure out what the plan was: the intelligence men could report only that something sinister was afoot. Was it just troublemakers? Was it containable? If they had known more about the recent history of Rwanda, perhaps they could have more accurately interpreted the warning signs. But they didn't. All that Dallaire and his officers at UNAMIR headquarters in Kigali could sense was what Conrad described as "the stillness of an implacable force brooding over an inscrutable intention."

Among the Belgians who arrived in November, one officer formed a special bond with Dallaire. Colonel Luc Marchal is a gaunt, serious-looking man with black hair and eyes. Though he appears dour, his disposition is to look on the bright side. Marchal served as Dallaire's Kigali sector commander and had many invaluable years of experience in peacekeeping, mostly in Africa. Dallaire quickly came to rely on Marchal's personal knowledge of the area, and Marchal attempted to "read the mood" for his friend and commander. "Rwandans genuinely want to live in peace," says Marchal. But their leaders didn't. "In Africa, when you have two parties and both want power, there is little chance for sharing." If there had been any possibility for the Arusha Accords, Marchal was certain the moment had been lost before he and Dallaire even arrived.

The general raised the UN flag on November 1 in the presence of armed forces from both the Rwandan government and the RPF, as well as his 150 blue berets. Dallaire proclaimed: "Today's simple ceremony is aimed at formally demonstrating to all concerned, but in particular to the Rwandan population, that the UN peacekeeping mission is launched and working." Dallaire knew the politicians in the crowd were desperate to form the transitional government; every lost moment made that seem less likely. He declared: "Moi, Roméo Dallaire, un petit gars de Québec," will be dedicated to peace. "Good luck to all of us who are committed by duty and loyalty, by patriotism, by hope and by the fundamental optimism that all men and women are born with the desire for peace and love, that we will together succeed in this magnificent adventure of a lasting peace in Rwanda."

Dallaire announced to those assembled under the hot equatorial sun that his major contingent of troops would arrive in about ten days. On November 17, Dallaire held another ceremony to officially open the UNAMIR headquarters and, again, he told the crowd he expected to see his UNAMIR contingent arrive within ten days. In his speech, he addressed President Habyarimana directly: "Your presence, your excellency, monsieur president, is a demonstration of your conviction to the success of the peace process in your marvellous country." But Dallaire knew that any commitment to the peace process on Habyarimana's part was rapidly eroding.

Dallaire knew it would take an accomplished diplomat to navigate these tricky political waters. But he wasn't so lucky as to get one. Boutros-Ghali appointed Jacques-Roger Booh Booh, a former foreign minister of Cameroon, to the job of special representative. Booh Booh was to keep the implementation of the Arusha Accords on schedule, and he was supposed to be fully briefed on the politics of the region. But he didn't arrive until November 23, and he was blatantly unprepared for the job.

Booh Booh never seemed to grasp exactly what was going on in Rwanda. Major Beardsley (the "other Canadian," as everyone called him) attempted to bring Booh Booh up to date on what the mission was doing, and came to doubt that the special representative had read the Arusha Accords before he arrived. To the horror of the two Canadians, Booh Booh quickly jumped into the delicate negotiations, issuing ultimata and threatening to report political players to the UN if they failed to co-operate. Dallaire and his small military staff had been in Kigali for four weeks; they didn't know much about diplomatic subtleties, but you didn't have to be too astute to see that the political situation was fragile.

Since the Burundi coup, the Clan de Madame and other extremists had accelerated their drive towards "the final solution" Rwandan-style. Members of a volatile and growing youth movement called the Interahamwe ("those who attack together") were actively training in various camps around the countryside. Belgian intelligence officers reported that they had seen such camps and had noted that Israelis, probably mercenaries, were conducting the training.

Broadcasters like RTLMC warned that there was work to be done in "cleaning" the country of the "cockroaches." Dallaire was deeply alarmed by the radio hate messages. Some of them were directed at UNAMIR and others were directed at his African friends, such as Landoald Ndasingwa. All requests to New York for some way to block this death talk were met with the argument that it was beyond the mandate of the UN to censor the media or to impose its will on a sovereign state.

Hutu Power leaders spread throughout the country, staging rallies and meetings, calling for support against the Tutsi menace. At one rally, people were warned: "Look for what is within us. The enemy among us here. We cannot sit down and think what happened in Burundi cannot happen here, since the enemy is among us."

Under UNAMIR's nose in November and December, unidentified assailants murdered dozens of people known to oppose the Habyarimana regime, some of them high-profile political leaders. Dallaire had his Belgian troops by then but it's not clear what he could have done about the murders. The Belgians' equipment hadn't arrived and even when it did Dallaire found much of it in a state of disrepair. His force had only a handful of armoured personnel carriers; Dallaire himself moved around the country in an un-covered Jeep. When some high-ranking Rwandans and some of Dallaire's officers suggested it was undignified and would diminish his stature in the eyes of Rwandans, Dallaire said his open car would show people there was nothing to fear.

By the end of December, fourteen hundred troops had arrived, which at last allowed Dallaire to act on some of the requirements of the Arusha Accords. Peacekeepers escorted six hundred RPF troops into Kigali as part of the power-sharing arrangement, but with Burundi refugees in Rwanda warning of impending disaster and the hate radio pouring more gas on the fire, the spectre of *inyenzi* rebels marching into the centre of the capital did more to provoke war than to promote peace.

Dallaire believed the only hope for stemming the violence was to get the new government in place and to allow the peace agreement to take its course. Booh Booh was so ineffectual that Dallaire tried to take on more of the diplomat's role. But even Beardsley could see it wasn't the general's strength, either. Beardsley had seen professional diplomats in action who were persuasive and even cunning, and had found it breathtaking to witness what they could accomplish. Dallaire was no such magician.

Habyarimana, meanwhile, was playing a game of divide and destroy. Sworn in as head of the yet-to-be-formed transitional government, he thwarted every effort to sign up ministers. He insisted that terms of the Arusha Accords be renegotiated, and that a number of smaller parties, including extremist ones, also become part of the transitional government. This wasn't because he wanted to broaden the base but because he thought, quite correctly, that it would set the various political groups to squabbling among themselves. The president knew what effect this would have on the fragile coalition: instead of sticking with mixed parties formed around ideological principles, people began to organize themselves along ethnic lines.

Habyarimana demanded that one of the most extremist parties, the Coalition pour la Défense de la République (CDR), be included in the new government. The CDR had been vehemently opposed to the Arusha Accords even before they were signed, and certainly had no interest in supporting the transitional government. A human-rights group working in the country had evidence that CDR members were attacking civilians in the countryside, and the party had issued a press release telling the Hutu they should be ready to "neutralize by all means" the enemy and its accomplices (which were any Hutu who resisted the anti-Tutsi message). Booh Booh may have been confused by the range of parties and rivalries, and he made a huge blunder: he agreed to Habyarimana's demand for CDR recognition. Booh Booh consequently lost the confidence of Dallaire and the country's political moderates.

If anyone thought they would get more help from the United Nations when things went wrong, they were sadly mistaken. An African bureaucrat at the UN, Kofi Annan, headed up the Department of Peacekeeping Operations (DPKO) — a relatively new office that was meant to deal exclusively, and promptly, with the needs of the various missions. But Annan was overwhelmed by the magnitude of the task and he lacked adequate staff and resources. Dallaire depended on the fact that he had a friend at the DPKO in New York. Maurice Baril, a Canadian general whom Dallaire had known for years, had been appointed as the chief military adviser to the secretary-general. Dallaire felt that he could call Baril and get his message across, that his old friend would cut through some of the red tape. But Baril was often sidetracked by other matters, one of them being the

UN mission in Somalia, which took a nasty turn for the worse just after Dallaire arrived in Rwanda.

On a dusty Mogadishu street, eighteen members of a U.S. Delta Force made up of commandos and rangers were killed and more than seventy injured in a botched attempt to abduct two top aides of a Somali warlord. Under a hail of bullets, the remaining U.S. troops attempted to shoot their way to safety through a mob of angry Somalis. Media reports indicate as many as one thousand Africans were killed in the shootout. Malaysian and Pakistani peacekeepers were sent to rescue the Americans and they sustained ninety casualties. The Somali rebels tied the naked corpse of an American ranger to the back of a pickup truck and drove it around the streets of Mogadishu while the crowds cheered. All of this was beamed back into the living rooms of America through their television news.

The deaths, and these images, would affect U.S. military and foreign policy for years to come. Why were American boys allowed to die in an African country no one needed or cared about? The reaction to the Somali incident crystallized in Presidential Decision Directive 25, a limitation on all further peacekeeping missions. PDD25 is informally called the Mogadishu Line — the barrier the U.S. will no longer cross to help anyone. That included Rwanda.

Dallaire had got the RPF into Kigali, but all the other important deadlines for the Arusha Accords came and went. The good news was that his soldiers were slowly arriving. At the same time, Dallaire was pleased that, as part of the deal brokered by the UN, French soldiers there at the behest of the Rwandan government were finally to leave. These ground troops had stayed on after UNAMIR arrived ostensibly to protect French citizens still in the country. But their presence was destabilizing: the French government made no secret of its opposition to the Tutsi rebels. Dallaire was happy to see them go, though he suspected that a number of them stayed on in an unofficial capacity. Belgian intelligence, as well as the RPF, reported seeing white French-speaking soldiers in the countryside wearing the uniform of the Rwandan armed forces.

Dallaire had been told he would get a full battalion of Belgians, but instead he got a force half that size — 450 troops. He had planned to make the Belgians his rapid-reaction force, training them for emergencies and to deter conflicts between the belligerents, but now he would have to give that job to the Bangladeshis, the only full battalion on the ground. The

Bangladeshis had almost no technical training, however, and it was soon obvious to Dallaire that they were not psychologically ready for even the relatively mild state of tension existing in Rwanda. They had no equipment or supplies, not even food and water, and they expected that the UN would provide for them. (Many poorer nations send peacekeeping forces abroad as a way for their soldiers and their governments to make money from the UN.) The Bangladeshi commander told Dallaire he hoped his troops would gain some experience and training, but his soldiers could not even be away from their base for more than twelve hours at a stretch. They didn't have sleeping bags.

Luc Marchal discovered that the Bangladeshis were not a battalion at all but an assortment of soldiers pulled out of different units who had never been together before Rwanda. Their commander showed up weeks late and turned out to be a professor from the Bangladeshi military school who would act only on written orders submitted well in advance.

The total UNAMIR force of 2,548 soldiers came from twenty-four countries, principally Bangladesh, Belgium, Ghana, Tunisia, Senegal, Congo, Togo and Mali. The last of them arrived in March 1994, just weeks before the genocide began—and eight months after the Arusha Accords had specified the immediate need for UN soldiers.

Getting equipment was as difficult. Dallaire wrote: "The APCs had arrived in late February [1994] and early March without tools, spare parts, mechanics, manuals and with limited ammunition. The main weapons on the APCs had never been testfired in Rwanda." Almost all of the six hundred vehicles that would eventually arrive were "soft-skinned": Jeeps and pickups with no protective armour. They came without radios, and many of them were hopelessly broken down. They had been driven in from whatever African country had last used them. Some of the soldiers didn't even know how to drive an APC, let alone repair one.

In January 1994, Faustin Twagiramungu, a moderate Hutu who was the prime minister designate for the transitional government, told UNAMIR he had a source who wished to provide some sensitive information. Heeding the UN's rules about intelligence gathering, Dallaire was wary of talking to an informant. Also, he worried it could be a trap. He designated Marchal and his Belgian intelligence officers to meet with the man and suss him out.

Luc Marchal remembers the encounter as being like something out of a James Bond movie. The informant, called only Jean-Pierre, was a military trainer with the Interahamwe who said that he supported the struggle against the RPF, but that he was against killing Tutsi civilians. And that was exactly what he was being told to prepare people to do. Jean-Pierre had precise and detailed information on the Rwandan government's preparations for mass murder. In exchange for the information, he wanted protection for himself, his wife and his children. The Belgian officers were highly sceptical of his extraordinary information. But Jean-Pierre also told of a cache of rifles that he was supposed to distribute to Interahamwe members. Dallaire immediately dispatched someone to secretly check this out, and he concluded that the man was telling the truth.

On January 11, Dallaire sent a coded cable to New York that has come to be one of the most loaded documents in UN history. The cable predicts all that is to happen in the coming months, straight from the mouth of the informant. Written entirely in capitals, the missive was titled "REQUEST FOR PROTECTION FOR INFORMANT," and it was addressed to Maurice Baril.

Dallaire told Baril that the informant had shown UNAMIR the location of an arms cache, and that Dallaire intended to raid it within the next thirty-six hours. Jean-Pierre had also outlined a plot to kill Belgian UNAMIR soldiers in order to create a kind of Mogadishu effect—an immediate pullout of all Belgian peacekeepers from Rwanda, just as the Americans had pulled out of Somalia. Next, the cable told New York that the informant was paid by the Rwandan government forces to train and equip Interahamwe members for a massive assault. "PRINCIPAL AIM OF INTERAHAMWE IN THE PAST WAS TO PROTECT KIGALI FROM RPF. SINCE UNAMIR MANDATE HE HAS BEEN ORDERED TO REGISTER ALL TUTSI IN KIGALI. HE SUSPECTS IT IS FOR THEIR EXTERMINATION. EXAMPLE HE GAVE WAS THAT IN 20 MINUTES HIS PERSONNEL COULD KILL UP TO 1000 TUTSIS."

Dallaire wasn't entirely confident—"POSSIBILITY OF A TRAP NOT FULLY EXCLUDED"—but he wanted the UN to allow the man protection just in case the information checked out. Dallaire concluded with: "PEUX CE QUE VEUX. ALLONS-Y." *Where there's a will there's a way. Let's go!* Dallaire and Marchal, along with Beardsley, who typed it, carefully drafted the cable for maximum effect, but the final inscription was the only French, and it was from Dallaire personally.

Maurice Baril acknowledged receipt of the cable and wrote that he would "get back" to Dallaire. Within hours, a message arrived from Kofi Annan, then the head of peacekeeping, addressed to Jacques-Roger Booh Booh, who was really the man in charge of the mission. "Information is cause for concern but there are certain inconsistencies," the message read. "Wait for further instruction." The next morning, two pages of specific orders arrived in Kigali for Booh Booh and Dallaire. Not only did New York deny permission to protect the informant, but it forbade Dallaire to seize the arms cache. Dallaire had not asked permission to take the guns; he had just decided it made sense. But Annan's message read: "It clearly goes beyond the mandate entrusted to UNAMIR under resolution 872." Dallaire was struck dumb by this instruction, but it got worse.

New York told Dallaire and Booh Booh to confront President Habya-rimana with this information and get *him* to do something about the guns. Since Dallaire knew the guns were being stored at the president's party headquarters, this seemed absurd, but it was completely consistent with the convoluted codes of peacekeeping neutrality. UNAMIR wasn't there to pro-tect people. It was there to help the Rwandan authorities protect people. It was Habyarimana's government that had invited the UN in, and it was to the president that Dallaire should address himself.

Before meeting with the president, the cable ordered, Dallaire and Booh Booh should go and see the ambassadors of Belgium, France and the United States, and inform them of the news in case their countries wanted to take action. Dallaire knew this instruction was also absurd—the French and the Americans had sophisticated intelligence gathering in the country, and they probably knew more than Dallaire did. In the interests of keep-ing the country stable, Dallaire had often passed information collected by Belgian intelligence to the French and American ambassadors, only to find they were already aware of it.

The final message of the New York cable was: "We wish to stress, however, that the overriding consideration is the need to avoid entering into a course of action that might lead to the use of force and unantici-pated repercussions. Regards."

That exchange of messages, in a nutshell, explained everything that was wrong with the UNAMIR mission, and much that was about to go seri-ously wrong in Rwanda. Dallaire dutifully went to the ambassadors and the Rwandan president to tell them what they already knew. The president was asked to inform UNAMIR within forty-eight hours as to what action he had taken.

Booh Booh wrote New York the next day to report that all the tasks had been completed and that the president had seemed surprised by the information about the arms cache. "My assessment of the situation," wrote Booh Booh, "is that the initiative to confront the accused parties with the information was a good one and may force them to decide on alternative ways of jeopardizing the peace process." It's not clear exactly what that was supposed to mean. Dallaire, on the other hand, wrote a situation report based on another meeting with the informant. Jean-Pierre stated that the president's party had been very shaken by UNAMIR's visit. According to Jean-Pierre, the militias were immediately ordered to step up the distribution of weapons before UNAMIR got hold of them. They needn't have worried: UNAMIR had been ordered not to interfere.

In February 1994, the Belgian foreign minister, Willy Claes, visited the mission in Rwanda, and Luc Marchal took him aside and told him of the problems. They needed weapons and ammunition desperately. UNAMIR was unable to stop the flow of guns to extremists because the force was so ineffective, and so undermined by instructions from New York. Willy Claes knew all too well how bad things were: Belgian intelligence reports filed to Brussels and the country's ambassador in Kigali had provided dire warnings, including indications that Belgian soldiers were to be targets. Claes subsequently tried to persuade the UN to change Dallaire's mandate to give him more freedom to act, particularly to raid and confiscate weapons caches, but to no avail.

Marchal wasn't the only senior officer with UNAMIR to pressure his government for added assistance. In a confidential memo obtained from the Canadian government under the Access to Information Act, the African attaché with External Affairs reported on a February 1994 meeting with Dallaire in Rwanda. The general had issued a desperate plea to Ottawa, describing Canada's small contribution to UNAMIR as "scandalous and il-logical." Dallaire called for the immediate deployment of a battalion of soldiers from his old command at Valcartier, Quebec, and told the attaché that he knew those particular soldiers could work miracles in a country where "Canada is placed on a pedestal" for its contribution to such things as the National University. "The expertise of Canada could make the difference between success and failure in Rwanda," says the memo. No response to Dallaire's plea was released by the government but it's obvious the reply was negative. A handwritten marginal note on the memo reads, "many of Dallaire's arguments are unconvincing."

The general was deeply alarmed by the imbalance of force. Covert weapons shipments were continuing to come in from countries like South Africa and, especially, France, and Habyarimana's people were distributing them to the extremists. Dallaire didn't realize that the guns were only a small part of his dilemma: there were more machetes shipped into the country in 1993–94 than in all previous years. With documents from shipping companies, Human Rights Watch estimates that Rwanda imported 581,000 machetes in that period — one for every three adult Hutu males in the country. Even if Dallaire had known of such shipments, he probably would have considered them farm tools, which of course they were.

While Willy Claes recommended a stronger mission, Britain and the United States opposed him, and favoured complete withdrawal over strengthening UNAMIR. Only the Security Council could authorize more firepower, and it wouldn't.

By March, Operation Zero was upon them. Both Booh Booh and Dallaire reported the slide into anarchy — murders, political assassinations, weapons and grenades fired off after dark each night. They knew of death lists and had been warned that opposition leaders would be killed first. No one in New York could be rallied, though the Security Council did warn the Rwandan government that UNAMIR would be pulled out if the interim government was not installed post-haste. For the death squads and the extremists, that was more a reward than a threat.

Much later, when the January cables were leaked to some journalists and the world learned about Jean-Pierre, about Dallaire's attempt to alert his masters and about the New York peacekeeping office's extraordinary lack of regard for the information, there was much tearing of hair and pointing of fingers. Non-permanent members of the Security Council said they had never heard of the cables and had never been warned that a genocide was planned. The Permanent Five must have withheld information. Certainly, they wailed, things would have turned out differently if they had only known. But that's not entirely likely.

Iqbal Riza was the person in the Department of Peacekeeping Operations who actually wrote the replies to Dallaire's cables for Kofi Annan. He says their first reaction, when they read that Dallaire was going to raid an arms cache, was: "Not another Somalia!" There was no political will in New York or Washington to cross the Mogadishu Line.

And what if Dallaire had intervened in January and February? What if he had resisted the death squads before the world saw what they were capable of doing? What if his men had been in a few shootouts, met violence with violence? Would any country have supported him or come to his aid? Could he claim, after the fact, that he was trying to prevent the deaths of nearly a million people? Who would have believed him? No, the story was just too fantastic, even if it did turn out to be true.

The third of April, Easter Sunday, was the most important day of the year for the people of Rwanda. It's a country of devout Christians, and they filled the churches. The priests broke bread for Communion and told the congregations Jesus Christ had risen: salvation was theirs. Within the next few days, these Christians would dutifully follow the orders of the government to kill their neighbours—brutally and without mercy—whether they were men, women or babies. Many of the priests would actually help. Not salvation but the apocalypse was upon them.

On Wednesday, April 6, President Habyarimana went to Dar es Salaam for meetings with other African presidents about the situation in Burundi. When the talks were over, the president of Burundi asked Habyarimana if he could bum a lift home with his fellow Hutu. Habyarimana had a beautiful Falcon 50 jet with a three-man crew, compliments of French president François Mitterand, and it could take the two presidents back to their respective capitals in no time. They would stop first in Kigali, to drop off Habyarimana, and the craft would go on to Burundi and then return home.

At 8:30 p.m., the Falcon dipped to come in for a landing at Kigali airport just as two missiles were fired from nearby. The presidential plane was struck and crashed near Habyarimana's own garden. Everyone on board was killed.

Dallaire had warned New York weeks earlier: "Time does seem to be running out for political discussions, as any spark on the security side could have catastrophic consequences." Dallaire now had his spark—a ball of flames, in fact—and he would also have his consequences. The red-eyed devils had joined with the papier-mâché ones. The effect would be devastating.

3

THE PRESIDENT IS DEAD – THE GENOCIDE BEGINS

All correspondence referring to the matter was subject to rigid "language
rules," and, except in the reports from Einsatzgruppen, it is rare
to find documents in which bald words such as "extermination," "liquidation,"
or "killing," occur. The prescribed code names for killing were
"final solution," "evacuation," and "special treatment".... The net effect
of this language system was not to keep the people ignorant of what
they were doing but to keep them from equating it with the old,
"normal" knowledge of murder and lies.
—Hannah Arendt, *Eichmann in Jerusalem:*
A Report on the Banality of Evil

Technically speaking, the story should end here. When the president of Rwanda was killed at 2030 hours on April 6, Brigadier General Roméo Dallaire and his UNAMIR force no longer had a job to do. It's not a minor point. Another force commander might have ordered all his men back to the barracks to await word on when and how they would be evacuated from the country. UNAMIR was in Rwanda to help the fractious military and political parties join forces and become one country, living in peace. In the simple semantics of his mission, Dallaire was to "monitor," "contribute," "supervise" and "help" the peace process. But the only member of the interim government who had been sworn in was the president, and he was now dead. Within twelve hours of the assassination, the Rwandan Patriotic Front of Colonel Paul Kagame was at war with the Rwandan government forces. Dallaire no longer had a mandate.

"My first reaction was, This is going to be a catastrophe," Dallaire said months later. "With the president gone there was no dauphin in the wings that we knew of." That was just on the political side. On the military side it was even messier. Who had shot down the plane? Was it a *coup d'état*? "I was very keen to know with whom I was going to do business."

To his relief, Dallaire got a call almost immediately on the night of April 6 from someone in the Rwandan military asking him to attend an emergency meeting at army headquarters. Théoneste Bagosora, a retired colonel with the Rwandan armed forces, chaired the gathering of sixteen high-ranking officers. Dallaire knew little of Colonel Bagosora, but he got a crash course. A member of the Clan de Madame, Bagosora was born in the same region of northern Rwanda as Habyarimana. He was a man whose lust for power was well known among the other extremists. He had little interest in politics, though he supported the CDR—at least its racist ideology. Bagosora believed the struggle was really between Tutsi and Hutu, not between political parties, and he maintained that the Tutsi rebels were really trying to reinstate the old monarchy, forcing Hutu into servitude once again. He had been in Arusha when the accords were negotiated, and was quoted as saying, after the documents were signed, that he was returning to Rwanda to prepare for the apocalypse. Luc Marchal had passed on his own hair-raising encounter just a week earlier: Bagosora told Marchal that the only way to solve Rwanda's problem was to get rid of the Tutsi. Marchal didn't know at the time that he meant it.

Human Rights Watch obtained some of Bagosora's papers and diaries after the war, and these revealed that the colonel was a principal—and very early—organizer of the Rwandan final solution. Through the winter and spring of 1994, Bagosora had been working out detailed plans for the deployment of "recruits" who would "defend" Rwanda from the enemy. His diary included directions for the distribution of guns and grenades to Interahamwe and ideas for messages to be broadcast on Rwandan hate radio. Bagosora was an extreme anti-Tutsi militant whom Dallaire quickly realized he could not trust.

Dallaire reported later that it wasn't clear whether Bagosora had unqualified support from the people in the room—a range of police chiefs and military officers. Colonel Marchal arrived late, but he had the same sense as Dallaire—that Bagosora wasn't the unanimous choice for leader. Bagosora was anxious to assure the foreigner that he was trying to maintain order. He also declared that the military would now take over the role of government, which clearly meant *he* would take over. Dallaire told him it just wasn't on: he'd have to establish a civilian head of state or incur the wrath of the international community. And he told Bagosora that the rightful successor was the Rwandan prime minister, Agathe Uwilingiyimana. Bagosora rejected that idea repeatedly but agreed to meet with Special Representative Booh Booh—a man the extremists trusted because he had supported the CDR in its bid to be represented in the transitional government.

Colonel Bagosora and General Dallaire went off to find Jacques-Roger Booh Booh, who had acquired his own private house in Kigali, and Booh Booh and Dallaire spent much of the evening trying to persuade Bagosora to allow for a civilian government. Colonel Marchal stayed at the meeting after Bagosora and Dallaire departed in order to monitor developments, but it soon deteriorated into a banal discussion of the historic significance of the president's death. With more pressing concerns on his mind, like the safety of his peacekeepers, Marchal departed.

He was struck by how calm the city seemed. Bagosora's reassurances that he was trying to maintain order hadn't satisfied Marchal; he could not shrug off his sense that something really bad was about to happen. The old mystery novel cliché came to mind: "Everything was quiet. Too quiet." The streets of Kigali converge on a few roundabouts, with roads leading off each like spokes on a wheel. To shut down or control the city, one need only take those hubs, and that's exactly what the Interahamwe militias were doing. Marchal saw roadblocks going up. Mobility would soon become difficult, if not impossible. At about 2:00 a.m., Dallaire called Marchal with several orders regarding the security of Rwandan VIPs and strategically important facilities throughout the city.

Protecting Rwandan politicians and opposition leaders from harm was never specifically Dallaire's job, but in his private notes he describes it as a personal priority. Since early December, when he was first informed that the militias had lists of people to be assassinated, he'd assigned units of four or five soldiers to guard, alongside detachments of Rwandan gendarmerie, all VIPs he considered at risk. Most members of the Rwandan political elite said they would have left the country weeks or months earlier if not for those blue berets parked at their door and Dallaire's own personal assurance that he would protect them. Dallaire knew that if the politicians left, there would be no chance for the Arusha Accords.

Dallaire considered Agathe Uwilingiyimana one of the most important and vulnerable of the VIPs. Mme Agathe, as everyone called her, was a tall, affable and trustworthy woman who had once said, "If you are afraid of dying, then don't become a politician in the conditions we are living in now." She had a master's degree in chemistry and was thoroughly modern, a role model for Rwandan women.

As per the orders from Dallaire, Marchal was to instruct the commander of the Belgian contingent, a cool and detached lieutenant colonel named Joe Dewez, to send out his units on several important assignments. Dewez is a Belgian of Flemish extraction who has no time for overheated emotions and hyperbole. Dallaire needed Dewez's soldiers to carefully manoeuvre themselves into strategic places in order to reassure Rwandans that everything was under control.

Some of Dewez's soldiers were to go immediately to Radio Rwanda, a state broadcaster not working for the militias, to secure its premises, while another unit was to head towards the prime minister's house to reinforce the guard around her. At dawn the soldiers were to escort Mme Agathe to Radio Rwanda, where she would make a public address, telling Rwandans to stay calm. The third job Dallaire assigned to his Belgian contingent was to secure the airport and protect the crash site of the plane.

Dewez sent his best men.

Three hours later, Dewez reported back to Marchal that it was impossible to secure the crash site, and that it seemed, oddly, that a group of unidentified French soldiers had already been there. As for the unit he had sent to the radio station, they didn't have much success getting past the roadblocks and had abandoned the mission. But one very persistent group of soldiers pushed through to the prime minister's residence. First Lieutenant Thierry Lotin and nine other Belgian soldiers from the elite forces of the para-commandos arrived at Mme Agathe's home at 5:30 a.m., taking three hours to go a distance that normally took fifteen minutes. Their persistence would have fatal consequences—for them.

Immediately, the Belgians found themselves under fire from a mob of Rwandan soldiers. Mme Agathe had been preparing a written statement to deliver on the radio, but now neighbours and friends called to tell her that she had to escape, that the Belgian peacekeepers were pinned down outside her door and would not be able to protect her family. She fled out the back way with her husband, Ignace Barahira, and they attempted to scale the garden wall. When it proved too difficult, Mme Agathe headed to a rented UN building, where she hoped she could hide, while sending her five children off for safety in another direction.

The Belgians at Mme Agathe's radioed back to base. Joe Dewez told them not to surrender their guns, but some had already done that and were pinned down on the ground. Dewez—in an order he will regret for the rest of his life—told the others to do the same. He had no way of knowing how grave the situation was and admits today that he failed to properly "read" the situation. Lotin told him: "They are going to lynch us, my colonel." Dewez thought he was exaggerating.

Dallaire had been trying to do Booh Booh's job for much of the night: put a political leadership in place to fill the vacuum left by Habyarimana's death. He didn't know what was happening to the Belgians. Bagosora was still proposing that the military take over, but both Dallaire and Booh Booh told him he would have to allow a civilian interim government until they could sort out the mess. Dallaire insisted Mme Agathe take charge; Bagosora said she wasn't "effective." The dickering continued.

What Dallaire and Booh Booh didn't know, however, was that all night Bagosora had also been orchestrating a separate series of meetings with the Presidential Guard and the Hutu militias that would ensure there were no civilian leaders left alive by the next day.

On the Presidential Guard's lists of people to be exterminated were both Tutsi and Hutu who had opposed Habyarimana; the death squads were going house to house rounding them up. Those they sought lived principally in the same neighbourhood, a comfortable residential area that also included embassies and residences of foreigners. Since Kigali was under curfew, most people were at home, guarded by the combined patrols of peacekeepers and the local gendarmerie. Neither offered much resistance as the Hutu militias swept through.

Some of the Rwandans who were attacked claim that the peacekeepers actually co-operated with the death squads that had come for them—a claim Dallaire argues to this day that no one can prove. But it's true that the peacekeepers were under orders to work with the authorities, not against them. Some of them didn't realize the degree to which the power structure had suddenly changed. In addition, a number of peacekeepers were simply intimidated by the better-armed Presidential Guard.

Landoald Ndasingwa was an obvious target, as he was a prominent Tutsi and a leading member of the Liberal Party. He had heard his name on hate radio, but he told his family that he felt he would be protected by UNAMIR and particularly by the good Canadian general. In February, Hotel Chez Lando had been ambushed in a grenade attack, and ever since, a unit of peacekeepers from the Ghana contingent had been guarding Ndasingwa and his family. They thought — or hoped — it was enough.

In the early morning of April 7, Ndasingwa picked up the phone and called Luc Marchal at UNAMIR headquarters. It was one of dozens of calls Marchal got asking for more bodyguards. He could do little about it. Militias blocked almost every route through the city, particularly the roads leading to the homes of political leaders. He didn't know yet that his own soldiers were becoming casualties, but Marchal suspected there was trouble. As he tried to assure Ndasingwa that help was coming, he heard gunfire over the phone and what was probably a grenade going off. Ndasingwa told him it was too late. The phone went dead. The family, including Ndasingwa's mother, his wife, Hélène, and the two children, were executed in their living room.

The peacekeepers who were to guard Ndasingwa and the other VIPs fled for their own lives or hid out as soon as they saw the Presidential Guard and the militias arrive in groups of twenty or thirty. Some of the Ghanaians were caught and beaten: the rest of them quickly got the message. Judge Joseph Kavaruganda, a moderate Hutu who was president of the Constitutional Court, and the man who could swear in the new government, had been guarded by Bangladeshis. Just days before the president was killed, Dallaire and Marchal had decided they needed to replace the completely ineffectual Bangladeshi contingent. They never got the chance. Now the Bangladeshis offered no resistance to the members of the Presidential Guard, who took the judge away instead of killing him on the spot.

The Rwandan militias became emboldened as they realized the peacekeepers would not get in their way. Although Dallaire's rules of engagement (particularly paragraph seventeen) would have allowed his troops to protect these people, the general had warned the soldiers in the weeks before the genocide to use their weapons only in the worst-case scenario. This wasn't just because New York was on his case constantly to prevent any violence involving UNAMIR (lest it draw them into more complex, and thus more expensive, operations) — he knew his people were simply not capable of handling much more. The Belgians were his best-trained force, and even they couldn't do much with light arms against an angry mob. There was also animosity between the Belgian soldiers and the Hutu militias, and Dallaire had heard of numerous threats to the lives of those troops. If the Belgians got into a scrap with the Hutu, it would jeopardize other contingents like the Bangladeshis, who were incapable of defending themselves. Also, UNAMIR was responsible for thousands of foreign workers and unarmed military observers throughout the country. If the delicate balance between UNAMIR and the Hutu was disrupted, they would be immediately at risk. Dallaire was more than willing to push the terms of his mandate to the limit, but he didn't have the resources to back it up.

In another house that morning, Faustin Twagiramungu—the man who would have been prime minister if the Arusha Accords had been implemented—asked his Bangladeshi guards if they were going to protect him when the Rwandan soldiers came. But the peacekeepers were already looking for someplace to hide. Just before she herself fled, Mme Agathe phoned Twagiramungu and told him to run. He hid his family in the basement and jumped the wall of his garden, landing in the yard of an American businessman. The man was terrified, according to Twagiramungu, and didn't want any trouble. Still, he hid Twagiramungu in a broom closet and got the U.S. ambassador to call UNAMIR for help.

Dallaire sent one of his five functioning APCs to rescue him and, when it arrived, Twagiramungu asked if they could go back and pick up his family. But the Belgian driver had already been to the house, looking for him, and he'd found no members of the family. Instead, he had loaded up the Bangladeshi peacekeepers, who were now cowering in the back of the APC. There was hardly any room for Twagiramungu in the vehicle, and he was compelled to sit on the lap of one peacekeeper for the ride to UNAMIR headquarters. Twagiramungu discovered later that one of them had stolen his pen. (Twagiramungu's family managed to escape.)

The calls of desperation came in to the headquarters all through the early hours of April 7. Dallaire and Marchal took most of them. "There was a lot of shooting going on," Dallaire explained later. "So I'm afraid on a number of occasions we simply either said we would try [to] get to you and never did or simply listened to them screaming as the door was being beaten down and then the phone [went] dead. So what do you do? You hang up and say, What next?"

As the morning progressed, Dallaire was uncertain about his options. He had sent a message to New York saying, "Give me the means and I can do more." Human Rights Watch reports that the response was that nobody in New York was interested.

Dallaire wasn't sure what was happening with his peacekeepers. He knew that the unit of Belgians led by Thierry Lotin had been arrested and taken to Camp Kigali—a military base only a few minutes' drive from

Mme Agathe's. The peacekeepers who had been sent to the airport had been abducted by the militias and they were now also missing. None of the other units in Kigali could negotiate their way through the roadblocks, unless they wanted to take on twenty possibly stoned militia men with Kalashnikov rifles slung over their shoulders.

Then there was the Bangladeshi battalion.

Dallaire had had a problem housing all of his soldiers when they first arrived. The only place large enough to hold a full battalion was the Amahoro stadium ("Amahoro" means peace in Kinyarwandan), the sports complex adjacent to Dallaire's headquarters. Having the Bangladeshis in one place and close by, Dallaire hoped, would allow him and Marchal to keep an eye on them. But now the Bangladeshis had retreated into the complex and barricaded the gate.

The Belgians had been spread out all over Kigali in fourteen smaller quarters. Dallaire had hoped that deployment might help him keep in touch with all parts of the city, but now it meant that the Belgians were trapped behind the roadblocks. A determined Belgian officer, Major Petrus Maggen, managed to make it to work that morning, and Dallaire immediately recruited him as a driver. Dallaire had heard at the military meeting the night before that about a hundred Rwandan officers were congregating at a nearby school—the military college—and he wanted to be there. Maggen and Dallaire set out in a Jeep.

They didn't get far before they were stopped by the inevitable roadblock. Even Dallaire was unwilling to take on the men who controlled it: he simply climbed out of the Jeep and announced he was going on foot. Maggen followed as Dallaire took a turn into the residential neighbourhood where many of the VIPs lived. Dallaire didn't say what he was doing, but Maggen guessed he was looking for the prime minister. UNAMIR headquarters had been told that Mme Agathe had climbed her garden fence and landed in the yard of a house rented by the UN. Dallaire went there, but there was no sign of Mme Agathe—or anyone else. They returned to the main road and kept walking.

A Rwandan Army officer drove past and offered to give them a lift. Dallaire told the officer he was headed to a meeting, but to Maggen's surprise he gave the wrong location for it. Maggen figured that Dallaire wanted to take a small detour in order to drive by Camp Kigali. As they passed the gate, Dallaire could see bodies on the ground inside the compound. They were Belgian peacekeepers.

Dallaire asked the Rwandan to stop the car so he could enter Camp Kigali, but the terrified driver said it was far too dangerous. The soldiers inside were out of control, he said. As they drove away, Dallaire made one of the most important decisions of his career. It was — he realized later — one of those occasions when everything you are and everything you've been trained to do mesh: "A commander must be able to make certain decisions in a nanosecond. And this was one of those moments. Before we arrived at the school for the meeting, another thirty seconds' drive away, I had decided on my course of action." Dallaire concluded that he could do nothing to save the Belgians trapped inside Camp Kigali — even to attempt a rescue would jeopardize any number of his other personnel. He had lost radio contact with his headquarters (his Motorola telephone was attached to the jeep he had been forced to abandon) and he could not notify Marchal about the Belgians. But Marchal had heard about the capture and — independently — he had come to the same conclusion. It was too dangerous for a rescue operation.

The meeting at the school was already in progress when Dallaire and Maggen arrived uninvited. Dallaire could see that Colonel Bagosora was now completely in charge and there appeared to be no dissent in the ranks. Bagosora had assured Booh Booh that he would find a civilian leader, and in the coming days he would appoint a puppet prime minister, Jean Kambanda, a Hutu politician. Kambanda had been fleeing over the back wall of his own garden when the Presidential Guard arrived at his house. Instead of killing him, they installed him as head of state.

Dallaire followed the meeting closely for about an hour and asked about his Belgian peacekeepers only when it was over. "I had to find out first just what I was up against. Were all my soldiers and my observers now at risk? I had to assess the people at that meeting." But according to the Rwandan senior officers there, everyone, even Bagosora, had lost control of the soldiers at Camp Kigali. There was a rumour that the Belgians had shot down the president's plane, and that the Presidential Guard, never a well-disciplined group, was out for blood. Camp Kigali was also overrun with two thousand Hutu militiamen who were on a killing mission. If Dallaire sent in his troops, how many would come out alive? He decided to stick with his nanosecond decision. It would haunt him for years to come.

The quiet night had turned into a noisy day. There was shooting everywhere — no one in UNAMIR could really determine from where or from whom. At one point, a group of Belgians under attack from a mob of soldiers and paramilitaries arrived at Amahoro stadium seeking protection, but the Bangladeshis would not let them in. After a brief firefight with the Hutu, the Belgians leapt the fence. Before the afternoon was out, the RPF in Kigali broke out of their garrison and were in full-scale battle with the Rwandan government forces. Dallaire continued to look for Mme Agathe, and he eventually discovered the hiding place of her five children. They frantically told the general of their night of hell and how the Presidential Guard had fired on them. Their mother was presumed dead, but Dallaire couldn't find her body.

Rwandan soldiers eventually reported they found her outside the UN building where she had taken refuge—very close to where Dallaire and the Rwandan officers had had their meeting. It seemed that Mme Agathe had not put up much of a fight. She had apparently tried to persuade the soldiers to take her away, but they had had other plans. A member of the National Police shot her point-blank in the head. Witnesses interviewed later by Human Rights Watch say that her body was left half-naked with a beer bottle stuck in the vagina. Mme Agathe's husband was also killed.

Colonel Bagosora made a show of issuing calls to stabilize the country, but he was saying one thing and doing another. It didn't take Dallaire and Luc Marchal long to figure this out. Still, even then it didn't appear to be a hopeless situation, at least not to diehard optimists like Dallaire and Marchal, especially when they learned that some senior officers of the army and many of the gendarmerie wanted to join forces with UNAMIR to stop the killing.

On the evening of April 7, Dallaire went to see his Belgian commandos. Their mutilated bodies, some with their testicles severed, had been tossed in a heap in the morgue of Kigali Hospital. In the dim light of the wretched room, Dallaire mercifully couldn't see all the details of what had happened to them. They had been brutally tortured before they were killed. The last soldiers had survived into the afternoon before the militias murdered them. For the first time, Dallaire says, he was overwhelmed.

Faustin Twagiramungu saw Dallaire that night, back at the headquarters, where UNAMIR was now hiding him. "His face was so sad," remembers Twagiramungu. "He was so disappointed. His mission was a complete failure. The president was dead. The prime minister was dead. He was humiliated. He kept saying, 'My soldiers; they killed my soldiers.'" Twagiramungu tried to reassure Dallaire that there was nothing he could have done: "He could not ask the Devil to stop if God was not interested."

On April 8, UNAMIR sent a coded cable to the peacekeeping headquarters in New York that should have been a wake-up call. But it was in two different voices. The first part, from Jacques-Roger Booh Booh, outlined the deteriorating political situation, saying that the country's leading political figures had been abducted and presumably killed. But it talked encouragingly about meetings with a new "crisis committee" that wanted to work with UNAMIR to establish peace. "The death of the President of the Republic, and the still unconfirmed deaths of the Prime Minister and the Presiding Judge of the Constitutional Court as well as a number of ministers has created a power-vacuum which could pose new problems for the peace process." (News of the murder of Mme Agathe had not yet reached the special representative, perhaps indicating the degree to which Booh Booh and Dallaire were no longer communicating.)

The second half of the message came from Dallaire and was written in capital letters. It described a situation that was utterly devastating. "THE APPEARANCE OF A VERY WELL PLANNED, ORGANIZED, DELIBERATE AND CONDUCTED CAMPAIGN OF TERROR INITIATED PRINCIPALLY BY THE PRESIDENTIAL GUARD SINCE THE MORNING AFTER THE DEATH OF THE HEAD OF STATE HAS COMPLETELY REORIENTED THE SITUATION IN KIGALI." Dallaire went on to describe the massacres of Tutsi, the attacks on UNAMIR and the mounting casualties. "THE PARTICULARLY BARBAROUS MURDER OF THE 10 CAPTURED BELGIAN SOLDIERS EMPHASIZES THIS SITUATION. IS THE MANDATE OF UNAMIR STILL VALID?"

Dallaire told those at the New York office that they'd better decide soon what they wanted him to do. There was food enough for the mission for two weeks, though only enough drinking water in some places for the next two days. Most critically, according to Dallaire, there was only enough diesel fuel for at most the next week. He had hardly any ammunition, almost no medical equipment and the local telephones were down. UNAMIR had one satellite phone that had been damaged by mortar fire and temporarily knocked out.

During its meetings after the president was killed, the Security Council debated what role UNAMIR should play. If UNAMIR was not to be expanded and reinforced, what should it do? The Americans talked of pulling the operation down altogether and calling everyone home, but a principal concern was how to protect the hundreds of foreigners and UN workers in the country at the time. Boutros-Ghali and some of the Security Council members thought UNAMIR's mandate should be changed to allow it just to evacuate foreign nationals. But that presented a sticky problem: How could UNAMIR justify not helping Rwandans as well? What would it look like if the UN was trying to save only the lives of white people? The council decided that countries that had significant numbers of nationals in Rwanda could send in troops to evacuate them. But what about the Rwandans? Who would help them? What should they do with UNAMIR? No one had an answer.

On April 12, based on a first quick assessment of his needs, Dallaire submitted a request to New York for a rapid reaction force of five thousand properly equipped and motivated soldiers. Dallaire had identified, by that date, that the killing was not a war but a civilian slaughter (he was careful to use the accepted UN term at the time — ethnic cleansing). With such a force, he thought he could stop the killing, which he believed to be still mostly confined to the capital. Dallaire told New York he could accomplish the task under the existing chapter six mandate, since he had included his paragraph seventeen in the ROE, allowing UNAMIR to intervene with lethal force when human rights were threatened. "The plan was simple," says Dallaire. "I would take that brigade and blow through the barriers. And I would blast them [the Interahamwe] if they got in the way." Dallaire heard nothing back in response to his ideas.

Over the next two weeks, as the genocide expanded, Dallaire slept on a cot in his office and spent hours in his operations room, working and reworking his plan for stopping the violence. It became a more detailed multi-pronged military strategy. He wanted to shut down the hate radio, dismantle the roadblocks, confiscate weapons, raid the Hutu militias' arms caches, secure Kigali and key locations in the countryside, and arrest the perpetrators. To do this he would need a chapter seven mandate.

Dallaire's plan — both the initial and the more complex version — was ultimately rejected. The Permanent Five, particularly the U.S., thought it was ill-conceived. There was no problem finding the soldiers. Members of the Organization on African Unity were prepared to send in all the troops needed: this was Africa's problem, and Africa wanted to solve it. But those countries had no equipment and no "strategic lift" — the ability to actually get themselves into the country and mobilized. The United States could do that but claimed it was restricted by PDD25, the presidential directive preventing involvement in "dubious" peacekeeping missions (i.e., anything that resembled Somalia). The American ambassador to the United

Nations, Madeleine Albright, said that obviously the first UNAMIR mission had failed and they shouldn't rush into a second, equally disastrous one. According to the U.S., the Dallaire plan would be just such a disaster. Casualties were inevitable, something Dallaire could hardly dispute.

Instead, UNAMIR was ordered to be prepared for a complete pullout. Dallaire was to do whatever possible to prevent more peacekeeping casualties and to avoid getting involved. UNAMIR was instructed not to criticize either "side" in the conflict, nor to appear to be helping one party or another, either Hutu or Tutsi. The UN didn't state it quite so baldly, but the orders clearly meant the peacekeepers were not to help civilians, since that would shatter their neutrality.

While deciding the fate of the mission, the Security Council thought an appropriate role for UNAMIR would be to negotiate a ceasefire between the RPF and the government forces in order to stop the war. In all of its dispatches and declarations, the SC denounced the killing but described the conflict in Rwanda as a civil war. Technically, this was true. The RPF was now at war with the Rwandan government forces. But the war was a sideshow to the main event—the slaughter of civilians. As the days and weeks passed, the UN couldn't—or wouldn't—come to terms with the fact that war was the least of its problems: Rwanda was in the midst of a planned, organized, systematic genocide.

While Dallaire resisted a pullout and argued for the right to intervene, Jacques-Roger Booh Booh urged UNAMIR to refrain from criticizing the interim government of Prime Minister Jean Kambanda. As his priority, Booh Booh took up the UN's call for a ceasefire between the forces of Colonel Bagosora and the Rwandan Patriotic Front of Colonel Kagame. In diplomatic terms, Booh Booh asserted, there was nothing to be gained by making enemies with either side.

Booh Booh's boss, the secretary-general, gave out a similar message. In a report on the slaughter dated April 20, Boutros-Ghali echoed the explanations handed out by Bagosora and his puppet president. He wrote, "Reliable reports strongly indicate that the killings were started by unruly members of the Presidential Guard then spread quickly throughout the city. Despite the best efforts of UNAMIR, the RPF ... broke out and started to engage government troops, including elements of the Presidential Guard.... Authority collapsed, the provisional government disintegrated and some of its members were killed in the violence." Boutros-Ghali's conclusion—that rogue elements committed some acts of violence in response

to Habyarimana's assassination, and that Rwandan forces were then provoked into a war with the RPF — was an almost verbatim echo of the official line from Bagosora.

Observers such as Human Rights Watch and the London-based group
African Rights had already provided detailed evidence that the genocide
was planned well in advance and executed by the highest levels of the
Rwandan government. The UN Security Council chose to ignore such
reports. In other statements, Boutros-Ghali described the nature of the
conflict exactly as the Rwandan government did. There were "Hutus
killing Tutsis and Tutsis killing Hutus," he said. There were no good guys
or bad guys, only tribes locked in some ancient blood feud.

As the Security Council struggled to find the least obligating definition
of the conflict in Rwanda, the Hutu Power militias, under the direction of
Colonel Bagosora, continued their "defence" of the country. Through April
and into May, the death squads rounded up people by the thousands and
forced them into churches and stadiums, where they could be killed expe-
ditiously in groups. Throwing grenades into rooms full of men, women and
children wasn't very thorough, but the killers found that if they tossed in
tear-gas canisters afterward, they could catch any survivors when they
choked on the gas.

Although the Hutu Power leaders had distributed thousands of guns,
there were not enough for the task at hand. If about 9 to 12 per cent of the
Rwandan population were Tutsi, there were about a million people who
potentially supported the RPF and had to be eliminated. And there were
also those Hutu who opposed the government: a smaller number, but they
too would have to die.

Most Hutu Power recruits were trained to use machetes. It was a
slower method than shooting but proved efficient over the long run. The
killers needed only to sever the Achilles tendons of the victims so that they
couldn't run away. They could then go off and have a meal and return to
finish the job the next day. Though the work was strenuous under a hot
sun, some of the killers stacked the severed body parts in piles like wood —
separating arms, legs and heads. It gave the scene the macabre sense that the
men and women doing the killing thought they were actually performing
a job — the "work" that their leaders had ordered — and not just murdering
their neighbours. In one case, the pastor of a church reportedly speeded
things up by simply bulldozing a church full of people — many from his
own congregation.

Throughout April and May, the Rwandan Patriotic Front defeated the Rwandan military in many key areas of the country. The RPF was ruthless with those Hutu who were suspected of taking part in the killing, and during these months, it too murdered thousands of people. Kagame's well-disciplined forces had picked up many recruits along the way — survivors of the genocide — who were less well trained and far more vengeful than the regular RPF soldiers. Despite the reprisal killings, wherever the RPF arrived, the genocide of tens of thousands of Tutsi and of Hutu moderates would cease. Kagame's best troops fought in Kigali, of which the RPF soon controlled a large part, including the area in which the Amahoro stadium and Dallaire's headquarters were located.

The best that Dallaire was able to do was to protect a series of un-official "safe areas" throughout the city, places where mostly Tutsi had gone for help. Hotel Milles Colline was the most relatively secure base for refugees, but Dallaire's troops guarded other places, including two churches and the King Faisal Hospital, which was staffed by NGOs, including Médicins Sans Frontières (Doctors Without Borders). Some of these refuges were places that UNAMIR was able to visit only from time to time, but it was enough to keep some semblance of control.

The safe zones developed on an ad hoc basis, and they were not all successful. Such was the case of the École Technique Officielle (ETO), which was run by priests and foreign nationals. The ninety Belgian soldiers posted at the school to protect the foreign staff allowed Tutsi to take refuge within the school grounds. Luc Marchal told the soldiers the refugees shouldn't be there — he had no idea how long peacekeepers would be allowed to stay in the country — but Joe Dewez, who was in better contact with the troops, decided it was okay.

On April 11, all foreigners were evacuated from the school. The Belgian officers stationed at the ETO were deeply troubled as to what they should do; the school was being attacked by Hutu militias and it was risky for them to stay. Most other troops had been dispatched to the airport to help evacuate the foreign nationals. The ETO soldiers asked Dewez if they should join the others and Dewez agreed. To this day, Dallaire says he doesn't know who gave — or approved — the order for the Belgians to pull out of the ETO. His instructions to Luc Marchal were to consolidate as many troops as possible, for security and self-protection, in a few areas, but not to abandon people.

The soldiers had tried to warn the refugees that UNAMIR might have to leave suddenly, but no one had budged. There was no place else to go. Some of the Tutsi in the school asked the Belgians to shoot them before they left. Instead, the soldiers tried to sneak away. The refugees ran after the soldiers and begged on their knees to be protected. Much later, in testimony before a Belgian inquiry, the soldiers said they genuinely thought the RPF, who were nearby, would come to the rescue. But nobody did. All two thousand people at the school were slaughtered.

Dallaire kept asking for more soldiers and supplies, and in a curious way he got them. First France, then Belgium and finally Italy sent in a total of more than a thousand troops. But they weren't there to stop the genocide; they had come to evacuate the European expatriate population—a group of nearly two thousand people. It was called euphemistically a "humanitarian mission," but the only humanity it was helping were the foreigners. Dallaire and Marchal asked if they could use these well-equipped, highly trained soldiers to stop the genocide from spreading. But the international community would have none of it. The troops were on the ground for one purpose only.

They were under instructions to airlift out only foreign citizens— Rwandan nannies, friends, relatives or staff, even of the UN, would be left behind to almost certain death. Some exceptions were made: France evacuated Mme Habyarimana and a circle of her supporters, as well as the children from an orphanage she managed. Another thirty-four people, claiming to be caregivers for the children, were also permitted to leave with the French, along with the principal stockholder and the director of Radio Télévision Libre des Milles Collines.

It's curious that these Hutu felt they needed to leave, but Hutu in high places could see that the Rwandan government forces were no match for Paul Kagame. Many suspected that it was only a matter of time before the RPF took power, and they wanted to get out.

In addition to the troops that arrived to evacuate the nationals, Dallaire knew there were other foreign soldiers in neighbouring countries, including three hundred American marines in Burundi and eight hundred Belgian troops in Nairobi. Dallaire asked New York why they couldn't be recruited to the cause. They couldn't. End of discussion. The general was slowly beginning to realize that no one was coming to help. There was no cavalry, no white knights, no political will to save this little postage stamp of a country.

Booh Booh had been living in a private house with a unit of Belgian peacekeepers to protect him. Dallaire decided he needed those soldiers assigned elsewhere and so he had the special representative moved into the Hotel Meridien with the other foreigners. Dallaire never saw Booh Booh out of that hotel room again until he was evacuated from the country. (Dallaire learned later that Booh Booh was never dismissed, though the UN failed to renew his contract when it lapsed.)

With the special representative sidelined, Dallaire assumed all political negotiations, something that left the military side of the mission in a bad way. "I no longer had any leadership," says Luc Marchal. "The general was completely involved in the job of Mr. Booh Booh."

Colonel Marchal didn't have to put up with it for long. The Belgian government was reeling from the loss of its peacekeepers — the images on Belgian TV had been explosive. Rwanda had become Belgium's Somalia. The government in Brussels announced that either the UNAMIR mission had to be bumped up to a chapter seven intervention force (to be done with anybody but Belgian soldiers) or Belgium would have to pull out. Brussels didn't want to remove its own soldiers unless the whole mission was cancelled. But the UN wasn't ready for that yet.

Dallaire was told on April 14 that his Belgian contingent, the most experienced and functional part of UNAMIR, was to be withdrawn. The news was devastating. Luc Marchal tried to resist his orders, staying an additional three days so that Dallaire could secure the airport by calling back Ghanaian soldiers he had posted in northern Rwanda. But that was all Marchal could manage.

Dallaire recalls the departure of the Belgians as one of the lowest points of his career as a soldier. "Fifty years earlier, my father was fighting through Belgium with the Allies. And there I was in an ex-colony of Belgium — the country that had created some of the problems we were facing there — and right at the worst time the Belgians were packing up and leaving a Canadian to defend himself. The irony of that hit me as I watched the last Herc [Hercules] depart. I despised them beyond description." Dallaire kept his friendships with people like Marchal but he never got over his feelings of anger and betrayal.

After the Belgians were gone, Dallaire voluntarily sent the Bangladeshis home. They were a drain on resources and an easy target — he didn't want to be responsible for any casualties among them. The Bangladeshi officers were hoarding food and medicine from their subordinates, and they would do nothing to help the mission. When the airplane arrived to evacuate them, Dallaire was stunned to see the officers race to get on the plane first, leaving their troops on the runway. He had insisted that each soldier take no more than fifteen kilograms of baggage, to ensure that as many people as possible could get on each flight. But the Bangladeshi officers broke the rules.

Other countries followed suit and pulled their troops. By the third week of April, Dallaire was down to a force of 450—all African soldiers, except for himself and Major Beardsley. Henry Anyidoho, an avuncular and competent brigadier general from Ghana, became Dallaire's right-hand man, and they soldiered on.

On April 21, the United Nations finally decided what it wanted them to do: the Security Council passed Resolution 912—with the exception of a skeleton staff, all the rest of UNAMIR was to pull out. Anyidoho got the news first: "When General Dallaire got back, I told him the story that our mission was to be brought to an end. Then General Dallaire shouted, 'Henry, do you mean we've failed?' We would not accept any closure of that mission because history would associate our name with failure. The order has to be lawful, and I thought what they were telling us at that moment by the dictates of my conscience was not lawful, it was not the right thing. And then if we have to disobey that in order to save lives, then that was it. And we were prepared to face the consequences."

Dallaire appealed to Anyidoho to do something. The two men made a pact: they would disobey the order to pull out. Dallaire and Anyidoho then went over to the Meridien to see Jacques-Roger Booh Booh, who said they should comply with the order. Dallaire said no. "The disconnect between my political master and me was consummated. He stayed in his goddamn room until they pulled him out," Dallaire says.

With the 450 soldiers that remained, Dallaire literally held down the fort. He continued to negotiate the ceasefire—though he knew it was useless—because it gave him a plausible reason to be in the country and to continue to show the flag he had raised on November 17, when he had told the crowd that together they would bring peace to Rwanda.

The UN Department of Peacekeeping Operations and the secretary-general decided to ignore Dallaire's insubordination—they chalked it up to a lack of airlift—and the Ghanaians stayed. Anyidoho and Dallaire kept reworking their rescue plan and petitioning New York to do something.

When Dallaire paused even for a moment, the full realization of what was happening would sink in and fill him with terror. He recalled one such moment: "I was standing in my office, standing by the window, and I had a screen and there were houses across the street from the compound. To this day ... I'm never sure if what I heard was the wind coming through the screen or the cries and moans of women and children who were being slaughtered. And a couple of days later, because the smell and stench was so bad in the area, I sent a team across to those houses ... [to] see what we could do to stop that." Dallaire's people counted eighty-nine bodies before they stopped, just a hundred metres away from UNAMIR headquarters. What was happening throughout the country?

4

THIS TIME WE KNEW

*My force was standing knee-deep in mutilated bodies, surrounded
by the guttural moans of dying people, looking into the eyes of children bleeding
to death with their wounds burning in the sun and being invaded
with maggots and flies. I found myself walking through villages where the only
sign of life was a goat, or a chicken, or a songbird, as all the people were
dead. Their bodies being eaten by voracious packs of wild dogs. During those seven
to eight weeks of the war, with little mandate, no reinforcements in sight,
and only one phone line to the outside world (which a mortar round knocked out
for nineteen hours) I felt the ghost of Gordon of Khartoum watching over me.
Dying in Rwanda without a sign or a sight of relief was a reality we
faced on a daily basis.*
—General Roméo Dallaire, "The End of Innocence: Rwanda 1994"

Roméo Dallaire was now marooned in the middle of a country he
was hardly able to find on a map a year earlier, with only his NATO
training and a personal sense of right and wrong to guide him.
Nothing in his previous experience had prepared the Canadian general for
this: he defied his political masters when they demanded his force be
reduced; he refused to abandon the thirty thousand souls in the protected
enclaves who now depended on him for their existence; he pushed his soldiers to their limit every waking moment; and he tried to close his senses
to the horror around him, lest he succumb to despair. Dallaire couldn't
even be sure the United Nations would come to the rescue if he lost the
tiny bit of control he retained.

Tens of thousands of Tutsi were being murdered throughout the
country and hundreds of thousands of Hutu were fleeing, one step ahead

of the advancing Rwandan Patriotic Front. Dallaire's contingent of Ghanaian soldiers had come down from the north to secure the Kigali airport,
now the lifeline for his entire mission. He managed to find some of the
Rwandans who had previously run the airport, and he put them to work
again.

Force commanders of peacekeeping missions usually find there's only
one place to turn when you really need help, and that's to your own country. The Canadian government had let him down in February when he
had asked for a battalion, but this time, when Dallaire petitioned his superiors in Ottawa, they responded, rerouting two Hercules aircraft (and their
crews) based in Italy and running humanitarian aid to Sarajevo to Nairobi.
They became the only aircrews that would fly into Kigali.

At first, the job was to help evacuate the foreigners, but then the
Canadian Hercules made two flights a day with food, water, medicine and
supplies. They evacuated wounded soldiers and removed, clandestinely,
Rwandan refugees, including orphans and clerical people. Dallaire says
that without those flights, the refugees could not have survived. The UN
usually charters its relief flights from private companies, but those companies wanted $5 million in insurance on each flight to Rwanda.

The Canadian Hercules also brought another gift. Though four
months earlier, Ottawa had refused to send any more soldiers for UNAMIR,
Dallaire finally got twelve Canadian officers for his mission. He was desperate for them. While the Ghanaians proved their mettle time and time
again, and were rock-solid under fire, they were not leaders. Worse, they
spoke only English in a country where most business is conducted in
French. Dallaire's new officers spoke both languages.

He had other support lines, but he did not control them. A handful of
journalists had stayed in the country, while others came and went on the
relief flights, feeding out into the world Dallaire's urgent SOS. The general
hoped that if all else failed, he could shame the world into taking responsibility. "Unless the international community acts, it may find it is unable
to defend itself against accusations of doing nothing to stop genocide,"
he chided through a Reuters reporter. As long as journalists from TV, radio
and the wire services put out the stories, foreign governments would be
unable to pretend they didn't know what was going on. The journalists
became Dallaire's most important strategic weapon: "I fed them, I transported them, I guaranteed them a story a day and it would get out [by]

hook or by crook." The relationship was two-way. When a palette of beer arrived on one of the Hercules, no one reported it.

His other lifeline was the NGOs—the agencies that delivered food, medicine and treatment to people in the refugee centres. Some of the organizations that arrived, full of goodwill and prayers, were completely useless. "They landed with two bottles of aspirin, and we would have to take care of them," complained Dallaire. But others, like Médicins Sans Frontières and the International Red Cross, were indispensable. Dallaire wanted to nominate their members for sainthood. With the NGOs on one side and the media on the other, Dallaire hunkered down to wait for what he still believed would come: a new UNAMIR mandate, with soldiers and supplies to stop the genocide.

Major Philip Lancaster arrived one morning in mid-May, among the new officers from Canada. With twenty-five years of experience in the military, he was prepared for a lot, but not for what he encountered in Rwanda. "We landed in ninety-degree heat, and as soon as we were on the Tarmac we were being fired on. Everyone was running for cover." The drive to headquarters was not as bad as it could have been—there had been an order that week to clean up the cadavers. But the stench was still overpowering, and the bodies of bloated animals littered the sides of the road.

When Lancaster finally got to headquarters, he found the kind of chaos he had seen in other military operations, only here everything was ten times worse. At the Amahoro sports hostel—functioning now as both living quarters and offices for the mission staff officers—the water had been cut off for six weeks. Lancaster's first job was to try to clean out his toilet with a pail and shovel. The only source of fresh water was ten kilometres away: not impossible, except for the thirty roadblocks in between, all controlled by men high on drugs and alcohol, with loaded guns in their hands. Major Lancaster would remain in Rwanda for the next year. It would change him permanently.

In the midst of it all was General Dallaire, intensely involved in every aspect of his mission. The Belgian officers who had worked at HQ had marvelled at Dallaire's attention to detail and the way he kept on top of everyone's job. Lancaster was Dallaire's military assistant and he quickly learned his boss was exhausted beyond human comprehension but was still issuing orders and making decisions—every moment—that meant life or death.

Lancaster also discovered the food was hard rations, and that was only until the supply ran out. "We ended up picking through bags of tins that had been put aside to demobilize Rwandan troops," recalls Lancaster. "We could generally find one or two cans in each bag that had not been spoiled after sitting a year on tne docks in Mombassa."

Dallaire structured the day tightly. Lancaster remembers the drill: "0630 Reveille. Made sure Dallaire had his cup of tea by 0700. Picked up the inevitably full 'out basket' that Dallaire had produced during the night (the general was not sleeping). 0800 Morning prayers, full briefings, meetings. 0930 Field trips, discussions, visits. 1700 Evening prayers, more briefings, phone calls with New York. 2300 Bed." (Though the phone calls overseas often continued all night.)

Soldiers who had not accomplished their tasks by the end of the day needed very good excuses. Officers just back from some harrowing encounter with the Interahamwe still had to write up their reports, accurately. Those who had just finished a mission were immediately sent out on another one. "The only way that I found out to be able to handle the stress was work people till they dropped," Dallaire said. "You never let people get idle — you conduct forced stress." One officer showed up for the morning meeting decked out in full combat wear — he even had his flashlight with him. Dallaire thought he seemed okay otherwise, but they all kept an eye on him. By evening, the man was still dressed for combat, and Dallaire knew it was time to get him out. Sometimes, says Dallaire, it would just take a bath and some food to recover a man, and other times it was beyond hope. He said his rule was "to be ruthless but fair."

Dallaire talked to everyone from ambassadors to admirals. Some he reached on the phone, others called him. Occasionally, a diplomat or a politician would even visit, and experience the full force of Dallaire's wrath. "This was not an exercise in being hypersensitive to the diplomatic chain," Dallaire later told the CBC-TV reporter Brian Stewart. "I will not negate that I was not particularly sensitive to the process. Maybe that was a failing in not convincing people to come. I hope not. But no one in the world can play Pontius Pilate on this one. You simply can't do that. You cannot permit not only genocide but a holocaust — you can't let people be slaughtered and mutilated, and then debate the finer points. You've got to come here."

Dallaire had dropped all civilities with everyone — especially New York. Beardsley and Lancaster, who both worked in the operations room, remember a lot of hollering down the phone lines. Dallaire believed that Maurice Baril and Iqbal Riza, along with their ultimate boss in the Department of Peacekeeping Operations (DPKO), Kofi Annan, were doing everything they could for the mission. Dallaire maintained that the trouble was higher up, with the Security Council. Some of those who worked with Dallaire didn't agree with his assessment; they thought the people at DPKO were mostly just trying to cover their butts.

At the end of April, just three weeks into the genocide, an estimated 200,000 people were already dead. Boutros Boutros-Ghali finally conceded that the slaughter of civilians and the battle between the two armies were not really the same thing. He concurred that Rwanda was in the midst of a genocide, and that a genocide probably required a different strategy. A reduced force of 450 was enough to support humanitarian efforts and ceasefire negotiations, but it was clear that something else was required to defend the civilians. If Dallaire thought this was a signal that he was now to get some help, he was mistaken.

Of the Permanent Five members of the Security Council, only France had a genuine interest in Rwanda. France was covertly and overtly providing support to the Rwandan government forces and had supplied them with large amounts of weaponry. As for the other members, Madeleine Albright was under strict orders to steer a wide berth around this Rwanda thing. The UK derided those who tried to talk about genocide. As always, Russia and China fundamentally opposed meddling in any nation's affairs for purposes of human rights, fearing that one day the same would happen to them.

The ten non-permanent members of the Security Council had been going along with the Permanent Five. None has a veto, and as lesser powers they haven't the same intelligence-gathering abilities as the big players, who knew all too well what was going on in Rwanda (the CIA had reported to its masters the possibility of mass killings as far back as January). The Permanent Five didn't share their knowledge, however, and Boutros-Ghali wasn't passing on the dire messages that his DPKO had been getting from Rwanda for months, including the famous fax of January 11.

Another factor seriously affected the Security Council's ability to make the right decisions: one of the non-permanent members of the council at that time was Rwanda. The Rwandan ambassador—a Hutu—had been a Security Council member at the time of the president's assassination, and he had simply stayed on, since he supported the new regime. The result was that Colonel Bagosora and President Kambanda had their own spokesperson at the heart of the UN's decision-making apparatus.

The Rwandan ambassador to the UN, Jean-Damascene Bizimana, was a very effective spokesman for the Hutu Power cause. The message from his government—from the very people who were conducting the genocide—was that it was all self-defence. If Tutsi were being killed in large numbers, it was because they were conspiring with the rebel army to destabilize the country. Yes, there had been some civilian deaths, but what could you expect? The population was traumatized by the assassination of its president and had overreacted. It was only a few rogue elements—nothing like the threat the RPF posed to Rwandan stability. How could the interim government of Jean Kambanda stabilize the country while a rebel army was waging war?

In an interview with American television years after he had left the UN, Michael Barnett (who had been with the United States mission at the time) revealed the level of frustration of the many people who knew what was going on in Rwanda. "Nobody said, 'Stop it.' Nobody said, 'Your presence disgusts me,'" says Barnett of the day when the Rwandan ambassador gave a speech at the UN proclaiming his government's good intentions. "Nobody said, 'Why don't you get out of the room?' There was never a real moment in which they dressed him down, because if you did, you would be breaking the rules of the club."

As the killing continued, a group of like-minded Security Council members banded together to seek out the truth. The ambassador from the Czech Republic, Karel Kovanda, called Alison Des Forges of Human Rights Watch, one of the agencies in the front lines of the Rwanda conflict. He asked her over for coffee, along with the ambassadors from New Zealand and Spain, other non-permanent members. Des Forges walked them through the horrifying reality. On April 30, the group forced a debate in the Security Council that ended, finally, in the body condemning the massacres, though it still refused to use the word "genocide." Boutros-Ghali and the pope finally publicly called it a genocide the following week.

The "g" word, as it's called in polite company, is one of the most burning and difficult legacies of the Second World War. A 1948 UN convention states that genocide consists of killing, serious assault, starvation and other measures "committed with the intent to destroy, in whole or in part, a national, ethnical, racial or religious group, as such." It doesn't take an expert to figure out that genocide was taking place in Rwanda. But the problem is that genocide carries with it legal obligations. To recognize what was going on—what was *really* going on—meant that all the countries that had signed the Genocide Convention (including Rwanda, which signed in the 1970s) were obligated by international law to do something. And no country wanted to take that responsibility, least of all the one that had the ability to do something, the United States.

If it wasn't so tragic, the way the U.S. government avoided the issue would be comical. Washington reporters chided the State Department into admitting that the Rwandan government—which was recognized by the U.S. and had representatives sitting in the United Nations—was murdering its own people by the hundreds of thousands. From April until June—even after most of the killing was finished and the *génocidaires* were just mopping up—the State Department's spokeswoman, Christine Shelley, sweated through the same questions and still denied there was a genocide. Finally, at a press conference on June 10, 1994, she conceded that there might have been "acts" of genocide in Rwanda:

> *Shelley:* We have every reason to believe that acts of genocide have occurred.
> *Reporter:* How many acts of genocide does it take to make a genocide?
> *Shelley:* That's not a question I'm in a position to answer.
> *Reporter:* Is it true that you have specific guidance not to use the word *genocide* in isolation but always preface it with "acts of"?
> *Shelley:* I have guidance which...which...to which I...which I try to use as best I can. I'm not...I have...there are formulations that we are using that we are trying to be consistent in our use of. I don't have an absolute categorical prescription against something, but I have definitions. I have phraseology which has been carefully examined and arrived at....

This is not what the drafters of the Convention on the Prevention and Punishment of the Crime of Genocide of 1948 had in mind. The idea was that "never again" would the world stand by and watch something like what had happened to the Jews in Europe. But it *was* happening again, and now many people were adding: "This time we knew." The TV pictures of bodies floating down the river may have shocked and horrified the public, but apparently not enough to get the machinery of "never again" into operation.

In mid-May, the United Nations received the Rwandan foreign minister, Jérôme Bicamumpaka, and the leader of the radical CDR party, Jean-Bosco Barayagwiza. The two Africans would tell the world that it was the Hutu who were being killed by the hundreds of thousands, not the Tutsi, and that the Rwandan government was only trying to bring about peace. The RPF was the enemy, and they urged the UN to try to negotiate a cease-fire that would stop the civil war. Their presence was suffered politely. The United States refused to meet the two men at all. But they found a gratifying reception elsewhere.

The republic of France had been doing a very bad job of covering up its involvement in Rwanda, if it cared to cover it at all. For the French government, members of the Hutu majority were the rightful heirs to the Habyarimana government, which France had supported. And as far as Paris was concerned, Paul Kagame and his RPF, dubbed Khmer Noir, were terrorists. France wanted the RPF defeated.

The Tutsi were a minority in the country, and Kagame could hardly make the case that he represented the broad interests of the electorate. But members of the Habyarimana regime and its successor, the government of Bagosora and Kambanda, had proved themselves ruthless killers and were hardly worthy of sustained support from France. The French sociologist Gérard Prunier says France's support of the Hutu leadership goes far beyond any interest in majority rule. France has a profound loathing for anything Anglo-Saxon, according to Prunier, and that prejudice lies behind its support of Hutu Power leaders. Paul Kagame and his Tutsi-led RPF had lived in Uganda for a generation and were anglicized Africans. France was determined to protect French Africa from this English-speaking mob.

President Mitterand not only received the Rwandan delegation, but France continued to allow weapons shipments to the country. Research done by the arms division of Human Rights Watch established that either the French government or French companies under government licence delivered arms to Rwanda five times in May and June through the neighbouring (and sympathetic) state of Zaire. This was despite an arms embargo that the United Nations had slapped on Rwanda on May 17, 1994. Also, as Dallaire had noted, French soldiers were the first to arrive at the site where the president's plane had crashed, even as Rwandan government forces prevented UNAMIR from getting anywhere near.

Officers who served with Dallaire didn't consider him paranoid when he suspected there were spies in their midst, and they certainly didn't think it far-fetched when they were told there were French spies. Dallaire knew that the Rwandan government forces got a steady stream of weapons from the outside, and that France was most probably the main source. But Dallaire discovered other countries supplied them as well, including Albania and Israel.

On May 17, 1994, all Dallaire's efforts to get a new force seemed to have paid off when the UN Security Council voted to accept UNAMIR II. He would get fifty-five hundred troops from various African countries, with a mandate to protect civilians and bring in humanitarian aid. It should have been cause for celebration, except that Dallaire had learned the wisdom of waiting for the other shoe to drop. Even when the UN made promises and passed resolutions there was no guarantee of delivery. For example, the U.S. had agreed to send fifty APCs to Dallaire's mission, and he was initially thrilled with the news. But the Americans then decided they would only lease the vehicles to UNAMIR, and many months of dithering and horse-trading over the cost followed.

Sure enough, UNAMIR II wasn't ratified until June 8 — the U.S. was the principal obstacle — and the troops didn't arrive until August. By all estimates, the largest part of the killing took place in the first hundred days after April 6, and the lion's share of that "work" was completed in the first six weeks. If the UN's objective was to keep out of this mess, it had succeeded.

In late May, Iqbal Riza and Maurice Baril turned up in Kigali on a reconnaisance mission. It was clear that Riza had also come to tell the warring parties that they should co-operate with the ceasefire arrangements and try to salvage something from the Arusha Accords. It was the same old malarkey; everyone in Kigali knew there wasn't going to be a ceasefire until one of these sides, probably the RPF, won the war. (Dallaire defends Riza. He says that during his visit, the UN bureaucrat was able to obtain a temporary halt to the shooting that lasted long enough for UNAMIR to move some of the refugees.)

Baril took the opportunity of the visit to see how Dallaire was holding up. He seemed fine and determined to stay, but people who worked with him were worried. Phil Lancaster says, "I could see the strain clearly in his writing. At one time, he had been a very lucid writer. He was almost

incoherent on paper for most of the time I was with him." Dallaire sometimes went out on mysterious trips that seemed like suicide missions. In a
CBC Radio interview years later, Dallaire said he met the Devil in Rwanda:
"I negotiated with him. I shook his hand. We even exchanged jokes." Only
one thing gave him hope: if the Devil was there, God must be as well.

Dallaire knew he was targeted in a number of murder plots. Before the
war began, Brent Beardsley had received a bizarre call one day from someone who would not identify himself: "I want to confirm whether a certain
Canadian general was shot down in a helicopter in northen Rwanda," said
the voice, in flawless English with a slight American accent. Beardsley was
startled and said there had been no such incident. The man asked to speak
to Dallaire. The general took the phone. "This is Dallaire," he said. The
voice responded: "Bingo! You got it!" and hung up. Beardsley would have
thought nothing more of it, except that not long after, he was instructed by
an intelligence source that Dallaire should not fly in a helicopter in the following week. UNAMIR complied with the advice.

A highly confidential report from his own officers, dated May 24 and
addressed to Dallaire, warned that the Rwandan government of Jean
Kambanda considered Dallaire too partial towards the RPF and the government forces might have a plan to kill him. About this time, the RTLMC
programs started to name Dallaire as one of the *inyenzi* that should be
exterminated.

Dallaire had first wondered about his safety when his men had questioned Jean-Pierre, the whistle-blower from inside the Hutu killing
machine. Jean-Pierre had told the Belgian soldiers that he knew of a trai-
tor working within UNAMIR, and he said he had been summoned to Habyarimana's party headquarters on four occasions to listen to tapes of what
seemed to be a spy reporting from inside the Amahoro hostel. No one at
UNAMIR headquarters could figure out who the fellow was. But in the
middle of the genocide, the RPF sent a warning to UNAMIR. It had intercepted information that a man, working on contract to the UN, might be
involved in a plan to kill Dallaire. The RPF apparently identified the suspect—a UNAMIR staffer who worked with Booh Booh—and those in the
headquarters wondered if he wasn't the same character that Jean-Pierre had
told them about earlier.

Dallaire could confirm nothing of the story, but he did discover that
this alleged plotter was having unauthorized meetings with Bagosora's
forces. Others in UNAMIR say they had heard the fellow was offended when

Dallaire—a white man—had sidelined Booh Booh and taken over nego-tiations. Whatever the possible motive, UNAMIR's military staff couldn't be too careful: they isolated the suspect from their operations and eventually moved him out of the country.

Then Ottawa called one day to say that DND had been told, by sources it wouldn't reveal, that the general was the target of an assassination plot. Dallaire was ordered by his superiors to carry a gun—he had refused to do so until then—and Brent Beardsley was instructed to put a bodyguard detail on him. "We asked the Ghanaians to do it, and they put together a group of the biggest, ugliest, most frightening soldiers we had ever seen." They drove around with their shirts open, wearing reflector sunglasses. Two vehicles were involved, one on each end of Dallaire's Jeep, with four guards to a car. "They'd arrive at a checkpoint and the Interahamwe would practically swoon in fear." Beardsley says it was very effective. They started to hope that Dallaire might actually survive the rest of the mission. But Dallaire didn't know who to trust anymore. He sometimes went to the room of an NGO to use a private satellite phone to call New York.

As the weeks wore on, the Rwandan government forces were appear-ing more and more pathetic. The interim government, under the puppet leadership of Prime Minister Jean Kambanda, fled from Kigali and set up shop in the neighbouring town of Gitarama, southwest of the capital. From there, Bagosora directed his forces to finish clearing the country of Tutsi "opposition." Bagosora detested Dallaire, and the interim Rwandan government often accused the general of having sympathies with the RPF. This is unlikely: Dallaire was far more concerned with Rwandan citizens than with helping military leaders. But, admittedly, he was im-pressed with the RPF leader, Paul Kagame, if only because of his brilliant battle skills. Years later, Dallaire would ask a group of young officers who was the greatest military tactician of the 1990s. Before they could offer the names of various American generals, Dallaire told them the answer was Paul Kagame.

Kagame had fled to Uganda with his family when he was four years old, and he grew up in the troubled years of the country's dictators Milton Obote and Idi Amin. Like so many other Rwandan refugees, he joined the military at a tender age and proved himself a very capable soldier. He became a major in the Ugandan National Resistance Army and its deputy chief of military intelligence when he was in his thirties. The Ugandan army paid for its soldiers to go abroad for training, and in 1990 Kagame reported for training at the U.S. Army Command and General Staff College at Fort Leavenworth, Kansas. The courses in tactics would more than pay off in the coming years.

Kagame knew he was up against a formidable foe, not because the Rwandan army was so good but because it had been so well equipped by the French. Kagame's rebels had lost previous battles with the forces of Habyarimana mostly because the French military took an active role. But Kagame knew that, with the exception of a handful of soldiers engaged in mysterious tasks, the French troops had left and the Rwandan armed forces were without their old friends. The Hutu had a huge buildup of arms, including heavy guns, but against a tactical guerrilla force, their big weapons were not so effective. To stop the progress of the Presidential Guard and the Interahamwe, Kagame moved his RPF soldiers in the north southwards, to link up with the forces in Kigali. They then moved on three fronts: the east, the west and the centre.

The RPF advance was relentless. Hutu fled the country, both because they felt threatened by the RPF and because many of them knew they were responsible for the genocide and feared the consequences. Some went to Burundi in the south, but the majority headed north, toward Zaire and a camp in the city of Goma, just over the border. Dallaire saw another humanitarian crisis looming, and he warned New York that as many as two million Hutu were possibly on the move. He was right.

At the end of May, James Orbinski of Médicins Sans Frontières (MSF) arrived in Rwanda from Uganda. He and a few others were to replace doctors and nurses who had been in the country since the beginning of the genocide. "I knew immediately I had arrived in a place where something profoundly evil was happening," he says. The road that he drove in on was slick with blood; there were corpses piled in the ditches, and bloated bodies washed up on the riverbanks by the tens of thousands.

When he arrived at UNAMIR headquarters, the central coordinating point for the peacekeepers and all the NGOs, he found a mission close to breakdown. His own doctors babbled senselessly. The UN soldiers were living in appalling conditions, with toilets overflowing, cooking their meals in hallways surrounded by garbage and filth. Corpses were everywhere. Orbinski had been to every hellhole on earth, but he saw just about the worst in Rwanda. The dogs, feeding off the corpses, fighting over human remains, are what he remembers most vividly. "Dogs — I'll never forget," says Orbinski. "Fat and vicious and bold. They travelled in packs, and they were eating human flesh."

UNAMIR headquarters was surrounded by sandbags and barbed wire. There were shells landing close by and constant gunfire. Soldiers and aid workers went out daily in whatever vehicle worked (often siphoning the gas from the others), to try to visit the sites where the refugees lived. They would assess the needs and then return the next day, only to find everyone dead. MSF was trying to run a hospital among the ruins, where they could perform operations. They relied on everyone, including the soldiers, to give blood. Even Dallaire was called in whenever his type was in short supply.

Orbinski remembers days of trying to get a truckload of refugees past the death squads. "When you are a handful of UN soldiers with a lorry full of people and you come up against this veil of force, you're operating with the tenuous promise of support from the international community that you know, and they know, is a delusion. And you are standing against thirty or forty Interahamwe, who are drunk and have more equipment than the pea-shooter that's on your shoulder—the last thing you want to do is shatter the delusion. Because everyone knows it's false, and we're all behaving as though it's true. The UNAMIR was a masquerade."

The mission was also a delicate balancing act: Dallaire kept up relations as best he could with the RPF and the Rwandan government. His people arranged for the exchange of Hutu and Tutsi over enemy lines and stayed in touch with both sides of the war, though Dallaire eventually lost contact with Bagosora. At their last meeting, the colonel said to Dallaire: "The next time I see you, I'll kill you."

"People were profoundly traumatized," says Orbinski. "But Dallaire was clear, firm, strong and uncompromising." Orbinski recognized immediately what the general was doing. "I had been in Somalia, Zaire, Afghanistan—everywhere. What people needed was the semblance of clarity. What are you trying to achieve here? Dallaire knew that and acted on it." And there was another level of the masquerade, this time for his troops. There was no way they could do anything to protect anyone, least of all themselves. But within Dallaire's limited sphere of influence in Kigali, he had everyone psyched—particularly the Interahamwe. Orbinski realized that any false move could destroy the illusion.

Dallaire knew it too. His own men could have figured it out, but he wouldn't let them. He couldn't let them smell failure or defeat. He kept sending them out, even when it was dangerous. Some of them didn't come back in one piece, and some of them didn't come back alive. Dallaire's mission, as he saw it, was to protect civilians, and that was what he was doing. He presented a series of medals to some of his soldiers in late June and commended them on their work. But he added, "It must be pointed out, however, there are trying and blurred moments ahead of us. I can only advise that you all hold your composure and continue to perform your duties to the best of your ability. I am always ready and willing to give you direction that will lead you to the attainment of the mission goal—God willing."

The failure of the international community to come to the aid of Rwanda was also a profound failure to support Dallaire's troops, and for years after he would rail against those who he believes deserted him in the field: "I saw too many corpses, too many tears, too much suffering. I sent too many brave young men in blue berets home in body bags to accept that we can do business as usual."

On June 17, as he awaited UNAMIR II, Roméo Dallaire learned that his fragile little mission was about to be turned on its head. "I got a hint something was happening when a couple of French senior officials end[ed] up in my headquarters and start[ed] discussing what-ifs," Dallaire recalls. François Mitterand had dispatched a political aide by the name of Bernard Kouchner, along with a military attaché, to prepare the ground for the arrival of French soldiers. To his astonishment, Dallaire learned from the two visitors that France had unilaterally decided to set up a peacekeeping mission of its own. It seemed the regime in Paris had had a change of heart and was now deeply concerned that a genocide might be taking place. But the French also feared the consequences of an RPF victory.

Mitterand stated that he felt deeply betrayed by the Rwandan government's attack on the civilian population, but that the Hutu were the majority and France did not want Paul Kagame to run the country. "Maintaining Hutu power is the democratic thing to do," Mitterand declared. His Operation Turquoise was billed as a humanitarian mission whose goal was to save civilians. Rwandans—both Tutsi and Hutu—were convinced the French were returning to ensure an RPF defeat.

Dallaire suspected that as well. When the two advance men from France showed him maps of what territory would be under French control—most of the country, including Kigali—Dallaire became livid. "I don't want to see any French around here," he told them. If France wants to help, he said, why doesn't it provide the airlift for the African soldiers waiting to join his mission? A good question, if the purpose of France was simply to protect civilians.

But Boutros Boutros-Ghali had always believed there should be one highly motivated government to take the lead in Rwanda, and now France was making the offer. The French ambassador to the Security Council tried to recruit the U.S. to share the job so it wouldn't look like a strictly Parisian initiative (which it was), but the Americans weren't interested. France asked not just for the Security Council's blessing, but also for permission to run Operation Turquoise as a chapter seven mission. With conditions deteriorating rapidly in Rwanda and no other country willing to do anything, the Security Council approved the operation. It was only a rubber stamp: French troops were already on the ground when the vote was taken.

Since Dallaire opposed having the French in Kigali, Operation Turquoise established its base in Goma, Zaire, where the Hutu refugee camps were quickly filling up. Whatever humanitarian component this mission had, the soldiers on the ground didn't entirely share it. Many of them had been in Rwanda on previous occasions, under the Habyarimana regime, and had helped the Rwandan armed forces fight Tutsi rebels. In interviews with reporters, numerous French soldiers betrayed a loyalty to the Hutu-led army.

Operation Turquoise arrived in Zaire with eight helicopters, support from four Mirage attack planes, four reconnaissance aircraft, one hundred armoured vehicles and a vast array of heavy weapons, including a battery of 120 mm mortars. France sent twenty-five hundred soldiers, including paratroopers and naval commandos. What was anyone to conclude from this? (The one vehicle the French didn't supply in any quantity was ordinary transport trucks, which would have been able to take refugees to safety.)

Everything about Operation Turquoise was a disaster for Dallaire. The French were well-known allies of the Hutu Power leadership. If they had had a change of heart, how was the population to guess that? As the French troops entered the country by land, Hutu and the Interahamwe ran out to greet them and cheer them on as if they were liberation forces. People wore tricolour hats to honour the soldiers. The Rwandan government forces were certain the French had arrived as military reinforcements. Dallaire feared that the chapter seven mandate, allowing them to use lethal force, would only create confusion. One group of foreign soldiers, Operation Turquoise, could be aggressive but another one, UNAMIR, could not.

How was anyone to know just what the soldiers would do or how far they could go?

"All the credibility, trust and impartiality we had laboured to build up over all those months evaporated overnight," Dallaire said later. "The perception of France as a supporter of the former regime led to a vastly heightened animosity toward UNAMIR." Dallaire immediately had a problem within his own staff. A number of his officers were from French Africa, and the RPF in Kigali decided not to trust them any more. He had to evacuate about ten important personnel and reorganize his headquarters for the second time.

There was also the problem of French spying. Dallaire suspected French agents had been conducting espionage around the country. In fact, that's probably how the French knew that the genocide was a reality, and that France had better manoeuvre towards the right side of history. In the end, Operation Turquoise may have saved ten thousand to fifteen thousand lives. But the French Humanitarian Protection Zone (HPZ), established in southwestern Rwanda and running to the Zaire border, also allowed Hutu Power leaders to escape from the country. Members of their militias escaped the wrath of the RPF by hiding out in the HPZ and then fleeing over the border. Sam Kiley, of *The Times* in London, reported that French soldiers even evacuated Bagosora in the final days of the war.

Dallaire told his bosses in New York that he wanted to pursue the Hutu Power leaders over the border and have them arrested. "That went over like a lead fart," Dallaire said. "There was an opportunity to get into those camps [in Zaire] and get those bastards." According to Dallaire, in the first week after they fled, they had nothing, not even soap to wash themselves. He believes he could have arrested them. But New York regarded such a course as a violation of the codes of peacekeeping.

The French and their HPZ managed to slow and then halt the RPF advance, and a clash between the French and Kagame's forces became inevitable. When it did happen, Dallaire was compelled to sort it out. As he explained later, "I negotiated the separation line and monitored, with my small force, the line between Paul Kagame's rebel forces and the forces of Operation Turquoise, which included Jaguar jets, helicopter gunships, heavy mortars, APCs and twenty-five hundred special-forces troops. There were a number of confrontational situations during Op Turquoise, including two occasions when the rebels beat the French in the field, capturing twenty French soldiers. These incidents demonstrated that the best Western equipment and training do not necessarily lead to success. As General Kagame so shrewdly put it, 'Kigali can handle more body bags than Paris.'"

If there seems to be a bit of gloating in that statement, Dallaire can be forgiven. He, too, was humbled by what he encountered in Rwanda. Despite years of NATO training based on the collective knowledge of generations of fighting forces, he had never known of anything like this, a situation where such simple technology as propaganda and machetes could defeat entire populations. That a French military unit could be captured, even briefly, by Kagame's anglo-trained forces seemed a kind of poetic justice.

On July 4, the RPF took Kigali and the war was over. Three days after the RPF victory, the soldiers of UNAMIR II began to arrive.

The U.S. finally sent the promised APCs, but without radios or mounted guns. If Dallaire was frustrated with the French for their involvement in Rwanda, he was just as frustrated with the Americans for their lack of involvement. In late July, the U.S. deployed twenty-five hundred troops, long after the war and most of the slaughter was over. And twenty-two hundred of them were kept in Zaire and Uganda. "I faced a situation where one contingent [the Americans] possessed the ability to provide UNAMIR with a supply of water—water that was urgently needed because hundreds of displaced people under our protection were dying of thirst. But this contingent was forbidden to assist us, no matter how many people were dying, because of the grave concern for casualties," says Dallaire. He suspected that when American soldiers finally arrived with the water supply, it was only to present a photo opportunity for reporters at the airport. They never came into the city.

In a speech years later, Dallaire noted that Rwanda had been best known for the work of Dian Fossey and her mountain gorillas before it made history for its genocide. "I always wondered if the international community would have done more if 800,000 mountain gorillas were being slaughtered."

In July, Major Phil Lancaster was amazed to see new soldiers actually arriving—350 Canadians were among the first to land in Kigali to form the communications unit for UNAMIR II. It was like Christmas had come early.

"In June, I knew every white face on the street. By the end of July, you couldn't have fit them into a stadium." Suddenly you could get things done. Sandbags were filled and a twelve-foot wall went up around the head-quarters. The parking area, which had been a place where broken vehicles awaited servicing, was so busy that the arriving soldiers put up signs and directions. The city and UNAMIR headquarters was transformed by the arriving soldiers and NGOs. Cadavers had to be scooped up out of the water and buried. Everything had to be repaired.

Dallaire was now the only soldier who had been there from beginning to end since Major Beardsley had had to be airlifted out of the country when he became ill during the war. The phone calls to and from New York continued and Lancaster—who took most of them—says that Baril often asked him how Dallaire was coping. "Baril is not known for his human qualities," says Lancaster. "But to be fair, he did his best [for Dallaire]."

Lancaster remembers that after morning prayers, Dallaire would walk out on the balcony of his office at the Amahoro hostel and smoke a cigar. It was a five-minute daily holiday. "He'd kibitz with the military observers on the ground, trading jokes and insults. Sometimes in the evening, he would go down and have a drink with the technical workers, who were UN civilians. He could fit in anywhere." Lancaster thought Dallaire had the golden touch—an ability to make friends out of enemies, to defuse a situation, to command absolute loyalty from those under his command. But he also knew the boss was a burned-out case. The mask would slip from time to time, and Lancaster could see the utter fatigue.

By August, two million refugees had fled the country, taking with them the vast majority of NGOs that Dallaire had come to know during the months of genocide. Dallaire complained bitterly about the aid agencies that moved to the Goma camps, and maintained they went to Zaire only because there were more media outlets there and more chances of getting publicity for their agencies. "Remember the NGOs work on donations, they need to sell their product, and so they assist. But they also have to go where they get a lot of CNN points."

Indeed, business was booming in Goma, where the TV crews had what they needed: phones, satellites, hotels and a humanitarian crisis that was much easier to cover than the genocide. Dallaire saved his greatest venom for the United Nations High Commissioner for Refugees (UNHCR), one of the last to call the scene in Rwanda a genocide but one of the first to depart for the camps in Goma.

Dallaire believed that if the NGOs had held fast in Kigali, most Rwandans would have stayed and the country would have stabilized faster. He also knew that the perpetrators of the genocide were among the ranks of refugees, not just the Interahamwe recruits, but their bosses and political leaders. The NGOs were clothing, feeding and harbouring the death squads.

In August, Dallaire started to realize the impact stress and trauma were having on him. He was seething with anger half the time and grief-stricken the rest. Even though the war and the genocide were over, the Ghanaian bodyguards stayed with him, since UN cars were frequently stopped by militiamen who would demand to know if Dallaire was inside — they wanted to kill him. But Dallaire would frequently escape his minders and drive out of the Amahoro parking lot in his own Jeep. He would head off like a maniac into the countryside and be gone for hours as staffers fretted about his safety. The drive would clear his head and allow him space to think. But there was another purpose. "I was trying to get myself killed," Dallaire now admits. "I wanted to be ambushed."

Major Lancaster suspected the general was suicidal when he went with Dallaire on one of his drives. "He wanted to check out a certain position, and so we drove into this isolated area." An Interahamwe emerged from the bushes with his rifle cocked and ready. Lancaster was impressed with the amount of firepower the man had. "Usually they had two ammo clips over the shoulder, but this fellow had three," Lancaster recalls, and he noted the man did not look at all stable. "Where is General Dallaire?" the man asked in French. Lancaster had a sudden sick feeling about what was going to happen next. Sure enough, his boss couldn't resist the challenge. "Moi, je suis Dallaire," he said. The militiaman seemed caught off guard, especially when Dallaire reached out to shake his hand. "They talked for a bit and we parted without incident," says Lancaster, though he was first relieved of a pair of high-quality binoculars.

The suicide drives continued; at the time Dallaire seemed unaware of how close to the edge he was. Until, one day, it became pretty clear.

"I had issued an order that all dogs should be shot. They had got a taste for human flesh and were now dangerous and often diseased. So, we killed the dogs," says Dallaire. But the general also determined there was too much death around the Amahoro and so he was thrilled when his soldiers acquired a goat and installed it at the compound. Dallaire was amused by the animal though everyone complained about the goat droppings.

One day in early August, a soldier dashed into Dallaire's office and told him that dogs were attacking the goat. Dallaire grabbed his gun and headed out into the compound in a rage. "I ran up to the dogs and fired my pistol. I almost emptied it." He looked up to see everyone watching him and he realized how fanatical he must have appeared. "Once your men have seen you out of control they can no longer trust your judgement, and that's the kiss of death for a commander." It was time to leave.

Dallaire contacted General John de Chastelain, the chief of staff back in Ottawa, and told him he wanted to be replaced. De Chastelain agreed, but Boutros-Ghali said no. The secretary-general didn't want Dallaire to leave just as UNAMIR II was establishing itself. De Chastelain was finally able to persuade the UN to relieve Dallaire by stating that DND was concerned that the general was at serious risk of being killed within the coming weeks. But Boutros-Ghali insisted that Dallaire could only go if another Canadian took his position. Dallaire had strongly recommended that General Henry Anyidoho, the Ghanaian who had stood beside him throughout the genocide, be appointed, but his views were ignored.

When Phil Lancaster learned that Dallaire wanted to go, and that New York had arranged for a replacement FC, he concentrated on finding the right place for a goodbye party for the general. There wasn't much still intact in Kigali, other than Hotel Chez Lando. Lancaster had the roof repaired and the dead bodies removed from the grounds. A Pakistani businessman had a portable kitchen that could be used to prepare a meal, and the Canadian high commissioner managed to score half a case of champagne. They found tables and chairs, and borrowed a generator.

Dallaire wanted the guests to be only the people who had been there during the worst of it—not the strangers who now filled the city. About sixty came to dinner. It was, by all accounts, intensely emotional, and even more so since Dallaire could recall so many fine and happy meals in that restaurant, shared with Lando Ndasingwa and his family, and other Rwandan friends, all now dead.

Dallaire remembers a lot of tears and some anger. But mostly, the occasion was a celebration of the bond among people in uniform. "I came to realize," says Dallaire of the event, "that the camaraderie between soldiers is as intense as that of family."

The next day, the Ghanaians organized a change-of-command ceremony, during which Dallaire turned over his responsibilities to another

Canadian, General Guy Tousignant. The weather was miserable. A steady drizzle of rain fell as he met with his troops for the last time. The Ghanaians provided a small marching band, complete with snare drums, clashing cymbals and a horn section, and they played a series of almost tuneless military arrangements as they paraded around the Amahoro parking lot.

Dallaire walked down the row of black soldiers in blue berets, their boots polished to a mirror-shine. They stood tall and stone-faced, eyes straight ahead, ignoring the rain. Dallaire was ashen, his moustache now grey, his eyes filled with angst, his face showing every emotion known to man. He stopped from time to time to speak to the soldiers and later presented them with medals of service to the United Nations. Then the band played "Auld Lang Syne."

Major Lancaster went ahead to Nairobi to arrange Dallaire's departure from Africa, and he was at the airport when the general arrived in the afternoon. He couldn't believe how much Dallaire had changed in a few hours. "I saw him get off the plane. He didn't recognize me. I gave him his tickets and travel advance, but I then took them out of his hand and gave them to an aide." Dallaire later said the moment reminded him of the movie *Twelve O'Clock High*. "You know when Gregory Peck talks about maximum effort. And when the commander goes into a state… That happened. The war was over. The slaughter. We had gone through it all. UNAMIR II had some of the same trauma as UNAMIR I. I was getting nowhere."

Dallaire met his family in Amsterdam for a brief holiday, visiting the battlefields where Canadians had died defending Europe from Nazi tyranny and retracing the campaigns of his father and father-in-law. If nothing else, it seemed a fitting close to his tour of duty in Rwanda, a chance to reflect on the enormity of human folly.

There was a time when it took weeks or even years to return home from battle. Men serving in the great wars came back by boat; even those returning from Korea were withdrawn slowly and debriefed over long periods of time. Odysseus took most of his adult life to return to Ithaca. But modern-day peacekeepers are often back home within hours. The effect is that no one has any time to decompress, to sort out the collection of memories and impressions, to talk through the nightmares with those who shared them.

Roméo Dallaire was at work in Canada on September 3, 1994. After a flurry of debriefing exercises in New York, he was assigned one of the most demanding jobs in the forces: deputy commander of the army. He was also appointed to be the commander of the 1st Canadian Division with his headquarters in Kingston. His superiors told him the hard work would help him forget what had happened in Rwanda.

5

THE SEARCH FOR A SCAPEGOAT

I know now that there is a God, because I just shook hands with the Devil.
— General Roméo Dallaire

Years after they returned home, many of the officers who served with Dallaire in Rwanda still had a problem with the sound of wind. In the hot equatorial climate, there is often a stiff breeze, and at night, it would howl and bang through the windows of their rooms at Amahoro hostel and carry with it the sounds of horrors outside. At first, Brent Beardsley couldn't identify the sounds, and later, when he knew what they were, he didn't want to acknowledge them. For Lancaster, the wind seemed like the essence of evil—a moving tide of air swirling with the stench of rotting flesh and cries of pain.

That is the sound Roméo Dallaire carried in his head as he returned to work. He was assigned the two new posts and had been promoted to major general. But he felt little satisfaction with the perks and kudos. He found little satisfaction in anything.

Friends say he would never relax, never slow down. On a train or a plane, even after a long day, he would snap open the briefcase as soon as he took his seat. He often exhausted his associates. Those closest to him could see this wasn't the man they had known—gregarious and fun-loving. An old friend from the artillery, Colonel Ralph Coleman, says there was something around his eyes. Dallaire wasn't sleeping, and a workaholic who isn't sleeping is someone to worry about. "I told him he needed to take some time off and deal with the stress." But Dallaire wouldn't. He was reliving everything that had happened in Rwanda, every failure, every nightmare, every day. And he feared his memories would destroy him.

In September 1994, the CBC-TV reporter Brian Stewart snagged Dallaire for the general's first major sit-down interview since Rwanda; it was to be broadcast on *Prime Time News*. "I had debriefed Lewis MacKenzie when he came back from Bosnia, and I wanted to do the same with Dallaire," says Stewart. "It was a fascinating study in contrasts."

The media-savvy MacKenzie was totally comfortable before the camera, warm and engaging about his experiences in Sarajevo. But Dallaire was plainly ill at ease. "The man is immensely impressive," Stewart says about Dallaire. "There's iron there." But Dallaire fumbled around in the interview, trying to put things together. "He says, 'I haven't sorted it all out yet.' That surprised me. Because it was a major interview, and I thought he would have gone back in his files and really prepped. But he was struggling." (Dallaire's own recollection of the interview is that he was taken aback by how little Stewart knew about what had happened. He had presumed the world knew.)

During the three-hour conversation, only a part of which was shown on TV, Dallaire sometimes seemed lost in thought. His face showed little emotion, but he constantly rubbed his hands together. "No one can play Pontius Pilate on this one," he said in a chilly finale. In the whole three hours, Dallaire revealed almost nothing of the mission's problems. Stewart didn't think that Dallaire was trying to hide anything, but that he was genuinely trying to sort the events out. "After the interview, Robin Benjer [the producer] and I felt that there was a lot more behind this story than we had just heard in that room." Stewart was right. He and Benjer went on to do one of the first major exposés on the Rwanda war—a TV documentary showing that world powers, along with members of the Security Council, knew well in advance that a genocide was planned and did nothing to stop it. The London-based group African Rights published a damning report in September 1994. "Rwanda: Death, Despair and Defiance" documented the wilful ignorance of world powers, the careful cover-ups of the United Nations and the diabolical influence of the Rwandan government while it continued to sit on the Security Council. The trickle of critiques became a torrent. What had been regarded as "the little mission that tried and failed to stop the dark, random forces of hate and evil" began to morph into something more sinister.

Eighteen months after the slaughter had ended, and more than a year after Dallaire had returned to Canada, *The London Observer* reported the

existence of what soon became the most famous fax in the world—
Dallaire's Cassandra-like report, dated January 11, 1994. Shortly after the
Observer exposé, a Belgian newspaper published the fax in its entirety. The
government in Brussels was engaged in a frenzy of investigations and witch
hunts over the deaths of the ten Belgian peacekeepers and the national
reaction to the fax was explosive. What shocked the Belgians was not so
much that the memo had predicted the wholesale slaughter of Tutsi, but
that it had alerted the UN Department of Peacekeeping Operations that
members of the Interahamwe were planning to murder Belgian peacekeepers in an organized plot to drive them out of the country. Belgians—
particularly the families of the dead commandos—quite rightly wanted to
know why no one had acted on this message. It had been addressed to
Maurice Baril. Did he pass it on? Who read the thing? What did they do
about it? The United Nations went into damage-control mode.

When DPKO staff were questioned by reporters, they responded that
they got missives full of excess and hyperbole from the field all the time
—a response one Belgian senator, Alain Destexhe, found astonishing.
Destexhe was trying to launch a major inquiry in his country into the events
of the Rwandan genocide. "How often was the peacekeeping office getting
messages that warned of 'extermination' of an ethnic group?" Destexhe
asked. What if the UN had been around for the Holocaust? Would they have
sloughed off warnings as hyperbole?

Passing the buck went into high gear. Boutros-Ghali insisted he didn't
see the fax until months after the genocide. He had been travelling a lot
during the period of the genocide, he said, and hadn't been consulted.

The quest for someone to blame inevitably led to Dallaire's door.
Here was a man hailed as a hero, decorated and promoted for his work
in Rwanda. But according to his own fax, he knew of the threat to the
Belgian peacekeepers and to the Tutsi population months in advance. What
did he do to prevent the deaths of so many? On April 6, he had a force of
twenty-five hundred. They had guns. They had authority. Surely he could
have shown the *génocidaires* who was boss. Critics pointed out that when
the Belgian peacekeepers were locked out of Amahoro stadium by the
Bangladeshis, they had an actual firefight with the Hutu Power militia and
managed to scare them off after only a few rounds. Why hadn't Dallaire put
on a big show of force right at the beginning and frightened them all into
submission?

Iqbal Riza of the DPKO provided an answer. Riza had been the one to sign off on the faxes from Kofi Annan before they were sent to Dallaire in the months leading up to the genocide. He gave this astonishing interview to the PBS program *Frontline*:

> *Frontline:* Was it within the [UNAMIR] mandate to open fire to protect civilians?
> *Riza:* Not strictly, but in a situation like this, if they were to have done it, nobody would have blamed them.
> *Frontline:* So they could have opened fire to save lives?
> *Riza:* I believe some of them did.
> *Frontline:* Well, not very many of them.
> *Riza:* No, not very many, but not because they were told by New York not to fire.
> *Frontline:* They appear to have thought that they didn't have permission from New York and—
> *Riza:* They did not need instructions from New York. They have their weapons, those weapons are loaded and...while lives are threatened, in self-protection or to prevent loss of life, they could have opened fire. This is in the broad rules of engagement that apply to all peacekeeping operations.
> *Frontline:* But the United Nations soldiers on the ground told us that one reason they did not fire was because they didn't have permission.
> *Riza:* I cannot understand that.

Perhaps Riza didn't recall that the DPKO had been telling Dallaire that the peacekeepers were to avoid a firefight at all costs. The whole thrust of UNAMIR's task after the genocide began was to get a ceasefire between the two armies. And as useless as that effort was for those in the villages being massacred by their own burgomasters, that was what New York had wanted. When Riza came to Rwanda during the genocide, he held private consultations with the people in charge of the death squads. What has never been reported is that in the minutes taken at that meeting (Dallaire was also there), Riza is recorded as saying: "The United Nations cannot intervene in a civil conflict of an ethnic nature. With a cease-fire, it will be easier to control and supervise those villages." Dallaire got the message, as did the *génocidaires*: the blue berets were not to get involved.

Dallaire had few ways to defend himself against the suggestion that he was to blame. But obviously people on the inside thought the truth had to be known. More faxes and messages were mysteriously leaked and subsequently published, showing that the red-eyed devils had worked effectively with the papier-mâché ones. One day in 1998, the fax machine of a New York–based journalist whirred into action and kicked out another astonishing leak. Philip Gourevitch, a writer for *The New Yorker*, had just obtained the response from New York to Dallaire's January missive. A lot of reporters investigating the Rwandan genocide had been told this response existed—now Gourevitch would publish it. The contents were explosive.

The world at large learned that not only had the UN refused to protect Jean-Pierre and his family in exchange for information, but Dallaire had been told not to raid the arms cache. The fax also revealed that Dallaire was instructed to tell President Habyarimana about the weapons and get the Rwandan government to do something about them. This was news to the general public, and even to members of the Security Council. Kofi Annan and Iqbal Riza had never consulted the council about this.

Another leaked fax from April 17 (ten days into the genocide) apparently reflects what Dallaire had been reporting on the telephone for several days. In it, Dallaire writes about "ethnic cleansing," and he makes a personal plea to New York to change his rules of engagement and give him a new mandate. He explains that one contingent commander (the Bangladeshi) has orders from his own national government not to endanger the men and "not to protect Rwandan civilians." They were to hand them over to the belligerents rather than use their weapons to defend them. "This reticence to engage in dangerous operations, and the stated reluctance to use their weapons in self-defence or in defence against crimes against humanity, has led to a widespread mistrust of this contingent among its peers in other units and among staff officers at the headquarters."

Dallaire himself was both fascinated and appalled by what he learned following his return from Rwanda. He knew what had gone on at his end. What he hadn't realized, until he read it in the press, was the extent to which world leaders knew what was happening and did nothing. "When I read stuff, I wonder if I was set up to fail," he mused on one occasion.

Dallaire couldn't shake the feeling that the leaders in the international community had just left him there to cover up for their own lack of courage and moral conviction: "They put on a good show, but they didn't give a rat's ass." Dallaire had spent 70 per cent of his time just trying to get someone to send basic materials, from boots to flashlight batteries. Some of the food that arrived was rotten. "My tattered and logistically depleted force knew that no reinforcement or supplies would be forthcoming," Dallaire wrote later. "And throughout it all, we received no formal mandate. I called our situation the 'Counter Crimes Against Humanity Operation' and my soldiers believed in that mission.... Surely no single nation would have deserted its troops the way we were deserted by the world community in Rwanda."

The general was forceful in radio and television interviews, and he proposed many safeguards that the UN could put in place to ensure that there would never be another Rwanda. First of all, there should be some kind of rapid reaction force at the heart of the institution that would be always on standby to intervene in these types of emergencies. Dallaire wrote papers, drafts and reports, attended conferences, gave speeches — any forum he could find to get the message out. Canada gave him its highest honour, the Meritorious Service Cross, for the UNAMIR mission, and the Americans gave him their Legion of Merit medal.

Through all the post-war fallout, Dallaire was struggling badly. He endorsed the image that was emerging of a peacekeeping mission betrayed, and he was surely the source of some of the leaked material. But he couldn't shake his sense of failure. What if he had been more forceful, given a better account of himself? What if he had flown to New York to make the case before the Security Council? Could he have done more?

Dallaire's friend and colleague Dr. Jacques Castonguay noticed the changes almost right away. Castonguay was of another generation and had retired from the Canadian Forces in 1970. In post-retirement, he had become a teacher and the head of the Department of Military Psychology and Management at the Collège militaire royal de Saint-Jean, where Dallaire had been appointed commander in 1989.

Castonguay made thirty hours of interview tapes with Dallaire as part of a Canadian Forces debriefing project. Dallaire told him of all the horrors, all the efforts to get help, all the failed attempts to save people — and the few successful moments when they actually protected people. Dallaire's angst is what one could expect from someone who had witnessed such events. But one day, Castonguay recalls, Dallaire suddenly said, "I think I could have done better." Someone else might have missed the shift, but as a trained psychologist Castonguay knew it meant something — the beginning of self-loathing.

Dallaire's family and friends noticed the changes, even if they didn't come across on the TV screen. Dallaire's wife tried to remain private throughout the difficult times, but Dallaire told his friends that Beth was suffering. Two of their children needed therapy in order to help cope with their father's ordeal. He was overwhelmed. The smell of fresh fruit in a grocery store made him break down and weep. While shopping in a farmer's market with his wife, the sight of ground and cut meat at the butcher's counter almost made him retch (it recalled the image of butchered babies and children). Even sticks and dead wood strewn on the sides of roads would overwhelm him as he drove by, reminding him of the bodies of humans stacked or strewn in the same manner.

In the fall of 1996, Dallaire was visibly sliding into severe depression. His public appearances became more rare, and when he did speak, he reiterated that he was the one who had to take full responsibility for what had happened under his command, including the death of the ten Belgian peacekeepers. That the commander should see himself as the ultimate person in charge sounded heroic and grown-up. But the weight of it was crushing him. He attempted suicide. When had the suicidal urges first surfaced? He confided to friends that he had contemplated killing himself when he was still in Rwanda. Other soldiers who were with Dallaire concede that is entirely possible. They had had the same thoughts.

Even as he fell into despair, the knives were out for him. Officers, many of them retired, stepped forward to point out how Dallaire had fumbled the ball in Kigali. Colonel James Allen (retired) — a former commander of peacekeeping forces in Iran and Iraq, and now a newspaper columnist — claimed that Dallaire's failure in Rwanda was a complete disappointment to the military: "Personal intervention, even if suicidal, would have been in the best military tradition, and may even have been successful in saving lives. Military history is replete with courageous acts by individuals and small groups against hopeless odds that brought success," wrote Allen in *The Kingston Whig-Standard*.

In another column, he claimed that Dallaire's failure to prevent the deaths of the Belgian peacekeepers showed that the Canadian Forces' problem "is at its core a moral one, a question of values," and that if the government didn't recognize Dallaire's moral failure, "the nation will never witness the Armed Forces recapturing its sense of purpose."

Dallaire's detractors could point to any number of senior officers who would not have failed in the mission — Lewis MacKenzie, for instance. Dallaire should have been used to it — the ranks of the armed forces are rife with backstabbers — but for someone in his mental state, it was excruciating.

When a *Saturday Night* magazine article in the fall of 1996 trashed his performance in Rwanda and argued that he had been cavalier with the lives of Belgian soldiers, Dallaire lashed back. In an angry five-page letter to the editor, Dallaire wrote: "It is most unfortunate that although the article concentrates on my leadership he [the author] could not arrange to travel the relatively short distance within Canada (from Calgary to Ottawa), talk to me personally, and fully present the facts upon which he would ultimately base his inaccurate and personally damaging conclusions."

After the *Saturday Night* article, it became almost impossible to interview Dallaire about anything. Using the excuse that the Great Lakes region of Africa was still unstable, the Department of National Defence decided that Dallaire should give no more public interviews. Letters and correspondence released under the Access to Information Act reveal that the DND was concerned with Dallaire's controversial role in Rwanda and with the media fallout. Though much of the material is censored, the occasional exchange between top bureaucrats at the DND shows that they were uncomfortable with what he had to say. The assistant deputy minister (personnel), D. N. Kinsman, wrote: "Dallaire's dynamic, outspoken style precipitates a huge number of invitations for him to speak as well as occasional discomfort or disagreement for those who do not share all his views." Kinsman's note actually supports Dallaire's right to speak openly and criticize the United Nations. But those in DND policy clearly didn't agree with him. A memo dated February 5, 1997, is a gag order from Rear Admiral J. A. King, the associate assistant deputy minister (policy): "I recommend that no further requests for Mgen Dallaire's participation be entertained except under exceptional circumstances where it would be clearly in the interest of the Department to do so."

The man who didn't need a gag order because he never spoke about these events, the man who seemed to be walking away from the Rwanda debacle with no blood on him, was another Canadian general, Maurice Baril. Cut from the same cloth, steeped in the same history, affected by the politics of Quebec's Quiet Revolution, married to the Canadian armed forces, he and Dallaire had climbed through the ranks of ambitious soldiers almost in lockstep.

"Baril is more laid-back, serene and cool," says now retired Colonel Michel Drapeau, a forceful critic within the armed forces who keeps a watchful eye on the mettle of up-and-coming officers. Drapeau was fascinated by the contrast between Dallaire and Baril: "Dallaire is tactile, enthusiastic. He has the common touch." They're both French, but Baril has "the anglo cool" while Dallaire is the "Latino."

The point of such a comparison for Drapeau is to try to figure out what happened between the two men during the war in Rwanda. Baril had been appointed to the prestigious position of military adviser in the Department of Peacekeeping Operations shortly before Dallaire was appointed force commander of UNAMIR. It's clear that Dallaire relied on their history together. "They drank together; they met in the mess and in the field. They had lived in each other's back pockets for thirty years. It's impossible to have any miscommunication between the two," says Drapeau.

After the war in Rwanda, *The Globe and Mail* reported that Baril said he had to keep Dallaire "on a leash," that Dallaire was a cowboy and too willing to go off half-cocked. Human Rights Watch's Rwanda expert, Alison Des Forges, says it is her understanding that Baril never made much of the Dallaire communiqués from Rwanda, which he considered a bit over the top.

For Michel Drapeau, it doesn't add up. Baril would not have been in a position where he could just ignore a fax warning of genocide. Dallaire has never said anything publicly against Baril, and still maintains that his only ally in New York was his old military classmate. If the game is to find someone to blame for what happened in Rwanda, Drapeau says you can't make a case against Baril: "Baril is not the take-charge type of guy. He is a facilitator. A conciliator. It's unlikely he would independently decide not to pass on an important fax." Drapeau says Baril had just started the job as military liaison at the DPKO and, given his nature, he would want to do everything by the book. Blame, according to Drapeau, probably does not reside with Baril.

In 1999, the new secretary-general of the UN, Kofi Annan, commissioned a study of communications in the peacekeeping office to determine just what went wrong. Annan, a key player at the time, picked the panel and set the terms of reference, which made the exercise appear dubious from the start. But he allowed the panel access to everything that had been written — every cable, fax and document.

The panel found the famous fax exchange to be an astonishing breakdown in communications and couldn't believe that UNAMIR wasn't told to do everything in its power to maintain contact with the extraordinary Jean-Pierre. But it blamed Dallaire for addressing the fax only to Baril. It suggested that if he had addressed the memo directly to the secretary-general, perhaps it would have reached higher places. The fax from Dallaire to Baril is written in English, however, not in their native tongue. Why? Everyone who worked with Dallaire says it's because English is the language of the United Nations, and clearly Dallaire intended the fax for general consumption.

Critics of Dallaire and the UNAMIR mission, and they are legion, say it wasn't just Baril who failed to convey the reality of Rwanda in the early days. They point out that Dallaire himself never used the "g" word when he talked to the media. In interviews and press scrums he spoke of massacres, but not of genocides. However, Brent Beardsley points out that the UNAMIR mission was under instruction to maintain relationships with both sides in the conflict. To have accused the Rwandan government of genocide publicly would have ended any chance of further contact. But private messages back to New York, he says, were filled with such urgency from the beginning.

Beardsley remembers when he realized that he was witnessing a genocide. On April 10, 1994, he went to a Polish mission to help evacuate the priests there. He arrived to find that most of the women and children who had stayed at the mission had been hacked to death. The priests told him that the Presidential Guard, accompanied by the gendarmerie, had arrived and taken everyone's ID cards. Tutsi were murdered and their records, kept at the civil registry in town, were also destroyed. It was a systematic slaughter of civilians combined with an attempt to expunge even their identities. Beardsley knew this was not random revenge killing as a result of the president's assassination. Something else was going on.

He reported his observation to Dallaire, who called New York and said that Rwanda was now experiencing "ethnic cleansing." Beardsley said no one in the mission said *genocide* in the first weeks because the word had not occurred to them. "The language of the time was ethnic cleansing. That's what they were calling it in Bosnia, and that's how we described it."

There were dozens more phone calls like that, says Beardsley. There are no records of those calls—some of them were made to people's homes in the middle of the night. But it's clear there was a stream of communications back to New York describing a genocide—a stream that exists now only in memory. Beardsley says they presumed that Baril and Iqbal Riza were passing those messages on to the secretary-general, and that the Security Council was receiving them.

Beardsley had one disturbing experience with Baril when he was in Rwanda. Dallaire had gone out on a reconnaissance mission, and while he was away, Baril called to speak to him urgently. Beardsley told Baril that Dallaire wouldn't be back until the next day. "General Baril was very tense, and he asked me if we had the land-evacuation plan worked out. I told him, 'Sir, we haven't. We had planned on an air evacuation.'"

If one side or the other in Rwanda had turned on UNAMIR, the plan, as far as Beardsley knew, was for a Service Protected Evacuation from the Airport—a SPEA. That's what UNAMIR HQ had been counting on. It was the same procedure when the American rangers had to quickly leave Mogadishu a year earlier: they had been airlifted out. But Baril was now telling Beardsley that UNAMIR personnel would have to leave by land. "This was impossible," says the major. "We had only a dozen trucks, and we didn't even have enough fuel to get our Jeeps around town. We would siphon off gas from abandoned vehicles in order to get back to the headquarters. And now General Baril was telling me we would have to evacuate by road."

Baril's voice was cracking as he talked. "You have to understand, there is no cavalry coming," Baril said to Beardsley. "The Security Council will not agree to an airlift of any kind." Beardsley was stunned. "For the whole night, I contemplated this news. That we were on our own. There would be no rescue. I thought, If we have to go, we'll go on foot. But we're not abandoning those people. We'll take them with us, and we'll walk out."

When Beardsley told Dallaire this the next day, the general just shrugged. "That's okay. We're not going anywhere, anyway," Dallaire told him. UNAMIR and Dallaire were doing a dangerous dance and one false move would have meant the end of them. And yet, says Beardsley, he felt strangely relieved. There were no more mysteries: everything was now a matter of life or death.

Baril will not talk about what happened while he was military adviser at the DPKO. He gave one long interview to Jacques Castonguay as part of the debriefing exercise at the DND, but Castonguay says that Baril revealed very little. Baril dismissed criticisms of the DPKO. "In the month of February," he told Castonguay, "no one could predict exactly what was going to happen, exactly. After the coup, the Monday morning quarterbacks came to say that you should have seen it. But no one came to tell us that before." Baril didn't think his department should take any responsibility.

Dallaire and Baril should have been contenders for the top military job in Canada. But there was too much controversy around Dallaire's role in Rwanda: the Belgian senate launched a massive investigation in 1996, and a number of Rwandans were trying to sue the United Nations and the general for failing to protect their families. In September 1997, Prime Minister Jean Chrétien appointed Maurice Baril the new chief of defence staff. When asked about his role in the Rwanda affair, Baril told reporters that he wouldn't be standing there today, sworn in as the country's top soldier, if there were any doubts about him.

In his new capacity as chief of defence staff, Baril continued to watch Dallaire carefully for cracks as he had done during the war in Rwanda. Dallaire's family had stayed in Quebec City, where the children were in school, and he had moved to Ottawa to work as chief of staff and assistant deputy minister for human resources. He was advised in 1996 to get professional help and he did: Dallaire was overreacting to most situations and was frequently irrational. But his slide into depression continued, unabated. Dallaire commuted to Quebec City to see his family (only on the weekends when he wasn't working) and it was on one of these drives—in the winter of 1997—that he attempted suicide for the second time. He calculated that if he aimed his car for the snow bank on the meridian while driving at top speed he could crash the vehicle and it would look like an accident. "But a Jetta, which is what I was driving, has a very low base of gravity," says Dallaire. "The car only bounced off the bank and sent me back into traffic." The vehicle went out of control briefly and Dallaire came to his senses. The impact knocked him out of the spiral of despair, but he wept for the duration of the drive.

Dallaire appeared in a DND video in 1998 in which he described his mental condition, post-traumatic stress disorder (PTSD). The program is called *Witness the Evil*, and it's an unusually emotional and confessional in-house training video. Canadian soldiers who arrived during and after the war in Rwanda tell the stories of what they encountered there. Phil Lancaster talks of his feelings of futility, of wearing a blue beret and representing all the best thinking in the world, only to find "it didn't mean a damn thing" against a genocidal machine.

Another soldier talks of the foods he can no longer eat because they have associations with death. Corporal Chris Cassavoy has a hard time looking at children because it reminds him of what the Hutu militiamen did to them. "Especially newborns. They were toys [to the Interahamwe]," Cassavoy says.

But the most forceful account is from Roméo Dallaire. He talks of losing his sense of self-preservation in Rwanda: "By mid-July, I was running ambushes, daring them. I'd lost my sense of humour." He describes how it took two years before the full impact of Rwanda hit. "Not being able to cope, to hide it, to keep it in a drawer," he confesses. "I became suicidal. Because there was no solution. You couldn't live with the pain, the sounds, the sights, the smells. I couldn't sleep. I couldn't stand the loudness of silence."

Dallaire admits to having death wishes after he came back to Canada, but he doesn't reveal that the "ambushes" he was running in Rwanda were really suicide attempts. He wanted someone to kill him.

He is intensely emotional in the video, but ever conscious that this is an educational tool, he urges others to get help for what the military has identified as a crisis within its ranks of post-traumatic stress disorder — almost all of it attributed to peacekeeping missions. "If you lose a leg, it's obvious. You lose your marbles, it's hard to explain or to get help. But those who don't get help are a risk to all of us. If I didn't get help I wouldn't be promoted because I would be dead." Dallaire was subsequently accused of getting preferential treatment. If a rank-and-file soldier confessed to such a condition — some complained — they would be treated with suspicion and not concern. Breaking down is seen as a betrayal of the codes of soldiering. (Many soldiers in the Canadian Armed Forces, however, have sought help for PTSD since Dallaire's disclosure.)

Dallaire made even fewer public appearances in 1997 and 1998. His doctors — a psychiatrist and a psychologist — told him to stop talking about the experiences because it was only making his condition worse. Dallaire apparently hadn't the "filters" left to sort out the events any more. His understanding was becoming irrational. Dr. Castonguay published a book about UNAMIR using his interviews with Dallaire. *Les casque bleus au Rwanda* is the definitive textbook of the mission, and it contains many of the important documents and letters that Dallaire issued. It describes the general's efforts as heroic. Dallaire's doctors began to use the book to help snap him back to reality — to remind him of what he had accomplished in Rwanda, not what he'd failed at. But the nightmares were too haunting.

September 24, 1998, was a watershed day for Dallaire. He had not slept the night before—he rarely slept at all anymore: "I couldn't go into a bed-room and lie down. The sound of the silence was deafening." Instead, he plowed through two briefcases of paperwork and finally dozed for a few hours close to dawn. Dallaire had worked out a system with his staff that, on days when he was on the road, which were many, he would leave his briefcases of completed work from the night before just inside the door of his rented Hull apartment to be picked up. The staff would replace the briefcases at the end of the day with new paperwork for the next night.

At 7:30 a.m., with the briefcases in place, he was out the door, en route to Kingston.

Dallaire remembers each moment of the day with vivid clarity: the half sandwich he had for lunch, the meetings and the debriefing sessions at the Royal Military College. Dallaire told the staff of the school that he wanted the curriculum of the college changed in order to reflect a new role for Canadian soldiers. He wanted them to study as much philosophy and anthropology as history and political science. He argued that officers needed to understand more about people and their cultures if they were to work as effective peacekeepers in the New World Order.

Dallaire returned to Hull that evening from the long day. "I was just opening my briefcases and deciding which junk food I would order for supper that night when the phone rang. It was General Baril." Dallaire immediately briefed his boss on everything he was doing, presuming that is what the chief of defence staff was calling to hear. But it wasn't. "I want you to take some time off," he told Dallaire. "I protested. I had too much to do. He said 'Roméo, go home. Don't even go to the office. Just go home tomorrow.'"

As soon as Baril said it, Dallaire broke down. The next day, he drove to Quebec City and didn't return to work for nearly six months. When he finally came back, he took the less challenging post of special adviser to the chief of staff on officer professional development, reporting directly to his boss at DND, Maurice Baril.

6

THE BELGIAN LEGACY

*For the Belgians ... Rwanda mattered. It was an important part of
their colonial empire. They tried their best to understand it, control it and
develop it. But "understanding," given the accepted scientific vulgate of the time,
proved an ambiguous process. On the basis of what was more an ideological
than a scientific evaluation, an ancient, rich and complex society was
modernised, simplified and ossified.*
—Gérard Prunier, *The Rwanda Crisis: History of a Genocide*

IN the Belgian town of Ottigny, about an hour's drive from
Brussels, Luc Marchal attends to the essentials of life. These days,
six years after the genocide in Rwanda, his haunting memories
of that time jostle each other for opportunities to torment him. He does
what he can to control his thoughts: he performs a lot of volunteer work
in his community, and he and his wife, Cathy, are very involved in the
affairs of their church. He passes much of his time in the exquisite gardens
around his home.

Before he was sent to Rwanda, Marchal had spent five years in Zaire
living in rural villages. "I discovered the real value of life there," says
Marchal. "We are too civilized. Just to see the stars at night there, it ...
brings sensations. It's a spectacle. My time in Africa was the richest time of
my life." When Marchal was given the opportunity to go on the Rwandan
mission, he'd been thrilled. "I liked the philosophy of the Arusha agree-
ments. I thought, Here is a chance to make peace, even though we are
trained to make war. I was optimistic, thinking we would reach a happy
conclusion." Dallaire shared that feeling with Marchal. But both men soon
saw the reality.

What went wrong? Marchal has heard that question too many times since he returned to Belgium. He shakes his head, and for a long time he just stares out the window at the garden. "I didn't know much of the Rwandan language. But they taught me that the word MINUAR [the French acronym for UNAMIR] actually has a meaning in Kinyarwandan. The word means that your lips are moving, but they don't really say anything. And that's what we were from the beginning. After a few weeks, the extremists knew we had no power."

When the Belgians were ordered home from Rwanda in 1994, Marchal considered mutiny: instead, he stayed with his friend Dallaire three extra days, until a Ghanaian contingent could come down from the north. Marchal says the emotional intensity of those three days was almost too much to bear, and he can't talk about it. He is ashamed of the Belgian military for "deserting" UNAMIR. Marchal offers a letter he wrote to Dallaire, dated April 18, 1994, just before they parted. But the letter reflects none of the sentiment of close friends. Curiously, it's written in the language of heroic poetry, like something from *The Iliad*. Perhaps more than anything, it reflects how Dallaire and Marchal saw themselves. "For a soldier," Marchal wrote, "it is so difficult to abandon the battlefield at the moment when everything requires him to be side by side with his brothers-in-arms."

The Belgian soldiers landed in Brussels in April 1994, and they tore up their blue berets on the Tarmac. Marchal knew there would be fallout from the deaths of the peacekeepers, but he couldn't know it would be directed at him. Within months, he was charged with involuntary manslaughter. He was the first officer in Belgian military history to be court-martialled. The Belgian military panel regretted that General Dallaire was out of its reach, protected from prosecution by the UN. The next person in line was Luc Marchal: at least he could be charged under the laws of the country.

The prosecutors prepared the case against him for nearly a year. Marchal asked to see the file. It was three metres thick. He went through every page, and at the end he was elated: the file didn't contain a single incriminating fact against him. And then he sank even deeper into despair. If there was no case, why was he on trial? With a Kafkaesque sense of semi-reality, Marchal realized his trial was political. "The court martial was my darkest hour," he says.

The legal machinery of the United Nations kicked into gear as soon as the investigation began and erected protective firewalls against the Belgian authorities. The court was told it could not have Dallaire, even as a witness — anything the judges wanted to know they could get from UN documents that were already on the record. Dallaire wanted to testify but was told it was not up to him. The UN legal advisers said that if he went to Belgium, he could perhaps be arrested and charged. The UN did agree to let him reply in writing to questions put to him by the court, but even these went through a vetting process in New York. When Dallaire discovered that the UN had censored his answers, he protested strenuously. His responses ultimately went off to Belgium intact.

Dallaire had not seen Luc Marchal since the last day on the Tarmac in Kigali, when they'd said goodbye. And now Marchal was being tried for failing to do what the Belgians believed Dallaire should have done. The families in Belgium publicly conveyed their horror and anger that Dallaire was decorated for bravery in Canada and the United States. In Brussels, Dallaire was regarded as the anti-hero.

In January 1996, after the UN had decided he could not testify, Dallaire wrote an open letter to "all personnel serving under my command in land force Quebec area." Over eight single-spaced pages, Dallaire defended his orders and the actions of the Belgians who obeyed him. "I fully support the decision of Colonel Marchal to order Belgian peacekeepers to carry out my direction," Dallaire tells his soldiers. "Colonel Marchal and the other Belgian officers demonstrated sound operational judgement and great moral courage in not ordering a suicidal military intervention to attempt to rescue the captured peacekeepers. Had either Marchal or his subordinate commanders requested authority from me to conduct an assault on Camp Kigali, my response would have been outright refusal to do so."

Dallaire was the man Marchal admired most of all the people with whom he had ever served. When Marchal heard, just before his trial, that his Canadian general was struggling with depression and was riven with self-doubt, he was truly alarmed. "If such a man was falling apart, what of me? Would I be able to resist?" Marchal asked himself. Did Marchal have more glue? Did he have more staying power? Marchal's wife is a devout Catholic, and he hoped her faith would rub off on him. He had little more than that to keep himself together.

Evidence presented at the Marchal trial revealed that the Belgian commandos had been tortured and beaten savagely by the Hutu soldiers.

Some of them were still alive in the afternoon. Why had no one come to help them? The evidence presented indicated that Dallaire had seen the bodies of the men lying on the ground inside Camp Kigali. But it seemed he was so obsessed with going to a meeting that he didn't even bother to stop to see them, let alone rescue them. When he did get to the meeting, it seems he dilly-dallied for about an hour before he even asked Colonel Bagosora about the Belgians. When Bagosora told him that there was nothing to be done — that even he had lost control of the men in that camp — Dallaire appeared to have done nothing more. As for the other Belgian officers — where were they? Why was no one sent to fight for the men? It's in the tradition of Belgian commandos — the *crème de la crème* of the armed forces — to look after each other. But no one came to the rescue. These men didn't even die with their weapons in hand, but were naked and mutilated.

Dallaire could only explain, in writing to the court and in his open letter to his personnel, that he firmly believed he would have lost many more men that day if he had allowed a rescue operation, and Marchal had agreed. That didn't soothe the souls of the Belgians.

The Marchal trial lasted for three weeks, and the court acquitted him of all charges. It seems to have been a show trial, whipped up by the government to take the heat off its own foreign affairs department and the Belgian military brass. But it didn't work. The final judgement ran to ten pages and exonerated Marchal completely.

At first, the relatives of the ten Belgian peacekeepers kept quiet, following the paternal tradition of military families, allowing the organization to take care of them. But the wives and parents of the peacekeepers had been treated appallingly. Sandrine Lotin, wife of Thierry Lotin (the one who had radioed back to headquarters that day: "They're going to lynch us, my colonel"), was told in the middle of the night that her husband was dead. Perhaps because she was very visibly pregnant, perhaps because her husband was the only officer, her messengers were actually polite.

The other wives, mothers and fathers were treated rudely, coldly, and even lied to about the details of the murders. They were not allowed to pay their final respects to the men when their bodies were sent home. The government took over the funeral arrangements and marginalized the families. And when the commander who had been in charge of the men, Joe Dewez, turned up to meet the families wearing Bermuda shorts, it was all too much. They went public. They denounced the Belgian government and the military for the death of the ten commandos and created a huge public outcry.

In 1996, as the court martial began, the Belgian government was presented with a petition. Two hundred thousand people demanded an inquiry into what had happened in Rwanda. The steady leak of information that found its way into the media leading up to the Marchal trial had painted a nasty picture. The mission was poorly prepared, poorly informed. The Belgian military had agreed to send 450 soldiers into a hostile environment without being properly briefed on what they should expect.

Available information could have told them the Belgians would be a target. But the decision-makers either ignored or failed to acknowledge that reality. And what did the Belgian authorities know about Roméo Dallaire before they entrusted their soldiers' lives to him? Surely they should have realized he wasn't up to the task? The groundswell of support for the families, and against UNAMIR, became a full investigation, led by the Belgian senator, Alain Destexhe.

The senate inquiry into the failure of UNAMIR went on for more than a year, through 1996 and 1997, much of it broadcast on Belgian TV. Marchal testified. So did Colonel Dewez. One of the saddest and most pathetic testimonies was that of Petrus Maggen, the officer who had managed to get to work the morning after the president's plane crash. Maggen told the inquiry that he heard Dallaire say, as they passed Camp Kigali, "Some of my men are in there." But the inquiry checked that statement against other testimony by Maggen (there had already been two investigations) and discovered that he had quoted Dallaire differently each time.

He was charged with perjury, and also accused of dereliction of duty by his own department of defence for failing to give assistance to people in danger. Apparently, he should have jumped from the Jeep that day, run into Camp Kigali, where almost two thousand heavily armed Rwandan soldiers were on a rampage, and saved the ten soldiers. Maggen testified that Dallaire attempted to do just that, and that the Rwandan driver had prevented him. How was Maggen then supposed to jump from the Jeep and perform a suicidal task?

Those who watched his testimony on TV found it profoundly depressing. This small, nervous soldier—who had the bad luck to show up for work in the middle of a genocide, and then failed to hear correctly, or remember correctly, or report consistently—was being held accountable.

Not Kofi Annan or Iqbal Riza or even Roméo Dallaire—those people had protection. The buck stopped with a little man who played a small part in a big drama.

Maggen has not recovered from the grilling he took. He was told, as a consequence of the inquiry, that he would never have a command in the army. That decision was later overturned, but not before Maggen felt the full sting of his humiliation. Maggen today says the several inquiries left him confused about the events and not sure who had done what. Speaking in an interview six years later, his eyes fill up with tears; he turns his wedding band around and around on his finger as he remembers: "Sometimes, I thought this ring was all that was left of my marriage."

Maggen blames Dallaire for almost nothing. In fact, he reveres him, as do many other officers. Maggen had followed Dallaire around that day after the president's plane crash like a loyal puppy. He described the general as preoccupied with finding out what had happened to the prime minister, and terribly worried about his peacekeepers inside the camp. He believed at the time that Dallaire was on top of everything. Now he wonders. Could Dallaire have saved them? Maggen turns away when the question is asked and says he doesn't know why Dallaire didn't do more. When he saw the bodies at Camp Kigali, why didn't Dallaire radio back to headquarters and order a rescue party?

Dallaire never appeared before the Belgian parliamentary inquiry. His written responses to the Marchal trial were forwarded to the inquiry instead. Senator Destexhe says the commission never got full and adequate testimony from Dallaire and consequently, he says, the inquiry was left with a number of grey areas. Dallaire maintains the inquiry's questions were the same as those he answered for Marchal's trial.

As the Belgian hearing was going full bore, the controversy spilled over into Canada and Dallaire faced a lot of flak at home. The damning *Saturday Night* article was by a Calgary-based writer, George Koch, who depicted Dallaire as a commander with an utter disregard for the lives of his soldiers. Koch interviewed friends and family of the Belgian peacekeepers, and they accused Dallaire of negligence: "As an artillery man, Dallaire had no background in the kind of commando tactics that his Belgian troops specialized in—tactics that might have worked in a civil war in a city like Kigali," writes Koch. "What Lotin's men find particularly galling is that they weren't allowed to make the effort. 'It's difficult to accept leaving ten guys to be hacked to bits with machetes,' says Sergeant

Didier Hutsebaut, a member of the 2nd Battalion. 'There would have been a risk to the other soldiers, but a soldier's job is to fight and perhaps die. In Rwanda, it was decided to not even try. I reproach Dallaire for seeing our guys and then going to a meeting and doing nothing.'" The *Saturday Night* article led the Canadian attack on Dallaire, which continued throughout the Belgian inquiry.

Dallaire did not contradict many of these charges—he said in the few interviews he gave that he deeply regretted the death of the soldiers, but that he would do it again exactly the same way. Soldiers should be prepared to die in the course of their service, he believes, and if not, "why not send Boy Scouts then?" Dallaire wrote his angry response to the Koch article, but he couldn't deny its conclusion: he had been willing to risk the lives of Belgian soldiers to save the lives of Rwandans. The mission came first.

You could almost hear the sharp intake of breath in the Canadian military. This is not how many in DND see peacekeeping. Lewis MacKenzie summed up the Canadian Forces sentiment for Koch: "Major General Lewis MacKenzie (retired) says that, for commanders, only in wartime is the mission clearly more important than the lives of individual soldiers. 'Peacekeeping is different. I can't think of a UN mission that was clear. So you have to determine if the mission is reasonable. I have my own philosophy. My view is, can I write Mrs. Jones and say, Your son/daughter died fighting valiantly for a good cause? Or would I have to write, Your son/daughter was massacred and I'm not sure why.'"

Roméo Dallaire believed he had been in the middle of a war and had to act like it. His critics say that though it was a war, it wasn't his to fight, and the peacekeepers were not his soldiers to lose. That thirty thousand people are still alive because of what Dallaire chose to do is often lost in the debate, sometimes by the Rwandans themselves.

A half-hour down the road from Luc Marchal, through the rolling farm fields of Belgium, in the town of Namura, Annonciata Kavaruganda lives in exile with two of her children. It is a miracle family. They should all be dead. Joseph Kavaruganda, a Hutu moderate and the president of the Constitutional Court—the man legally in charge of the government—was protected by a detail of five Ghanaian soldiers, but they deserted him when the Rwandan military arrived the morning of April 7, 1994.

Judge Kavaruganda was still in pyjamas. His wife asked the Rwandan soldiers to wait while he got dressed and she prepared some clothes for him to take. No, it was unnecessary, said the soldiers. The judge would not need clothes where he was going. They took him away, and that's the last time his wife and children saw him. According to Annonciata's testimony, the Ghanaian soldiers were friendly with the Rwandan militiamen, having a few drinks and laughing while some of the Presidential Guard beat her and her children.

They eventually escaped to a neighbour—the Canadian representative in Rwanda—who shuffled the family off to the Canadian embassy downtown. The door was locked. The family lived on the embassy's terrace for a week, eating fruit from the garden and listening for news on the security guard's radio. Finally, UNAMIR came to rescue them, and they were flown out of the country in the middle of the genocide.

Sitting in her chilly apartment in Belgium, with a photo of Joseph on a shelf above her, Annonciata talks of the failure of UNAMIR. The so-called bodyguards were useless. General Dallaire had promised to be there for the families, but no one came to their rescue. When the judge called for help, they told him they would try to send reinforcements. No one ever came. Annonciata just shakes her head when asked about the Bangladeshis. "Were they really soldiers?" she asks, with a touch of sarcasm in her voice. She has heard that Dallaire is being held responsible for the ten Belgian peacekeepers. She laughs. "Ten dead peacekeepers. What does that mean up against the genocide, compared to the number of Rwandans who died?"

For many of the Belgian soldiers who were part of UNAMIR, their biggest failure was not really the loss of the entire political elite of Rwanda in a bloodbath, or even the murder of ten of their soldiers in an ambush. What haunts them most is the day when they pulled out of the ETO compound, where two thousand people had gone seeking protection. UNAMIR soldiers were ordered to help with evacuation of the foreigners. When the Belgians abandoned those people, some of them lay down on the road to prevent the trucks from leaving without them. Major Brent Beardsley had been asked about this by a reporter at the time, and he categorically denied that the Belgians had left: "I didn't know for a fact, but I just knew it couldn't be possible." Beardsley was devastated to learn later that it was true.

In the summer of 1996, thirty relatives of those who were killed that day filed a lawsuit against the United Nations and also named the force commander of the UNAMIR mission, Roméo Dallaire: "UNAMIR and its

members consciously abandoned defenceless people, knowing that a genocide was ongoing and that they and their families faced certain deaths."
It was the first time in history that a specific peacekeeper had ever been
sued for failing to protect the citizens of the country. The thirty suitors
demanded $250,000 each in compensation.

William Schabas, the Montreal lawyer who filed the suit on behalf
of the survivors, admits that it was more to make a point than to get compensation. The host-state agreement established between Rwanda and the
United Nations before the mission began gave members of UNAMIR immunity in the Rwandan courts but allowed people to file cases before an
arbitration panel. That panel had a statute of limitations of three months,
however, and those months had long since passed. Schabas had no place to
launch his civil action, no country's court in which to file the claim. He sent
it to the office of Boutros Boutros-Ghali, still the secretary-general of the
UN, and was told that the UN cannot be sued. Schabas dropped his case.

Undaunted by the failure of Schabas, Annonciata Kavaruganda and
the sisters of Landoald Ndasingwa launched a legal action in 1999. The two
families retained a crackerjack Australian attorney and former crown prosecutor named Michael Hourigan; he had been an investigator for the
International Criminal Tribunal for Rwanda when he quit over the way he
believed the UN was obstructing his work. He admits to being the source,
or the conduit, for some of the incriminating documents that have ended
up in the public domain, which he says were leaked to him. On behalf
of the Ndasingwa and Kavaruganda families, Hourigan is pursuing the
United Nations for damages. He principally blames Kofi Annan for not
responding to the dozens of warnings from Dallaire. But the families were
shocked to learn that Dallaire knew that they were specifically targeted by
the death squads.

A leaked inter-office memorandum from an intelligence officer to
Dallaire, dated February 17, 1994, warns of a plot to assassinate specific
people: "We have been informed that there's a serious threat against Chez
Lando Hotel. The 'Death Esquadron' is planning to conduct sabotage in
the building and murder against Mr. Lando and Mr. Joseph Kavaruganda,
president of the Constitutional Court." The memo goes on to list the
names of people who would kill the two men.

The families were amazed that no one came to warn them, and that
no one arrested the men listed as part of the death squad. Both families
now say that had they known of the memo from intelligence, they would

have left, or at least, according to Landoald's sister, sent the children out of the country. But diplomats in Rwanda at the time recall that Dallaire did send covert messages warning people he suspected were in danger, though he was careful to always communicate this intelligence through civilian agents, lest UNAMIR find itself accused of biases.

In many cases, Dallaire had thought it was enough to put the security units on duty and give the families phone numbers to call if something went wrong. But the morning of the assassinations, the phone systems were jammed by those needing help. The roadblocks prevented UNAMIR from getting around. Dallaire didn't know until too late just how many people were involved with the extremists. He had thought he had the support of the gendarmerie. He wasn't completely wrong about this: a number of senior officers with the police and the military did resist Colonel Bagosora's forces.

But Dallaire knew that people had stayed because they believed he would protect them. In November 1994, he made an astonishing admission: "The UN mission, and later, the very civilians whose lives it was intended to secure, fell victim to an inflated sense of optimism which I myself participated in formulating, thereby creating high expectations which the UN did not have the capacity to meet."

In his letter to the UN seeking reparations, Hourigan writes: "Without question, more could and should have been done with respect to the critical information received by General Dallaire concerning death plots.... Both families were assured that they were safe from harm and, as a consequence, they relied completely on the United Nations troops for their safety." While the people of Belgium demanded to know why their peacekeepers were sent to their deaths in a futile attempt to protect Rwandan politicians, and why Belgium was even in Rwanda in the first place, the victims of the genocide wanted to know why the peacekeepers didn't fight until the last man to protect them.

Annonciata Kavaruganda doesn't really blame Roméo Dallaire, whom she describes as a man of courage. No, he didn't protect them and he didn't stop the genocide. But at least he didn't insult them by pretending the genocide wasn't even happening, like the papier-mâché devils in New York. She thinks that Roméo Dallaire wasn't terribly good at his job. But at least he tried to do it. In fact, none of the litigants really wants to bring down General Dallaire. They just want someone to be held accountable.

Even those allegedly involved in the death esquadrons have turned on Dallaire as the villain. The chief of the gendarmerie is the most recent character to file suit against him. General Augustin Ndindiliyimana was arrested early in 2000, in Belgium, and transferred to the International Criminal Tribunal for Rwanda. He charges that it was Dallaire who should have stopped the *génocidaires*, since he was the person best positioned to know what was happening. His suit for damages against Dallaire has been filed in Brussels.

The mad search for a culprit sometimes looked like a witch hunt, but that was understandable. Even as the classified documents kept turning up on people's fax machines, the United Nations remained stone-cold silent on what had gone wrong. The Belgian senate's final report, tabled in December 1997, ran to seven hundred pages and concluded that the Belgian military was unprepared, the government was ill-informed and UNAMIR was poorly equipped and badly led by Roméo Dallaire. The report also recommended that Belgian soldiers should never do any peace-keeping in a former colony.

The U.S. Committee of International Relations also held an inquiry, and it too got little help from the United Nations. Shaharyar Mohammad Khan, who replaced Jacques-Roger Booh Booh as special representative, testified but was unable to explain why some of UNAMIR's decisions were made — he hadn't been there. The congressional committee was furious that Dallaire was not allowed to testify, even though the general made it clear that he would like to. The members of the committee suggested that the UN was involved in a cover-up.

The French government had its own inquiry and concluded that it did nothing wrong. One tragicomic headline was worthy of note: "France Finds France Not Responsible."

Finally, in 1999, the new secretary-general of the United Nations, Kofi Annan, could take the pressure no longer and appointed his own independent inquiry into the events of the Rwandan genocide. A former Swedish prime minister, Ingvar Carlsson, was chosen as its chairman, and he was to have access to all the papers, documents and reports.

In the fall of 1999, the dying days of the century in which the United Nations had been invented to ensure that "never again" stood for something, the Carlsson report declared that the United Nations had failed the people of Rwanda. "It is a failure for which the United Nations as an organization, but also its member states, should have apologized more clearly, more frankly, and much earlier."

The report confirmed all the criticisms that had been made in the media for the past six years: the mission leaders didn't have important information about Rwanda; Booh Booh lacked the skills and knowledge necessary to run the political activities of UNAMIR; Dallaire had enough people but not the right people, and he didn't have the necessary equipment. The report also asked where Boutros Boutros-Ghali had been hiding during most of this crisis. It acknowledged that the secretary-general was a busy man with places to go, but if he had been there to push, nudge, cajole and shame the member countries into action, then maybe more could have been done, sooner.

The UN peacekeeping office's obsession with ceasefires really puzzled the commissioners—why bother with the war when you've got a massacre in progress? "Records of meetings…show continued emphasis on a cease-fire, more than moral outrage against the massacres which was growing in the international community." And even without ceasefire obsessions, why were representatives of the United Nations having meetings with those doing the killing? At some point, the commission asked, shouldn't we cut ourselves off from such people?

Which brought the inquiry to the whole sorry business of "impartiality" and "neutrality," the sacred code words of peacekeeping, which have helped so many missions stand by and say "not my problem" when things turn really ugly. "In effect, there can be no neutrality in the face of genocide, no impartiality in the face of a campaign to exterminate part of a population," says the report. Decision-makers should have dropped the whole mandate immediately, "and indeed the neutral mediating role of the United Nations was no longer adequate and required a different, more assertive response, combined with the means necessary to take action." The inquiry judged that the "institutional ideology of impartiality" needed a serious rethink.

But in the end, what really went wrong with the UN response? The inquiry came to the same conclusion as Dallaire: the handful of countries on the Security Council simply did not want to get involved. They shamefully ignored the warning signs and then refused to use the "g" word. The problem was the Mogadishu Line, the barrier that powerful sovereign nations decided not to cross to help victims of conflict and chaos.

The final report wasn't really necessary—the principal players had already apportioned blame and responsibility. President Bill Clinton, anxious to deflect attention away from the Monica Lewinsky scandal, had already flown to Rwanda for a few hours on March 25, 1998, where he issued an apology. He said the United States had failed to call the crisis in Rwanda what it was, a genocide. Two months later, Kofi Annan issued his apology to the Rwandan parliament. The French thought they had nothing to apologize for and the Belgians were waiting for the UN to apologize to them.

Roméo Dallaire declared to the world that he was the one responsible for what had happened. Yes, the Security Council was to blame, certainly the United States acted shamefully, and what the French did was a scandal. But Dallaire said, on Canadian television in September 1997, "I'm fully responsible for the decisions of the ten Belgian soldiers dying, of others dying, of several of my soldiers being injured and falling sick because we ran out of medical supplies, of fifty-six Red Cross people being killed, of two million people being displaced and made refugees, and about a million Rwandans being killed—because the mission failed, and I consider myself intimately involved with that responsibility."

EPILOGUE

LESSONS LEARNED

Honoured gentlemen of Argos, go to your homes now and give way
to the stress of fate and season. We could not do otherwise
than we did. If this is the end of suffering, we cannot be content
broken as we are by the brute heel of angry destiny.
—Aeschylus, *Oresteia*

Dallaire spent the end of the 1990s—and of his career as a soldier—trying to develop a set of "lessons learned" from the Rwanda crisis. He repeatedly told the UN, and anyone else who would listen, that peacekeeping needed a rapid-reaction force—a sharp, well-trained, eager international militia that could go to the world's hot spots and douse the fires immediately.

Dallaire's own best lesson was driven home in 1996, at a UN Lessons Learned Conference in New York. Dallaire couldn't attend and Brent Beardsley went without him. The group took a break in the afternoon and went for lunch at the UN cafeteria. A few tables over, quietly eating his lunch, was the man who had allegedly been part of a plot to kill Dallaire in Kigali in 1994. Dallaire had reported the incident and the individual when he returned from Rwanda. And there he was, still employed by the UN, enjoying all the perks and privileges. Beardsley wanted to go over and drown the man in his own soup, but his colleagues told him not to bother. He reported the astonishing encounter to Dallaire. Life could hold no more surprises.

The real lesson to be learned from Rwanda is that no one gives a damn. The missing ingredient isn't a special force or better communications—it's political will, courage, morality. Dallaire knows all too well that what is truly missing is a genuine desire to make the world a better place. As

Pollyannaish as that may sound, it's what is required if another Rwanda is not to happen. That image of the potential assassin quietly drinking soup in the cafeteria might convey the idea that nothing fundamental is going to change, that Dallaire's clear sense of right and wrong is a liability in the *realpolitik* of the United Nations.

Is Canada at war? Dallaire asked a group of soldiers not long after he returned from Rwanda. Not in a traditional way, was his answer, but perhaps there's a war against tyranny, no less relevant than the great wars, which is now being fought by diplomats, peacekeepers and the media.

Who is willing to die in such a war? "We're on a terribly steep learning curve in this village," Dallaire says. "We fought the Second World War because there was a threat to us. Now we've gone to 'We have to do something because it's a threat to humanity.' That's a big step." It wasn't one the Belgians were willing to make, and it may not be one many other countries are willing to take either.

Roméo Dallaire was very hard on the soldiers under his command. Was he negligent about their interests? Was he cavalier with their lives? Only if you conclude that Dallaire had no business trying to save people in Rwanda. Another force commander would have retreated to barracks, called his troops in and declared he had no mandate. But Dallaire couldn't have looked himself in the mirror again had he done that, and he believed, rightly or wrongly, that the people who served under him felt the same way.

"I maintain that commanders who insist on clear mandates and unambiguous decision processes should not be involved in conflict resolution, because the challenges they will face will be too complex and subtle to be explicitly addressed through simple short-term tactical objectives and readily identifiable milestones," he says. He determined that his mandate was still viable after the president's plane was shot down, and he acted on it. The mission was first, the fate of his men second, his own fate third.

Dallaire's reduced force of 450 soldiers met with the devils of the genocide and tried to get their co-operation. And they fought with the UN every day for more help. They ate their bad food while sitting next to corpses. They lived with their own shit and garbage and fear. By all accounts, including their own, the effect they had was marginal, even if the effort was courageous.

At the 1995 Vimy Awards, commemorating the extraordinary victory of Canadian troops during the First World War, General Dallaire gave a speech related to the war in Rwanda that warrants repeating here:

I have sent men to serious injury and even to their deaths in accomplishing near impossible military and humanitarian tasks. We have seen thousands hacked and dying, mothers holding dehydrated children, children surviving among the corpses of the rest of their family. We have witnessed hysteria drive people to murder, and others throw their children at us for protection as they ran in mortal fear. We have witnessed Dante devils from hell run amok in what was once paradise on earth. I have seen fear in the eyes of officers and watched soldiers cower in mortal dread. I was—as others were—on occasion left for lost in battle behind belligerent lines. Many Canadian military personnel are living these types of experiences…. These peacekeepers are the new breed of full-fledged veterans of Canada.

General Dallaire retired from the armed forces in April 2000, seven years after he got the call to go on an exciting adventure in Africa, six years after he returned home from a genocide. He planned to see more of his family, to put his feet up, to write a book. Those who know him wonder if he is capable of any of those things.

The general has good days and bad. Medication helps and hinders: it keeps his spirits up but prevents him from sleeping. His doctors don't want him to think or talk too much about the experience of Rwanda—he seems to lack the ability to deal with the memories, which are much too vivid. According to those close to him, he has lost the ability to rationalize and he still sees only what he failed to do, not what he accomplished.

Dallaire is considered a chief witness for the International Criminal Tribunal for Rwanda, and he spends much of his time with his Montreal lawyer, Harvey Yarosky, preparing his testimony. Dallaire considers the tribunal work to be an extension of UNAMIR; the mission is not finished until the perpetrators are in jail. The most important trial the court will undertake is that of Colonel Théoneste Bagosora, the man who ran the Rwandan military during the genocide. Chief Prosecutor Richard Goldstone indicted Bagosora and he was arrested in his hiding place in Cameroon in 1997. His trial is scheduled to begin in the fall or winter of 2000, and Dallaire has been called as a witness for the prosecution. The last time Dallaire saw Bagosora, the colonel said he was going to kill him the next time they met. That now seems unlikely.

Dallaire spoke for five hours almost without stop during a final interview for this book and he appeared lucid and strong. His memory of dozens of events proved accurate. But I also met a man anxious and grey, intense and sad. He paused during conversations to deal with searing head pains. A flood of emotions crossed his face every minute. He talked freely about his condition, how easy it is to lapse back into thoughts of suicide. He was open and often eloquent but extremely unhappy. "It was all futile, right from the beginning," he said of his many attempts to get international intervention in Rwanda. "The big boys had decided they weren't going in. Period." Dallaire doesn't blame the UN, but he says the institution has to evolve. "The UN can change—it's within its power. But it can't do massive change without co-operation from the big boys—the Permanent Five members on the Security Council. They won't change it because they need the UN to hide behind, to be a scapegoat for them."

The death of the Belgian peacekeepers haunts him, but he says he does not regret what he did that day. "A commander must be ready to make a nanosecond decision like that and live with it. All my training in NATO and years of experience came to bear as I made that single commitment." But he wonders what would have happened if they had been Canadian peacekeepers. "What is the Canadian resilience to that? That doesn't inspire our troops, not knowing when or if the commitment to them and what they're doing will change. How many casualties does it take? Five? Ten? We don't know." Should Canada accept the deaths of peacekeepers as part of the business? Dallaire asked then answered his own question: "Well, shit! They're soldiers."

At Vimy Ridge, the Canadian Corps took more than ten thousand casualties.

In a movie that plays over and over in Dallaire's head, he relives all the events of that period, all the mistakes, all the deaths, his own private horror show. In a letter to me about what he did, and failed to do, in Rwanda, Dallaire concludes with a kind of haiku, a personal declaration of intent, typed in bold italics:

> **To command is to hurt**
> **To command is to cry**
> **To command is to love**
> **To command is to keep the "_mission_" first and foremost.**

On April 18, 2000, he cleared off his desk and retired from the Canadian Forces. In late June 2000, the day after his fifty-fourth birthday, the

Ottawa-Hull police were called to a city park where they found Dallaire, curled on the ground in fetal position, unconscious and apparently inebriated. He was released from hospital into the hands of relatives in Ottawa who took him home to Quebec City. Colleagues say, only days earlier, he had seemed better than he had in months.

In an open letter to the CBC radio program *This Morning*—where he had been interviewed about his stress disorder—he explained that incidents such as the one in the park were not uncommon but that they normally happened in private. He wrote: "The anger, the rage, the hurt and the cold loneliness that separate you from your family, friends and society are so powerful that the option of destroying yourself is both real and attractive." Dallaire's doctors say the collapses are the result of the human trying to emerge from behind the military leader's ethos of: "my mission first, my personnel, then myself." In his letter Dallaire made an open commitment to the public that such behaviour "will be the subject of a lot of work over the next while."

BOOK TWO
The Fox

1

BIRTH OF A NATION

The last thing that a peacekeeper wants to know is the history of the region he is going into. It complicates the task of mediation.
— Major General Lewis MacKenzie to the
Royal United Services Institute, December 9, 1992

Af[ter breaking through the clouds and starting the final descent into Sarajevo, you can see only a few apartment buildings and houses in the suburbs surrounding the city that still bear the blight of bombs. For a large part of the 1990s, most of these buildings lay in ruins, their once-charming red-clay roofs shattered. Now, in the year 2000, people are slowly, finally, reconstructing.

Your plane lands at an airport that is typical of those in most post-Communist European republics: small, nondescript, cramped. But here is an airport that was once a crucial factor in one of the most misunderstood and devastating conflicts since the Second World War. Your plane taxis down the single runway—a piece of track that Major General Lewis MacKenzie once considered using as a car-racing course. He was so certain the Bosnian war would be a fleeting event, he asked his wife to send over his racing togs in anticipation that he and the peacekeepers under his command were going to need amusement during their leisure time. The racing suit arrived, but he never got to use it.

Halfway to the terminal, your plane passes over a piece of history, though you wouldn't necessarily notice. During the war, local commanders of the ragtag Bosnian army dug a tunnel—it started inside a house across the road from here and continued right under this runway—and opened a lifeline out of the besieged city. Mainly a conduit for importing guns and ammunition for the poorly supplied Bosnian defence force, the tunnel also became a crucial pipeline for consumer goods. On the other side of the Sarajevo airport was a relative paradise, a free world where a fistful of Deutschmarks could buy anything. Some people who had access to the route would purchase goods in bulk and sell them at extortionate prices to people in Sarajevo — a horribly exploitative system, but it kept the city alive.

Leave the airport and drive into town. A veneer of normalcy coats everything and everybody. Struggling saplings have replaced the city's beautiful old chestnut trees, cut down during the war for firewood. The so-called Snipers' Alley is now an unexceptional part of the route down-town, though the ghosts of the men, women and children shot dead there surely must haunt it. According to one story that was current during the war, the sharpshooters who controlled Snipers' Alley got extra money for gunning down pregnant women. Serbian leader Radovan Karadzic was filmed bringing foreign guests to the hilltops looming over Sarajevo to take target practice on the local population just for the pure sport of it. Tele-vision crews knew where to station themselves to get the gory pictures the world expected to see on its evening newscasts.

Along the route you notice that the Holiday Inn has been restored to its original ghastly mustard-coloured prominence. It was built nearly twenty years ago to accommodate some of the tens of thousands of sports fans who came to this enchanting city for the 1984 Winter Olympics. The hotel's Communist utilitarian architecture and garish colours didn't take away from its breathtaking location: from its rooms, tourists could see the glorious mountain ranges where the best of the world skied and luged their way to gold. Not far away, the Olympic figure-skating pavilion has been restored. The former speed-skating track is a bit more of a problem. It is now a giant graveyard.

Unfortunately, during the war, the neighbourhood's open spaces and broad avenues made the Holiday Inn vulnerable to mortar attacks. From a reporting point of view, this was both good and bad. Even after an entire wall had been ripped from the structure, journalists continued to use it as their home away from home during the Bosnian war — it had an electrical generator and its dining room served real food. The exposed parts of the hotel offered a ringside seat on the action, but the hotel desk staff took it for granted that guests did not want a room with a view.

All around Sarajevo now, the lush green mountains that cup this city like hands are silent. Absent is the ring of artillery positions from which gunners pounded the city year after year. On the worst days, locals esti-mated that up to two thousand shells landed.

A newcomer to Sarajevo, strolling its avenues, stopping in at one of its dozens of inviting cafés and bistros, checking out the shop windows for the latest Benetton or Armani fashions, may have trouble imagining the place as those who lived through its horror experienced it. No water, gas or elec-tricity; no phones or food; no contact with the world nor sympathy from it — the people of this city took a beating that started in the early spring of 1992 and lasted for a total of 1,395 days.

In the early 1990s, Bosnians were just getting accustomed to the new post-Communist world order and wondering what their place in it would be. They were faced with an array of homegrown nationalist leaders vying to replace the old roster of Yugoslav socialist politicians, and it wasn't certain what anyone could expect from these people. In the front ranks was Alija Izetbegovic.

Izetbegovic is a slim-built man with sharp blue eyes and a convoluted way of reaching decisions that baffles everyone, perhaps with the exception of his daughter, Sabina, whom he trusts absolutely. The two stretches of time served in Marshal Tito's prisons — on charges of conspiring against the Communist regime — hardened the man and made him private and suspi-cious. He is a founder of the country's Muslim party and a devout follower of Islam.

While his life is informed by his faith, Izetbegovic's politics are decid-edly secular. He wrote extensively about his beliefs and political theories over the years, and although his writings are infused with his religion, his love affair with the principles of Western democracy often overwhelm everything else. In his book *Islam between East and West*, written in 1984, he argues for a state that joins the values of Western commerce and civil rights with the religious inspiration of the Koran. Izetbegovic's Islamic national-ism is a passive part of his politics, but it nonetheless became a provocative piece of his reputation when he became president.

Marshal Tito, who died in 1980, suppressed national identities during his many decades of rule. With the collapse of the Eastern Bloc in 1989, and without Tito's iron hand to yoke them together into one people (Yugoslavia means "the union of south Slavs"), these identities resurfaced with a vengeance, largely with the encouragement of the politician who lobbied to succeed Tito — Slobodan Milosevic.

Nationalist leaders such as Milosevic declared to each other, and to the world, that they could not live with people who were not their kind. A common Slavic identity was an illusion; their other religious and cultural histories, as Croats, Serbs or Slovenes, took precedence. Ten years after the death of Tito, the multicultural nation he had forged was slowly dying.

Of the six Yugoslav republics (Serbia, Croatia, Bosnia, Macedonia, Montenegro and Slovenia), Slovenia departed the Yugoslavian federation first, in 1990, following a short war. Croatia's subsequent bid to separate caused eighteen months of bitter fighting with Belgrade. President Franjo Tudjman lost one-third of his territory before Croatia became an independent and ethnically homogeneous republic in 1991.

These nationalist wars set off a fear throughout the rest of Yugoslavia that a sense of security lay exclusively with one's own kind. Only Bosnia — the most ethnically mixed of the republics — made a political effort to sustain the Titoist ideal of multiculturalism. In the Bosnian election of 1990, the first multi-party campaign in the republic's history, all three nationalist parties — Muslims, Croats and Serbs — did very well, while the Communists and the other secular parties fared poorly. Izetbegovic's Stranka Demokratske Acije (SDA) garnered the highest percentage of the votes.

Izetbegovic's political enemies painted him as a religious fanatic and claimed he represented the threat of Islam in Europe. But even before the elections, the SDA had agreed to govern in a coalition with the other nationalist parties if it was successful (the principal objective they all shared was a desire to defeat the Communists). After the elections, two representatives from each of the Croat, Serb and Muslim parties were awarded a place within the Presidency, the executive branch of government. Izetbegovic was declared president; Momcilo Krajisnik, a strident Serb nationalist, became parliamentary speaker; and the Croat, Jure Pelivan, became prime minister. Few people believed this fractious, divisive government would last for long, though no one could have predicted how savagely it would be attacked.

The American ambassador to Yugoslavia, Warren Zimmerman, thought highly of Izetbegovic, and found him sincere in his desire to maintain a Bosnia where every ethnicity could live in relative harmony. Zimmerman reported to his government in 1991 that the Bosnian president was trying to avoid a move towards independence for his republic, since he feared the consequences would be civil war. In his memoirs, Zimmerman recalls Izetbegovic's "moderate nature" and his openness towards his political enemies.

He adds, "While charitable, Izetbegovic wasn't naive." The Bosnian president knew what the radical Serb ultra-nationalists were planning.

If it is true that Izetbegovic wasn't naive as Zimmerman believes, the Muslim leader certainly didn't demonstrate a savvy nature. Izetbegovic continued to deny the possibility of war until events were already upon him. He may have been motivated by the best of intentions, but Izetbegovic was perhaps not the charismatic, decisive leader Bosnia needed at the time. While he was able to keep an uneasy consensus among his coalition partners, it was more because of their survival instincts than any loyalty to him. Even his own supporters, who admired him as an intellectual, often found him bumbling and incompetent as a politician. For instance, Izetbegovic sometimes turned to other Islamic countries for support: on a visit to Turkey in July 1991, he asked to join the Organization of Islamic Countries. Such a move was foolish and did nothing to quell the nationalist fires in Bosnia. But Izetbegovic's sins were minor compared to the sins of those who opposed him.

Before he became the poster boy for Serbian ultra-nationalism, Dr. Radovan Karadzic was a psychiatrist who specialized in treating depression. He was also a published poet. He is actually not a Serb but a Montenegrin from a tiny mountain village where every single resident is a Karadzic. In fact, the village people will tell you that even today, five hundred years after the first Karadzic brothers founded it, only Karadzics are permitted to live there. An ill-informed interloper recently bought a property from the Karadzic family (or clan), unaware of the village's quaint medieval attitudes towards outsiders. Soon after he built it, somebody burned his new house to the ground.

The Montenegrins are kissing cousins of the Serbs—both embrace Orthodox Christianity—but Montenegro has a greater reputation for success on the battlefield. During the medieval wars and invasions that have marked so many Serb communities with a heritage and a mythology of victimhood, it was never conquered by the Turks. Montenegro was one of the jewels of Yugoslavia, famous for its stunning Adriatic coast, but its entrenched system of clans makes it more like Sicily than the Riviera.

Radovan Karadzic also spent time in Tito's jails, not for his politics, but for corruption. In Sarajevo, he practised his psychiatry, and he joined the ranks of the nascent Srpska Demokratska Stranka (the SDS), a Serbian nationalist party that emerged just months after the Muslim SDA. The flamboyant Karadzic was elected the first president of the SDS, and he quickly proved himself to be a persuasive politician able to articulate — and exacerbate — the deep historical fears of his Serbian constituency.

Karadzic warned that any new Bosnian nation that tried to lump all ethnicities together as one would be stillborn. Serbs, who formed a majority in Yugoslavia, would become an orphaned minority in Bosnia, he argued, and Karadzic said he would never stand by and allow Bosnian Serbs to be separated from the rest of their ethnic group. Along with warning that the Serbian minority would have no guarantees of protection for their religion, culture and property in an independent Bosnia, he argued strongly that Bosnia had no right to self-determination. Muslims were merely Slavs who had been conquered by Turks, and according to Karadzic, that wasn't enough to give them a legitimate claim on nationhood.

As for the Croat population, another minority, they should go to the newly independent Croatia to be with their Slavic, and Roman Catholic, brethren. Karadzic believed it was really the Serbs who were entitled to most of the territory of Bosnia. From his SDS headquarters in the Sarajevo Holiday Inn, he organized and directed his resistance to the elected Bosnian president.

Karadzic had a vision of a united Bosnia, a pure Serbian territory that would keep close links to the former Yugoslavia and the regime of President Slobodan Milosevic (who is also a Montenegrin). The capital of the new Serbian republic would be Sarajevo, though Karadzic would tolerate specific sectors in the city where Muslims and Croats could live. When asked how a minority of the country — the Serbs — could lay claim to the lion's share of the territory, Karadzic's deputy, Biljana Plavsic, declared: "They like to live on top of one another. It's their culture. We Serbs need space." Karadzic would show anyone who visited him maps of the carved-up territory, indicating where walls, like those that had only recently come down in Berlin, would be constructed to separate the ethnic groups.

That they needed walls came as something of a surprise to Bosnians, who had been living together for five hundred years. In the pre-war 1990s, Bosnian Muslims formed 44 per cent of the country's 4.4 million population. Just as Karadzic said, the ancestors of these Muslims were Slavs who had converted to Islam, though people rarely identified themselves as such in modern Yugoslavia.

Serbs made up 31 per cent of the population of Bosnia, and Croats 17 per cent. The balance was a mix of other races, including Romanies, Jews and Hungarians, who had co-existed comfortably and with thriving commerce since the Middle Ages.

Sarajevo is a dense, congested city, sprawling up the sides of the mountain flanks. The city's different cultures are clustered in the downtown core: a stroll through the city centre takes you past a mosque, a Catholic church, an Orthodox cathedral and a synagogue. Intermarriage was common, particularly in the city, where few households could claim anything like homogeneity. Half the population would need blood transfusions to achieve the racial purity the Montenegrin psychiatrist was championing.

But Karadzic and his fellow Serb nationalists had a lot of supporters, principally in rural Bosnia, where ultra-nationalist sentiment ran high for all the ethnic groups and where the type of propaganda campaign that launched Rwanda's ethnic war dominated the TVs and newspapers. The citizens of this former Communist country were accustomed to believing what they heard: they had been told what to think by Tito's regime for many decades. In the countryside, people had few media alternatives on which to build an understanding independent of the Belgrade-produced propaganda that warned of an approaching genocide and reminded the Serbs, day after day, of their history.

That history tells of one slaughter after another, starting with the medieval Turks, who defeated them on the battlefields of Kosovo. In the twentieth century, the Serbs' killers included the brutal Croatian Ustashe, who ran concentration camps for their Nazi allies, and the German Fascists themselves, who wiped out hundreds of thousands of Serbs throughout the country during the Second World War. Suggestions of a planned mass murder perpetrated by marauding bands of Muslims (read Turks) fed an underlying paranoia that had existed for centuries and created a general atmosphere of panic. Reports that the new Bosnian president was instructing his Islamic followers to feed Serbian babies to the wild animals at the Sarajevo zoo were accepted in their entirety, and even today one can meet Serbs who claim they actually heard the screams of the infants as they were devoured by lions and tigers.

The wily Dr. Karadzic, with his mop of grey hair and his trademark white silk ascot, became a fixture on the evening news for anyone following the tragic demise of Yugoslavia. Ambassador Zimmerman had many encounters with Karadzic leading up to the war, and he saw a man who would be foppishly funny if he wasn't so lethal: "In his fanaticism, ruthlessness, and contempt for human values, he invites comparisons with a monster from another generation, Heinrich Himmler."

The European Community's special envoy, Colm Doyle, was one of the best placed to give an assessment of Karadzic. Doyle was an officer in the Irish army who had been awarded a civilian observer's job in Bosnia. His responsibility was to meet with all the nationalist leaders and to treat them as equals, though his efforts to remain impartial were frequently challenged. Doyle remembers a series of meetings that best illustrates the political reality of the place: "When I met with Izetbegovic, I asked what would happen if Bosnia declared independence? Izetbegovic said, 'Well, at first the Serbs won't accept it, but eventually they'll come round.' I went up to see Karadzic and asked him the same question. Karadzic says, 'All our enemies will be killed.'"

Australian brigadier John Wilson, who headed a group of military observers for the United Nations in Sarajevo, says he was often frustrated with Izetbegovic. Wilson and Colm Doyle were among a small group of foreign observers in Sarajevo before the war even began, and they got to know the players better than anyone. Wilson says the Bosnian president would agree to one thing and then do the opposite, particularly if he felt he had been manipulated into a decision. But overall, Wilson found Izetbegovic to be a man with a lot of integrity and an ability to articulate the Bosnian position well.

Wilson said he avoided showing preference for one side or another, as is the UN way, but he disliked Karadzic. He found the Serb leader to be a weak personality with no moral courage, and worse, "He was a whimperer." Wilson suspected that Karadzic was merely a puppet of the regime that controlled him. It was clear to outside observers that Yugoslav president Slobodan Milosevic had been orchestrating the wars throughout Yugoslavia from the backroom. "Karadzic's strings were pulled elsewhere in Belgrade."

Such was the environment in which the international community was struggling to find a solution before things got out of hand. The hapless Izetbegovic should have been easy to manipulate, given his lack of experience. But years of prison confinement and house arrest had made the president uncompromising. That unbending nature was coupled with a personal conviction that the world would never sit by and watch innocent Bosnians murdered. If events turned ugly, he was certain that other countries would come to Bosnia's rescue. His assumption was founded on little more than his own trust in Western democracy and his belief that the international community was full of fair-minded people.

Milosevic claimed from the very beginning of the breakdown in Bosnia to be a man of peace who hardly knew the wily Dr. Karadzic. But Yugo-watchers knew that Milosevic was the source of efforts to unite all Serbs in the former federation. He had aspired to replace Marshal Tito as the supreme leader of Yugoslavia; now he figured he would have to settle for being the supreme leader of Greater Serbia. That would require forcing out non-Serbs and carving out the Serb republic. Milosevic had manoeuvred to take one-third of Croatia's territory during the war in 1991, and in 1992 he set his sights on Bosnia. The ultra-nationalist rhetoric was thick in the political corridors of Belgrade, and anyone with the slightest knowledge of the players knew that he was organizing something big.

The European Community (EC) slowly realized that Slobodan Milosevic and Croatia's rabid ultra-nationalist president, Franjo Tudjman, had a plan to divide up Bosnia between them. The parts of Bosnia that Karadzic had his eye on would become part of Serbia; the rest of the country would be annexed by Croatia. These men were like real-estate agents run amok. What was to become of President Izetbegovic and the Muslim population that formed almost half of Bosnia's citizenry? Since they were merely Slavs who had been conquered by the Turks, these Bosnians would be "liberated"—if they survived. Upon hearing that the two men wanted to partition his country, Izetbegovic remarked that choosing between living with Tudjman or living with Milosevic was like choosing between leukemia and brain cancer.

In the early 1990s, various EC conferences attempted to find a way to parcel Bosnia into ethnic enclaves in order to avoid bloodshed. But Izetbegovic rejected these efforts, recognizing that, as desirable as cantonization might be—and he often said it was—it was impossible. The population of Bosnia was just too mixed, especially in the cosmopolitan capital, Sarajevo, where very few people could tell you their national origin, much less explain why on earth it mattered.

In early 1992, Izetbegovic could resist the pressure from the hardliners in his own party no longer, and he held a referendum on secession. The referendum question was fairly straightforward and might serve as a model to Quebec nationalists. It was simply: "Are you in favour of a sovereign and independent Bosnia-Herzegovina as a state of equal citizens and nations of Muslims, Serbs, Croats and others who live in it?" Karadzic called for a boycott of the vote among Serbs and he was successful in many parts of the country, particularly where his party refused to allow polling booths to set up. The Muslim and Croat populations voted overwhelmingly in support of the question, as did Serbs in Sarajevo. Izetbegovic held off a declaration of independence until the EC decided if its members would recognize the other breakaway nations. Without the recognition, these new states would be banana republics, European-style. What Izetbegovic feared the most was this: if the EC accepted the secessionist governments, Bosnia would also have to ask for nation status in order to protect the Muslim population from the designs of Serbia and Croatia. The EC could predict that outcome as well, and most of its members had decided not to recognize Croatia and Slovenia. But Germany became the spoiler.

Anxious to cement its relationship with Croatia (despite the unfortunate conclusions the world would draw from this allegiance, given that the Croatian Ustashe had fought alongside the Nazis), the German government offered recognition to Slovenia, Croatia and any other former Yugoslav republic that met certain basic criteria. In an effort to keep up EC unity, other countries in the EC capitulated and agreed to Germany's declaration. The United States and Britain resisted recognition, but not with enough vigour to do any good.

It's not certain which is the factor that finally sparked the war in Bosnia, but this premature recognition of Yugoslav states, before they had worked out the problem of minorities living within their borders, was crucial. No matter what the EC did after this, the dominoes would begin to fall.

2

WAR IN BOSNIA

*You can't understand. How could you?—with solid pavement under your feet,
surrounded by kind neighbours ready to cheer you on or to fall on you, stepping
delicately between the butcher and the policeman.... These little things make all the
difference. When they are gone you must fall back on your own inner strength,
upon your own capacity for faithfulness. Of course you may be too much of a fool to
go wrong—too dull even to know you are being assaulted by the powers of darkness.*
—Joseph Conrad, *Heart of Darkness*

Radovan Karadzic had made it clear to everyone that if Bosnia declared
independence, "rivers of blood" would flow; no Muslim would survive, because the Muslims had no way to defend themselves. Bosnia
had no military to speak of outside the Yugoslav National Army (JNA) and
Karadzic already had reassurances from Milosevic in Belgrade that the
JNA would back up the Serb nationalists. Despite the dire predictions, in late
1991, the Bosnian Presidency voted to ask the European Community to
recognize the territory as a separate state (the two Serb members of
the Presidency, Nicole Koljevic and Biljana Plavsic, voted against it).

As Bosnia awaited a response from the EC, Karadzic and Milosevic
prepared for war. By the spring of 1992, Karadzic's SDS supporters along
with his militias had set up barricades throughout Sarajevo and had taken
control of the central police station. On April 5, 1992, a large peace
demonstration formed in the streets of the city, despite a palpable atmosphere of violence. The demonstrators, determined to show the world they
would not be bullied by a rump of extremist Serb nationalists trying to run
the country from the Holiday Inn, defied the barricades and marched on
the Bosnian government buildings.

Aida Alibalic remembers watching the peace march as it moved past her street and feeling tears of pride stream down her cheeks: "I was so happy to see those people walking and [feel] their strength." She was sure that the renegade Karadzic crowd could never defeat a city like Sarajevo. Unlike the voters in rural Bosnia, a population Sarajevans frequently derided as "peasants," those in Sarajevo had voted against the nationalist parties and there was a strong multicultural sentiment in the city. But the peaceful character of the demonstration changed in an instant. Serbian sharpshooters suddenly opened fire on the protesters, killing a young woman and scattering thousands of others in every direction.

Karadzic claimed he had nothing to do with the shooting, but Sarajevo had seen the first casualties of an incipient war. Now it was clear to Alibalic, and everyone else, that the nationalist differences, so recently resurrected and redefined, were not going to disappear so easily.

If there had still been room for compromise between the nationalist parties in Parliament, the killings in Sarajevo eliminated it. Karadzic gathered up his supporters and regrouped, first at the Hotel Srbija in the Serb-dominated suburb of Ilidza and then, a month later, they all headed up to the mountain village of Pale, twenty kilometres from Sarajevo, among the ski slopes of the 1984 Olympics. Koljevic and Plavsic resigned their seats in the Bosnian Presidency and joined Karadzic (Izetbegovic replaced them with two other Serbs). In Pale (pronounced Pa-lay), Karadzic set up a government in exile for the self-styled Serbian republic, the Republika Srpska. For the duration of the war, he and his followers would be known as the Pale Gang.

On April 6, 1992, Canada, along with the European Community, recognized Bosnia as an independent state. The United States followed suit the next day. It was clear—or it should have been clear, given the shootout of the day before—what the consequences would be, but the international community went ahead anyway. There wasn't much else other nations could do after Germany and the EC had made their decision to support the recognition. There were more gunshots in Sarajevo the afternoon of the EC declaration; this time, the snipers opened fire from the top of the Holiday Inn, killing six people and injuring dozens more. Sarajevans would soon get used to seeing pools of blood on their streets.

The attacks outside the city were more frightening. In northeastern Bosnia, during the first week of April, Serbian paramilitaries fresh from ethnic-cleansing campaigns in Croatia moved in on a series of strategic border towns, driving out or murdering women and children and taking the men away to the first of the prisoner of war camps. The notorious war-lord Arkan and his Tigers, who had distinguished themselves by brutaliz-ing towns all through Croatia, were joined by other paramilitaries, such as the White Eagles, led by the psychopathic Vojeslev Seselj, who had report-edly ordered his men to gouge out the eyes of their Croat victims with rusty spoons. Whether they ever performed that particular act of savagery is unknown, but foreign aid workers and war crimes investigators who examined the corpses of victims can attest to any number of inventive forms of torture devised by the paramilitaries. (The Serbs weren't alone in that. Croat paramilitaries met the enemy with their own formidable volley of abuse, and it's a debate as to which side committed more atrocities than the other in the Croatian war.)

Radovan Karadzic claimed he had no control over the Serb rene-gades. International observers reported that the Yugoslav National Army was also operating in the northeastern section of Bosnia, near the border with Serbia, and that JNA tanks and artillery pieces were providing backup for the Serb nationalist paramilitaries.

This came as a shock to most Bosnians, who still saw the JNA as the people's army. It was a formidable fighting force, among the largest and best equipped in Europe, and it had been Tito's pride. Bosnia, pro-tected by its high mountains and nestled in the interior of the federa-tion, had been a principal armoury for Yugoslavia; a large part of the JNA arsenal was housed in a series of barracks in and around Sarajevo. When they were part of Yugoslavia, Bosnians took for granted their important defence role. They had no idea that their army could be turned against them.

But Milosevic had anticipated the day when an independent Bosnia might want to expel the JNA, and in January 1992, he began reorganizing his Yugoslavian armed forces. Any JNA officers and soldiers based in Bosnia who were not natives of that republic were replaced by those who were. He was effectively turning part of the Yugoslav National Army into a Bosnian Serb force that was loyal to Belgrade but sympathetic to the Karadzic nationalists. When the time was right, the renegade Republika Srpska would inherit a professional army—ninety thousand well-disciplined fight-ing men—who were already entrenched in the Bosnian countryside.

Belgrade's support wouldn't end there. Once the war was under way, there would be a steady influx of reinforcements, and for the duration, officers and soldiers would continue to take orders and get their pay packets from the Yugoslavian capital.

In the first half of 1992, there was probably still time to stop a full-scale war if there had been the international will to do so. With a few exceptions, such as Ambassador Zimmerman, who spoke Serbo-Croatian and had met all of the players in the Yugoslav drama many times, the Americans were not terribly interested in Bosnia. Secretary of State James Baker made it clear throughout the early part of the Balkan breakdown that the United States "didn't have a dog in this fight," and that his president, George Bush, asked frequently to be reminded what the conflict was all about.

Washington maintained that this was Europe's problem, and that Europe should figure out a solution. It wasn't an unreasonable position. Ever since the collapse of the Soviet bloc and the end of the bipolar political world order, the European Community had been attempting to redefine its political leadership role on the European continent. Trying to keep Yugoslavia from disintegrating into chaos and a bloody war seemed to be a worthy test of the EC's skills and its influence.

The United Nations was the only other body that might have been able to prevent the inevitable, but it was riven with competing interests. There were Security Council meetings and a flurry of UN resolutions, among them a ban on the export of arms to the former Yugoslavia. That initiative was suggested by none other than Slobodan Milosevic. UN members wanted to believe he was trying to contain the war and prevent the spread of violence, but he was really attempting to freeze the power balance in favour of his friends in Pale. The effect of the resolution was to stop legal shipments of weapons to Bosnia; Yugoslavia (and, by extension, its Bosnian Serb clients) already had more than enough firepower. And if the inevitable war was to drag on, the JNA and the Bosnian Serbs would have no problem replenishing their arsenal from Yugoslavia's own munitions factories.

In early 1992, the UN was preparing a peacekeeping mission to neighbouring Croatia. That country's independence struggle with Belgrade had left a series of small, disputed "pink zones" as the UN called them — orphaned enclaves of mixed nationality with Serb minorities who needed protection as the JNA was forced to withdraw after the war in 1991. Boutros Boutros-Ghali decided to locate the headquarters of the Croatian peacekeeping mission in Sarajevo, hoping that the mere presence of the blue helmets would encourage an atmosphere of calm, and that the UN soldiers might avert all-out war without too much expense or effort.

Canada was one of the first countries to offer peacekeepers. Prime Minister Brian Mulroney had strong personal feelings about the conflict: his wife, Mila, was a Serb born in Sarajevo and she and the prime minister had honeymooned in the Balkans. Aside from the personal connection, Canada had a deep attachment to Yugoslavia: another "middle power" much admired in Ottawa political circles for its independent posture during the Soviet era. Yugoslavia had managed to resist Soviet hegemony and to become an important player in the United Nations, with an independent foreign policy and a flourishing economy. All of this appealed to a Canadian sensibility shaped by its relationship with the world power next door. Canada also had a significant Serb and Croat community, which was pressuring Ottawa to get involved.

Canada's former ambassador to Croatia, Graham Green, was a player from the start, as he then was serving in the Canadian mission to the UN. Green admits that Canada was deeply confused by the crisis in Yugoslavia. "We made a lot of decisions from the beginning based on believing in Belgrade. We didn't want the rest of Yugoslavia to break up, and we accepted the German position. The Germans claimed if we 'internationalized' Croatia by giving it recognition, then we could control the situation. We went along with that."

Canada was also a strenuous defender of the arms embargo — a position that it stuck with throughout the war, long after other countries had realized how unfair it was. Canada supported the ban even when it was pointed out that it was probably illegal to prevent a country from acquiring the means to defend itself. And Canada resisted calls for air strikes on Belgrade after others, including the United States, had recognized that bombing was the only way to end the conflict.

Canada selected many of its most experienced peacekeepers, including the then brigadier general Lewis MacKenzie, for the mission to Croatia, with its tagged-on Bosnian agenda. When he was appointed chief of staff for the United Nations Protection Force (UNPROFOR), to be based in Sarajevo, MacKenzie was already a veteran of eight UN tours, from Gaza to Central America, and had twenty-nine years of experience as a peacekeeper.

MacKenzie was thrilled at the prospect of this assignment—in fact, he lobbied for it. As he later wrote in *Peacekeeper*, his best-selling memoirs of his exploits in Sarajevo, a soldier needs experience to brag about. This mission looked like it would provide bragging material for years to come. "I'm sure some military personnel do volunteer for peacekeeping duty for higher reasons, such as alleviating human suffering wherever it may be found," he wrote, "but for the majority of us, it's the excitement and camaraderie that beckon."

MacKenzie was born near Truro, Nova Scotia, in 1940. His father, Eugene, fought in the Canadian army during the Second World War and again in Korea in 1952. Initially, Lewis MacKenzie had no interest in the armed forces, having had more than his fill of military life living on army bases in British Columbia and Nova Scotia during his teens. But as a young officer cadet, MacKenzie finally took to the profession; he was attracted to the idea of leading soldiers rather than just being one.

After he finished his infantry officer qualifications at Camp Borden in Ontario, MacKenzie joined the Queen's Own Rifles of Canada. His unit was just heading out for NATO training in West Germany, and the twenty-year-old soldier wanted to be part of it. He never looked back.

MacKenzie's early resumé reads more like that of a recreation director than a soldier. His earliest work with the armed forces was as sports coordinator, a talent that got him to the Gaza Strip, where the bored and dispirited Canadian peacekeepers needed some team coaching. In Gaza, he also acquired a reputation for showmanship. Having arranged for a screening of the movie *Lawrence of Arabia*, MacKenzie arrived at the theatre dressed in Bedouin clothing and riding a camel. From Cyprus to Saigon to Central America, MacKenzie's career curve climbed steadily. He rose through the officer ranks to general while keeping the soldiers under his command secure, content and often amused.

MacKenzie is a hard-living man whose love of thrills and excitement is legendary. Swashbuckling and unpredictable, the sandy-haired general with blue eyes and an expression of amusement permanently stamped on his face cuts an attractive figure. Men find him roguish and women find him sexy. He loves fast cars, and he's won awards for his daredevil formula four racing exploits. People who worked with him over the years knew he loved to drink, party and play practical jokes. MacKenzie always made it clear that his first priority on a mission is the well-being of his soldiers, and when he arrived in Bosnia he brought extra weapons and high-explosive ammunition with him, contrary to the rules of peace-keeping. Nobody was going to catch his soldiers underarmed, and this defiance of the bosses in New York City just made him more popular in the ranks.

MacKenzie landed in Sarajevo on Friday, March 13, 1992, three weeks before the first shots were fired there. He quickly declared that he had no mandate for Bosnia other than to offer his "good offices" whenever necessary to help the peace process—he was really there for a mission in Croatia. He was doubtful he could do anything to help Sarajevo, though he stated in his memoirs, "[W]e hoped the UN was right and our modest presence here would help to keep the lid on the ethnic tension."

Izetbegovic had been pleading with the UN to send peacekeepers. For ordinary Bosnians, the idea that this multinational UN force based in their capital city had no mandate for Bosnia didn't register. The blue helmets represented security and the Canadians symbolized the best of the world's good intentions.

While the cardinal rule of peacekeeping is neutrality, one of the unof-ficial verities is that it's prudent to be particularly friendly to the people who have the largest number of guns. For the peacekeepers, it was imme-diately clear who was in charge in Bosnia, and it wasn't President Izet-begovic. To get to Sarajevo, MacKenzie and his entourage from the United Nations had flown first to Belgrade (in fact, they were in Yugoslavia at the behest of the government), where they got a full briefing on the situ-ation from the Serbian regime of Slobodan Milosevic—not exactly the most impartial source of information. From that point, they depended entirely on the services of the Yugoslav National Army to get them into Sarajevo. They would, in fact, depend on the JNA for just about everything in the coming months, as it controlled all the air space and the territory in and out of all the zones of operation, and quite obviously enjoyed an enormous advantage in firepower. Whoever controlled the JNA controlled the country.

In their first weeks in Sarajevo, the UN soldiers busied themselves with making plans for peacekeeping in Croatia while the Bosnian war clouds formed all around. MacKenzie tried to ignore it. It wasn't his mandate. He noted the shootouts of April 5 and 6, and he was certainly conscious of the barricades around the city. He assigned a couple of locally hired observers to monitor the radio and TV, and to keep him at least superficially briefed.

He was a spectator, watching the final desperate attempt of the Bosnian government to save the country, and he described the drama in his diary as "riveting stuff."

In April, while MacKenzie prepared for Croatia, Milosevic prepared for Bosnia. After his campaigns in Slovenia and Croatia, he had redeployed his artillery and heavy weapons to the Bosnian countryside. As the army grew around them, it still wasn't clear, even to Karadzic, what would happen when the hostilities began in earnest. And it wasn't at all clear whether senior JNA officers would go along with a war waged against Bosnia. Many of them were, after all, Bosnians. In Bistrik barracks, for example, in the centre of Sarajevo, JNA general Milutin Kukanjac, a Serb, had made it clear to his superiors that he was not prepared to use his considerable firepower against the local people.

President Izetbegovic knew that his enemies were trying to marshal the JNA against him, and he could certainly see that the airport was under Serb control. He tried to raise his own army to protect his budding new nation, issuing a call-up to a reserve army known as the Territorial Defence Force (TDF). He appealed to Bosnians of all nationalities to come to the defence of their republic. This nascent Bosnian army was certainly multi-ethnic—a number of Serbs offered to lead—but it was a motley crowd consisting of anyone who had a gun and knew how to use it. In Sarajevo, along with the legitimate reservists came a mix of policemen and armed thugs. The TDF was led by a Muslim named Sefer Halilovic and his deputy, the Serb general Jovan Divjak. They were to throw themselves against one of the best-equipped and -trained armies in Europe.

The most valued unit in the fighting forces of Sarajevo was the special police, a force of 180 well-trained and disciplined men under the command of a Croat named Dragan Vikic. Vikic knew the underworld of Sarajevo well and he put out a call to the criminal community to bring its guns and come to the defence of the city. Hundreds of young toughs with no experience lined up behind a common thief named "Juka," who became legendary during the war for feats of bravery—though his "boys" were the worst trained and often the first killed. There were other militia units that would distinguish themselves one way or another over the coming years—the Green Berets and the Patriot League, the military wing of Izetbegovic's SDA—but in these early days of war in Sarajevo, there was little to define this "army" except for enthusiasm.

Lewis MacKenzie and his officers at UNPROFOR headquarters started an office pool shortly after they arrived in Bosnia, trying to guess when the war would begin. A major who picked April 5 at 2:30 p.m. got closest to the moment when a twenty-one-year-old woman walking in a Sarajevo peace demonstration was killed—and won the pot of $250. In April, as fighting intensified in Sarajevo and spread across the country, MacKenzie wrote a letter home, summing up his views: "Well, it's springtime in the Balkans, and history is repeating itself as the various ethnic groups (Muslims, Croats and Serbs) seek to exterminate each other; except this time it's by artillery rather than by swords." His letter summed up the attitude Europe and North America would adopt and cling to during the coming years: "Tragically, there is no solution I can postulate. Hatred is deep and everyone has a gun and calls himself a sniper. Hundreds of years of ethnic violence are dredged up at every meeting; everyone thinks theirs is the just cause. From my impartial view, there's more than enough blame to go around for all sides, with some left over."

MacKenzie's views grew to have enormous cachet abroad. The international media began a love affair with the Canadian general not long after he arrived in Sarajevo. Few reporters had known a military leader so willing to talk and to share his world view. *The Washington Post* writer Peter Maas was amazed when MacKenzie, upon meeting him on the airport Tarmac one day in the middle of a pitched battle, pulled up two lawn chairs and gave him an exclusive interview. Canadian journalists swelled with pride and added considerably to the legend in the making. *Saturday Night* described him as "strong and sinewy"; another reporter said "tall and beefy." They portrayed him as a straight-talking soldier who told it like it was: "He embodies the qualities Canadians think they share—modesty, tolerance, fair-mindedness, and a capacity to make the world a better place," said *Saturday Night*.

From his vantage point in the hills surrounding Sarajevo, Special Envoy Colm Doyle was only too aware of the impending danger. Doyle stayed at the Hotel Srbija where he had first-hand knowledge of what Karadzic was up to. Doyle also made regular visits to the hot spots and he had toured the Serb positions above the city. He advised a group of local reporters who came to see him in mid-April, on one of their last excursions out of the city, that there were at least two thousand guns in the hills of Sarajevo and they were all pointing downtown. The firepower, he said, was overwhelming, and the city could not last a week under its awful force. Doyle wanted the reporters to warn President Izetbegovic that Sarajevo was about to be crushed.

He was right about the guns but wrong about the crushing. Bosnia's thrown-together army would actually defend its capital city and its territory for the next three and a half years, with its men on the front lines often sharing one gun among three soldiers. The United Nations would dither and pass resolution upon resolution, more than for any other conflict in its history, but that only made matters worse. And the local population of Sarajevo would come to wish they had never laid eyes on the roguish, sandy-haired general from Canada.

3

THE PRESIDENT IS KIDNAPPED

[President Izetbegovic] did not know that there had begun, that morning, the greatest single bombardment to date, the targeting of many government buildings and the destruction, by sabotage from within, of the city's central post office and telephone exchange. Forty thousand phone lines had been knocked out, including all those serving the city centre where government buildings were located. It was May 2, 1992. Unwittingly, the President was flying into the eye of the storm.
—Laura Silber and Allan Little, *The Death of Yugoslavia*

[May] the second was a relatively quiet day; only a couple of hundred rounds of machine-gun fire in the Old City. But the firing continued all night, so I was unable to get to a colleague's flat to watch the Spanish Formula 1 Grand Prix. It was just as well—the flat was partially destroyed by artillery fire during the afternoon.
—Lewis MacKenzie, *Peacekeeper: The Road to Sarajevo*

It was a watershed moment for the people of Bosnia, and especially for the citizens of Sarajevo. The battle for control of the nation's capital on May 2, 1992, is regarded by many journalists and historians as one of the five or six most decisive events of the war.

It was the day when Serbian forces, controlled from Belgrade, moved on the Bosnian Presidency building. It was the day terrorists conducted a well-planned sabotage of the city's central post office and telephone exchange, destroying the old stone structure with fire and explosive devices. It was the day when Radovan Karadzic attempted to execute his plan to divide Sarajevo. And it was the day when the president of Bosnia was kidnapped.

For Gordana Knezevic, it was the last day her family would live together for years to come. That morning, she and her husband, Ivo, took two of their three children, Igor and Olga, down to the bus station to send them off to safety for the duration of the war. Like most people in Sarajevo, one month into the often confusing conflict, the Knezevic family still believed it would be only a few months before the crazy nationalists burned themselves out. Then the tranquility of their city would be restored.

As Gordana and Ivo trudged back up the hill towards their apartment building, they saw the first trucks in a convoy of military vehicles, laden with weapons and soldiers, stream down the street, heading towards Marshal Tito barracks. Gordana stopped to count: seventeen in all. Later in the afternoon, she planned to report to her job as deputy editor of the *Oslobodjenje* daily newspaper, where she could publish news of the extraordinary convoy along with other stories of the day. But she never got there. By the time she and Ivo reached their apartment, they knew what the trucks meant: the Serbs were pounding Sarajevo with all the force they had. The bus with their children aboard passed the city limits just as they reached their gate, and was the last regular bus to leave the city for the duration of the war. The siege of Sarajevo had begun.

Bosnian vice-president Ejup Ganic was in a panic that morning. His security personnel had told him the Presidency building was surrounded by a heavily armed SWAT force of combat soldiers who had entered Sarajevo from Serbia intent on storming the head office of the government. Ganic is a tall, gaunt, easily rattled man—an intellectual with a degree in engineering from the Massachusetts Institute of Technology. He left academic life to join the SDA party and the new government. Though young and inexperienced, Ganic was smart, and he quickly moved up the ranks to become Izetbegovic's deputy. Now he was in big trouble, and he had no idea what to do.

His boss had flown to Lisbon two days earlier to take part in European Community talks aimed at stopping the war. Izetbegovic was expected back at any moment. In the president's absence, it appeared that some elements of the Yugoslav National Army, under the leadership of the rogue Bosnian Serb government in Pale, were staging a *coup d'état*.

Ganic's security forces urged him to leave the building before he was murdered—they told him of a series of tunnels that were installed by the Austro-Hungarians under the old government offices when they built them. If the passages could be found and cleared, Ganic could flee to safety. But he knew this was a bad idea; as soon as he left the complex, it would be the beginning of the end. It was impossible to know who were friends and foes among the tangle of political interests that had become the government of Bosnia, but there was one thing Ganic was sure of: if Izetbegovic returned, he would thwart this coup attempt. But where was the president?

Negotiations in Lisbon were going badly. The European Community was trying to keep the Bosnian Humpty-Dumpty from falling off the wall, and things didn't look good. Ambassador José Cutileiro of Portugal, the chairman of the EC group, had tried for weeks to persuade Croat, Bosnian and Serb leaders to accept some kind of partition of Bosnia, but for differing reasons they all balked. The Serbs and Croats had already discussed dividing up Bosnia between them, with little regard for the fate of the Muslims. No borders drawn up by the EC could be acceptable to them. And Izetbegovic wouldn't deal because he believed cantonization was impossible. Cutileiro threw up his hands in frustration and declared the meeting over. Delegates headed for home, which would be a lot easier for some than for others.

Colm Doyle had arranged for Izetbegovic to attend the meeting, knowing that without the Bosnian president this Portugal conference wouldn't have much legitimacy. Both the Serb and Croat members of the meeting had relative ease of movement. Not Izetbegovic.

Doyle went to see him at the Presidency days before the conference. "Well, Mr. President, are you all ready to leave for Lisbon?" he'd asked with a chuckle. Izetbegovic told Doyle what the Irishman already knew: there was no way to travel without the permission of the Serbs, who controlled the airport and all roads in and out of Sarajevo. It would endanger his life to even attempt to go.

Doyle made a bold commitment: he would arrange for a plane and a pilot from Europe, and he would guarantee an armed escort of peacekeepers to get the president to and from the airport. Lewis MacKenzie, UNPROFOR chief of staff, had been in his headquarters in the vacated Communications Engineering building on the outskirts of town, near the airport, since March and was quite preoccupied with his mission in Croatia. But the UN soldiers were the only internationals with guns, and MacKenzie was instructed from New York to offer VIPs safe passage and to provide his "good offices" for any peace negotiations. MacKenzie agreed to provide the escort. Without UNPROFOR assistance, Izetbegovic would never be able to attend the meeting in Portugal.

On April 29, after a few false starts, Doyle got the president to the airport, along with his daughter, Sabina, who acted as translator and as a kind of chief of staff. Also on the mission was Zlatko Lagumdzija, a Muslim by birth but the leader of a non-nationalist party in the coalition government and also deputy prime minister. Izetbegovic wanted Lagumdzija along on the ride to show Lisbon that his views were not those of Muslim nationalists with a plot to "Islamize" Europe, but were held by secular members of government as well. Doyle bid the party farewell and braced himself for the difficulties he was sure to face when the group came back on the second of May.

There are many theories as to why the Serbs chose May 2 for a major assault on Bosnia. Colm Doyle suspects it was because the Lisbon talks had failed. But most observers agree that in the absence of the president, the Serbs grabbed an opportunity to take the territory they wanted. On this same day, the JNA forces in the northeast carved out a land corridor between Bosnia and Serbia, which they needed to ensure a resupply of arms, and they brutally cleared all non-Serbs from the area in their bid to create an ethnically pure state.

In Sarajevo, the assault began with an attack on passengers of a streetcar in the centre of the city. By noon, the convoy of Serb soldiers rolled through the downtown area toward the Presidency building, and in late afternoon, the Serb nationalist forces blew up the main post office and telephone exchange in the heart of the city. This deliberate act of sabotage, planned well in advance as a diversionary tactic, managed to take out most of the phones in the city, cutting off residents from a crucial lifeline. From this day forward, the people of Sarajevo would have little information from other parts of the country and the outside world, and it would come to have a powerful psychological effect on them. They would freeze, starve and be bombed to death over the next four years, all in a state of primitive isolation.

Serb forces established a front line in the middle of Sarajevo, effectively partitioning it for the duration of the war. May 2 was a fierce battle for as much control of the city as possible: it left the streets strewn with corpses that no one was able to drag from the urban battlefield for days.

The new Bosnian army was an awkward, disorganized beast, but it understood two things: do not let the Serbian forces take the Presidency building (they came within two hundred metres); and do not let the JNA take the arsenal out of the city. On the morning of May 2, the army used to its advantage a superior knowledge of the city's narrow streets to fight off the attack that had Ejup Ganic pinned down. The next task was to capture the Bistrik barracks, where the guns were stored. As long as the Bosnians had the arsenal, there was a tiny chance of winning this war.

By midday, they had Bistrik surrounded, with several hundred JNA officers and their leader, General Kukanjac, trapped inside. Not bad for a band of thugs, cops and reservists.

In Lisbon, Sabina Izetbegovic was trying to call the Presidency in Sarajevo. The phone lines appeared to be down. The president's daughter is a small-framed, willowy blonde with the same strong facial features as her father, including the sharp blue eyes. She and her father were anxious to get back to Sarajevo that day. As soon as the little Cessna twin-prop that had brought them to Portugal was ready to fly, the party of four — Izetbegovic, his daughter, his bodyguard and Deputy Prime Minister Lagumdzija — left for home.

Their plane touched down in Rome to refuel. It actually had enough petrol to make it, but not enough to cover for any emergencies — such as having to turn back. The French flight crew wanted to be prepared for anything. While in Rome, Sabina again made desperate attempts to contact home, without success. With no news of the siege, they flew on towards Sarajevo.

Since Belgrade controlled the airspace over the former Yugoslavia, Belgrade would now determine the fate of the president. From the air, the French female co-pilot made several unsuccessful calls to Sarajevo airport to confirm their landing. She immediately set up contingency plans and established that the plane would be able to turn back to Zagreb or Belgrade. Izetbegovic wanted to risk the airport, but for the sake of his daughter's safety he agreed, if necessary, to go to Zagreb. Just as this decision was made, the co-pilot made contact with Sarajevo. The controller told the crew they could land, but only at their own risk. Since this is what the tower had been saying routinely to flights in and out since before the war began, Izetbegovic instructed the pilot to carry on.

Sabina peered anxiously through the tiny aircraft window as the plane taxied to the Sarajevo terminal. She decided that no one would disembark until they saw Colm Doyle. At first, all she could see were JNA soldiers, mixed with an alarming number of paramilitaries and a ring of tanks around the perimeter. Izetbegovic asked his daughter for a verdict. Sabina was about to tell the pilot to take off again when she saw what appeared to be the familiar figure of the Irishman striding across the Tarmac. Though he was flanked by a dozen JNA officers, she knew the presence of the EC envoy meant UNPROFOR wasn't far away. Sabina breathed a sigh of relief and declared it was safe to leave the plane. But it wasn't.

Colm Doyle was actually downtown, trying to find out what was going on. It was clear to everyone that a major assault on the city was under way, perhaps a decisive one, and the EC special envoy needed all the information he could get his hands on. He also had been watching the time so he wouldn't forget his most important task — arranging the convoy to greet the president upon his return, a hellish job under the circumstances.

In early afternoon, the satellite phone rang at his headquarters, and when he answered the caller claimed to be from the Bosnian Presidency.

"Izetbegovic will not be returning from Lisbon today," said the man.

"Thank God," Doyle thought, not questioning the authenticity of the message, just happy to get it. He radioed UNPROFOR headquarters. "Stand down the escort for the president. It won't be needed." That meant one fewer task to perform on this frightening day.

As JNA guards shepherded Izetbegovic and his party into the terminal, Zlatko Lagumdzija realized that the man in the suit was not Colm Doyle but the airport manager, and they were being taken to his office. The pilot helped carry their baggage into the building before departing again, and Lagumdzija took him aside and briefed him on what he was to do: notify all authorities that no one had been at the airport to meet the president and his party. They were being taken into custody and clearly they were in danger. The plane departed in the dying light of the day. The president, his bodyguard, his daughter and Lagumdzija were now prisoners, their fate, and the fate of the Bosnian nation, in serious doubt.

As the Serb officers installed Izetbegovic in the airport manager's office, they told him that the city was in ruins, the phones no longer functioning. He demanded a radio phone to call the police and was told that they did not work either. A group of young soldiers surrounded them, their guns aimed and ready. The JNA officers said they were prepared to take Izetbegovic and the others to their nearby base—the Lukavica military barracks—where their future would be decided. Sabina remembers feeling desperate and fearful. And then, suddenly, the telephone on the manager's desk rang.

They all froze. Sabina jumped to grab it before her father could, certain the young men would shoot him if he moved. On the other end of the line was a woman from a suburb of the city that still had phone service. She wanted to know if a plane carrying her daughter had been able to take off that day.

The call was so unexpected that no one was sure what to do, and in the moment of confusion, Izetbegovic grabbed the receiver. He ordered the woman to call the Presidency and tell them he had been arrested and would be taken to Lukavica barracks. The woman was clearly startled and disbelieving, but Sabina was certain her father's message would get through.

When they got to Lukavica, an unidentified colonel, gun in hand, threatened to throw Izetbegovic and his daughter to an angry mob that had gathered outside, baying for blood. A group of drunken civilians with guns had surrounded the barracks with the connivance of the Serb soldiers, and they were calling for the president to be turned over to them for "questioning." Sabina could hear soldiers barking orders into their radios—clearly to the troops in the hills surrounding Sarajevo: "Hit them hard, hit them again. Don't let them breathe."

Despite the threats, it was becoming clear to those in the room that the Serbs had no idea what to do with the president. Whatever the plan had been, it had never included this, and while there were certainly those in Lukavica who would have arranged a swift execution, a number of the JNA officers were still squeamish about what they were doing.

Meanwhile, as the drama with the president was unfolding at Lukavica, dozens of JNA officers and troops, along with General Kukanjac, were pinned down in the Bistrik barracks in downtown Sarajevo by the ragtag Bosnian army. A general in one barracks, a president in another. Perhaps there was potential for a deal. Izetbegovic began negotiating for his own life in a most unorthodox way.

"Imagine how you'd feel if you were reading the news and, after about fifty minutes, you were getting ready to sign off, and you heard that the president had been kidnapped. I didn't know what to say." Senad Hadjifejzovic anchored the evening news on Bosnia-Herzegovina TV, and that night he made history for, if not the longest, then certainly the most bizarre newscast in television history.

The woman who had phoned the airport had dutifully called in the alarm that the president had been detained. Ganic had contacted the TV station, and they were able to hook up a link to Lukavica barracks. The only connection between Izetbegovic and his office that night was a telephone hotline that ran from the Presidency to the TV station. All the negotiations for releasing the president were conducted on national TV. The extraordinary newscast began at half past seven in the evening and ended at five o'clock the next morning. Every possible player was involved in the program, which was hosted by the exhausted news anchor.

There were calls with Ambassador Zimmerman and the JNA leadership in Belgrade, Ganic, and of course the president. The remarkable news event was carried throughout Europe, with parts of the dramatic live broadcast even turning up on the BBC and CNN.

Every Bosnian who still had electricity tuned in, knowing that the fate of their country was hanging by a thread. Gordana and Ivo Knezevic were among them, huddled in their apartment with their eldest son, Boris. Everyone knew the consequences if Izetbegovic was removed from power. Bosnia's institutions were simply not strong enough to survive such a crisis, and Radovan Karadzic, backed by the government in Belgrade and its army, would be free to swiftly finish his campaign.

Lewis MacKenzie has only a fleeting recollection of these events. His diary entry for May 2, published in his memoirs, reads as follows: "... a relatively quiet day; only a couple of hundred rounds of machine-gun fire in the Old City. But the firing continued all night, so I was unable to get to a colleague's flat to watch the Spanish Formula 1 Grand Prix. It was just as well — the flat was partially destroyed by artillery fire during the afternoon."

The half a dozen key people involved in the day's events believe it's impossible that General MacKenzie did not know that the president had been kidnapped. Stjepan Kljuic, one of the two Croat members of the Presidency, monitored the movements of Izetbegovic that day through radio communications. He knew the president's plane had left Lisbon before anyone could get a message to him about the ambush. By monitoring radio communications from the airport, which Kljuic was able to do from the Presidency building, he says he knew that the plane had been turned back and then given permission to land at Sarajevo. UNPROFOR must have had at least the same rudimentary technology as he had, and would have had the same basic intelligence. Says Kljuic: "General MacKenzie certainly knew. He simply let the delegation arrive. MacKenzie was the guarantor for Izetbegovic's escort. If there had been no guarantee, the flight wouldn't even attempt to go to Bosnia." Kljuic's theory (eventually to be held by many in the city) is that MacKenzie was somehow complicit in the kidnapping. But the truth is much more mundane.

In an interview some years later, after a number of accounts had emerged about the day, MacKenzie says he probably knew the president had been kidnapped. He knew there had been a long local newscast and suspects that someone probably monitored it for him. But as the chief of staff for UNPROFOR in Sarajevo, he didn't consider it important to his Croatian project. To get involved would be considered "mission creep" — a term used often by soldiers to indicate the worst of what can happen to a military operation. "We didn't really know the players in these events," says MacKenzie, and he could hardly remember the president's name. He and his fellow officers at headquarters would help each other recall "Izetbegovic" with the phrase "It's a bagel."

Even without a mandate in Bosnia, three hundred UN soldiers from a half-dozen different countries were in Sarajevo at this point, in addition to unarmed monitors, who relied on the peacekeepers for protection. Doyle argues that the president's kidnapping presented an enormous security issue for all internationals on the ground. But MacKenzie disagrees. "It was really minor at that stage. We hadn't taken over yet."

Could MacKenzie have prevented the kidnapping of the president? "Well, if we had known he was going to arrive... I don't even remember the event of Izetbegovic going away. It wasn't a big event for us. It wasn't a big event for HQ."

By dawn on May 3, Izetbegovic and his captors had come up with a plan: there would be an exchange. General Kukanjac would never get out of the Bistrik barracks alive if he couldn't get past the desperate line of Bosnian army soldiers. And Izetbegovic would never get out of Lukavica alive if the JNA didn't help.

Both sides agreed—a general would be swapped for a president. In the course of the night, Ganic says he told MacKenzie about the plan and asked him to provide armoured vehicles. MacKenzie called Doyle to tell him there would be a meeting at the UNPROFOR headquarters the next morning.

That morning would drag MacKenzie deep into the reality of Bosnia and its war. And it would launch a chain of events that would ultimately result in the premature end of the general's military career.

4

DAY OF THE GENERAL

If the United Nations had existed in 1939,
we'd all be speaking German now.
—Fred Cuny, Sarajevo aid worker

Ejup Ganic was in no less of a panic on May 3 than he had been the day before. He had slept badly for a few hours on a bed in the Presidency building, and he awoke to the horrible recollection that during the night, Izetbegovic had made him deputy president. He couldn't deny it: the whole proceeding had transpired on national television. Now a greenhorn university professor was in charge of a country at war, with its state leader in the custody of the enemy.

Lewis MacKenzie didn't know it yet, but May 3 wasn't going well for him, either. Later, he would describe it this way in his memoirs: "Definitely the worst day of my life." He continued, "Around mid-morning, Bosnian Vice-President Ejup Ganic came to my office and met me with Colm Doyle of the EC. Ganic explained that President Izetbegovic, on his return visit from Lisbon, had been kidnapped at Sarajevo airport; he was being detained by the JNA at their Lukavica camp, just east of the runway." If that wasn't enough of a challenge, one of the JNA's most important generals, Milutin Kukanjac, along with his officers and men, was being held captive by Bosnian forces at the Bistrik barracks in the centre of Sarajevo. MacKenzie says that he got involved that morning only because he believed Ejup Ganic was desperate. According to MacKenzie's memoirs: "Ganic said he was not a strong leader, and needed the President back in order to control the radical officers within the Bosnian TDF, who were rapidly getting out of control."

Ganic had gone to see MacKenzie at UNPROFOR headquarters along with Colm Doyle to make the arrangements for an armed escort. He spelled out the details of the plan to swap President Izetbegovic for General Kukanjac. Looking for all the world like a lost schoolboy, Ganic then headed back to the Presidency to try to keep his unpredictable armed forces under control, while MacKenzie headed out to Lukavica barracks with Colm Doyle.

At the gate of Lukavica, the MacKenzie party met the same band of crazed "citizens" who had been baying for the blood of Izetbegovic all night. Thinking they were Sarajevans concerned for the safety of their president, MacKenzie called for a translator (a Serb from London, Ontario, volunteered) and proceeded to tell the mob not to worry about their leader—MacKenzie was there to save him.

The general's presumption that the group was pro-Izetbegovic when it had actually come with hopes of lynching him was perhaps the best thing that could have happened: the bemused crowd parted and allowed them passage. Fate often has more to do with chance than with knowledge.

Inside the compound, MacKenzie and Doyle eventually found Izetbegovic: he was on the phone with General Kukanjac and they were changing the plan. The JNA had decided it wasn't getting enough in exchange for the president and it insisted that the entire barracks of four hundred men plus their weapons be removed from Sarajevo. The idea was mad. MacKenzie declared he couldn't possibly guarantee the security of such a group, but the president was desperate. "Izetbegovic said *he* would guarantee their safety," says Doyle. "I knew he couldn't possibly, but the man was afraid for his life and especially afraid for the life of his daughter."

Time was passing quickly, and if there was to be an exchange, it would have to be in daylight. MacKenzie agreed. Without his help, it was possible the JNA soldiers would also be murdered.

Zlatko Lagumdzija remembers the plan as being utterly insane. He was placed in the lead vehicle with MacKenzie; fluent in English, he was able to follow most of what was going on. MacKenzie, curiously, doesn't recall, either in his book or in interviews, that there was another person in the Izetbegovic party in his car and under his protection. Izetbegovic and his daughter were put in an armoured personnel carrier, while the bodyguard and Colm Doyle were left behind as hostages.

From the lead car, Lagumdzija could observe their progress through the streets towards the barracks in downtown Sarajevo. The scene was out of Hades: burnt corpses lay strewn in their path and the vehicles had to swerve to miss them; blown-up cars, buses and tanks littered the sides of the roads; everywhere there was the acrid smoke from the burning fuel oil of wrecked vehicles. MacKenzie was rapidly gaining a first-hand understanding of just what had happened in Sarajevo over the past twenty-four hours.

When they finally arrived at Bistrik barracks, the Bosnian forces allowed the UN vehicles and a number of JNA trucks to pass their line. MacKenzie instructed Izetbegovic and his daughter to go and sit with General Kukanjac in the office, where they would all have coffee. Sabina remembers the scene as being surreal. "The [Bosnian] forces were all around the barracks, and they had not slept all night. They were untrained and very edgy. We were inside, surrounded by the JNA and having coffee!"

General Kukanjac is a beefy man with a bouffant of thick, dark hair and a flair for the dramatic. Although a Serb nationalist, he also fancies himself a free thinker; he had been a disappointment to Karadzic when he failed to immediately make the Bistrik arsenal available to Bosnian Serb paramilitaries. In the coming weeks, Kukanjac would be replaced by a more forceful general, Ratko Mladic, who wouldn't hesitate to follow the wishes of Pale. Belgrade would eventually tire of Kukanjac altogether, and the general would be sidelined. But in Sarajevo that day in May, he was at the peak of his career and importance.

Sabina says Kukanjac quickly launched into a tirade about the Bosnian leadership, but Izetbegovic was much too tired to participate with any zeal. MacKenzie, however, tried to join the discussion and asked her to translate. "General MacKenzie wanted to know what everyone was saying, what points they were making about Serbian nationalism. We were in a sovereign country, surrounded by an army that had no legitimate role in Bosnia any more, and MacKenzie wanted to hear both sides of the argument. I was terrified of what would happen next and also exhausted."

MacKenzie remembers the coffee party as being very informative. He found General Kukanjac an interesting man who offered his services as a peacekeeper. "He had floated the idea that he could stay and keep the warring parties separated in Bosnia, and that it might be a good use of his skills. But I guess Belgrade disagreed."

The barracks were housed in a handsome stucco building of the Austro-Hungarian period. Its splendid architecture betrays the real purpose of the complex. Beyond the façade there's a large open courtyard with room to accommodate a concentration of heavy guns, vehicles and troops.

While Kukanjac was drinking coffee and haranguing the president about Serbian nationalism, his soldiers were loading trucks with as much of their arsenal as they could possibly carry away. The barracks had served as a base when Serb military officers were planning the assault on Sarajevo, and there was a mountain of incriminating files and papers there. What the packers couldn't get onto trucks, they attempted to burn. The paperwork is believed to have contained blueprints for a campaign of ethnic cleansing.

Finally, everything was pronounced ready and the convoy could begin. MacKenzie put Sabina, her father and Kukanjac together in the same APC and closed the door. With the trucks groaning under the load of weapons and filing cabinets, the convoy began its slow progress out into the narrow, tree-lined street.

Sabina was frightened. MacKenzie had permitted Kukanjac to keep his pistol (a soldier's honour), and Sabina recalls that he had his hand on it during the entire ride. Her concerns were later proven to be legitimate. In subsequent interviews, Kukanjac confessed he had planned to kill Izetbegovic and then himself. He says he changed his mind only when he realized he was probably too valuable to the cause to be wasted.

No two people agree on what exactly precipitated the disaster that followed, but it would affect relations between UNPROFOR and the Bosnian leadership for the rest of the war. It was a long procession and before it was entirely through the barracks gates, people riding in the lead car heard gunfire.

MacKenzie ran back to see what had happened. He later recalled that a Volkswagen Golf had suddenly cut into the convoy, splitting it into two sections. The street was so narrow, MacKenzie says, that one small car effectively stalled the entire operation. Horrified, he could also see that Bosnian soldiers were shooting JNA officers at point-blank range, confiscating their weapons and piling them into their own vehicles.

The general was appalled. People for whom he had taken responsibility were being killed. And worse, they were men in uniform like him. It seared the psyche of a man who prided himself on keeping soldiers safe when they were under his command. He tried to stop the Bosnians but quickly realized that they were so exhausted and pumped on adrenaline that they were out of control.

MacKenzie demanded that the leaders of the Bosnian forces do something to stop the chaos. The most experienced soldier in their ranks, the deputy commander, General Jovan Divjak—an anti-nationalist Serb who opposed Karadzic's vision of an ethnically pure Bosnia—did his best to intervene. Finally, President Izetbegovic poked his head out of the APC to reassure the troops that he was still alive and to dispel the rumour that he had been assassinated. The shooting finally stopped.

In the end, seven men were murdered. Compared with the rest of the carnage in the city that day, it was minor, but for MacKenzie it was a turning point. He would never forget or forgive. He believes the Bosnian Muslims, almost undoubtedly Ejup Ganic, betrayed him and ordered the convoy cut and the soldiers killed. So strong was his conviction that he was unable to trust the Muslim leadership for the rest of his time in Sarajevo.

Sabina Izetbegovic saw it differently. The deal called for a very limited number of vehicles to leave the compound, and that was what the Bosnian forces on the outside had expected. The JNA were supposed to take only their personal weapons with them. That was what MacKenzie had agreed to. "[The Bosnian army] knew precisely how many trucks had been negotiated for, and when they saw the last of those trucks pull out they said, 'Enough! No more!'" she says. "The Serbs broke the deal by attempting to empty out the barracks of all the weapons plus files." General Divjak remembers a plan for thirty trucks—enough for the soldiers in the barracks to leave, carrying only their personal weapons. And yet, the convoy attempting to leave Bistrik that day was seventy vehicles long.

Ganic says he was never informed that the president was to be exchanged for the entire barracks and, frankly, he would have had a lot of problems with that if he had known. But he also denies he gave the order to break the convoy. In any case, the Bosnian army was too disorganized to take a command from the deputy president; the incident only reaffirmed for Ganic that without Izetbegovic at the helm, there would be anarchy.

The reality is that the Bosnians had very few weapons; they certainly weren't going to watch the entire JNA arsenal leave the city to be used against them. The Bosnian forces were poorly armed for the duration of the war. As for assault weapons, they had only what they could steal—a few machine guns and mortar launchers. They survived the attack on Sarajevo on May 2 mostly because of the tactical advantage provided by the city's narrow streets. But such advantage wasn't going to hold if they didn't get some firepower.

An angry and frustrated Lewis MacKenzie finally manoeuvred his convoy to the designated exchange point just before a bridge that cuts Sarajevo in two. His plan was to put the general in one car, the president in the other, and send them in different directions.

Lagumdzija remembers the moment of exchange: "In the midst of this battlefield on the street, with both fighting forces lined up on either side and nerves frayed, MacKenzie brought Izetbegovic out and put him in one car, with Kukanjac in the other." Lagumdzija climbed out of MacKenzie's car and clambered in with the president. "It was the first time I would believe my life was over." (Lagumdzija would face another close encounter with death a year later, when he was seriously wounded in a mortar attack. He survived it and is today considered a likely successor to the presidency in Bosnia.)

By happenstance and fate, the principal players departed the scene safely. But seven Serb soldiers had died, and most of the others who had been caught behind the Volkswagen—approximately 150 men—had become hostages.

Back at Lukavica barracks, Colm Doyle was dealing with his own private nightmare. The crazed colonel who had terrorized Sabina Izetbegovic all night was now doing an effective job on the EC representative. The Bosnian Serb's radio crackled with the misinformation from downtown that JNA soldiers were being stripped naked and summarily executed. "The colonel waved his gun and declared me personally responsible for what had happened. Which amused me only in later years, when I was cut out of Lew's account of the negotiations," says Doyle. "But at the moment I genuinely believed I would be killed."

He mustered some latent talent for blarney and told the colonel that the international community would execute him if the JNA did anything to harm the special envoy to the Balkans. That seemed to work. But when MacKenzie returned to fetch Doyle and the president's bodyguard, he too was detained. Everyone spent an uncomfortable night at Lukavica before cooler heads prevailed and MacKenzie and Doyle were released (there would be further negotiating for the president's bodyguard).

For years to come, MacKenzie would recount this story in interviews and speeches, describing the details of his plan to rescue the president and the general, and the act of betrayal by the Bosnians. He gives a similar account in *Peacekeeper*. But few remember it the way MacKenzie does.

Doyle was the one asked to chair the meeting that morning at UNPRO-FOR and make all the arrangements, because Lewis MacKenzie didn't want to get involved in something that smelled of mission creep. A few years later, Doyle was surprised to see, in an episode of *Death of Yugoslavia* (the seminal TV series on the war), that the meeting at UNPROFOR headquarters had been recorded on videotape. MacKenzie had recorded the session and passed the tape to the British TV producers, and then he had been interviewed for his account of that fateful day. On both the videotape and in the MacKenzie narrative, the EC special envoy has vanished from the event.

Doyle jokes about it now. "As I don't appear in the account of Lewis MacKenzie, nor on the videotape in *Death of Yugoslavia*, I began to wonder if I had just imagined it all!" It only matters, according to Doyle, because he clearly remembers how reluctant MacKenzie was to get involved in the first place. Ganic was also surprised to see MacKenzie's account of the day. He'd had no idea the meeting was being videotaped either.

Yet MacKenzie says he was really in charge that day: "That was our first event. Everything until then had been the European Community." Doyle had told him that the EC would soon have to pull out since it was becoming too dangerous for the observers. "There was no official document signed," says MacKenzie. "But all of a sudden we took the lead." In twenty-four hours, between the kidnapping and the rescue, apparently everything had changed, yet no one in the Presidency knew about it.

On May 4, in his new capacity as a UN facilitator, MacKenzie demanded that the Bosnian armed forces release all the JNA soldiers and officers they had arrested the day before and allow them to depart the city on buses. Ganic had hoped to keep them to bargain with, but Izetbegovic was also troubled by what had happened the day before. He had given his guarantee for the safety of the convoy. He felt honour-bound to release the hostages and did so. Some decided to switch sides and join with the Bosnians. Some of them had already disappeared.

In the coming years, Izetbegovic would reorganize his army under the command structure of the national police — the most accomplished of his forces. And he would also begin to separate his soldiers along ethnic lines. But he would never be able to acquire the weapons his troops needed to defend the country.

MacKenzie lobbied throughout the war against providing the Bosnians with weapons, claiming on numerous occasions that "there were more than enough weapons to go around." He had personally seen what they had acquired from the Sarajevo barracks. Other JNA arsenals were emptied out after negotiations under the auspices of UNPROFOR, and the departing Serbs were forced to leave a large supply of material behind for the Bosnian forces.

But what MacKenzie didn't say — possibly didn't know — was that the JNA sabotaged most of their heavy guns before abandoning them. Of the roughly six thousand rifles they turned over, most were models that were nearing obsolescence.

With hindsight, Sabina Izetbegovic believes she and her father were supposed to have been stranded in exile, where the president would spend the next months, and perhaps years, trying to retake his legitimate place as head of state. When they actually arrived back from Portugal and the Cessna was given clearance to land, however, there was a change in plans. She thinks her father's enemies saw the perfect opportunity to seize the president and use him as a bargaining chip to get General Kukanjac and his troops out of a jam. Lagumdzija is sure Izetbegovic would have been assassinated that night if the Bosnian Serbs had been better organized.

For Izetbegovic, the kidnapping was the first of many eye-opening experiences. He and his coalition government had celebrated the arrival of UNPROFOR on Bosnian soil as though the cavalry had arrived. So sure were they of the validity of their government and its right to sovereignty, Izetbegovic and Ganic could not have imagined that the United Nations would become involved in presiding over their country's dismemberment.

5

THE BREADLINE MASSACRE

Anyone who remains neutral in this war is a shit.
—Susan Sontag

ON the morning of May 27, 1992, word circulated in a downtown neighbourhood that there would be bread. This was cause for celebration. The Serbs had set up a number of roadblocks when Bosnia declared its independence; movement in and out of the city was almost impossible. The JNA forces in Bosnia (now the army of the Serb republic) had been shelling the city for nearly two months, and Sarajevo had been under siege since May 2. Water and electricity supplies were sabotaged. Almost everyone in Sarajevo was being harassed by snipers as they dashed about gathering necessities. The announcement that there would be bread was a rare occasion of good news in a city cut off from the world.

Sulejman Hebib heard about it and immediately called his brother to tell him, "We will eat bread tonight!" The once-husky young Sarajevan had become familiar with hunger, like everyone else in the city, and since the siege had begun he had lost a lot of weight. Hebib ran a popular restaurant/bar called Ragusa, an establishment that had remained open because it was tucked away down an alley, steps from the most popular walkway in Sarajevo, Vase Miskin. It was also only twenty metres from the bakery. People still came to this street, though there were few goods to be had, because it was sheltered from snipers by surrounding buildings and difficult to target because the passage was so narrow. Hebib entered Vase Miskin around ten that morning to join the already sizeable breadline queue.

He immediately became depressed. He was standing on what was perhaps the most agreeable street in all of Bosnia — a place where only weeks ago, people strolled arm in arm while choosing which of the many coffee bars to retire to for a pleasant afternoon. Now he was part of a column of hungry people with hollow, mournful faces waiting to buy some bread.

"I couldn't do it," says Hebib. "I couldn't wait in that line with those people, no matter how hungry I and my family were." Dejected, he headed back to the restaurant. Moments later, he heard the first shell land.

People who grow accustomed to being shelled learn to anticipate a certain response pattern after an explosive impact. First, there's a kind of eerie silence as victims take stock. People are stunned; even birds stop chirping. Then there are the shrieks and groans of pain. One artillery shell is almost invariably followed by a second, calculated to arrive as people rush to help the first victims. On that hideous morning in May, Hebib arrived back at Vase Miskin just after the second bomb and confronted a scene that overwhelmed him. The two mortars had landed in the middle of the bread queue and had scattered body parts all over the pavement. Hebib saw a man he knew and ran to help. "I grabbed his arm and the arm came off in my hand. I grabbed his leg; it too pulled away."

In all, seventeen people were killed and more than a hundred injured in a callous act of war terrorism. Moments after the impacts, a camera crew from the Bosnia-Herzegovina TV network arrived. They had been taping an announcement in a nearby building and were the first media on the scene. They were there filming even before ambulances and volunteers arrived to take the bodies away. The attackers in the hills had scored a direct hit. International television crews working in Sarajevo at the time beamed the pictures via satellite to a horrified world. Surely to God the foreign powers would have to intervene now, given the impact of those images. Or so thought a hapless Bosnian population.

In Lisbon, Colm Doyle was taking part in fruitless meetings with the Bosnian Serb leadership, trying to persuade them to move some of the heavy guns away from the Sarajevo area. The EC's presiding chairman, José Cutileiro, was consulting with Doyle when a horrified aide rushed into the room and told them to turn on Sky TV, the British all-news network. Karadzic, who was part of the negotiations, rushed in right behind. "We didn't do it!" he breathlessly declared.

"I knew he couldn't possibly know that for a fact, since no one had telephone contact with Sarajevo that day," recalls Doyle. "He was bluffing."

The Irishman decided to seize a momentary tactical advantage. He advised Cutileiro to try to get concessions from Karadzic while the Bosnian Serb leader felt vulnerable. "Cutileiro said to Karadzic: 'That may be so. But the world will believe that you did it. So perhaps you better start negotiating.' We immediately asked him for an agreement on opening the airport," according to Doyle. "And we got it."

If Karadzic had waited a few days, he wouldn't have bothered agreeing to anything. People in Bosnia were only just beginning to realize how United Nations peacekeeping really works. And they would make the astonishing discovery that the UN would go to extraordinary lengths to remain neutral, even to the point of blaming an atrocity like the breadline massacre on the victims.

Lewis MacKenzie was in the Yugoslavian capital of Belgrade on the day the breadline massacre occurred. The United Nations had finally agreed with the Canadian general and others that the Sarajevo base was an untenable site for their mission in Croatia, and they were deciding how and where to relocate their headquarters. Nevertheless, MacKenzie kept in close contact with Sarajevo, not just because he was chief of staff, but because he was genuinely fascinated by the developments there.

The general had travelled overland to the Yugoslavian capital for consultations in mid-May, and he spent three weeks doing the rounds politically and diplomatically. He made a number of important contacts at this time, including one that arose from a meeting with the Serbian-American congresswoman Helen Bentley. The following winter, Bentley would help to organize a series of paid speaking engagements for the general, during which he would be able to expand on theories and opinions he formed while in the Balkans. One of MacKenzie's most forceful opinions would grow out of his theory about the breadline massacre.

Radovan Karadzic and the rest of the Bosnian Serb leaders were soon insisting at every opportunity that the attack on the people in Vase Miskin did not come from a Serb mortar position in the hills but from a remote-controlled detonating device set off by someone inside the city, probably close by. A press release from the Milosevic government in Belgrade stated: "Attention should ... be directed to the behaviour of the casualties; some of them, although both their legs are torn off, are still conscious and watching what is happening around them."

Apparently, this was evidence of injury from a bomb rather than from a mortar attack, which, because it is airborne, causes more shrapnel wounds to the upper body. The fact that people had their arms blown off didn't seem to have registered with the Belgrade propagandists. The government press release also pointed out other "irregularities," stating as fact that the Bosnian TV camera crew had been tipped off in advance in order to be there for the photo opportunity.

According to the Serbian leadership, both in Bosnia and in Belgrade, the breadline massacre was planned and carried out by Bosnian Muslims and orchestrated to look as though the Serbs did it. Communiqués like these would regularly emerge after particularly hideous attacks that had the potential to direct international wrath towards the leadership in Pale or Belgrade. The Serbs would charge that the Muslims were bombing themselves. During Belgrade's ethnic war in Croatia, the Serbs made a similar accusation — that the Croats were bombing themselves.

The Serbian leaders would also claim, repeatedly, that there was no siege of Sarajevo and no war at all. The Bosnian conflict was only a struggle in which innocent Serbs were trying to defend themselves against the Muslim aggressors. On one occasion, Dr. Karadzic informed an international conference that it was actually a Muslim force, not his army, attacking Sarajevo. The wily Muslims were cleverly creating the illusion that Serbs were on the attack when it was clear to the psychiatrist-poet that the Serbs were the only true victims.

No self-serving denial or assertion, when dispensed with bold confidence, was too preposterous for people from the outside world. Though perhaps Dr. Karadzic was as surprised as anybody when some influential people believed them.

MacKenzie's diary entry sums up his take on the gory event outside the bakery on that awful Wednesday morning: "May 27. Disaster in Sarajevo. People lined up for bread [were] attacked, and at least seventeen killed. President claims it was a Serb mortar attack, Serbs claim it was a set-up using explosives. Our people tell us there are a number of things that didn't fit. The streets had been blocked off just before the incident. Once the crowd had been let in and had lined up, the media appeared but kept a distance. The attack took place and the media were immediately on the scene. The majority of people killed are alleged to be 'tame Serbs.' Who knows? The only thing for sure is that innocent people were killed."

"Tame Serbs" referred to people of Serbian background who held moderate political views and refused to participate in the ultra-nationalism of the Pale Gang. As time went by, the world would learn that there were a lot of these tame Serbs in Sarajevo.

No one from the international community went to investigate the site and reach an independent finding about what happened that morning. Had someone done so, the cause of the carnage would have been as clear as day. There were two craters caused by mortar shells in the pavement — identical to many others in the streets of Sarajevo. The observers would have discovered that moments before the two shells landed on the people in Vase Miskin, there was a similar explosion just a block away.

They would also have learned for themselves that the victims bore the obvious signs of shrapnel from a mortar attack, including wounds to the upper parts of their bodies. There is no evidence that the street had been blocked off; the reporters who arrived at the scene had been at another event in the neighbourhood, and had reacted to the explosions. But at the time, neither UNPROFOR nor any other outsider spoke to the survivors or to members of the television crew to see whether there was any foundation to the bizarre speculation that the Bosnians were blowing up their own people to win international sympathy.

From his vantage point in Belgrade, MacKenzie insisted he had no way of knowing which side bombed the breadline: all he knew was that it was very suspicious. He later wrote in his memoirs that the people on the ground told him all signs indicated it was *not* a mortar attack, and that there was no way of determining who was really responsible. As far as he was concerned, it didn't look good for the Bosnian government and was a setback in the Bosnians' attempts to claim the moral high ground in the conflict.

But who were his sources? Who were the people "on the ground"? The only UN personnel who were there say they never reported anything because they just didn't know. John Wilson was the senior military observer based in Sarajevo at the time. He says that undoubtedly someone from his team went down to have a look at the scene of the impact, but he had no qualified ballistic expert on staff to do even a cursory investigation. "You have to understand, at the time, before MacKenzie arrived [back from Belgrade with a peacekeeping force], there were very few of us in the city." Wilson also adds there was no one from the international observer ranks who was down in the streets that day and could have noted that the road had been blocked off before the incident or that the media had been tipped off. No one could have reported with any credibility that the bombing might have been done by the Bosnians. "We went down to have a look at where it landed, but that's about it," says Wilson. He says he has no opinion either way on culpability. He discussed the massacre with General Ratko Mladic, the new commander of the Serbian army, and "he told me in such a convincing way that he didn't do it that I tended to believe him." But he never filed a report to his UN superiors, including MacKenzie, and he doesn't believe anyone else did either.

That Mladic was a man of his word was something many UN soldiers believed during the war. They found him belligerent and often nasty, but they say he always did what he said he would do. In military terms, this represented a kind of integrity. He was a soldier's soldier. But outside the comradely ranks of the military, people will cite dozens of documented cases where Mladic lied. The most stunning example came close to the end of the war, in an event captured on TV. In the designated safe haven of Srebrenica, Mladic offered candy to children and announced over a loudspeaker that none of the civilians who had taken refuge there would be hurt if they left peacefully and voluntarily. Mladic would subsequently be indicted on charges of genocide for directing the murder of seven thousand of those people at Srebrenica.

General MacKenzie says it wasn't the Serbs who told him that the Bosnians had bombed their own people; it was a conclusion he reached based on his own deductive reasoning. In MacKenzie's own account, "Whenever there was an incident I would say to myself, 'Who benefits from this?' And the first one of these would have been the breadline massacre. 'What advantage was there for the Serbs in that operation?' And I couldn't come up with any reason except to kill a lot of people of which paradoxically a number were Serbs in the breadline. 'What advantage was there for the Bosnian government?' A number of them."

The Serbs were thrilled to find such a sympathetic interpretation in such an influential place. Biljana Plavsic, the only member of the original Bosnian Serb leadership who is neither dead nor wanted for war crimes, fondly remembers the willingness of MacKenzie to at least question who was to blame. She told UNPROFOR what she had heard: that someone had gone door to door that morning and told only the Serbs there would be bread in order to lure them out. The Muslims in the neighbourhood knew about the conspiracy, as did the reporters, who were part of the planning, and they stayed away, she claims.

Sulejman Hebib says this account would be laughable if it were not so tragically false. No one ever came to ask him questions about the day, though he was a primary witness. Instead of speaking with people like him, the UN formed its own independent theories and, through innuendo and off-the-record remarks, began to propagate the Karadzic/Mladic line.

It fell to an American reporter, Tom Gjelten, to reconstruct the event a year later when he was preparing a story for *The New Republic*. He visited the site of the massacre with a Dutch crater-analysis expert, who concluded that the damage could only have been caused by shells and not a ground explosion. He also said that marks on the walls beside the mortar splats were typical of damage caused by a shrapnel spray.

Why was it so important to UNPROFOR to cast doubt on the Bosnians' character? The most common theory is that it was a perverse result of the United Nations peacekeepers' need to stay neutral, no matter what was going on around them. MacKenzie and UNPROFOR had to acquire a level playing field in Bosnia, and principally in Sarajevo, to maintain good relations with both sides. Peacekeepers argue that they must strike this balance to be in a position to negotiate with everybody, but that's difficult if one side is overwhelmingly more belligerent than the other, which was the case with the Serb side in Bosnia.

The business of making the good side of a conflict look bad in order to cast the bad side in a better light (or at least give an aggressor the benefit of the doubt) is called moral equivalency. It isn't official policy, but it is such a widespread practice that critics of the United Nations point to it as evidence that the organization is morally bankrupt.

Moral equivalency allows peacekeepers to pretend that they are dealing with two equal sides in a conflict, not with aggressors and victims. Their only task is to keep them apart and help them reconcile differences. In Rwanda and Yugoslavia there were two armies in conflict, but one side was also terrorizing the civilian population in a parallel campaign that was inseparable from the overall military project. The United Nations peacekeeping office had developed no plan for what to do in such cases.

For his part, MacKenzie says his position on the breadline massacre had absolutely nothing to do with any UN doctrine of moral equivalency. He says he genuinely suspected the Bosnian government could do something like that: "I would if I were in their position."

According to interviews and his own writing, the general became convinced, even before he had a mandate in Bosnia, that if President Alija Izetbegovic sat down with the Serbian republic's president, Radovan Karadzic, and negotiated, they could end this war, establishing a zone of separation, and the United Nations could come into Bosnia with a peace-keeping force. Without such an understanding, there was nothing that the international community could do.

MacKenzie didn't know that the two Bosnian leaders had spent a great deal of time negotiating these points long before UNPROFOR arrived on the scene. But the leaders had found no point of compromise. Karadzic had declared that Serbs could not live with the Turkish aggressors, that the ethnic groups of Sarajevo could never co-exist, that an independent state of Bosnia would be stillborn and that there would be blood in the streets.

Izetbegovic had a pretty good idea where he stood. He was the consti-tutional head of a state that lacked the military muscle to survive in the face of an aggressive campaign of destruction. His only hope was for interven-tion by the international sponsors of law and order—the United Nations. In the first two months of war, April and May of 1992, the Bosnian Serbs had consolidated most of the territory they wanted in the countryside sur-rounding Sarajevo. All they needed for victory was to subdue the city and make it the capital of their rogue state.

In such circumstances, the Serbs were more than willing to negotiate. The Bosnians were not. In their view, the Pale Gang had hijacked a legally constituted nation. Izetbegovic wanted his country back. Bosnia was a state that had been recognized by the international community, and he didn't think he should have to make deals with a terrorist group backed up by a foreign government.

But UN personnel say there was another significant factor in the polit-ical equation: MacKenzie came to distrust the Bosnian Presidency. Senior officers at the time say that Izetbegovic and his right-hand man, Ganic, were considered the problem. "We hated the Presidency and we saluted General Mladic," admits one senior officer who served with MacKenzie.

The JNA and the Bosnian Serb paramilitaries blamed UNPROFOR, and MacKenzie specifically, for the humiliating experience of being captured by the Bosnian army and the deaths of the soldiers in the convoy. MacKenzie knew he had lost face with the Serbs, and he recounts in his book, in a tone of great discouragement, that after the incident his rela-tionship with the Serbs was at an all-time low. But it wouldn't stay low for long. It was Belgrade that had agreed to let the peacekeepers into the region. The United Nations was beholden to the Serbs, and the Serbs were not going to let MacKenzie forget that. The imperatives of *realpolitik* meant that the UN had to play by the rules of Belgrade and with the friends of Belgrade.

Shortly after the breadline massacre, a group of children visiting a gravesite were killed; the international observers in Sarajevo said the killings appeared to have been the result of a bomb, rather than artillery or a mortar shell. UNPROFOR couldn't prove it: the incident just looked suspicious.

A year later, a mortar attack on a makeshift school in west Sarajevo killed several children and their teacher. According to reports, the mortar round destroyed the building, "spraying their remains all over the walls of the classroom." UNPROFOR took the position that the shell could have come from either side. An exasperated Izetbegovic speculated that if the Serbs killed him, UNPROFOR would find a way to call it suicide. He eventually refused to answer interview questions about charges that members of his military were killing his own citizens for tactical reasons.

However, on one occasion well into the war, he rhetorically asked a reporter to explain why, if he was really bombing his own people, he would continue to do so for such a long time when the tactic clearly wasn't making much of an impression on the international community. Sarcasm, Izetbegovic discovered, was as futile as everything else.

To this day, Sulejman Hebib lives in the rubble of Sarajevo — literally. His Ragusa restaurant displays fragments of buildings and statuary blown up during the war. There's a bit of ceramic from the ornate, rococo library, a marble horse's head from the cemetery. And behind the door there's a wanted poster from the international criminal tribunal featuring mug shots of all the men indicted for crimes in Yugoslavia, including Mladic and Karadzic, who are charged with the crime of destroying Sarajevo. Hebib declares that the UN's chief peacekeeper in Sarajevo, Major General Lewis MacKenzie, was as responsible as any of them.

Just steps from the restaurant, on Vase Miskin, one can clearly see the imprints of the two mortar rounds that landed on the pavement there, and beside them a plaque dedicated to the people killed and wounded while waiting for bread on May 27, 1992.

6

A TIME FOR APPEASEMENT AND A TIME FOR WAR

*The dons of the political world had, with winks and nods and euphemisms,
put out a contract on Bosnia. The dons who, in political parlance,
are called presidents and prime ministers do not carry out the dirty work
themselves, and they deny being involved in it, or having ordered it,
and in fact they would argue that they would never consider
doing anything of the sort because it would be wrong, they would
never appease or reward aggression.*
—Peter Maas, *Love Thy Neighbor*

By May, the European Community monitors, led by Colm Doyle, were finding their positions becoming more and more untenable. The EC had taken a principled position on the conflict and had refused to include Radovan Karadzic or the Pale Gang in a marathon week-long peace negotiation held just after the kidnapping incident. But such principles did nothing to help the monitors on the front lines, who had become an endangered species. They were frequently targeted for attacks by the Serb militias and one German monitor had to be spirited out of the country for his own protection. The EC finally ordered all the monitors out of Bosnia before dawn on May 12.

That left Lewis MacKenzie and his UNPROFOR colleagues as the chief go-betweens in the Bosnian conflict. MacKenzie welcomed this opportunity to plunge into the dark waters of Balkan politics.

Before leaving for Belgrade on May 17 to help reorganize the Balkan mission, MacKenzie had made it clear that UNPROFOR would work only if both sides were at the table, and so his first order of business was to reinstate the Serbs in the negotiations. MacKenzie believed that Biljana Plavsic had the ear of Radovan Karadzic, and best of all, she still lived in Sarajevo, not Pale. He invited her to participate in the process.

Plavsic is like a character from a Wagner opera, a kind of Brunnhilde without breastplates. Blonde, plump and matronly in tailored suits and trim blouses, she looks pleasant enough — until she pronounces on the importance of Serbian purity and the quest for the Promised Land. She is probably the only Bosnian Serb leader who really believed in the odious vision of Greater Serbia. Her counterparts in the Pale Gang were, for the most part, opportunists for whom ideology offered a fast track to the spoils of the black market. Bosnians had got their first glimpse behind the mask of the Rhine Maiden when she showed up to review the paramilitary carnage in northeast Bosnia in early April 1992 and warmly planted a kiss on Arkan's cheek in gratitude for his superb job of ethnically cleansing the region.

Plavsic developed an early friendship with Lewis MacKenzie that she cherishes to this day. Shortly after publication of his book, the general sent her an autographed copy, which she counts among her prized possessions. She regarded MacKenzie, as others in the Bosnian Serb leadership did, as a man who truly understood them.

There was one small difficulty for Plavsic in taking up MacKenzie's invitation to join the peacemaking negotiations. Yes, she was living in Sarajevo, but she was staying in her mother's apartment in the Serb-dominated borough of Ilidza, and she could not leave the old woman alone for any length of time. If UNPROFOR could escort her brother from his apartment in central Sarajevo to stay with her mother in Ilidza, then she would have more freedom to attend the meetings.

MacKenzie was uncomfortable with the idea, since it would appear to be favouritism and there was already enough suspicion of pro-Serb bias on his part. He declined. But UNPROFOR did agree to escort Plavsic herself to the meetings, and she gratefully recalls how the peacekeepers would arrive to pick her up with food for her mother. None of this went unnoticed by Sarajevans, who wondered just what the UN was trying to prove. A number of high-profile Serbs were petitioning the UN to move Plavsic and her family out of Sarajevo to Pale, the de facto headquarters for the Serb faction. John Wilson, who was put in charge of this operation, says he was under enormous pressure: "I had calls from all kinds of people from the pretender to the Yugoslavian throne on down, saying you have to get her mother out." Plavsic even threatened Wilson: "She told me, 'You know I can be very kind or very cruel to the UN.'" Satish Nambiar, the force commander for the whole UNPROFOR mission, eventually relented and ordered his soldiers in Sarajevo to help.

It would prove to be a costly misstep. Wilson regards it as one of the biggest mistakes of his life — and an important learning experience. Ever since, he says, "It doesn't matter when someone else tells me to do something. If I feel bad about something or it doesn't seem right, I'll never do it again."

UNPROFOR launched this operation to move the Plavsic family just days after the breadline massacre. The aged mother had to be carried seventeen storeys down to the waiting armoured vehicle (the elevator did not work). Two vehicles transported Plavsic, her mother and their belongings to her brother's apartment building near the hospital, where he and his family were waiting with their luggage and some furniture.

Wilson is certain the Bosnians intercepted a phone call from Nambiar approving the relocation, because there was a large crowd of civilians and Bosnian military waiting for them at the brother's apartment. They surrounded the car in which Plavsic was riding and forced it to drive on to the Presidency building. Izetbegovic was away, and the eager Ejup Ganic saw an opportunity to grab an important hostage. Ganic ordered his forces to bring Plavsic inside the building, but the peacekeepers wouldn't let her go. Plavsic remembers the day with terror. The French UN driver kept radio contact with all the parties and tried to negotiate her release; she, meanwhile, pulled out her rosary and held the hand of her French escort, the rosary pressed between their palms. And so they sat for several hours, until Plavsic was finally allowed to leave.

The incident caused an uproar in Sarajevo. The public was furious that a woman of Plavsic's reputation should have an escort when innocent people were being killed on the streets daily. MacKenzie argued that moving Plavsic was part of the peace process and an appropriate expenditure of UN resources, though he said that he himself had refused to move the family only weeks earlier and was in Belgrade when Wilson got the order. MacKenzie, however, wasn't as far out of the loop as he might have appeared.

Plavsic gratefully remembers that it was MacKenzie, negotiating from Belgrade on the phone with the Bosnian Presidency, who engineered her release as she sat clutching the cross of her rosary so tightly that it left an imprint on her hands. People made obvious parallels. MacKenzie had done nothing to prevent the capture of the Bosnian president. Now he was going out of his way to help a minor Serbian leader. Whether or not the criticism was fair, Bosnians gave UNPROFOR a new nickname: the Chetnik taxi service ("Chetnik" was the resurrected—and derogatory—label for a Serb nationalist, a throwback to the Second World War).

By the first of June, tension between the international community and the citizens of Sarajevo was close to the boiling point. UN representatives, including MacKenzie, persisted in referring to the people of Bosnia as Muslims when they were actually dealing with people of many ethnic backgrounds. Croats had authority over many of the military operations, Serb officers helped to command the Territorial Defence Force and there were 100,000 people of Serbian heritage living in the city. As multicultural Sarajevans, most wanted the world to know that they were united against the vile ultra-nationalists.

Moving Plavsic out of Sarajevo under UN guard seemed to be tacit acceptance by UNPROFOR of Karadzic's assertion that Serbs could not safely live in the city. It was a grim indication that the international community didn't understand the fundamental issue in the dispute—that this was a war about ideology as much as it was about territory.

Plavsic would later complete her relocation by secretly arranging for a Red Cross ambulance to remove her family members from Sarajevo to Pale. The project was relatively straightforward, since the Red Cross in Pale was run by none other than Radovan Karadzic's wife. Karadzic, however, soon got tired of his Brunnhilde and shut her out of the little rump government. She retreated to Belgrade, where she took over relations with the Bosnian Serb diaspora, aided by that Serbian-American congresswoman, Helen Bentley.

As the weeks of war stretched to a month, then two, the international community was becoming more squeamish about the goings-on. Sarajevo was almost completely out of food. *Oslobodjenje*'s deputy editor, Gordana Knezevic, whose youngest children were safe abroad, remembers her first occasions of real hunger: "I would be somewhere in the city working and I would start to get hungry. There was no food to buy, no restaurants, so I would begin to wonder if I knew anyone in that neighbourhood that might feed me. It was an odd sensation to really not know when you could eat again." The prospect of starvation in a modern European city was enough to provoke even the indecisive international community to turn up the heat.

In the first week of June 1992, the United Nations had brokered what seemed to be a breakthrough deal between the Presidency and the radical Bosnian Serbs. The no-nonsense Wilson and an Irish diplomat named Cedric Thornberry managed to persuade both sides to sign a document that would lead to the withdrawal of all heavy guns from the airport and allow UNPROFOR to take charge of the facility.

Karadzic put up a brave show of resistance, claiming that while Belgrade's JNA had controlled the airport since before war began, many of his soldiers had defended the territory around the airport with their lives and their blood. Serb blood made it Serb territory, and compromise wouldn't come easily.

His posturing obscured the reality that the deal was really of primary benefit to Karadzic and General Ratko Mladic. They were turning the airport over to the UN, but by keeping control of the area around the airport, they would be in a position to benefit more than anybody from the arrival of food and medical supplies.

The Bosnian president, on the other hand, suffered a major setback because of the deal. Izetbegovic had strenuously resisted signing any document that recognized the existence of a Serbian republic and the legitimacy of its leadership. He refused to attend meetings with Karadzic, claiming the doctor and his army were illegally occupying territory in Bosnia and murdering his people. He foresaw, quite accurately as it turned out, that once Karadzic was recognized as an official player in the negotiations about Bosnia's future, his case for a Bosnian Serb republic would achieve political legitimacy. The president's stubborn refusal to deal with Karadzic drove Lewis MacKenzie to distraction. But Izetbegovic stood by his claim that he was the leader of a sovereign country under attack by a rogue faction, and that his enemies were sponsored by a foreign power — Yugoslavia. Many European leaders agreed with him and insisted that they should be negotiating with Slobodan Milosevic or Mladic, the chief of the Yugoslav army in Bosnia, not Karadzic.

Wilson and Thornberry, however, were bent on opening the Sarajevo airport and starting a flow of humanitarian relief into the country. They warned Izetbegovic that the deaths of thousands, indeed millions, might be on his shoulders if he refused to deal with the people who were trying to destroy his country. The devout Muslim was stubborn, but such warnings plagued his conscience. Vice-President Ganic proposed that in exchange for their opening the airport, all the guns should be withdrawn from the city to a distance of twenty kilometres, which would effectively end the siege of Sarajevo. The Serbs had most of the guns, and so, predictably, they resisted.

Cedric Thornberry asked Izetbegovic to consider separating the two issues. Opening the airport would be phase one of the negotiations and withdrawing the guns would be phase two. With extreme reluctance, the Bosnian president agreed. He might have anticipated that there would never be a phase two, that once the main objective was achieved, the secondary concern (silencing the guns around Sarajevo) would be shoved to the back burner, if it even stayed on the stove. He was about to learn yet another lesson in *realpolitik*: any agreement that by itself brings an end to an immediate crisis will be deemed sufficient by the people in charge of the deal-making. Issues of less urgency will be deferred. With the airport agreement in hand, the UN and the EC observers basically had what they wanted. In months to come, when Ganic and Izetbegovic reminded observers of the pledge for phase two—a daily life-and-death concern for the people of Sarajevo—they were accused of obstructing the peace process.

The airport agreement brokered by the United Nations is among the most ambitious and important achievements of the war. It allowed brave pilots, aid workers and peacekeepers to bring crucial relief supplies into the country. But it was also seriously flawed from a strategic and political point of view, and would eventually be revealed as one of the most cynical exercises in expediency in the Bosnian tragedy.

Izetbegovic had signed a document, agreeing to withdraw his heavy guns from the airport and to cease armed conflict nearby. *His* heavy guns? What heavy guns? His heavy guns amounted to a handful of mortar launchers, three tanks and an assortment of machine guns. The president's critics in the city argued that by agreeing to remove something he didn't have, Izetbegovic played into the hands of those who insisted on treating the conflict as a civil war when it was really an aggressive external attack on a sovereign country.

The Bosnian government never recovered from this loss of principle. For the rest of the war, it would be treated as one side of a conflict between parties of equal legitimacy and strength. From a strategic point of view, the situation was even more serious. The Serbs had agreed to point their thousands of artillery pieces, tanks and heavy guns away from the airport, but not to move them away from the city. In fact, the Serbs would continue to fire on or near the airport any time they thought they could get away with it. And they would continue to maintain a military chokehold on the suffering city.

John Wilson had demanded that the international community be allowed a safe access corridor in and out of the city. But somehow the Serbs managed to establish a checkpoint even there, and thus were able to control the flow of supplies and people. In case anyone doubted who owned the road, a popular Bosnian politician was murdered at that checkpoint while sitting in a French armoured personnel carrier.

A high proportion of the goods entering Sarajevo went straight to the Bosnian Serb army, and there was nothing aid organizations could do about it. Once the supplies were inside the besieged city, it was the turn of the Bosnian army to pick through them for what they needed. Civilians came last.

Through it all, UNPROFOR found the Serbs mostly co-operative and predictable. As long as the foreigners didn't interfere with the siege and didn't obstruct any part of the Serb military operation, aid workers could bring food and medicine into the country and UNPROFOR could replenish its supplies.

John Wilson says this is not surprising, because the airport agreement was never designed to affect the Serbian military operations. "There was always the concession to the Serbs that they would turn over the airport and reduce the threat to the airport, but it would not affect their ability to continue with the siege." That was part of the deal.

Among the peacekeeping nations there was a lot of jockeying to see who was going to take charge of the airport and this new mission, perceived as an international success story. It would be a neat, self-contained and high-profile assignment for whoever got it. Lewis MacKenzie makes it clear in *Peacekeeper* that he was fairly salivating for the assignment and went so far as to dupe his own UN commander into appointing him head of the mission.

By his own account, MacKenzie had been up all night planning his strategy. First, he had to persuade Satish Nambiar that the Canadian troops already stationed in the Croatian UN protection areas were the best suited and situated for the job. He argued plausibly that predictable UN foot-dragging would delay the arrival of new personnel by months, and that in that time the momentum of the airport agreement would be lost. As the

Balkan mission's chief of staff, MacKenzie knew that the Royal Canadian Regiment and the Royal 22nd Regiment—then based in Sector West of Zagreb—had the lightest workload of all the battalions in the area and, thanks to his bending of the peacekeeping rules, were the best equipped. Nambiar agreed that it made sense to send in the Canadians.

Then came the hard part: persuading Nambiar that MacKenzie should be appointed to lead the force. Nambiar wasn't sure that MacKenzie could be spared but, ever the wily tactician, MacKenzie easily manoeuvred around that obstacle. He told Nambiar that Ottawa would never agree to send a Canadian battalion to Sarajevo unless it was led by a Canadian. There was no UN mandate to operate in Sarajevo, argued MacKenzie, and because of that: "There's not a country in the world that would send troops [in those conditions]. But if you send me as the commander, there's a very good chance we can get approval. I don't think Canada will do it unless you send me." MacKenzie wanted to avoid the proposed deployment going before Parliament, where it would be delayed and perhaps even scuttled. It was, after all, probably the most dangerous mission Canadian soldiers had faced since the Korean War.

Nambiar was sceptical and he told MacKenzie to call Ottawa to verify this. MacKenzie went into his office, closed the door behind him, put his feet up on his desk and smoked a cigarette. Then he went out and told his boss that the Department of National Defence had taken exactly the position he'd anticipated: there would be no deal without Lewis MacKenzie. Nambiar's hands were tied and he agreed. MacKenzie was going back to Sarajevo, and the Canadians would go with him.

7

THE AIRPORT IS OPEN – THE CITY IS CLOSED

It never ceases to amaze me that the people you were helping
wanted you dead.
—Lewis MacKenzie,
Peacekeeper: The Road to Sarajevo

The highway that runs beside the airport and heads out into the mountains is an endless strip of greasy auto-repair shops and dull little coffee bars. There are still rows of shattered apartment buildings that have, somehow, missed out on the reconstruction funds. Salem Mujezinovic sits comfortably in a rattan deck chair amidst the grime of his mechanics shop on the side of the highway. His place is identified only by a handmade sign on plywood. But his reputation as a Class A mechanic is widely known, and these days his modest shop attracts a steady stream of customers. They are usually men in dark sunglasses with brand new Audis and Mercedes-Benzes. People with expensive cars in Bosnia usually work for the underworld or the foreign community, but Mujezinovic doesn't care. He pulls his wiry frame out of his deck chair, peers under the hood and knows immediately what's wrong.

Many of the tough-looking characters who drop by are not just looking for a good mechanic. Curiosity is another factor. And admiration. Mujezinovic is one of the heroes of Bosnia's war.

While his two assistants finish work on the car he's been repairing, Mujezinovic folds himself back into the chair, pours a glass of Sprite and lights up yet another cheap cigarette. He is a long, lanky man with a bristle of salt-and-pepper hair and shockingly intense blue eyes. His gaze is so severe you assume it has to be from some deep trauma or grief. Then his two brothers show up, and they have the same startling expression. They laugh when the resemblance is pointed out: their eyes come from their mother.

There was another brother; his name was Ejub. He was killed at the age of thirty-eight, attempting to escape from the besieged city of Sarajevo. The only relatively sure route was across the airport runway and out toward nearby Mount Igman, one of the few Bosnian strongholds in the country. Yes, the peacekeepers controlled the airport, but with that responsibility came the unwelcome task of enforcing the agreement under which the Serb forces allowed it to operate. The airport was not to be used as an escape route for Sarajevans. And so the peacekeepers trained powerful lights on the runway. The Serbian snipers did the rest. They shot fleeing Sarajevans like deer caught in a car's headlights. Ejub Mujezinovic was one of them.

Since the airport agreement effectively made flight an act of war, the UNPROFOR officers felt they had no alternative but to work with the Serbs to catch refugees from Sarajevo. UN soldiers patrolled the airport perimeter and the runway. Most of the escapees they simply dragged back to the Sarajevo side where they often confiscated any food or goods returning Sarajevans were carrying. But David Rieff learned that military vehicles once ran over some people who were lying on the Tarmac waiting for a chance to flee. Radio reports gave the death count of those who failed the airport road crossing much in the way that pop radio stations in the West update traffic reports. The Bosnian authorities rarely complained about this: they, too, wanted the Sarajevan people to stay in the city in order to help defend it.

The surviving Mujezinovic brothers walk with a variety of limps from their war wounds. Theirs is the story of Bosnia's military reservists, a citizens' army fighting with Kalashnikov rifles and very little training against an army equipped with tanks, heavy artillery and a mountain of ammunition. The Bosnian soldiers in their Sarajevo trenches often found themselves sharing a gun and down to the last round of ammunition. Salem Mujezinovic was a commander, though there were no fancy uniforms, paycheques or citations for exceptional service, only the dubious distinction of being the one responsible for telling a wife or a mother that another poorly trained fighter had been killed.

Ninety metres from where Mujezinovic now repairs cars, there's a nondescript house that once provided a doorway to freedom and hope for those trapped in Sarajevo. After a year of siege, as people were starving to death, Salem Mujezinovic and his company were ordered to dig a tunnel from the basement of this house, tucked away in the suburb of Dobrinja, to the other side of the airport runway and the village of Butmir, at the foot of Mount Igman.

The Dobrinja-Butmir tunnel's alleged purpose was to supply the Bosnian army but its function quickly expanded. The line between military and citizen was so blurred—as was the line between the criminal and the law-abiding elements within the army—that the tunnel was often "rented" for private use. Through its narrow, dangerous passageway, people would drag boxes and bags of food and supplies to be sold in the city. The UN claimed to know nothing about it (Sarajevans came to call it "the non-existent tunnel") and it also became the route for Izetbegovic to travel when he needed to visit other parts of the country (his aides would trundle the frail man through the tunnel in a wheelbarrow).

When commercial operators came to get as much, if not more, use out of it than the army, the tunnel's managers were accused of smuggling, but the black market by then was the only functioning market in Sarajevo. With the exception of the starvation rations that aid organizations managed to get past the checkpoints, just about everything else came through the passage. Prices were fixed by the criminal cabals that arranged most of the smuggling. In any case, it was that long, black, dirty hole that made it possible for people in the city to survive. And it also provided a safer flight path than the deadly surface route, under the peacekeepers' lights (the Bosnian army later dug a second tunnel passage).

The Mujezinovic brothers can hardly contain their rage, even today, when they're asked about UNPROFOR. They don't entirely blame the peacekeepers for what happened to their brother. Like most people of Sarajevo and its suburbs, they admit that they needed the United Nations' intervention and the humanitarian aid that UNPROFOR helped to get into the country. They loathe General MacKenzie not because he was the worst (MacKenzie was not in charge when Ejub was killed) but because he was the first, and he was the commander who established the rules. The bizarre symbiotic relationship that developed between the Serbian army and the blue helmets is beyond their comprehension.

Back in June 1992, as UNPROFOR was preparing to open the airport, the Serbs realized that they would have to strengthen their control of the suburbs that ring the city. Obviously a key objective would be the suburb of Dobrinja, which was right beside the airport.

Bosnian forces, including the Mujezinovic brothers (all of them alive at the time), put up a fierce resistance, but the Serbian guns pounded Dobrinja for days. A steady procession of ambulances took civilian and military casualties to hospital.

This combat zone lay directly in Lewis MacKenzie's path as he made the difficult overland trek back from Belgrade to Sarajevo to take up his new mission. The only passable road at the time took travellers through Pale and down the mountain towards the airport. With the battle for Dobrinja raging, the MacKenzie party couldn't get past the airport and decided to bunk in for the night at the nearby Lukavica barracks. For this, MacKenzie got a quick reaction from the Bosnian Presidency, a warning that if UNPROFOR stayed in Lukavica, it would be considered to be consorting with the Serb enemy and would be bombed. Go ahead and bomb, MacKenzie replied, and I'll move into the basement. He told the Bosnians that as far as he was concerned, their mortars were the ones making it impossible for him to get all the way into town. Nobody bombed him, but it was a graphic reminder to the general of what life was like in Sarajevo.

MacKenzie had originally planned to return by helicopter, and the JNA had arranged for the flight. Warnings went out to the Bosnian forces not to shoot at the aircraft carrying the chief of UNPROFOR, and they agreed. At the last moment, however, the Serbs told MacKenzie the weather made it unsafe to fly, and the general started his journey by road. No one told the Bosnians of the change of plans. That afternoon, Serb helicopters took advantage of the confusion to conduct a serious bombing raid on Bosnian positions. MacKenzie blames the Bosnians for not letting him into the city, but the Bosnians had been fooled once that day and were in no mood to trust anybody.

After a meeting with Biljana Plavsic the next morning, MacKenzie made his way into Sarajevo. He met with Ganic, who told him the airport could not open until the Serbs agreed to move their guns twenty kilometres away from the city. That was the deal, according to phase two.

But that wasn't the deal that MacKenzie had come to enforce. He was interested only in phase one—getting the airport back in service—and he immediately determined where he was going to have problems. His memos back to UN headquarters reported examples of Bosnian intransigence and Serb co-operation. At the time, there was no Department of

Peacekeeping Operations as Dallaire would know it; MacKenzie sent most of his missives directly to New York and later, when New York began to have problems with MacKenzie, he sent them through Satish Nambiar.

Now back in his old office at UNPROFOR HQ, MacKenzie started to keep score of the death threats he got on a whiteboard behind his desk, marking it each time someone from either side of the conflict called to say they wanted him dead. The most telling message he received wasn't a death threat, however, but a simple letter of rebuke from a group of people living in Dobrinja: "General MacKenzie, we want you to know that we, citizens of Dobrinja, residential area of Sarajevo, will start collecting signatures of our fellow citizens on a document which will bring you to court."

The letter went on to say that in the eyes of the people, the general should be prosecuted as a war criminal for bringing this assault on their suburb. The letter might not have been entirely accurate or fair, but it is important because it reflects the overall sentiments of many people in Sarajevo. "Dobrinja is being constantly shelled and bombed by the Serbian heavy artillery and tanks.... However, knowing you very well now, we're inclined to believe you will now make a statement in which you will say 'both sides are responsible.'...

"Thousands of signatures on that document including [those of] our Serbian neighbors, will confirm that this is not an 'ethnic war' as you're trying to put it all the time, giving the Serbian side more room to continue killing civilians and destroying our homes." The letter concludes with what would become an enduring grievance among Sarajevans: "We are very disappointed that a person like you ever came to our city...."

And yet the overall attitude towards the peacekeepers wasn't at all negative. When the Canadian battle group that was to run the airport finally arrived on July 2, Sarajevans cheered. Canadian soldiers were highly regarded—even Ganic declared them to be among the most professional of the UNPROFOR troops. And Stjepan Kljuic, the Croat member of the Presidency, declared the Canadians the best in Sarajevo. In the early days of the war, two of them became the most celebrated of peacekeepers—Captain Guy Belisle and Sergeant Mario Forest pulled some women to safety under deadly sniper fire. The people of Sarajevo had a problem with only one Canadian peacekeeper—MacKenzie.

He decided that this was a public-relations problem that could be fixed if the Bosnian Presidency would act to improve his image. Izetbegovic and others had been openly complaining in the local media about what they believed was clear evidence of partiality by MacKenzie. The general threat-ened to tell New York that Izetbegovic was the real problem and that finally pushed the Bosnian president to do some PR. Izetbegovic delivered a glowing series of accounts to the press about the fine work of the UNPROFOR chief. But his effort did nothing to improve the general's image, and MacKenzie continued to blame Izetbegovic for deliberately prolong-ing the war.

Kemal Kurspahic, the editor of *Oslobodjenje*, was alarmed by the hos-tility towards the Canadian general. Whatever the flaws in the UN mission, the men in the blue helmets were the last thin line of protection from the Serbian extremists. Kurspahic was no fan of MacKenzie, but he recognized that the city needed UNPROFOR and couldn't afford this bad relationship. He sent his most trusted reporter, Gordana Knezevic, to interview the general with instructions to go easy on him. But going easy on him wasn't as easy as they anticipated.

MacKenzie was perhaps the most interviewed person in the Balkans. But it turned out that his openness was limited to the foreign press. It took Knezevic days to get an appointment with the man who had become famous for giving interviews on the spot. The general was being wary: he wasn't sure if this was an ambush.

She finally booked an early-evening interview at UNPROFOR head-quarters. MacKenzie and his staff worked out of a big concrete building, formerly a communications centre, located on the notorious Snipers' Alley. The *Oslobodjenje* offices had once been directly across from head-quarters, but the newspaper's building was blown to smithereens in the early weeks of war. Most of the editorial staff had decamped downtown. Without an armoured vehicle, it was a treacherous journey to the general's office, especially late in the day. And Knezevic had another problem: local reporters didn't have the same access to fuel that foreign reporters did. The car had only enough gas to get her there, not back. She went anyway.

Travelling with a man from the newspaper who would take photo-graphs, Knezevic arrived at MacKenzie's office with a series of questions designed to put him in the best light possible. She had decided in advance not to challenge him on any subject, and to publish the interview, un-edited, as a series of questions and answers. She found MacKenzie cool but co-operative, and at the end of the interview, she raised a subject that was of enormous concern to the struggling newspaper—the availability of newsprint. She asked if UNPROFOR would allow the import of newsprint on relief flights to Sarajevo. The answer was no. MacKenzie told Knezevic he couldn't be seen to be helping one side of the conflict.

She was shocked. Knezevic had never considered herself or *Oslobodjenje* as being a "side" in the conflict. The newspaper had been highly critical of all the nationalists in Bosnia—whether they were for Karadzic or Izetbegovic. In fact, Kemal Kurspahic was so critical of Bosnian Muslim extremists and the foibles of the Presidency that he was amazed that Izetbegovic had not shut down his presses long ago. The Bosnians could have easily declared a state of emergency and censored all media, but this had not happened.

The paper had also gone out of its way to maintain an ethnic mix among the employees. Knezevic herself is Serb, and the photographer with her, Elvedin Kantardzic, a Muslim. As the only newspaper still printing regularly, *Oslobodjenje* was a crucial source of communication in a city that no longer had a functioning telephone system, and it had become a vital source of information on everything from food to hospitals.

MacKenzie couldn't be persuaded. He went by the UN list of what was considered humanitarian aid, and newsprint wasn't on it. So Knezevic made another request she was sure he couldn't refuse: Could UNPROFOR provide her with enough fuel to get back to her office? It was getting late, and they had passed several corpses on the way. Again, MacKenzie said no. He couldn't help one side of the conflict. No gas.

Knezevic was feeling desperate and tried her plea once more. At the door she asked one of MacKenzie's senior officers, a Palestinian, if he could spare some fuel, but she got the same chilly response. Using Arabic expletives that she'd learned as a foreign correspondent in Egypt, she told the Palestinian what she thought of him before she left. But it didn't help her get back to town. Predictably, the car ran out of gas, and she and her photographer were forced to hide out overnight in the ruins of the nearby TV building. Their bosses and families didn't have a clue where they were, or that they were safe, until the next day.

To Knezevic's surprise, she subsequently had a phone call from the Palestinian officer. He wanted to apologize. And he also realized that it might be appropriate for him to come downtown and actually meet some of the people of Sarajevo. It was the first such gesture from UNPROFOR, and it broke the ice: there followed a number of important encounters between citizens and officers who wanted to know more about the people they were trying to help. But the one person who remained conspicuously absent from this genuine and useful exercise in "public relations" was the Canadian general who was in charge of the whole show.

UNPROFOR's relationship with *Oslobodjenje* eventually became friendly. A Belgian lieutenant general, Francis Briquemont, who later took over MacKenzie's post, immediately arranged to have newsprint classified as humanitarian aid and included on the relief flights. When the reporter Knezevic went out to interview him, once again low on gas, Briquemont not only procured two cans of petrol for her but brought it to the car himself.

After MacKenzie was gone and the regime had changed, whenever the electricity grid was down, which happened often, UNPROFOR would supply gas for the generators so that the presses could roll through the night and the daily newspaper could make its deadline. "I would phone the UN," recalls Knezevic, "and very often it was [Canadian lieutenant colonel] Barry Frewer who would go in the middle of the night himself to get the gasoline for the generator." It wasn't just the newspaper—the bakery and the hospitals got the same treatment. And it wasn't a one-way relationship: when special envoys or visiting VIPs came to Sarajevo, UNPROFOR would call *Oslobodjenje* and ask on very short notice if it could arrange a tour of what had become an international *cause célèbre*—the newspaper that defied the war. The printing presses functioned in the basement bunker of the demolished building and never missed an edition. Throughout the war, *Oslobodjenje* gleaned countless international awards and won tens of thousands in prize money for its perseverance in the face of adversity.

But all of that was under subsequent commanders. "For MacKenzie it was an aboriginal operation and he was not interested," says Knezevic, still angry to this day.

Eventually, as the Serbs tightened the knot of control around Sarajevo and throughout Bosnia, a lot of UNPROFOR personnel would come to realize they were being had. But in these early months under MacKenzie, they were frequently being shot at and didn't know who was responsible. It was easy to believe that members of the disorderly, unruly Bosnian Defence Force were the most likely culprits, and in fact they *were* repeatedly caught in the act. Whatever their politics, the Serb soldiers could observe military discipline and follow orders. When they said they would do something, even if it was odious, they would do it. Not like the "Muslims."

MacKenzie never would define the conflict as an attack on an unde-fended civilian population. When it came to discussions about lifting the arms embargo, he insisted there were more than enough guns to go around. Discussing ethnically motivated atrocities, MacKenzie insisted there was more than enough blame to go around. MacKenzie's suspicions of the Bosnian government coloured the tone of his communiqués back to New York and to his boss, Satish Nambiar, the commander of UN forces in the former Yugoslavia, who supported and shared MacKenzie's views.

MacKenzie kept telling his masters that the real peacekeeping problem in Bosnia came not from the Serbs but the Bosnians. He could have put this in context: the Serbs had already gobbled up 70 per cent of the country by force and had ethnically cleansed the area. But this, to MacKenzie, was a side issue. The enemies of the peace process were Izetbegovic and Ganic. In one memo, MacKenzie asserts: "UNPROFOR is being subjected to a smear campaign by the presidency side, which is denied by their leadership, including the president [Izetbegovic] but is extremely effective. The attitude of the people of the presidency side is very negative, and there has been a number of incidents with our personnel being threatened in the performance of their duties." In another missive, he writes, "Indications in Sarajevo point to a desire by the presidency to perpetuate the current crisis. Most of the Serb guns are silent. However, they themselves are not entirely free from blame. The presidency on the other hand continues to initiate exchanges as they attempt to improve their tactical position."

MacKenzie and his civilian counterparts in Sarajevo arranged any number of ceasefires, which were almost immediately broken. As soon as the shooting stopped, the Serbs would attempt to move their heavy guns into better positions at the outskirts of the city. The Bosnians would shoot at them. They'd shoot back. MacKenzie would report to UN headquarters that it was almost always the Muslims who broke the ceasefire arrangements. They were unwilling to stop the war, MacKenzie declared, and didn't deserve the help they were getting. Another message to Nambiar says: "[The Presidency] is in fact perpetuating the current conflict while the Serbs are showing considerable restraint. I can only speak for Sarajevo."

While his relations with Izetbegovic and Ganic were becoming ever more tattered, he was getting along well with Radovan Karadzic and his sidekick, a Shakespeare scholar turned ultra-nationalist named Nicole Koljevic. They had a number of fruitful meetings with MacKenzie, and they actually listened when he told them to lay off their action in the suburb of Dobrinja. If they didn't, he said, he wouldn't be able to open the airport and they, the Serbs, would get the blame. They saw his point.

On the morning of June 28, President François Mitterand of France, in a daring display of Gallic chutzpah, decided to brave the shelling of Dobrinja and fly into Sarajevo airport. He initially wanted to arrive the night before, much to the horror of everyone on the ground. They persuaded him to wait for daylight, but nobody was in the dark about the importance of this visit.

This was to be a day of reckoning. The European Community wanted to believe that the entire Bosnia debacle could be solved by humanitarian airlifts. If Mitterand reached a different conclusion during the fact-finding mission, both the EC and the United Nations would have to go back to the drawing board and come up with a new strategy for the troubled region. MacKenzie and company nervously prepared for the president's arrival.

MacKenzie, recently promoted to the rank of major general by the defence department in Ottawa, wasn't going to miss an opportunity to share his analysis of the Bosnian situation with an influential world leader. He was the first to greet the president of France as he climbed down from his helicopter in the company of Bernard Kouchner, his humanitarian aid adviser.

Nobody knew exactly how long Mitterand would be in Sarajevo, since his chopper had taken some machine-gun fire as it descended and needed some repairs. MacKenzie asked for an hour of the president's time before he began his tour. At UNPROFOR HQ MacKenzie explained to Mitterand that it didn't really matter any more that the Serbs had started the war. They had their reasons, and in any case, it was now the intransigence of the Bosnians that was the big obstacle to peace. As he recalled it later, his spiel went something like this: "Izetbegovic has determined that this is a war of outside aggression controlled by Belgrade. Karadzic, on the other hand, insists it's a civil war." Now that the Serbs had captured most of what they wanted in the way of territory, "Izetbegovic wants the entire country back. Quite frankly, the only way he can get it back is by convincing the international community to intervene with massive military force, ridding him of his Serbian enemies."

MacKenzie explained to Mitterand that he had tried and failed to point out to Izetbegovic the folly of such a venture, and he asked the French president to use his own powers of persuasion to bring Izetbegovic round to UNPROFOR's way of seeing things.

MacKenzie says he told Mitterand that while it was true that the

Serbs, overall, bore most of the responsibility, "whenever we arrange any kind of ceasefire, it's usually the Muslims who break it first. In addition, there is strong but circumstantial evidence that some really horrifying acts of cruelty attributed to the Serbs were actually orchestrated by the Muslims against their own people, for the benefit of an international audience." What MacKenzie is referring to here can only be the bread-line massacre. At the time of Mitterand's visit, it was the only such incident that had been cited and the only one, of that early period, that MacKenzie had ever mentioned. The effect this had on Mitterand is not clear. According to MacKenzie, he responded to his speech with only a polite "*Merci.*"

Mitterand then announced his program for the day, which was principally to greet the French UNPROFOR soldiers in Sarajevo and then to meet the president of the country he was visiting: Alija Izetbegovic. MacKenzie was horrified to learn that Mitterand had no plans to visit Radovan Karadzic.

The Canadian general went into pitch mode again, insisting that Mitterand see the Bosnian Serb leader. It didn't seem to have registered with MacKenzie that the United Nations Security Council had just passed a resolution denouncing the Bosnian Serb leadership. He insisted that a courtesy call was crucial. Mitterand was doubtful, so MacKenzie played his best card: If the French president came to Bosnia, landing safely at the Sarajevo airport thanks to the goodwill of the Serbs, and then snubbed the Serb leadership, UNPROFOR and MacKenzie would almost certainly face reprisals for the diplomatic slight.

Kouchner suggested it was probably a good idea—for the sake of security, if nothing else—to have a brief moment with the man who was really in charge here—Dr. Karadzic. Mitterand finally agreed.

While the president of France went off to meet with Izetbegovic, MacKenzie got in touch with Koljevic, the Shakespeare professor, and they set up a meeting with Karadzic and Mladic, to take place later that day. After Mitterand visited Izetbegovic, he placed a flower at the site of the breadline massacre and went off to the airport. The president's executive jet had arrived to take him away since the helicopter was still being repaired.

On the Tarmac, surrounded by dozens of international reporters and TV cameras, Mitterand met with Karadzic and Mladic, along with Koljevic. The Serbs invited Mitterand to sit down for a longer talk, but the French president declined. It seemed that the meeting was over, a mere diplomatic formality. Then, as if on cue, a firefight broke out somewhere nearby and MacKenzie quickly escorted Mitterand into the safety of the terminal building.

This was the opportunity Karadzic needed. MacKenzie says he had expected such a ploy to trap Mitterand into participating in a full-fledged meeting. Karadzic briefed the French president on his theory that there was a Muslim fundamentalist threat on Europe's doorstep (this suggestion of "Islam at the Gate" would begin to have the desired effect on European leaders later in the Bosnian war). He asked if the French president agreed that it was reasonable for the Bosnian Serbs to want to have their own state. According to MacKenzie, Mitterand's reply was quick and firm: "Perhaps. But you are going about it the wrong way." He coolly shook hands with the Bosnian Serb leaders and went on his way.

In *Peacekeeper*, MacKenzie expressed his disappointment that the Serbs had not made a more effective impression on Mitterand: "The coherence usually evident in their argument was missing. If they were looking for a glimmer of understanding or sympathy from Mitterand they didn't get it." And he wonders why the Shakespeare scholar didn't make the case, because he was usually very persuasive: "I was disappointed that Professor Koljevic did not intervene, since he was certainly the most articulate of the three. Presumably, he was deferring to his leader, but I could tell that he knew a valuable opportunity had been lost here."

But overall, Mitterand's visit was an important validation for the controversial airport agreement. It proved to the world that the airport could operate and that aircraft could land there.

MacKenzie describes the Mitterand visit as the one time in his life when all of his military and diplomatic skills jelled. It was — he says — his finest moment. He had had only a few hours to persuade the French president that the airport could open for business: "When he and I discussed it and when I asked him to send humanitarian aircraft, I knew the media would cover it. And I knew that every friggin' country in the world watching TV would want to be part of the action for their six o'clock news." Within days, MacKenzie was able to get the first planeloads of aid into the Bosnian capital — first from France and eventually, as MacKenzie predicted, in a flood from the rest of the world — and without interference from the Pale Gang.

The Canadian battle group charged with running the airport would have a bit more difficulty arriving. The UN had agreed that the Canadian peacekeepers would only be deployed to run the airport if MacKenzie and his reconnaissance party determined it was safe. Mitterand's gesture was enough to satisfy Nambiar, and New York, that it was.

The Canadian battle group was actually two large companies from the Royal Canadian and the Royal 22nd regiments, all under the command of Lieutenant Colonel Michel Jones. They had hoped to arrive for Canada Day—July 1—but they were a bit late: Jones's arrival was delayed on the road to Sarajevo by a Serb force of two thousand troops backed up by a dozen tanks, under the command of an inebriated Bosnian Serb officer who held up the Canadian convoy for eighteen hours. Jones eventually tired of it and made threatening gestures to his hosts who immediately backed off. It was just a taste of what was to come.

The UNPROFOR mission was under a chapter six mandate—the soldiers were to have only light arms and use them only in self-defence. MacKenzie unofficially redesigned the rules of engagement for the Sarajevo mission—"I declared it a chapter six and a half," he says. The UN's restrictions on weapons didn't faze the general, who authorized Jones to bring as much firepower as he could. "I told Michel Jones, 'Bring every missile you've got. Put every high explosive round you can bring for the mortars, cram those vehicles full of that stuff and bring it to Sarajevo. 'Cause you're going to need it. 'Cause you guys are going to have to defend that airport.'"

How Canada came to have such firepower in Yugoslavia is a story in itself. According to MacKenzie, someone in Ottawa was "using his noggin" and approved what he thought the troops might need, including one hundred APCs—about eighty-five more than the limit (the UN was very conscious of the petrol costs). But MacKenzie says he asked Canada to also send "through the back door" its relatively new tube-launched, optically-controlled, wire-guided anti-tank missile system—TOW. Jones brought four of them. The UN could sanction the TOW deployment because a night vision system that came on the vehicles would be useful for securing the airport. But the UN would permit only illuminating mortar rounds—used to light up the night sky—and not high-explosive ammunition. MacKenzie declared that ridiculous: "These guys in New York thought this was still nice quiet peacekeeping!" MacKenzie "cheated"—as he describes it—and had Jones bring the ammunition anyway. "After all, if the situation turned nasty and we had to make a break for the Adriatic coast, we would be three hundred kilometres from the nearest border to the west," MacKenzie declared. With the TOW system he believed they would be able to hold off the tanks.

Under his self-styled chapter six and a half, MacKenzie authorized his soldiers to use lethal fire not just when they, themselves, were threatened but when anyone from UNPROFOR was threatened or even if airport operations were threatened — "Which means if those bastards fired at the aircraft when it was landing, unloading or taking off, then we could take them out," MacKenzie says. They didn't have to wait until someone took the first shot at them — a standard chapter six rule. If an UNPROFOR soldier saw a sniper, he was to wait until he was sure the sniper saw him. "And they would normally disappear. If they did not disappear and they engaged the aircraft then our people killed them," says MacKenzie. This turned out to be not a "what if" scenario but a reality. MacKenzie will not hazard a guess at how many belligerents his soldiers shot at — or killed — in defence of themselves or the mission. "Most of them were just thugs with guns," he says. MacKenzie believed his soldiers needed to know they had the full support of their commander to do whatever was necessary to defend the airport and themselves.

Jones (now a brigadier general) remembers his time in Sarajevo as being one of intense violence where his men were constantly under attack. He came first in June with a reconnaissance mission and watched the city being bombed and engulfed in flames for the duration of his visit. The UN headquarters was directly across from the *Oslobodjenje* building, and Jones had watched it being destroyed. "It was a towering inferno," he recalls. "Things were far more violent than I had thought they would be." It was his first peacekeeping mission but even now, with much more experience under his belt, Jones is still astonished at how dangerous the mission was.

When Jones returned with his soldiers on July 2, not much had changed, except he was now in the middle of it. Half of his battle group dug themselves into trenches surrounding the airport while the rest unloaded the planes and transported the aid as deeply into Bosnian territory as was safe (which wasn't very far). Jones's force took eighteen casualties in one month. Many of the attacks came from mortars and grenade launchers fired from too great a distance for the soldiers to determine who had done it. "But I told both sides that I held them responsible. That's the way we stayed neutral," says Jones. The worst of the attacks came from the snipers in the vicinity of the airport grounds. He says he doesn't know which side they were from. "We neutralized them. That is the word I used at the time. We don't know if we killed anyone."

MacKenzie filed no reports on these incidents and he made no investigations. But he believes each occasion was warranted. "It was an act of peace enforcement," MacKenzie said in an interview. "I made up the rules as I went along. I knew I shouldn't have done it. But I'd do the same thing again, absolutely." The peacekeepers were controlling "no man's land," he says, "making sure people didn't sneak around the airport and sneak up on our guys. And Michel Jones had full authority to do that." The French colonel who replaced Jones after MacKenzie and the Canadians departed immediately rescinded the orders to shoot at the airport. "But *we* could not have accomplished what we did otherwise," MacKenzie says.

Soldiers who served under the general speak fondly of "fighting Lew" and his fearless concern for their personal safety. But the Canadians might well have asked themselves what they were doing there in the first place. MacKenzie had volunteered himself and the Canadians for a tour of duty in what Boutros-Ghali had described as "the most dangerous city in the world."

The mission with the misleading name — United Nations Protection Force — did everything but protect the people of Sarajevo. It became an essential part of the civil infrastructure, providing services from garbage pickup to food drop-offs. No Bosnian politician could move without the peacekeepers' escort or transportation, and no foreign journalist could tell the story of Sarajevo without their assistance. But they were not present in the city to protect people from the daily rain of shell- and sniper-fire. UNPROFOR, paradoxically, was there to expedite an agreement that required the people to acknowledge and co-operate with their sworn enemies.

John Wilson, who negotiated the airport agreement, says, "If people won't agree to the moral solution, then you have to get the best deal you can get, as unsavoury as that might be." Wilson believes there was not the political will to do much more. He acknowledges now that the airport agreement actually had a devastating effect, in that it stabilized the conflict in a particularly murderous phase and allowed the war to continue. He says, "The moment [for stopping the war] was lost with the airport negotiations." According to him, the international community was becoming outraged by the siege of the city. Even Mladic, Karadzic and Plavsic believed the Americans were going to launch air strikes. Opening the airport created the illusion that the siege had been lifted and removed the immediate threat of air strikes. "We continued to threaten air strikes on a number of occasions until 1995," says Wilson, "but it became the boy crying wolf. It had lost its impact. The moment was then, in May/June 1992."

Today, MacKenzie admits that the decision to open the airport was probably a mistake. He now maintains that the United Nations should have turned down the plan and rejected his own offer to lead the mission. The agreement was unenforceable and endangered the peacekeepers. Over the coming months and years, peacekeepers would be taken hostage and used as bargaining chips by the Serbs to extract even more concessions from their Western "minders," and to press the international community to withdraw any threats of force.

But MacKenzie didn't raise his concerns during the two months he led the UNPROFOR mission and entrenched the policy of accommodation that characterized UN relations with the Serbs for the duration of the mission. Had he uttered such warnings back then, he might not have become the poster boy of Canadian peacekeeping and a globe-trotting expert on the war in Bosnia.

Salem Mujezinovic and his brigade dug their tunnel beneath the airport runway in 1993, cursing UNPROFOR and the "Chetniks" in equal measure.

8

MAJOR GENERAL SUPERSTAR

If the international community is not ready to defend the
principles which it, itself, has proclaimed as its foundations, let it
say so openly, both to the people of Bosnia and the people of the world.
Let it proclaim a new code of behaviour in which force will be the
first and the last argument.
—Bosnian president Alija Izetbegovic, May 22, 1993

Lewis MacKenzie had a natural gift for speaking to the media, and he hit his stride in Sarajevo. In July, with the airport open for relief flights and his men engaged in frequent gun battles, MacKenzie appeared in complete control and was even good-humoured. He fired off provocative comments for the journalists who had come to cover the war, and he had a particular talent for the TV sound bite. He became a fixture on CNN and the BBC all-news programs, reducing complex operations to simple, quotable little nuggets, and he was always considered an objective observer, with his macho "tell it like it is" kind of style.

MacKenzie also had a captive audience: the only show for the media to cover in Bosnia was the siege of Sarajevo and its heroic airport peacekeepers. The reporters had yet to get into the rest of the country, where the horrific campaign of ethnic cleansing was under way.

The American journalist Roy Gutman, who won a Pulitzer Prize for his coverage of Bosnia, remembers how MacKenzie was always ready with a damning declaration, whether in a scrum or a formal interview. *The Washington Post*'s Peter Maas described MacKenzie as a character from central casting: "He wore his flak-jacket like a badge of honour and he shined his own boots.... Canada is known for producing hockey stars rather than war heroes, but MacKenzie was becoming one, and if a movie is ever made about Sarajevo, he should be cast to play himself."

Like many of the foreign reporters, Maas would become quite critical of MacKenzie in the following months, and he later expressed his profound disappointment with the general's behaviour during a panel discussion on television. But that was in the future. In Sarajevo at the time, MacKenzie quickly became a valued asset for quote-starved reporters.

As MacKenzie became a media superstar, Ottawa developed misgivings. The military brass had no way to assess whether what he was telling the media was accurate or even true. But that didn't bother Ottawa as much as what might seem to be his crass self-promotion. DND never likes it when soldiers stand out in a crowd, and MacKenzie was becoming quite conspicuous.

Even before he really hit his stride, the DND's chief of defence staff, General John de Chastelain, fired off a subtle warning: "I just want you to know that, so far, it's all playing pretty well." The subtext? Don't blow it.

Sarajevans, obviously, saw matters in quite a different light. The MacKenzie they got to know was quite a different personality from the one appearing on CNN. The typical Sarajevan salute to the general was an upright middle finger as he drove past them in his APC.

When MacKenzie told Izetbegovic that if he didn't do more to improve public perceptions of UNPROFOR and its general then maybe Bosnia didn't deserve any help at all. Izetbegovic told MacKenzie that he could do a lot to improve his own image if he'd only stop lunching at the Lukavica barracks with the Serb Republican Army or up in the mountains of Pale with the Karadzic crowd.

Sabina Izetbegovic had her qualms about MacKenzie ever since the day he put her and her father into an APC with General Kukanjac. She had watched the steady deterioration in relations with the Canadian general since then. And one day, she decided Bosnia had finally had enough of Lewis MacKenzie.

The American embassy in Belgrade was still functioning, even though Ambassador Zimmerman had been recalled, and Washington could still send messages to Sarajevo through Belgrade. Sabina Izetbegovic remembers that one day General MacKenzie arrived and handed her a letter from the United States. It was a list of fifteen questions that Washington wanted the president of the republic of Bosnia and Herzegovina to answer.

Izetbegovic's written response was to be returned exactly the same way — sealed in a double envelope to protect its sensitive contents, and passed back through Lewis MacKenzie. What did the State Department want to know? "Let's just say it was material that the Bosnian Serbs would [have loved] to get their hands on," says Sabina Izetbegovic.

The president's daughter had all fifteen responses typed in English and sealed in the proper envelope. She distinctly remembers handing the letter to MacKenzie. But seven days later, the U.S. embassy called to ask what had become of this important document.

"General MacKenzie was meeting at the time with Ejup Ganic, and I went into the office," recalls Sabina. "'What happened to the letter?' I asked him. 'What letter?' he said. I couldn't believe it! He said he would ask his assistant if he knew of any letter, and the next day he told me no one knew of any letter. I contacted the American embassy and told them, 'MacKenzie lost the letter.' A few days later, MacKenzie came to our office, quite agitated, and asked for [a copy of] the lost letter, saying he would deliver it. I told him I had made other arrangements."

MacKenzie says he doesn't recall the incident and claims it's unlikely he would have carried such a letter. Had he been caught at a Serb checkpoint and the letter discovered, he could have been accused of acting as an agent for the Muslims. But Sabina Izetbegovic says it happened just as she describes. MacKenzie concedes it would be unlikely for her to lie, but he just doesn't remember.

After that incident, Sabina Izetbegovic bundled up all the written messages MacKenzie had sent since he arrived in Sarajevo — messages telling her father that if he truly wanted peace, he should negotiate with the Bosnian Serb leader, Radovan Karadzic — and she shipped them off to the American embassy by a secure route. Relations with MacKenzie would never recover.

By July, the death threats were no longer simply addressed to MacKenzie but were directed at anyone thought to be working with him. Peacekeepers in the field reported that they would often hear some variation of the slogan "MacKenzie Must Die" before a round of machine-gun fire would go off close to their heads. When General de Chastelain came to Sarajevo for a visit, MacKenzie took his boss aside and told him he wanted out. De Chastelain agreed, and a plan was hatched to remove both MacKenzie and the Canadians from Sarajevo, replacing them with a mixture of Egyptians, Ukrainians and French UN peacekeepers. The makeup of the new force

(Muslim-Orthodox-Catholic) was a telling admission that New York had accepted MacKenzie's (and the Serbs') characterization of the war as a civil conflict along religious lines.

The French soldiers who replaced the Canadians were shocked to discover how bad relations were between the peacekeepers and the people they were ostensibly helping. A French colonel, Patrice Sartre, says their first order of business was to find out why everyone hated the Canadians. As far as anyone knew, they had been doing a good job and had been cited for several acts of heroism. As a veteran peacekeeper, Sartre had never seen this kind of animosity.

He concluded that MacKenzie was only partly to blame. Half the problem was the airport agreement itself. "UNPROFOR became part of the siege," says Colonel Sartre. Whether they were preventing people from crossing the airport road or ignoring the shells that fell on Sarajevo, the peacekeepers were complicit. MacKenzie's perceived biases didn't help the situation, according to Sartre, but there was really nothing anyone could have done once the UN had decided that the airport should be kept open at any cost.

Colonel Sartre eventually paid personally for the flaws of the airport agreement. It was Sartre who opened the door of the French APC at the Serb checkpoint to reveal a popular Bosnian politician, Dr. Hakija Turajlic, who was sitting inside. A soldier—presumably a Serb since it was their checkpoint—shot over Sartre's shoulder into the vehicle, killing Turajlic. David Rieff dedicated his book *Slaughterhouse* to "the memory of Dr. Hakija Turajlic, vice-president of the Republic of Bosnia-Herzegovina, who was killed by Bosnian Serb fighters on the airport road in Sarajevo while riding in a French armored personnel carrier and ostensibly under the protection of United Nations soldiers." And Sartre took another drubbing, from French TV, when he was ambushed by a live interview after the network had just broadcast video of people being captured by peacekeepers while crossing the Sarajevo airport runway. He couldn't possibly defend the policy and he was privately contemptuous of it. In fact, Sartre's real problems with the "escapees" began after he relaxed the policy of shooting at people considered a threat to the airport.

While the newly arrived peacekeepers prepared to take over from the Canadians, MacKenzie continued to be the spokesperson for UNPROFOR.

At a press conference on July 23, however, he let the mask of neutrality slip just a little. Among the heated questions directed his way was one asking him to explain why he persisted in claiming that both sides were to blame. "At no time did I say both sides are equally to blame," answered the general. "What I did say is that there is plenty enough blame to go around. The Serbs started the shelling and therefore have to accept the majority of the responsibility. But the Presidency has to accept a good deal of the responsibility for keeping the fighting going." He then unleashed some of his frustrations. He couldn't get a ceasefire in Sarajevo, he said, "Because I can't keep the two sides from firing on their own positions for the benefit of CNN. If I could get them to stop, perhaps we could have a real ceasefire."

MacKenzie later charged that the print media twisted the remark to read: "If I could convince both sides to stop killing their own people to impress CNN, perhaps we could have a ceasefire." However, he concedes that that phrasing still accurately reflected what was in his mind. And significantly, that's the quote that appears on the jacket of his own book. (It is now recorded in the annals of career-shortening comments.)

MacKenzie claims he had never betrayed his suspicions about the Bosnian government in public before and, in his book, says this is the first time he declared his real sentiments. But Gordana Knezevic was at the press conference and says the local media felt there was nothing new or noteworthy in the general's remarks that day. No one much cared, Knezevic says, since everyone had heard through the very efficient grapevine that MacKenzie was leaving.

MacKenzie maintains it was this single moment of candour that got him into hot water with the United Nations and it was only then that he was ordered out of Sarajevo. Nambiar notified him that he was to gather his kit and come to Belgrade for "consultations." MacKenzie knew what it meant. He was offended by the UN attitude to his remarks, since he was convinced that he had been doing a lot to bolster the image of peacekeeping. Just a week earlier, he had informed New York: "I have been told by those who should know that the airport opening has endured more coverage, and that I have been interviewed more times, over the previous ten days, than anyone else in the world in the last half century." MacKenzie suggested that if New York people could spin the Bosnia story any better than he had, they were welcome to try. He reminded the UN of the stellar job his assistant did in getting international coverage for the recent Canadian rescue of the Sarajevo women.

MacKenzie was right. The UN couldn't have asked for more. He'd given them exactly what the international community wanted and needed.

With his gift for media relations, he had turned the war in Bosnia into a humanitarian crisis like a natural disaster, to be solved with food and medical aid. MacKenzie had activated the moral equivalency that the UN calls impartiality and persuaded the world the UN was doing everything possible. What more could the UN want?

Biljana Plavsic was very disappointed when she learned that MacKenzie was leaving. "He was the only one who was truly objective," she says. Plavsic remembers the splendid hotel dining room in which the Bosnian Serb leadership held their final tribute to the general who had done so much for them. It was mid July, on Jahorina mountain, the old resort area for Sarajevans and now Bosnian Serb headquarters. She can't precisely recall the location, but the restaurant had a panoramic view. MacKenzie characterizes it as a routine business lunch but for the Pale Gang it was their farewell party for the general, a lamb barbecue with all the trimmings, attended by a huge crowd of well-wishers, including Karadzic, Krajisnik, Koljevic (the Shakespeare professor) and countless others.

MacKenzie said publicly that he had asked to leave the mission because the death threats he was getting could endanger the Canadian soldiers on the ground. Plavsic says he gave a different explanation for his premature recall to the Bosnian Serbs who had assembled for this party. "He gave a final little speech in which he said he had to leave because he had become 'inconvenient to Izetbegovic.'"

Plavsic says the occasion was truly sad. She remembers standing with the general, staring at the view. "He looked out over the terrain, and I asked him what he was thinking. He told me it would be very difficult to take this territory."

On July 25, MacKenzie was on a Russian UN cargo flight on his way to Belgrade. In his memoirs, he says he put his head in his hands and cried like a baby. "I just felt like—a great event was over. I was totally and absolutely confused because I was leaving people behind. I had never done that before in my life." Why did he cry? "I had too much adrenaline rush. And all of a sudden, Kabam! It was all gone. I looked down and everything looked normal and pretty. Everything was green. I couldn't see the damage. And I thought, 'Is this a dream? Is it real?'" The UN gave him one reprieve, allowing him to return long enough to say a proper goodbye to the departing Canadian troops and presumably to take care of any unfinished business. But by the first of August, he was gone from Sarajevo—and his command—for good.

For Alija Izetbegovic, his daughter, Sabina, Ejup Ganic and the entire Presidency, that was the end of it. They didn't know that while Major General Lewis MacKenzie was going away, he wouldn't soon be forgotten. MacKenzie the peacekeeper was finishing up. MacKenzie the oracle was just getting started.

On August 6, 1992, MacKenzie was lunching at Harrington Lake, the prime minister's summer residence just over the Quebec border in the Gatineau Hills. Brian Mulroney hosted the intimate gathering to celebrate the return of Canada's most famous peacekeeper—the country's best-known soldier in peacetime.

It's not surprising that the prime minister, who was always deeply sentimental about such things, wanted to rub shoulders with a real hero. He and his Sarajevo-born wife, Mila, peppered MacKenzie with questions about who was responsible for what was going on back in Bosnia, and the general was only too happy to tell them.

It was a crucial moment in the evolution of Canada's Balkans policy. According to the former Croatian ambassador, Graham Green, Canada made all its key decisions on how to deal with Bosnia during the first six months of the crisis. Even when observers were reporting, in 1994 and 1995, the full story of the horrors that international policy had inflicted on the Bosnian population, Canada was locked into a position that had taken shape in mid-1992. "We couldn't say that we blew it," says Green, "so we had to keep propping it up on this bad foundation." Canada wasn't the only one; other countries may have had better information, but they were even more reticent about military intervention.

The most important government of all was in Washington. As sympathetic as the American public was in the face of a daily barrage of tragic images from Sarajevo, no one wanted to participate in a messy little war that had no strategic purpose for them. As the Bush administration approached the end of its mandate in 1992, Washington had better things to do than get involved with a bunch of crazy ethnic clans who were killing each other as they had for a thousand years.

Of course they couldn't ignore it entirely, and Mulroney wasn't surprised when he was called away from his lunch with MacKenzie to take a pre-arranged phone call from the U.S. president. The conversation was about the Balkans, and when the prime minister returned to his lunch party, he told MacKenzie that George Bush wanted the general to go down to Washington and speak to the Senate Armed Services Committee.

MacKenzie could hardly refuse. The Pentagon had already been pestering him to appear for a debriefing, and many in Congress saw the Canadian peacekeeper as the authority on events in Bosnia. He wasn't some academic pipe-smoker or bleeding-heart human-rights activist—he was a military man who had actually dodged bullets.

From the moment he arrived back in North America, it seemed that MacKenzie was hardly ever out of an interview chair—every American and Canadian network program wanted a piece of him. From *Larry King Live* to *USA Today*, from CFRB in Toronto to *The Washington Post*, MacKenzie explained it for all of them. After lunch with the prime minister, he began a whirlwind tour that reached the inner chambers of world power: the American military, NATO, the most influential committees in Washington, the Commons and Senate committees of Ottawa, the supreme allied commander of Europe, the British Defence Committee, and even Her Majesty, the queen of the Commonwealth.

In an austere congressional committee room on Capital Hill, on August 11, 1992, MacKenzie addressed one of the most powerful groups in Washington—Republican Sam Nunn's Senate Armed Services Committee. Congress was wrestling with a decision: America was not about to get involved in the war, but the committee was trying to figure out if it should support a UN resolution to use force to ensure that humanitarian aid could get to the regions of Bosnia outside Sarajevo. Here's some of the exchange that the committee heard:

> *Chairman Nunn*: What do you believe, General, the United Nations should do now? What is your advice based upon your own experience, your own personal view?
> *MacKenzie*: My personal view is there is no military solution. There is no way that intervention will do anything but escalate the fighting, and more people will be killed—
> *Chairman Nunn*: When you say intervention will escalate to violence, if anything, do you include in your definition of intervention humanitarian assistance, or is that not intervention?
> *MacKenzie*: I'm afraid so, sir.

MacKenzie went on to warn the Americans that anything they did would risk drawing them into this messy war, and that, in fact, was precisely the desire of President Izetbegovic. All of MacKenzie's hypothetical examples of trouble placed the burden of responsibility on the Bosnians and not the Serbs. "Halfway down the chain of command you run up against one of these warlords that says, 'This is my area.' I do not care what Izetbegovic has said," MacKenzie asserted.

Senator John Warner, one of Elizabeth Taylor's ex-husbands, asked MacKenzie, "Have you ever witnessed anything like it?" MacKenzie told them that he'd seen it all, from the Sandinistas to the Viet Cong, and that after the fighting you could have a coffee and talk about the good old days. Bosnia-Herzegovina was different.

What, then, was the solution? MacKenzie responded: "Rip the rug of intervention out and force people to sit down and discuss. One side has already said it is prepared to do that. The other side has not got the message yet."

There was no confusion as to which side was which: Major General MacKenzie made it clear that Americans would come back in body bags if they even tried to force humanitarian aid convoys into the countryside. Where would it all end? he wondered aloud. He couldn't say for sure, but he made it clear the Bosnian Muslims were the greatest potential source of grief for the Americans.

He claimed that Izetbegovic resisted all reasonable negotiations because he believed the world would intervene to help. He said he had repeatedly told Izetbegovic not to expect such intervention, and he had told foreign leaders it was their responsibility to convince Izetbegovic the cavalry was not coming. Failure to get that message across would only prolong this conflict, and the Bosnians would never agree to sit at the negotiating table.

MacKenzie then offered the senators his seminal theory and "just a little bit of history." The Serbs and Croats were traditionally farmers, which gave them an appreciation of and entitlement to land. The Muslims, on the other hand, were mostly business people, a population that was concentrated in a few towns and not entitled to much land. So the country should be divvied up accordingly, giving the Muslims "not a heck of a lot" — Sarajevo and some of the land around it.

If the senators had been up to date in their reading of Serb propaganda, this would have sounded familiar to them. This was precisely the argument Karadzic was shopping around Europe's capitals while his deputy, Biljana Plavsic, elaborated that Muslims were accustomed to living on top of each other in cramped quarters while Serbs needed room to breathe.

If they were privy to what was really going on, they'd have known that the farm theory was simply preposterous. The Serbs were ethnically cleansing Bosnia's rural countryside of at least a million people and the majority were Muslims. In the very month that the committee members met with General MacKenzie, August 1992, the Serbs and Croats were discussing how they would divide up that territory after the anticipated capitulation of the Bosnian government.

What about the arms embargo? "There is no shortage of weapons over there," MacKenzie testified. Senator Levin wasn't sure he'd heard right, since the statement contradicted everything the committee had been previously told:

> *Senator Levin*: [O]ur understanding is that the *Serbs in Bosnia* have a significant number of tanks, armored personnel carriers and modern artillery pieces, perhaps as many as a thousand altogether. Does the Bosnian government have anywhere near that number?
> *MacKenzie*: You are talking about Sarajevo, or at least I am talking about Sarajevo. *The Bosnians would outnumber the Serbs in and around Sarajevo.* [Emphasis added]

The American congressmen must have had an idea that the Serbs had an overwhelming advantage in firepower. By September, congressional records show a report that the Bosnians had two tanks and two APCs while the Serb army in Bosnia had three hundred tanks, two hundred APCs, eight hundred artillery pieces and forty aircraft. Presumably the congressmen knew at least some of these numbers in August, but they were evidently relieved to learn the siege in Sarajevo was not as uneven as they had thought.

By the end of the session there was no doubt that the Canadian general had made a major impact on the policy-makers. Senator Exon thanked him warmly. "I have had an opportunity to see you on several television programs. You are obviously the most experienced person that we know of in that area." Senator Warner admired his "very persuasive" arguments against any kind of intervention in Bosnia: "We thank you personally and your government for making you available. Canada has a long history of trying to bring about peace in the world, and where necessary to use force. But Canada has always stood for trying to resolve conflicts by peaceful means."

United States president George Bush thereafter declared the Bosnian war a quagmire of historic proportions: an unruly people continuing a long history of killing each other. Why on earth would the world get involved?

How much influence did General MacKenzie have in shaping the president's position? There is no definitive answer to that intriguing question. But one State Department insider who had spent much time in Sarajevo says the MacKenzie effect on foreign governments was as significant as it was obvious. "Among people prepared to do nothing, the idea that the Bosnians are killing themselves is a heart-warming idea. It means that the Serbs are doing nothing wrong—it's the foul Bosnians who are killing themselves. We don't have to side with them, even if mothers are being gunned down in the streets."

Canada, of course, was part of this consensus that intervention would be folly. Graham Green remembers when the Mulroney government stridently opposed lifting the embargo, which would have enabled the Bosnians to properly arm themselves. The Bosnians claimed, and a number of outside military people concurred, that if the arms embargo had been lifted at the beginning of the war, they could have pushed the Serbs back in about six months. The Serbs had the firepower but often seemed to lack the determination. The JNA fought in Sarajevo as it had fought in Croatia, by lobbing hundreds of shells at a position, presumably to soften it up, before moving in. The Bosnians had the tactical advantage of being highly motivated—they were fighting for their homes. To have coupled that enthusiasm with sufficient guns would have brought the war to a quick and decisive end to Izetbegovic's advantage. But Canada would have none of it.

Canada also opposed intervention, heeding the warnings of General MacKenzie that it would be difficult and too risky. Air strikes against Serb positions, Canada argued, would endanger the lives of peacekeepers in the field. The presence of peacekeepers produced a supremely ironic situation, it seemed. While they were unwilling to do anything to stop the slaughter themselves, their presence would prevent anybody else from trying.

Green says, "I think the biggest role General MacKenzie had was conveying the message, whether it was fully supported or not, that all sides are guilty, all sides would shell their own people in order to curry international favour." He became an antidote for the gruesome pictures that were emanating from TV and for the newspaper reports about the deliberate slaughter of an innocent population.

"Who fired the first shot?" a journalist asked MacKenzie. "Some son of a bitch two hundred years ago," was his answer.

Mohammed Sacirbey was a bright young American who found himself in the unlikely position of being Bosnia's first ambassador to the United Nations. His family had moved from Bosnia to the United States when he was twelve, and he grew up as an all-American boy (the family name was originally Sacirbegovic).

In his New York office, surrounded by the classic memorabilia of an American life, including photos of himself on the Tulane University football team, Sacirbey still shakes his head and marvels at how MacKenzie undermined the Bosnian cause. He particularly remembers the Senate hearing of August 1992. It was just weeks before the London Conference, a thirty-nation summit that the Bosnians were hoping would bring the war to an end.

Sacirbey was worried about the extraordinary impact MacKenzie was having on international opinion. But he had high hopes that it would be offset by a new element in the flow of information from Bosnia: reports of the existence of prisoner-of-war camps.

In July, Roy Gutman was the first Western reporter to break out of the Sarajevo media pack and head into the countryside. He brought back tales of brutal detention areas — concentration camps — where Serbs held thousands of men in squalid conditions. He reported that people were being tortured and murdered there. A few adventurous British TV journalists from ITN followed, resulting in a series of shocking television reports in August. When MacKenzie was asked by the media and by the U.S. Congress about these camps, he replied that he'd been told both sides had such secret prisons, but he had found no evidence of their existence in and around Sarajevo. The general said he had no "eyes" outside the city, which is true, and he had no intelligence-gathering abilities.

But while MacKenzie had no confirmation of the camps, other people did. It would later be revealed that Western governments had inside reports about them months earlier and had kept them a secret. After

MacKenzie's appearance in August, the U.S. Senate Foreign Relations Committee revealed that according to American intelligence sources, Western governments and the UN had known about the ethnic-cleansing campaigns since May 1992 and had done nothing about them.

It was a frustrating moment for Ambassador Sacirbey, who had been trying to get Boutros-Ghali interested in these prisons. He had first reported them to the UN in May, when he received what he believed was reliable confirmation of the camps from sources in Zagreb.

The upside for the Bosnian ambassador was that—with the media reports—the world could surely no longer remain indifferent to the plight of his people. And they'd get the chance to do something in the upcoming summit in London. He was confident, as he prepared for the conference, that despite MacKenzie's interventions, the civilized world could no longer avoid action. But he was in for a nasty surprise.

Just days before the London Conference was to begin, the Bosnians were shocked to see this headline in Britain's *The Independent*: "MUSLIMS 'SLAUGHTER THEIR OWN PEOPLE': Bosnia Bread Queue Massacre Was Propaganda Ploy, UN Told." The story, by Leonard Doyle, was mostly a review of the old allegations. But the reporter cited anonymous "United Nations officials and Western military officers who believe some of the worst recent killings in Sarajevo, including the massacre of at least sixteen people in a bread queue, were carried out by the city's mainly Muslim defenders—not Serb besiegers—as a propaganda ploy to win world sympathy and military intervention."

This was serious. *The Independent* is a prestigious British newspaper, and it was referring to official "reports" from the United Nations. The article attributes other incidents to the Bosnians, including a series of mortar rounds that landed near the Presidency buildings while the British foreign secretary, Douglas Hurd, was visiting. In his memoirs, MacKenzie recalled the same incident; "everyone who witnessed the event had an uneasy feeling that it had been orchestrated by the Presidency to put the Serbs in to a bad light."

The UN officials mentioned in Leonard Doyle's piece never offered any proof for the allegations, and no one was named as the source of the story—except the UN force commander in the Balkans at that time, Satish Nambiar, who received all reports of Sarajevo from his chief of staff, Lewis MacKenzie. Nambiar concluded that "the Bosnian forces loyal to President Izetbegovic may have detonated a bomb."

MacKenzie has no recollection of the article by Doyle, or of ever being interviewed by him. But he admits that he could have been. He recalls that he gave a number of interviews on that very subject at the time—not for attribution—and he certainly held those views. "I would have talked about those things, yeah. But I would have made it very clear I didn't know. But I was suspicious. It took me a while, a couple of weeks, before I started qualifying what I was saying."

MacKenzie doubts there would have been any official report on the breadline massacre at the UN, since the organization had no mandate for Bosnia at the time and there was no official investigation. Only John Wilson was there, and Wilson says there was no report—just his personal hunch that Mladic wouldn't have lied to him when he denied having any involvement.

Sacirbey could see the strength of the Bosnian government's case was being seriously diminished by this headline dominating the British newsstands. The thirty countries that took part in the late-August summit ended up condemning the Serbs for their prisoner-of-war camps and demanding an end to ethnic cleansing. They called for consideration of a war crimes tribunal as well. But the summiteers stopped short of what Bosnia wanted: "lift and strike," a lifting of the arms embargo (which would allow them to arm themselves) and air strikes on the Serb positions to end the war against the civilian population of Sarajevo.

The air strikes wouldn't come until three years later. And what happened to the idea of lifting the arms embargo? Boutros-Ghali declared that it was pure fiction that the Serbs had an advantage in arms, since he knew the Bosnians were getting secret shipments from Islamic countries. But it didn't really matter: it all had the desired effect—justifiable inaction.

According to one Balkans diplomat, Graham Green, "Those people didn't want to go in. On the one hand, they were seeing the results of the atrocities, so public opinion was forcing them to take decisions they didn't want to take. And it was very good to be able to point to a senior UN general in Sarajevo [who was] saying, 'Look, this is a hornet's nest, everybody's guilty here. You can't separate good guys from bad guys....' I think that may have been the biggest role General MacKenzie had—delaying the kind of intensive military involvement we ended up seeing three years later." Green also personally believes the reports may have been true. "The Muslims were desperate for intervention, and they may have been desperate enough to fire on their own people."

Sacirbey and Izetbegovic found themselves in a no-win situation. The more atrocities emerged, the more they appealed for help; the more they pleaded, the more they invited the accusation that the Muslims were desperate enough to savage their own people—and the more reluctant the international community became to help them.

At the London Conference in August, Radovan Karadzic had a role in the negotiations for the first time—though behind that of Slobodan Milosevic, who was still considered the statesman at such events, and sat at the negotiating table. But it was just the beginning. With his mop of grey hair and white ascot, Karadzic would become a familiar spectacle in the coming months. The president of the Serbian republic would soon show up on the doorsteps of all the important nations, stepping out of limousines in Geneva, giving media interviews about the importance of protecting Christian Europe from the Islamic hordes. The recognition that he longed for, and that MacKenzie tried to help him win, was building.

The delegates at the conference drew up a statement of principles and resolved that there would be no recognition of territory taken by force, that there had to be compliance with all codes for guaranteeing human rights, and that there had to be respect for national borders. These were all fine principles, but none of them could stop a war.

"It all could have been over in a few decisive months," Mohammed Sacirbey reflects sadly now. He agrees there was a genuine reluctance to get involved, but that Doyle's article in *The Independent* was "hugely influential."

As he departed the London Conference, President Izetbegovic could not have known how damaging the charges would become though he and Sacirbey made it clear they thought it was cowardly of the UN not to admit who was the source of them. *The Independent*'s East European editor Steve Crawshaw managed to get an exclusive interview with the president before he left for Sarajevo. Crawshaw reports: "[President Izetbegovic] complained that General MacKenzie had never put the allegations to him personally when still in Sarajevo, and called upon UN officials to put their names publicly to the new accusations. As we parted, however, the previously soft-spoken Mr. Izetbegovic suddenly returned with passion to the subject as though unbottling emotions that he had previously kept in check. 'Hundreds and thousands of shells have fallen on us. Why should we prove anything by shelling ourselves? Why should we prove something which has been proved already? One hundred times it has been proved that they have shelled civilians, why should we do it the hundred and first time? They have shelled the hospital seventy times. Is it necessary to shell ourselves for the seventy-first time, in order to make a big show?'" Crawshaw ended his article there.

The summer of 1992 came to a close with the airport open, the threat of air strikes gone, the arms embargo in place and the war unresolved.

Relations with subsequent UNPROFOR commanders and battalions would vary according to the individual personality, but not substantially. Ejup Ganic sums up his observations: "MacKenzie put the little bit of poison into the system right from the beginning. And we never got it out."

President Bill Clinton took power in the fall of 1992, and U.S. sympathies began to slowly shift to the Bosnians. But not in Canada. Even after the Mulroney government was defeated in 1993, the new liberal prime minister, Jean Chrétien, chafed at the American government and its subtle shift in favour of the Bosnians. In the House of Commons, he took the line that "it is not useful for anybody to encourage sides there."

Nader Hashemi, a PhD candidate in political science at the University of Toronto, has extensively researched foreign policy towards Bosnia. He says, "To speak of a Canadian policy in Bosnia is a misnomer. After recognizing the republic of Bosnia-Herzegovina in April 1992, Ottawa's policy was a derivative of decisions made in other capitals. Except for a few off-the-cuff remarks by Brian Mulroney, which he quickly abandoned after they were challenged, Canada put forward no independent initiative of its own. Ottawa's main foreign-policy concern was obtaining acknowledgement by the world powers that it existed as a state and should be consulted."

It got neither.

By August 1993, when NATO first considered air strikes against the Serbs, Canada was the only holdout. Clinton called Prime Minister Jean Chrétien and gave him seven days to change his mind. By that time, it didn't matter—the moment had been lost.

By February 1994, says Graham Green, "We had run out of ideas." Canada was excluded from the contact group on Bosnia, despite having a large peacekeeping force on the ground and a considerable investment in the area. Under Bill Clinton, the Americans took the international lead, but not before several high-profile resignations. The Yugoslavian desk officer, George Kenney, had left the State Department during the

Bush administration claiming the U.S. government was involved in a cover-up. A number of other resignations followed under Clinton. The U.S. had not seen such defections in protest against foreign policy since the Vietnam War. One State Department official who stayed as his colleagues quit over American intransigence in the Balkans was able to pull his country up short when he remarked that the U.S. "was sliding dangerously close to Canadian policy" (read inaction).

In Sarajevo, France's Colonel Patrice Sartre says it eventually became obvious that not only was there no moral equilibrium, but there were definitely white hats and black hats. For Sartre, the revelation came one day when he went to Serb military headquarters for talks about withdrawing some guns from the periphery of the city. Sartre thought once these professional soldiers realized that they were shelling more civilian targets than military ones, they would change their tactics. The man in charge of the operation, General Stanislav Galic, looked at Sartre with surprise. "But those are my orders. I'm to kill as many civilians as possible," he told the peacekeeper. Sartre turned on his heel and walked out. He subsequently refused to negotiate with the Serbs again.

But his new insight into the Serb mentality didn't help matters for his soldiers. The Bosnians never really noticed that in Sartre there was a sympathetic UN officer in the area. "Whenever there was an incident where one of my men was shot at," he says, "almost invariably it came from the Bosnians." He understood, however, that it was because they felt they had been betrayed by the UN as a result of the airport agreement.

In February 1993, MacKenzie's bosses in Ottawa were becoming uncomfortable with their superstar's pronouncements and found he was wandering into policy areas that were usually off limits for Department of National Defence staff.

They decided he should shut up for a while. The major general decided he would rather move on to a new career. He was by then a sought-after public speaker and TV panellist. In addition, he was writing a book about his years as a peacekeeper and his accomplishments in Bosnia that he knew might not sit well with some of his superiors.

MacKenzie took early retirement with a pension. He published *Peacekeeper* later that year and, shortly after, returned to Bosnia to make a documentary film based on his memoirs. He was considered *persona non grata* in Sarajevo; the Bosnian government refused to meet with him.

There was a different reaction up in the hills of Pale, where the Serb leadership celebrated the return of the Canadian general who was one of the few outsiders who really understood them. Radovan Karadzic was finally able to personally present the general with a gift he'd tried to offer earlier—a pistol MacKenzie says he had initially refused on principle because he was with UNPROFOR at the time.

MacKenzie later had the Yugoslav pistol modified to hold an ammunition clip that conformed with Canadian gun laws. He said he needed it for self-defence. Even though he was a civilian, living quietly in peaceful Bracebridge, Ontario, the death threats continued.

9

LIFT AND STRIKE

*[A] truly terrible massacre of the Muslim population seems to have
taken place. The evidence tendered by the Prosecutor describes scenes of
unimaginable savagery: thousands of men executed in mass graves,
hundreds of men buried alive, men and women mutilated and slaughtered,
children killed before their mothers' eyes, a grandfather forced to eat
the liver of his own grandson. These are truly scenes from hell written on the
darkest pages of human history.*
—Judge Fouad Riad, on confirming the indictments of
Radovan Karadzic and General Ratko Mladic, at the International War
Crimes Tribunal for the Former Yugoslavia, November 1995

The battle for public opinion was crucial during the Bosnian conflict.
The origins of the war were difficult for ordinary people to grasp,
even those who lived in Sarajevo, but winning support was necessary
for both the Bosnian government and the Pale Gang. For those familiar
with the events leading up to the war, it was an ideological conflict with a
fairly clear dividing line: multiculturalism versus ethnic purity.

But that clarity was lost on the general public because of the complex
history of the region, which seemed to support the claim that the country
was made up of clans that were really just settling old scores. A brutal media
image of a massacre or slaughter could change opinion overnight, even if
fleetingly, and it was necessary to exploit those moments to support the
broader political arguments.

That all sides were committing atrocities was well documented by the
earliest reports out of Bosnia. Helsinki Watch (a division of Human Rights
Watch) described forays by the Bosnian Defence Force into Serbian villages,

where it killed civilians, sometimes tying them up before executing them. These Bosnian army paramilitaries operated out of four enclaves that had survived the ethnic cleansing that was underway in Serb-held territory. The primary purpose of the military operations was to capture arms and ammunition from the well-equipped Serbs. Inevitably, the raids presented irresistible opportunities for committing acts of revenge.

Helsinki Watch reported the reprisals but noted that compared to Serbian atrocities, they were small-scale and generally unpremeditated. In the final months, hundreds of thousands of Serbs were driven out of the Krajina region. But CIA intelligence analysts calculated that 90 per cent of all the war crimes committed in Bosnia were done by the Serbs. With a few documented exceptions, most of the examples of Bosnian atrocities alleged by Radovan Karadzic proved to be unfounded. On the other hand, independent observers were able to confirm the existence of concentration camps and mass graves in Serb-held areas. In May 1994, the Commission of Experts headed up by the American war crimes investigator Cherif Bassiouni issued a damning report of Serbian army atrocities in Bosnia, and while the document spells out many of the Muslim war crimes and Croatian ones — including massacres — Bassiouni concludes, "It is clear that there is no factual basis for arguing 'moral equivalence' between warring factions."

The Bosnians never denied that their people committed murders, and the Izetbegovic government was the first (and for a long time, the only) party to the conflict to voluntarily hand over indicted criminals from its ranks to the international criminal tribunal in The Hague. But none of this seemed to register in the mind of Lewis MacKenzie, who became a leading commentator on the Bosnian war after he left the region. While he admitted he knew little about what was happening outside Sarajevo during the few months he served as commander in Bosnia, he began claiming, back in North America, that only 60 to 65 per cent of the atrocities were committed by the Serbs. The Muslims and Croats were responsible for the rest. The world didn't know about the latter atrocities, according to MacKenzie, because the media refused to report them. But where did the figure come from? Bosnians claimed MacKenzie was a mouthpiece of Serbian propaganda but the answer is much more simple. He admitted in an interview that he made the numbers up: "Right off the top of my head. To make a point." He says he first used those figures when he was asked by a Serb, back in Canada, who he blamed for the atrocities and plucked 60 to 65 per cent out of the air. But he believed the numbers to be true, "based on what I read and saw and experienced."

The Serbs were grateful to MacKenzie. The Serbian political lobby was anxious to gain acceptance for the position that their people were also victims, even the principal victims. The lobbying effort was seriously hampered by an ongoing United Nations campaign of sanctions against the former Yugoslavia. As a result of the boycott, no public-relations firms could openly work for the blacklisted government in Belgrade. A network of Serbian support groups took up the task. In the United States — possibly the most important battlefield for public opinion — Helen Bentley was a formidable force with strong connections to Biljana Plavsic in Belgrade.

Bentley had travelled to Yugoslavia, and she had been with Milosevic in 1989 when the Serbian president made his first war whoop in Kosovo, launching the ethnic policies that would lead to so much violence in the region. Back in the U.S., as a member of Congress, Bentley used her influence to lobby in support of the Serbian cause; she even raised money from the Serbian Orthodox Church for her SerbNet organization (Serbian American National Information Network). One of SerbNet's achievements was the production of a video called *Truth Is the Victim in Bosnia*, a propaganda documentary that claimed to tell the real story. The video features three interview segments with Lewis MacKenzie. He says he did not know he was used in the video and would not have approved it. But his presence gave it weight and credibility, and it was widely distributed to politicians and journalists to discourage support for the Bosnian Muslims.

Whether MacKenzie endorsed the views of SerbNet or not, he became a powerful voice for its cause. After his retirement from the Canadian Forces in early 1993, and without the constraints of the United Nations or the Canadian government to hamper him, he could speak freely. A series of public appearances cemented his reputation as a defender of Serbian interests.

He appeared before the House Armed Services Committee in May 1993 to tell the Americans — once again on the verge of deciding whether or not to bomb Serbian positions in Bosnia — that the conflict presented no threat to world peace and stability. His recommended solution? Partition. Divide the country up along ethnic lines. The UN was squeamish about enforcing such a solution because it would have rewarded the violence that had led to the status quo.

MacKenzie had a ready rebuttal for that view when he appeared before the House committee. "Now obviously the critics will say this rewards force and sets a bad example. I can only say to them, 'Read your history. Force has been rewarded since the first caveman picked up a club, occupied his neighbour's cave and ran off with his wife.'" He would go further, with a simile that would be picked up and quoted whenever a government committee or a political gathering would try to grapple with the intractable Bosnian problem. "Dealing with Bosnia is a bit like dealing with three serial killers. One has killed fifteen. One has killed ten. One has killed five. Do we help the one that has only killed five?"

It was a devastating pronouncement, and it stuck to the situation like glue. Never mind that the world was beginning to see the war as an act of aggression, organized and executed by one of the most heavily armed countries of the world—Yugoslavia—against the population of a country that was stealing guns and bullets to survive.

After his House committee appearance, MacKenzie showed up on *Larry King Live*. Substitute host Frank Sesno asked him if the Americans should vote to lift the arms embargo and allow the Muslims to defend themselves. MacKenzie responded: "If the Muslim forces were without arms, Sarajevo would have fallen thirteen months ago, on the sixth of April when the battle started. There's enough weapons to go around."

He told Sesno that he personally turned over a pile of JNA arms to the Bosnian Defence Force as part of the deal for allowing the Yugoslav army to depart from its barracks. MacKenzie didn't say that the Bosnian Serbs had shelled the barracks and destroyed the heavy guns they had left behind, or that they bored holes through gun barrels to disable them.

John Wilson says the Serbs had so many weapons they didn't have enough people to fire them: "They actually bused people between their concentration sites to fire their weapons. That's true! They had the artillery pieces laid out in normal firing deployment, and they would have a small crew to maintain security of the sites. But when they actually intended to fire them, a busload of troops would arrive, fire them and move off."

General MacKenzie claimed that the Bosnians were getting arms shipments from Islamic countries, and it was certainly true that the Middle East was trying to ship arms into Bosnia. Iran was one of the few countries to defy the embargo. But most of what it sent was intercepted and confiscated before it ever arrived in the land-locked Bosnian republic. In the second year of the war, Croatia launched its own offensive against Herzegovina, and the Croat arms embargo against Bosnia was even more effective than that of the international community.

On *Larry King Live*, MacKenzie reiterated his observation that all three sides were doing nasty things. And he made a grim prognosis, one that many people would repeat: "It stretches my imagination to the limits to think they could live together again side by side."

In an ideological war, ideas are truly powerful—and the more odious they are, it seems, the greater their impact. Bosnia's first government was multi-ethnic, and its Presidency was a coalition of Serb, Croat and Muslim leaders that lasted until well into the war. Serbs, Croats and Muslims stood shoulder to shoulder in the trenches of Sarajevo. Many of them intensely disliked Alija Izetbegovic and his SDA party, but they were prepared to fight for the idea that they could all live together. As the years of war went on, many abandoned that principle and succumbed to the notion that Bosnia —and multi-ethnicity—was a lost cause. Every defection to the other ideological side shook those who remained in the city to their foundations. For the hundreds of thousands of people who resisted the ultra-nationalist ideas of Radovan Karadzic, who sent their children away and didn't see them for years, who saw family members killed, it required an unceasing mental struggle to hold on to the principle that they could—and must— live together. In the United States, Canada and Europe, Lewis MacKenzie helped disseminate the defeatist view that these people could never do so. The world would be doing them a favour by forcing a settlement that reflected their entrenched ethnic hatred.

At the end of that interview on *Larry King Live*, Sesno asked MacKenzie if he had an anecdote he wanted to share, and the general told his version of the story of the convoy incident, when he was trying to get the Bosnian president to safety. In his telling, the president's own people betrayed him. Sesno then concluded the interview with an observation that all America would remember: "You've just cited an example of why we can't bring peace to this place."

The House committee and *Larry King Live* weren't the general's only stops in the United States in May 1993. MacKenzie gave more than a dozen speeches and interviews and met with key people in the American Congress. Some journalists were criticizing the line he was taking, but it was a bit late. The foreign reporters had created this media star and now he was using his influence to place his own stamp on the Bosnian story.

One of Roy Gutman's most significant scoops would emerge at the end of June 1993, not in Sarajevo but in the U.S. Gutman revealed that MacKenzie's two-day trip to the U.S. had been financed by SerbNet, an organization that was dedicated to propagating the Serb position in the United States. SerbNet had paid MacKenzie US$15,000 plus expenses to make the appearances that were calculated to generate some much-needed good press for the Serb side. SerbNet got a bargain.

MacKenzie's usual speaker's fee was (and is to this day) $10,000 for a forty-five-minute session. He made dozens of appearances during the Bosnian war. He spoke at discount prices or gratis for charity groups, but he made it clear that he was running a business. News agencies that sought him out for interviews were told to make the cheques payable to Major General MacKenzie Enterprises Inc.

MacKenzie never denied he was being paid, but he insisted he didn't know it was SerbNet that wrote the cheques because his agent, working with their agent, set up the engagements — which is entirely possible. One of the mistakes critics of the general often made was to claim that he was just giving out a pro-Serb line for the money, when in fact he was expressing what he truly believed... and still believes. It didn't matter who was paying him. As far as he understood, the gig had been set up by Congresswoman Helen Bentley, whom he had met in Belgrade. MacKenzie says he didn't know that Congresswoman Bentley was a key figure in SerbNet.

Ambassador Sacirbey tried to stop MacKenzie's speeches, but the UN's secretary-general declared that the retired Canadian soldier was free to say what he wanted. However, Sacirbey was able to persuade the UN to advise MacKenzie he couldn't wear a blue beret at his appearances. "That blue hat is like a halo," says Sacirbey. "It represents truth and integrity, and it was being abused." The UN agreed and the general was told not to wear the peacekeeping symbol, though the business cards for Major General MacKenzie Enterprises still sport a small colour decal of the famous soldier, complete with his blue beret.

Sacirbey had some limited victories, but he had little or nothing in his arsenal to match the charisma and public profile of Lewis MacKenzie. A New York public-relations company, Ruder Finn, offered its services to help raise the Bosnian profile in the world's capitals. "David Finn put a staff of five or six people on the Bosnian file for almost a year and offered most of the work for free," says Jim Harff, the man assigned the task of buffing the Bosnian image. But it was hard work. "The Bosnians were hopeless at getting their message across," says Harff.

Some foreign journalists, who covered the war and the political fall-out abroad, admittedly skewed their stories in favour of the Bosnians because they could see Izetbegovic's people were being creamed. Some reporters deliberately failed to report atrocities committed by the Bosnians, fearing it would play into the UN's moral equivocating. But just as often news agencies tried to find "Muslim" atrocities in order to appear more balanced.

By the end of May 1993, talks of possible air strikes against the Serbs came to an end. At a meeting in Washington on May 22, foreign ministers from Britain, France, Russia and the United States agreed they would also abandon a peace plan that proposed cantonization. They would, instead, allow for safe areas around Bosnia where people could seek protection, though the peacekeepers who guarded these areas would be under a chapter six mandate and unable to use their guns except in self-defence. The decision constituted the wholesale abandonment of Bosnia's claims to statehood. The war would continue.

Before it became an international symbol of inhumanity, the town of Srebrenica in the Drina valley of Bosnia was known mostly for its old silver mines. The United Nations now regards what happened in Srebrenica as one of the worst failures in its history. "Through error, misjudgment and an inability to recognize the scope of the evil confronting us, we failed to do our part to save the people of Srebrenica from the Serb campaign of mass-murder," reads the UN's report on the incident, released in 1999.

The Bosnian forces had been able to hold on to four enclaves in the middle of Bosnian Serb territory, and they had become extreme irritants for General Ratko Mladic. From these pockets, Muslim fighters conducted ambushes on Serb forces and carried out their revenge murders in the towns from which they had been ethnically purged.

In 1993, General Mladic decided to get rid of these pockets of resistance once and for all. Not only were they irritants, they stood in the way of his military objective: to conquer as much of Bosnia as possible for the vision of Greater Serbia. Thousands of refugees were streaming into one of those enclaves — Srebrenica — seeking protection from advancing Serbian lines. Aid workers who were able to get into Srebrenica were absolutely appalled by conditions there. While the world was focused on Sarajevo, people were dying of starvation and exposure deep in the heart of Serbian-held territory.

Philippe Morillon, the French general who replaced MacKenzie as head of the UN mission (which had expanded to all of Bosnia), decided to go and see Srebrenica for himself. In one of the most dramatic moments in the history of UN peacekeeping, Morillon was taken hostage by civilians who begged him to save their lives. They were unarmed and did not use force: thousands of men, women and children sat down on the road and blocked his exit.

Morillon could see the vulnerability of the refugees who were huddled there, and he was genuinely horrified. He ran a UN flag up a pole and declared Srebrenica a safe area under UN protection. He promised the people that he would not abandon them, but they wouldn't let him go. He tried to walk out of Srebrenica in the middle of the night wearing a raincoat to conceal his identity, but he had gone only a short distance when he encountered a scene from a nightmare. Hundreds of refugees were heading towards Srebrenica, soaked through with rain and carrying their children. They were seeking refuge in a place Morillon knew was doomed. When his escape vehicle failed to show up, Morillon returned to town in despair.

UN officials, when they heard about Morillon's gesture, thought their general had lost his mind. Morillon had made a commitment that was far outside the UNPROFOR mandate. He had broken the codes of peacekeeping neutrality. The understanding in UN circles was that Srebrenica was a base from which Bosnian soldiers launched military attacks. But most of the ambushes conducted by the men of Srebrenica were food-gathering missions, since the Serb militias would not allow any humanitarian relief convoys into the area. Morillon, by his action, was declaring that there were bad guys and good guys, and the good guys needed help. Thousands of innocent people were about to die.

The UN had no choice but to follow through on the general's impossible offer of help. UNPROFOR dispatched a company of Canadians, though they were convinced that the mission was folly and that General Morillon, by then back in Sarajevo, was mad. It was the job of the 140-man Canadian company to disarm desperate Bosnian fighters in the enclave, and then to protect the entire population of Srebrenica from the forces of General Mladic. It was crazy — they didn't have the men, the weapons or the backup, and they were up against the Bosnian Serb army. The United Nations was trying to save face and claim it was possible to protect a safe area, but it was a diplomatic dream in Technicolor. There was no world support for such an action, and no political will to support the UN with firepower. Morillon was later relieved of his command in Bosnia as a consequence of committing the UN to a deeper engagement than it was prepared to support.

Srebrenica and the three other vaguely defined safe areas — now under UN protection — limped along for another two years. (Sarajevo was eventually added to the list). The Bosnian fighters never gave up their weapons, and they continued their raiding parties in Serb-held territory. It was a formula for disaster, and in the end, nobody would be able to prevent the Serb militias from ignoring the UN and cleaning out Srebrenica.

In mid-July 1995, General Mladic was ready for a unilateral and final solution to his Srebrenica problem. He ordered the UN peacekeepers (now Dutch) to deliver any men who were of potential fighting ability to the Serbs, promising that nobody would be harmed — only detained. This, presumably, would put a stop to the Muslim "provocations" in Serb-held territory and make Srebrenica safer for the innocent people who were stranded there. Mladic seemed to be sincere. He offered candy to the children and told them that they would soon leave for a safer place.

The UNPROFOR soldiers actually helped to load the men onto the buses that would transport them to the safety of detention. It all seemed very efficient, except that many of the Bosnians didn't believe the Serbs and didn't trust the UN. Many tried to escape on foot. Mladic's soldiers drove along the rural roads, calling on the fugitives to come out of hiding, assuring them they wouldn't be harmed. Those who complied were immediately killed.

The men on the buses were taken to holding centres. From a distance, international aid workers who had managed to get into the area could hear the screams and the gunfire all night long. It took two days to kill approximately seven thousand people.

In Canada, Lewis MacKenzie confidently asserted that the Bosnians had brought this slaughter on themselves. In an article in *Maclean's* magazine, he said: "UN peacekeepers reported numerous atrocities by the Bosnian Army but were inadequately equipped to control the situation. Finally the Bosnian Serbs overreacted by cleansing the entire population centre of Srebrenica — all very explainable if not justifiable." It was as close as he could bring himself to a condemnation of mass murder.

Years later, in its own review of the massacre, the UN reported that the enclave had posed no real military threat to the Serbs and that the claims of Bosnian atrocities emanating from the Serb refugee community had been highly exaggerated—principally by the foreign observers on the ground. The UN report stated that the massacre of Srebrenica was an extension of the Serbian war aim. The UN report stated: "The extent to which this pretext [of Bosnian atrocities] was accepted at face value by international actors and observers reflected the prism of 'moral equivalency' through which the conflict in Bosnia was viewed by many for too long."

As the bloody events in Srebrenica unfolded, conditions in Sarajevo went from bad to worse. The Bosnian army had clearly given up on the idea of ever getting help from the international community; soldiers launched a daring assault on Serbian positions in the mistaken belief that they were actually ready to win the war for themselves. They sustained enormous casualties and a crushing defeat.

To punish them for this act of chutzpah, the Serbs cancelled the airport agreement, declaring that the Bosnians had violated the terms of the deal (which nobody denied). A year earlier a Canadian lieutenant colonel, Barry Frewer—the UNPROFOR spokesman at the time—had declared that there was no siege in Sarajevo, just "a tactically advantageous encirclement." Now the international community had to admit that Bosnia was cut off. Three years into the siege, the world finally saw it for what it really was.

In midsummer, there was another bloody mortar attack in Sarajevo's Markale district, the marketplace. The awful images were beamed around the world. Five mortar rounds had slammed into a downtown crowd, killing thirty-seven people and wounding ninety. It was getting hard to shock people with pictures from Sarajevo, but the Markale massacre provoked humanitarian organizations to clamber for intervention.

Taking a page from Lewis MacKenzie's doctrine, British general Rupert Smith, the last wartime peacekeeping commander of Bosnia, first told the media that he wasn't sure who had committed the Markale massacre or how UNPROFOR should react. President Izetbegovic gave his now routine expression of outrage and the Serbs continued their war effort, confident that the status quo would be maintained.

But it turned out that General Smith had been bluffing when he expressed ambivalence about who had caused the carnage. He never doubted that it was the Serbs who had launched the attack, and he only wanted to buy some time in order to get his peacekeepers out of the field as quickly as possible, without alerting the Serbs to the fact that the Bosnian war was now going to change course. He was about to bring an end to the international paralysis.

At 2000 hours on August 28, 1995, General Smith authorized air strikes against Serb positions. His NATO counterparts agreed and Operation Deliberate Force began its sorties—three thousand of them on sixty targets.

The Americans had covertly helped arm the Bosnian Croats, who were, at the same time, advancing deep into Serbian-held territory in co-operation with the Bosnian army. They would take a large swath of territory before the war was finally over. It was lift and strike, exactly what the Bosnians had been asking for since the summer of 1992. And within months, the war would end.

In November 1995, the U.S. envoy Richard Holbrooke cajoled and manipulated the three principal Balkan leaders, Tudjman of Croatia, Izetbegovic of Bosnia, and Milosevic of Serbia, to talk peace in Dayton, Ohio. The Americans eventually shepherded them into an agreement that none entirely liked but all grudgingly agreed to. The Dayton accords split Bosnia into two parts, one for a federation of Muslims and Croats, another for the Serbian republic. Everybody won something, but everybody lost something as well—especially a generation of Sarajevans who, under Tito, had come to believe in and live the dream of multiculturalism.

Radovan Karadzic got his republic but there was one clear moral victory implicit in the Dayton agreement: the process excluded Karadzic and General Ratko Mladic, who by then were indicted war criminals and international pariahs. They were wanted on charges of genocide and crimes against humanity for what they had wrought in Sarajevo and Srebrenica.

The United Nations' final report on this sorry chapter in international peacekeeping, published in 1999, is an abject admission of guilt. It condemns the inadequacy of its own response to the crisis and admits that the doctrine of moral equivalency was central to its failure. In an effort to make all things equal, it had ignored reality: an undefended population was being pounded and systematically slaughtered by a sophisticated armed force. The report blames the UN for responding to what was really a terrorist attack with humanitarian aid, and it condemns the decision to send peacekeepers to a place where there was no peace to keep.

"In the end, the only meaningful and lasting amends we can make to the citizens of Bosnia and Herzegovina who put their faith in the international community is to do our utmost not to allow such horrors to recur.... Bosnia was as much a moral cause as a military conflict. The tragedy of Srebrenica will haunt our history for ever."

The war had endured for nearly four years. Two million people, Serbs, Croats and Muslims, lost their homes; 200,000 died. The siege of Sarajevo lasted 1,395 days. In that city, more than ten thousand people were killed —sixteen hundred of them children. No one knows what nationality they belonged to, or what ethnic group, since nobody kept such statistics.

Sarajevo today is a city of wheelchairs, with special lanes on the sidewalks for the more than fifty thousand people wounded and crippled during the siege. It is a city of sorrowful memories, none more poignant than that of a lone cellist who, for the duration of the war, showed up periodically at the site of the breadline massacre to play a mournful lament he composed for the people who died there.

10

AN OFFICER AND A GENTLEMAN

I was more than upset over such disgusting fabrications.
My greatest concern was the impact these lies would have on the security
of our people on the ground, particularly the Canadians.
Anyone with a Canadian flag on his sleeve was immediately associated with
my reputation as a "rapist and murderer of Muslims" in Bosnia.
—Lewis MacKenzie, *Peacekeeper: The Road to Sarajevo*

Mustafa Bisic is a nervous little man in an oversized blue suit. He sits in his office, surrounded by mountains of case files, and gestures erratically as he discusses his truly impossible job. Bisic is the prosecutor for the canton of Sarajevo in the republic of Bosnia-Herzegovina. It's an impossible job because everything in the Bosnian government is impossible.

The Dayton, Ohio, peace accords that finally concluded the Bosnian war managed to stop the fighting, but they also partitioned the country and institutionalized its ethnic divisions—everything the Bosnians had been fighting against. A three-part presidency representing the major ethnic groups forms the leadership of a state that includes both Bosnia-Herzegovina (BH) and the Republika Srpska (RS).

Civil servants like Bisic have a limited ability to do their jobs. Though the two republics are theoretically joined, Bisic has no arresting powers in the RS and he can't bring anyone in for questioning from the Serb side. He is frequently threatened with physical injury, or worse, for trying to do his job. "I can't even go to the beach with my family," he complains.

Bisic has the distinction of prosecuting the first war crimes in Europe since Nuremberg. In the fall of 1992, the Bosnian Defence Force captured a Serbian soldier and realized immediately that they had a prize on their hands. Borislav Herak had been a guard in one of the most notorious concentration camps in Bosnia during the summer of 1992. Kod Sonje — Sonja's Place — was a small hotel on the outskirts of Sarajevo, in a village called Vogosca. Women were held in the motel complex, while a cement bunker out back, a relic from the Second World War, was used as a holding tank for men. Herak supervised the bunker, where the detainees lived for months at a time in subhuman conditions; about ninety men at a time stayed in the windowless building thirty metres from the motel's restaurant, the Kon Tiki.

Before the war, the Kon Tiki had been a swinging establishment, but in 1992 Serbian paramilitaries took over and used the restaurant and Sonja's Place as a regional headquarters. Women who were held there would later testify that they were frequently raped by their captors, and the complex became far more infamous as a rape camp than for what was happening to the men in the cement bunker. Testimony by the women now forms an explosive part of the international criminal tribunal's ongoing investigation of war crimes during the Bosnian conflict.

In a report prepared for the United Nations by a specially appointed commission of experts, Kod Sonje is described as a prison where as many as fifty or sixty Muslim women and girls were held in the motel (the Kon Tiki restaurant was downstairs). Approximately a hundred of Arkan's and Vojeslev Seselj's men stayed there and, at night, the soldiers chose women at random and had forced sex with them. In one instance, witnesses cited in the report described how two girls, aged seven and thirteen, were gang-raped by soldiers in front of their mother. The girls died from their injuries.

Herak said he was told it was his duty as a Serb soldier to rape women. During interrogation, he confessed to beating, torturing and killing men, and claimed he witnessed other Serb officers doing the same. He also confessed to having raped more than a dozen women at Sonja's Place. The confession was significant for a number of reasons: it was the first full-blown description of how the rape camps might have functioned, and it was the evidence the Bosnians needed to prove that rape was a systematic part of the Serbian ethnic-cleansing project. (The international tribunal is still having a difficult time proving that rape was anything more than a "normal" part of the ongoing brutality of a civil war. But at the time, Herak gave substance to the charges and pushed the United Nations towards a full investigation of "rape as systematic war crime.")

The international media broadcast the Herak trial far and wide. Herak turned out to be a valuable source of information, especially since he was willing to be interviewed by foreign journalists. But there was a number of problems with the trial, and they gave local Bosnian journalists pause. There were obvious signs of torture on Herak's wrists and his eyes had a glazed look. How credible was he?

Bisic concedes there were irregularities. Local police who arrested him admit that Herak was initially beaten to extract his first confessions of rape and torture. But after that, they claim, he was left alone. At trial, without any prompting from the prosecutor, Herak made a startling claim: he had seen United Nations personnel and UN peacekeepers at Kod Sonje during the summer months of 1992. No one had expected this bombshell.

Herak spent two days testifying on these matters. He said that he saw United Nations personnel—in full uniform—arriving for drinks and dinner, and that they often took women away with them in their armoured vehicles. He claimed that the women were later murdered by the Serbs to hide the evidence. Bisic was fascinated by the claims, and most of all by Herak's assertion that one of the officers who visited was none other than the commander of Sector Sarajevo for the UN, Lewis MacKenzie. Bisic had his concerns with other parts of Herak's prosecution, but this spontaneous offer of testimony about UNPROFOR officers was more than he had expected.

Herak was eventually found guilty of rape and murder and sentenced to death. His sentence was commuted.

Mustafa Bisic had no idea where the investigation would go—accusing a UN general of serious impropriety, if not crime, struck him as being daft. Nevertheless, the Bosnian prosecutor decided to launch a formal investigation, and he filed an official Demand for Investigation Execution in the District Military Prosecutor's Office of Sarajevo. It named General Lewis MacKenzie and alleged that "during his stay in the Republic of Bosnia and Herzegovina as commander of the United Nations peace forces, [MacKenzie] went to the territory controlled by the aggressor (i.e., Serbo-Chetnik forces) where the aggressor organized concentration camps and prisons."

His "Demand" claims that the general arrived at the women's concentration camp, picked up four Muslim women and drove them to a place "for the purpose of satisfaction of personal lust." It was a contravention of the Geneva Convention just to know about the existence of such a facility and do nothing about it.

The Sarajevo military court followed up on the charge two months later, sending a letter to the UN 's Boutros Boutros-Ghali demanding that he suspend MacKenzie's immunity from prosecution. The court also requested assistance from the UN in its investigation — asking that the organization turn over documents, daily logbooks and whatever else might help prepare the case.

Bosnia's ambassador, Mohammed Sacirbey, watched the astonishing development unfold with mixed feelings. For one thing, he saw it all as a giant headache. He knew enough about the way the world (and the UN) works to recognize a dead-end process when he saw one. Sacirbey sensed the charges would create a big flap and go nowhere. He also worried that making such charges would damage Bosnia's reputation at the United Nations, where he was trying to persuade the Security Council to take action against the Bosnian Serbs. "We were trying to get 'lift and strike' at the time," he says, referring to appeals for an end to the arms embargo and the beginning of air strikes to relieve the siege of Sarajevo. His main challenge was rebutting MacKenzie's effective message that all sides were equally guilty in the conflict.

Sacirbey had lashed out at the general for negotiating with the Serb extremists on the same basis as with the constitutional Bosnian government. "I feared that these sex charges would wipe out all the other points we were trying to make." Personally, Sacirbey didn't believe the charges. "MacKenzie did a lot of wrong-headed things in Bosnia, but not that," he says.

Mustafa Bisic released his letter to the media and made Herak available for interviews (at least until Herak started to deny everything he had previously said and claim he had been tortured) in the erroneous belief that publicity would pressure the UN to act. It was a naive assumption, especially since Bisic didn't seem to know that his own government, acting through Ambassador Sacirbey, didn't want to be bothered with it. News agencies in Italy, the United States, Canada and the Islamic countries were the first to cautiously report the story of Bosnia's investigation into the general's possible improprieties. There were a lot of reporters who simply wouldn't touch the story.

MacKenzie countered with a media campaign of his own. In February 1993, a Southam News story reported that he was the victim of a smear campaign by the Bosnian government. "I can understand why they would do something like that," MacKenzie offered generously. "If I were in their position and found that the peacekeeping force was not what I wanted, I can envision my devious mind working out a story to discredit them."

MacKenzie was certain that the Presidency had concocted this story and had it put out to the world through a public-relations company. How else could they have spread the word, since Sarajevo didn't even have functioning phones? The article then proceeds to expose Bosnia and Croatia for trying to influence public opinion by hiring spin doctors, just as the Kuwaiti government had done to lure the U.S. into Operation Desert Storm back in 1990.

That newspaper article, and a number of others, charged that the Bosnian government was up to its old devious tricks, trying to muzzle the critical Canadian general who was only trying to tell the truth. New York–based Ruder Finn was identified as the company that was probably responsible for planting the smear. David Finn, co-owner of the company, dismisses the accusation as being ludicrous.

This was exactly the distraction that Sacirbey had feared. The Bosnian ambassador had dutifully passed the letter from the Bosnian court to the secretary-general but, on the advice of his own government, had not made a formal complaint. Contrary to MacKenzie's claims of a giant smear campaign, there was actually a significant attempt by the Bosnian authorities to bury the story. But it wouldn't go away.

On February 23, 1993, in Washington, at a Helsinki Watch briefing for Congress, a Bosnian nurse testified that she had seen a videotape in which General MacKenzie was with a group of Muslim women and seemed to be hugging one of them. The women were crying, the nurse reported. The testimony was part of a discussion of what the American government should be doing about the increasingly lurid accounts of mass rape in the aftermath of the war.

Congresswoman Louise Slaughter was concerned enough about the allegations involving MacKenzie to convey them to Madeleine Albright, who was at that time the U.S. ambassador to the UN. MacKenzie quickly countered. He said that he knew all about the video, that it was recorded during his farewell party in Sarajevo. The weeping women are the people he describes in his book as "the Sarajevo girls," a group of secretaries and office workers who were crying because they were sad to see him go.

MacKenzie volunteered all of this to Peter Gzowski on the CBC's then-flagship radio program *Morningside*, and he stated that another humanitarian aid worker had also seen the video and confirmed it was an innocent social event. Nobody produced the actual tape, but the American reporter

Roy Gutman found the dust-up intriguing. He launched a six-month investigation for *Newsday*, travelling extensively and following up every lead. He never found the video, nor any conclusive evidence against MacKenzie. But in November 1993, Gutman reported: "United Nations peacekeepers in Bosnia regularly visited a Serb-run brothel outside Sarajevo, where some of them took sexual advantage of Muslim and Croat women forced into prostitution, according to Muslim witnesses and the local Serb commander."

Gutman tracked down twelve Muslim and three Serb witnesses, all of whom were still living in the area, to get their testimonies; one witness was the camp commander, Branislav Vlaco, who was in charge of the rape victims. They all reported seeing United Nations personnel and their distinctive white vehicles arriving at Kod Sonje and the Park Hotel, down the street, where female witnesses say they were also raped. Vlaco claimed that as many as fifty UN peacekeepers visited the establishment during the summer of 1992, including men from Canada, New Zealand, France, Ukraine and an African country. Some came only for afternoon visits and others stayed for parties.

The Muslim men detained in the cement bunker behind Kod Sonje could not see the UN soldiers from their vantage point, nor could anyone arriving at the restaurant have seen the prisoners. But on many occasions, according to Gutman's witnesses, the men were ordered to work at the restaurant, to cut firewood and prepare the traditional lamb barbecues and to clean up the mess afterward.

One prisoner reported that when he was cleaning up one morning-after scene, he found, along with the dirty dishes and wine bottles, both a Serbian and a UN flag. These prisoners also reported seeing women taken away in UN vehicles. "Two of the women told New York *Newsday* they had been raped at the brothel, one by a UN officer, one by a Bosnian Serb soldier. A third said she had witnessed Bosnian Serb officers rape and kill two Muslim girls in front of a crowd of captured Muslim women," Gutman reported.

But Gutman was highly sceptical of claims that Lewis MacKenzie was seen at Kod Sonje: "He was in Belgrade during one of the alleged occasions," says Gutman. And then there is the problem that a lot of people started referring to any peacekeeper they saw as "MacKenzie." When Serbs told their prisoners to look sharp because MacKenzie would be visiting, Gutman believes it could have been anyone from the United Nations.

It is difficult to dismiss charges that people in the UN visited, and hence knew about, Kod Sonje but didn't report it to their superiors. But UNPROFOR maintained that war crimes weren't a peacekeeping responsibility and sticking its nose into such affairs would constitute "mission creep." (This was the same defence UN peacekeepers offered in years to come, when they were told to arrest indicted war criminals. It wasn't their job and might even disrupt the delicate balance they had created with the locals.)

But Kod Sonje was on an official list of probable prison camps that the Bosnian government had submitted to the UN and its personnel when MacKenzie was still in Sarajevo. The Bosnians had demanded an investigation at that time. MacKenzie counters that he got requests like that from both sides, but it wasn't really his job to investigate.

MacKenzie told Gutman the visitors were probably UN observers and not UNPROFOR soldiers. The probable reason for the visits would be prisoner exchange. If women were getting into vehicles, he said, it might have been because they were part of an agreement to take them to safety.

MacKenzie offered a New Zealand colonel named Richard Gray as the likely UN visitor, a man considered to be somewhat of a loose cannon by UNPROFOR officers. Gray now admits that he went to the Kon Tiki restaurant, but only for lunch and only as part of a day-long negotiation process. He knew nothing about women captives or prisoners, he says, and it wasn't his place to ask about them.

The UN agreed to conduct an internal investigation of a number of charges of impropriety, including a claim (well founded, as it turns out) that Ukrainian peacekeepers were engaging in black-market exchanges, even acting as paid escorts for desperate Bosnians trying to cross the airport runway. Cherif Bassiouni is an American lawyer who was chairman of the UN Commission of Experts in the early 1990s. He exhaustively documented wartime atrocities in the former Yugoslavia and was asked to turn over his files on Kod Sonje to both the UN legal affairs department and the Yugoslavian war crimes tribunal. He says that "a lot of witnesses say they saw him [MacKenzie] there. But only for meetings. Nothing more."

MacKenzie continues to deny vehemently that he ever went to Sonja's Place for any reason. But the Bisic investigation seems to have taken on a life of its own and, regardless of its merit, has become a reality that haunts Lewis MacKenzie to this day.

"At the time, I was consulted [by the Canadian Department of National Defence] as to how we would deal with the charges," says MacKenzie.

"We all agreed that we would low-ball it and wait for the UN to clear me. In hindsight, that was probably a mistake."

The UN has never made its findings public. After numerous requests, MacKenzie received a single-page fax from Kofi Annan, head of the Department of Peacekeeping Operations at the time, telling him that the final report of the Greindl Commission (Major General C. Greindl chaired the investigation) into the conduct of United Nations personnel had dealt with the "prostitution activities" separately.

In March 1994, the Greindl Commission submitted its report, which dealt with the so-called MacKenzie Allegation. In its conclusion, the report states the following: "Allegations against Major General Lewis MacKenzie are unfounded. Evidence shows that General MacKenzie departed the mission area approximately one month prior to any allegation."

The UN has never released the complete findings of the Greindl report. But the flow of unsubstantiated allegations continues. Whether the stories are true or not is no longer an issue in Bosnia. They are part of the popular history of the war, much of which may well be rooted more in anger than in reality. There are unflattering anecdotes about MacKenzie scattered throughout the articles and books written in Bosnia about the war. It has become common currency that he was at Kod Sonje, just as it became common currency among Western governments that the Bosnians were killing their own people to get international attention. In the apocrypha of war, universal truths materialize and can never be changed, no matter their damage.

The Sarajevan evening paper *Vecernje Novine* recently published a series of articles on the alleged goings-on at Kod Sonje during the war. UNPROFOR figures prominently in the story: "On two occasions an UNPROFOR delegation headed by Lewis MacKenzie came to the 'Kontiki' pension. His first appearance saved my life," reports one witness the newspaper interviewed. The man was about to be killed when the foreign soldiers and their commander arrived, he says, and the Serbs had to abandon their plans. On another occasion, the man says that MacKenzie came for dinner: "It was expected that MacKenzie would tour the prison and see in what condition the inmates were living, whereas he, along with his escort, drank and ate lamb, spit-roasted especially for them."

The various commanders who ran the UNPROFOR mission during the war were a mixed lot: some were disliked more than others and they were often suspected of harbouring biases. MacKenzie is the only one of them the Sarajevans want to see punished: he's been convicted in the court of public opinion there and no evidence he can offer will unconvict him. "Only MacKenzie was charged with any crime," says Gordana Knezevic. "No other commander in UNPROFOR was accused of any sexual impropriety except for him." While Canadians think of MacKenzie as a hero, Sarajevans think of him as a criminal. "In Bosnia, MacKenzie will be remembered for rape," says Mohammed Sacirbey, "while in the minds of Canadians, he will always be the victim of that story."

Mustafa Bisic is like a dog with a bone. The Sarajevo prosecutor is still actively pursuing the case against the general. His other files are stacked all over his office in Sarajevo's palace of justice, but Bisic takes out a key to open the wooden cabinet that contains one item: a thick folio with the words "MacKenzie: November '92" scrawled on the front. The file contains a new allegation against the Canadian general, one made by a young woman who says she met MacKenzie not at Kod Sonje but at another secret place. That Bisic is willing to clutch at this slim straw is another sign of what people in Sarajevo are willing to believe of the Canadian general.

Bisic's new witness claims she was pulled from a busload of refugees departing Sarajevo in late June of 1992 and whisked away by Serb paramilitaries in old JNA uniforms. Her nine-month-old baby was taken from her and she was told she would never see the child again if she didn't cooperate. She says that after hours of interrogation, her captors discovered something that seemed to impress them: she spoke English quite fluently.

Days later, the English-speaking Muslim woman says she was taken up to Jahorina mountain, past Pale, to a hotel with a large dining room. It was there, according to her testimony, that she claims to have first seen Lewis MacKenzie and recognized him from his television appearances. Later, she claims she was taken to a secret location—a chalet of a type that is common in resort areas like Jahorina mountain. She says MacKenzie came there. At all times, he acted the gentleman. He arrived at the house, presented her with a rose, told her he knew she spoke English and suggested he might be able to help her. She claims she had sex with him, hoping that, by doing so, she'd save herself and her child: "He didn't beat me or force me to do anything but I was as helpless as a prisoner."

The woman was taken to Kod Sonje later in July where she says UNPROFOR soldiers came to rescue her and to reunite her with the baby. Her story has one of the few happy endings among the women held at the brothel.

The case is troubling. Bisic doesn't know the woman's real name. The incident involves an officer esteemed by the UN and awarded iconic stature in his own land. The story is also highly uncharacteristic of all other such testimonies: the alleged "crime" lacks the primitive brutality of the Kod Sonje testimonies.

Nonetheless, Bisic is pursuing it. He's now caught up in a legal wrangle with the organization that came forward with the testimony and that claims to be representing this witness and alleged victim. The Centre for Investigation and Documentation (CID) in Sarajevo—a privately funded agency—recorded the woman's testimony and it will only reveal her identity to the war crimes tribunal in The Hague if the ICTY decides to pursue the case. CID staff members will confirm only that the woman is a member of the Association of Former Camp Internees of Bosnia-Herzegovina.

The centre has published the woman's testimony, along with that of other alleged victims of rape, in a book that has been widely distributed in Bosnia. The introduction to the hefty volume declares that its aim is to reveal the truth about what happened to women during the war and it is signed by three members of the CID, including Dr. Nedzib Sacirbegovic, Mohammed Sacirbey's father, who also lives in the United States. There is also a short endorsement from U.S. journalist Roy Gutman. But the true identities of the victims are omitted from their accounts along with any details that might reveal who they are. Bisic has now made a representation to the war crimes tribunal to help him pry that information from the CID. So far, the ICTY hasn't given him much help or encouragement.

In an interview, MacKenzie says he has no recollection of such an encounter: "There's not even anything that can be the genesis of this story," says MacKenzie. "I never saw a rose the whole time I was in Sarajevo." Yes, he certainly went to Pale and to a restaurant for lunch—only once—but if there had been such a woman among the group, "they never would have let me talk to her." MacKenzie says he was never alone and always had a witness with him—quite often BBC reporter Martin Bell, who later became a British member of Parliament.

MacKenzie later submitted a detailed itinerary of his days in July and says—given that it would take eight hours to go up and back to Jahorina through all the Serb roadblocks—it's impossible that he would have had the time for such an illicit tryst.

Nonetheless, MacKenzie is now bracing himself for another round of Bosnian accusations. Bisic wrote another letter to the UN in late 1999, once again asking that MacKenzie's immunity to prosecution be waived and that the UN turn over all its documents, including its unreleased Greindl inquiry into the "MacKenzie Allegation." He's heard nothing back. "If I fail this time, then I'm ready to send this file down to the basement," he says as he locks the pile of papers away in his wooden cabinet.

EPILOGUE

NEW FRONTIERS

The Prince must be a lion but he must also know
how to play the fox.
—Niccolò Machiavelli, *The Prince*

hroughout the spring of 1999, Gordana Knezevic, along with her
husband, Ivo, and all three of their children, watched the televised
war in Yugoslavia from their home in east-end Toronto. First there
were the stories of the Kosovo refugees fleeing the Serb police and military forces; these were illustrated by evocative pictures of people being
loaded onto trains and expelled, shipped off to crowded camps in Macedonia and Albania.

And then they watched as NATO dropped its bombs on Kosovo and
Serbia. Ivo Knezevic cheered, and then he wept. Why could they not have
done this ten years ago? Why didn't they stop Milosevic and his war-
mongering in 1991, before he went on to ruin so many lives in their beautiful old city, Sarajevo? So much would have been different.

When the war in Bosnia started, they sent their two youngest children
away. Now they live in Canada, once again a family, but with a large hole
in their collective memory. Boris, the son who stayed with them in Sarajevo, is now a man. The other two—Igor and Olga—hustled onto a bus on
May 2, 1992, for a separation that everyone thought would be months at
most, grew up in exile.

The trauma of the Bosnian war for this family—for all those who
lived through it—is immense. In the spring of 1999, they watched television to see if Kosovo would turn into a re-run of what happened in their
country. But this time, whatever the motives for bombing Belgrade, whatever flak participating countries took for joining in, whatever mistakes the

bombers made, NATO members heard the clarion call and it amounted to a simple declaration: *We can't face another Bosnia. Don't fail to act again.* And they didn't.

People who followed the Yugoslav coverage on television would see a familiar face on *CTV News* with Lloyd Robertson. Major General Lewis MacKenzie, retired, bright as sunshine, gave a blow-by-blow account of the conflict from the Serbian point of view. His upbeat commentaries on how the Serbian people were coping with the NATO shelling often concluded with a trademark sign-off from Belgrade: "Cheers." He was also a regular in *The Ottawa Citizen*, offering the inside story of the war in Yugoslavia at a time when journalists were being expelled for objectively reporting the results of the NATO air strikes.

What the audience didn't know was that MacKenzie was in Belgrade as a guest of the Yugoslavian government. According to MacKenzie he obtained a visa for himself and the CTV crew after discussions with the embassy in Ottawa and with Yugoslavian ministers concerning what he might be able to do to help them out. One possibility was for him to negotiate the release of two American servicemen who had been captured near the Macedonian border. But for someone who had often demonstrated his understanding of the Serbian point of view, the possibilities were endless.

To help facilitate his double role in Yugoslavia, MacKenzie had a police escort while moving around the country, and he seemed to have unrestricted freedom of movement. Many reporters were being censored and kicked out, but MacKenzie says that everywhere he travelled in Serbia, people would mob him for his autograph.

The Yugoslavian government had warned him that he'd need to bring a supply of photos of himself—preferably signed—as people would want them as souvenirs. Indeed, the foreign media liaison officer for the Belgrade police department has a framed picture of the general on his desk, among the snapshots of his family. In restaurants, people stood to applaud when MacKenzie entered. When the indicted war criminal (and soon-to-be murdered warlord) Arkan encountered MacKenzie in his hotel lobby, he greeted him warmly.

After interviews with government members, the CTV crew would remove the recording equipment and close the door so that the general could continue speaking in private with the usually influential guests. He sometimes disappeared for private meetings without his CTV colleagues. What did Belgrade get for it? Not much. "I think the government thought he could do more for them than he really could," said one Serb who worked with the MacKenzie group.

In his commentaries, MacKenzie was openly critical of the NATO bombing campaign. He argued that the best solution for Kosovo was partition, and he denounced the Kosovo Liberation Army as a terrorist group whom Slobodan Milosevic had a legal right to try to crush. NATO bombed anyway. The NATO force included Canadian planes, fighting in Europe for the first time since the Second World War. In one article, MacKenzie claimed the KLA was being whitewashed by NATO just as these "terrorists" were *provoking* the Serbs to act: "And it's equally true," wrote MacKenzie, "that most governments facing a separatist or independence movement tend to react with a heavy hand; we invoked the War Measures Act over a few bombs in a mailbox and a couple of kidnappings."

As MacKenzie argued the legitimacy (if heavy-handedness) of the Serb campaign in Kosovo, the Yugoslavian authorities were up to their old tricks. The information ministry called a press conference to demonstrate that the so-called Albanian refugees were actually paid Hollywood actors who numbered only in the thousands; they were walking around in circles to give the illusion of hundreds of thousands. Belgrade then claimed the Albanians were killing themselves to make it look as though the Serbs were doing it. But this time it didn't stick. Too many Serb police and militiamen had been caught red-handed. MacKenzie never suggested that the Albanians were burning down their own homes and poisoning their own wells for sympathy, but he did insist that the atrocities committed against Kosovar Albanians had been exaggerated. MacKenzie says he objected only to the way Milosevic was conducting the campaign against Kosovo, by blowing up whole villages. "My way would be to go in there at night and slit their throats. Be a little selective." He shared his advice with Yugoslavian ministers but they failed to appreciate the merits of the MacKenzie method.

It wasn't MacKenzie's first trip back to Belgrade since he returned to Canada in 1992. Radovan Karadzic had invited the general back in March 1993 to discuss what the Serbs should do with a number of UN soldiers they had taken hostage. MacKenzie took along a CTV crew.

In 1995, as the general was getting ready to judge a Miss Apple Blossom contest in the Annapolis valley of Nova Scotia, he got another request for advice. This time it was a cellphone call from Nicole Koljevic, the professor-cum-ultra-nationalist who was Dr. Karadzic's right-hand man. The professor wanted to know what he should do with the Canadian peacekeepers they had taken hostage to prevent Western planes from bombing Serbian positions. One of the hostages was a Canadian officer, Philip Rechner, and Koljevic understood he was an old buddy of MacKenzie's.

Rechner's forlorn face had become famous worldwide when he was filmed handcuffed to a post during the hostage-taking incident. MacKenzie advised Koljevic that he had to let all the hostages go, not just Rechner. And he demonstrated a surprising familiarity with the military back roads around Sarajevo as he explained to the Bosnian Serb exactly what route to take to get the captives out of Serbian territory.

All these negotiations for the release of peacekeepers were unofficial. MacKenzie called the Canadian government to inform them about what he was doing but, according to the general, Ottawa wasn't particularly interested.

Lewis MacKenzie is as convinced of the success of his 1992 mission to Bosnia as Roméo Dallaire is convinced of the utter failure of his mission to Rwanda two years later. There's an unofficial debate within the ranks of the Canadian Forces: on the one hand, Lewis MacKenzie argues that the security of the soldiers come first, the mission second and the force commander third. Then there's the Dallaire view: it's the mission first and the soldiers second. MacKenzie opened the Sarajevo airport and made sure that all his soldiers left Bosnia alive. Saving the country from war was not his job. He did all he could, he says, to persuade the two sides to end the war. It's not his fault if they didn't.

Dallaire opened the Kigali airport to humanitarian relief and saved thirty thousand people. He never tried to end the war: only to stop the genocide. He lost ten peacekeepers and watched an entire country dissolve into a bloodbath. Dallaire believes his mission failed. MacKenzie believes his mission succeeded. In the calculus of geopolitical interests, they are both right. On the human level, however, there is another standard by which to judge their respective missions. Roméo Dallaire is welcome to return to the country he served in. Those who survived its horror believe that he, at least, did all within his power to save them. MacKenzie is not welcome in Bosnia, unless he wants to face Mustafa Bisic in court.

During the bombing of Belgrade in the spring of 1999, Lewis MacKenzie reported that the Serbs were holding up very well under the attack and their spirit was defiant. Gordana Knezevic, in her Toronto apartment, wished he could have admired and encouraged the people of Sarajevo half as much.

BOOK THREE
The Blasted Heath

1

RWANDA

Imagine the assault on your senses. First, the stench of bodies rotting; you cannot distinguish between the odour of slaughtered livestock and the odour of the people who once tended the animals. Second, there is a queer absence of sound: the clap of gunfire, the shudder of grenades and the reverberation of missiles slamming into the sides of mud huts have stopped. Bells do not ring, calling people to prayer — the church halls are still clogged with cadavers. Radio broadcasts that once incited people to kill their neighbours, to "exterminate the cockroaches and make sure even the baby cockroaches are dead," have now ended.

By the fall of 1994, Roméo Dallaire is gone and UNAMIR II is in place, trying to put together the pieces of a destroyed country. Once, there was hardly a square inch of Rwanda that didn't teem with activity — farmers working their red-clay garden plots or tending their cattle; women in brightly coloured tangas carrying goods to the marketplace; children in their indigo uniforms heading to school. That's all stopped.

The sorghum rots in the fields; the only harvesting of maize and beans is by hungry refugees who scavenge for food; the precious coffee and tea crops have been destroyed. All around are burned-out huts, damaged villages and, of course, corpses. A cattle-dipping pit is a mass grave. Latrines, holes, cellars, rivers, lakes — and whatever else might have helped to hide the evidence — have become tombs for butchered Rwandans. Eventually, the smell forces survivors to bury the bodies in shallow graves. The faces of people tell a story of trauma, loss and grief, the faces of people without the hope that anyone will ever be held accountable for what happened to their families.

October is the rainy season — spring in Rwanda, though there is more than one crop per year. Refugees who returned — or managed to stay close by — struggle to plant crops with farm tools and seed provided by the dozens of aid agencies arriving daily. Tutsi farmers have only the possessions with which they fled, and after several months of nomadic life, they have been reduced to almost nothing. If they can get back to their homes, they find them damaged and looted of everything of the slightest value — chair cushions, bedding, pots and pans, radios, clothing — stolen with the clear permission of the authorities, much of it traded for little more than beer.

A part of Rwanda's beautiful Akagera National Park was settled by returning Tutsi unable to find land anywhere else. Zoologists who had assumed the work of Dian Fossey tried to save Volcanoes National Park from the same fate. It is the heart of the mountain-gorilla research centre that Fossey founded; during the genocide, the gorillas actually had little trouble from potential poachers, who were busy either fleeing the country or helping the *génocidaires* in their "work detail." But after the war, with poverty raging, the gorillas were more vulnerable than ever. Without a functioning government in Rwanda, or at least one that considered the mountain gorillas a priority, people began encroaching on the valuable real estate.

Among the impoverished Tutsi returning to Rwanda in the months following the war were some relatively wealthy ones, those who had lived in neighbouring Uganda since the 1960s. They came with cash to open businesses and cattle to start farming. They returned to find the land they — or their parents — had fled nearly forty years before, and to reclaim it. These refugees shared none of the collective trauma and shock of those who had fled only months before, leaving behind the bodies of children, husbands, wives and parents.

Despite the extraordinary civilian death toll, Rwanda had very few funerals — too many bodies to bury. Temporary mass graves would become permanent because it was too much work to find and exhume loved ones who might be entangled in the compost of cadavers underground. French soldiers with Operation Turquoise had helped the Hutu bury many of the corpses during the summer of 1994, courting suspicion among the Tutsi that France was only trying to help the *génocidaires* hide incriminating evidence.

The Rwandan government — now under the de facto authority of Colonel Paul Kagame — ordered some of the graves opened and the cadavers reburied in marked plots. But the task was a symbolic gesture, and thousands more bodies were left scattered around the countryside. At least there were fewer dogs to fight over the human remains; General Dallaire had ordered the animals killed when he was still in charge.

Schools and churches had been the settings for some of the worst of the slaughter. The Tutsi who had sought refuge in those presumably safe places were butchered in groups. In some of the bloodiest places — like Nyarubuye, in the prefecture of Kibungo — the bodies were coated in lime, which slowed down decomposition, and sustained the unimaginable reality of the scene. Foreigners still visit such "shrines" to see first-hand the scale and the horrifying techniques employed in the massacres. Beheaded children lie beside women cut in half as they attempted to hide babies (still) tied to their backs. There are groups of people obviously shattered by grenades as they huddled together in what they thought was a sanctuary. A child's skeletal arms are still tied together, tiny hands crushed by some blunt instrument. A dull machete? A hammer? There is no one left to answer the questions that these scenes of carnage pose.

A three-hour drive from Kigali, on a hilltop overlooking the prefecture of Gikongoro, a group of red-brick buildings, formerly a school, is now a giant tomb where bodies are either neatly stacked or left strewn about just as they fell. Local people — the survivors — say that forty-seven thousand Tutsi were murdered in Gikongoro within just a few days in mid-April. The French soldiers from Operation Turquoise arrived there in June 1994, greeted like a liberation force by the burgomasters who were helping to conduct the genocide. The soldiers used a bulldozer to dig a mass grave for an unknown number of corpses.

A researcher who works with Human Rights Watch went to the Catholic church in Cyahinda, in the southern prefecture of Butare, eight months after the genocide began and found an eerie, haunted scene. The main doors of the church, pocked with bullet holes, had been left open.

The fifty-year-old brick structure was once a busy social centre for youth groups, women's associations and public gatherings—a place to talk, sing and laugh. It became a logical place for Tutsi to hide from the killers. But the hundreds who took refuge there found themselves in a trap.

There were burn marks on the walls of the church where grenades had exploded. "Bullets shot into the church had left holes on several walls and had broken some of the stained glass windows," said the researcher's report. "There were bloodstains on the floors and walls. Bleached bits of human bone were mixed with the dirt on the ground of the church. Just next to the church was the grave of the priest. Three mass graves lay behind and below the church and a long line of graves ran next to the church on the right-hand side. Behind the church, on the left-hand side, was a long row of latrines that had been stuffed with bodies."

In the months following the end of the war, many Hutu fled the country as the Rwandan Patriotic Front took charge. But RPF authorities quickly arrested thousands of Hutu men, women and children and charged them with murder. Many, if not most, of those caught up in the sweep had been involved in killing their neighbours. Some were actual organizers of the genocide. But thousands of those arrested probably had little to do with the atrocities. Petty crimes and old grudges commingled the truly wicked with the merely unsavoury and, in some cases, the baldly innocent in the country's teeming prisons.

By the Rwandan government's own admission, a number of the prisoners were guilty of nothing more than having a plot of land that someone else coveted. In one sector, the male Hutu population fell from three hundred to four individuals. The rest were killed or arrested. But what was to become of those in jail? Paul Kagame could have initiated his own slaughter, but his government knew that such conspicuous retaliation would jeopardize the flow of external assistance from aid agencies.

In the months following the war, there was no functioning legal system—judges and lawyers had been among the first to be rounded up and killed, whether they were Tutsi or moderate Hutu. Most of Rwanda's prisons had been severely damaged or destroyed. Out of seventeen, the government could use only four.

The arrested prisoners were first placed in local *cachots*, or makeshift jails, where the overcrowding quickly became acute. Aid workers in some regions got a glimpse inside some of these dungeons, where the authorities kept dozens of people in space designed for only a few. In one of them, local police had forced sixty people into a tiny room, closed the door and locked it. As it was reported later, guards heard prisoners inside banging on the doors and walls and calling for help, but they ignored them. When the cell was finally opened again the next morning, twenty-two people had suffocated; four others had to be put in a hospital, where two more died.

A transfer to one of the few functioning prisons was only a slight improvement. Women had more space, but many had no choice but to bring their babies and children along with them. Infants lived in fetid, disease-ridden quarters with their mothers. Young boys were confined with men of all ages. Strict hierarchies of prisoners formed. People paid for space to lie down, while others would wait in turn to sit or sleep on boards covering the latrines at night.

In the first year after the genocide, the authorities arrested and incarcerated ninety thousand. During the next year, the number climbed to 130,000. Wounds festered and sickness spread rapidly. A visitor to one prison "hospital" saw rows of people lying on the floor; instead of the smell of disinfectant, there was only the odour of rotting flesh. AIDS, tuberculosis and dysentery took hundreds of lives, but there are few records. Almost no paperwork exists. Families of people who suddenly disappeared in the summary arrests would inquire in vain to find out where they went. Only by standing outside the prisons, scanning groups of inmates from a distance, did they have any real hope of finding a parent or a child or a sibling. Locating the missing loved one was usually a matter of life and death, since prison food was barely sufficient to keep a person alive. Families fed those in jail.

The newly installed government was clearly anxious to get the country moving again; but with few functioning public systems, an estimated 800,000 people dead and two million refugees hiding out in other countries, there wasn't a lot of Rwandan expertise left to run the state. Within the surviving population, there was the question of reconciling the killers and their victims. How could Hutu ever again take up residence in the same villages and neighbourhoods as Tutsi? The notion of truth and reconciliation was gathering credibility in South Africa. But it would be a long time before anybody would be able to introduce such a concept here.

Some Hutu had become internal refugees, in camps established by foreign relief workers. By the beginning of 1995, the consensus among aid workers and the new Rwandan government was that these sprawling camps needed to close down if life was ever to return to normal. But for obvious reasons, Hutu were reluctant to leave a place where foreigners protected and fed them, for the uncertain perils of life in communities now run by their enemies.

Major Philip Lancaster stayed on in Rwanda after Roméo Dallaire had departed to work as a military observer in the outlying regions of the country. One day he arranged for a reconnaissance party of Hutu refugees from Kibeho camp, near the scene of one of the worst of the April massacres in Gikongoro, to visit their home sector to see if a larger return by the Hutu might be possible. The local burgomaster was the first to spot the Hutu as they tumbled out of the UN vehicle. He had lost eighty-seven members of his family — and he immediately identified the visitors as *génocidaires*. The few who had been so unlucky as to get out first were marched away to jail; no one else would get out of the vehicle. That was the end of any plans to repatriate the internally displaced refugees, and Lancaster took the rest of them back to Kibeho camp.

As the months went on, the insurgent RPF and its now separate military wing, the Rwandan Patriotic Army (RPA), finally decided it was time to force these people out of the internal camps; by March 1995, only Kibeho camp remained. At last count in March, according to Major Lancaster, it had 120,000 inhabitants. The RPA plan was to cordon off the camp and slowly tighten the military loop until people had no choice but to leave. The refugees would then have to run a gauntlet of "security checks" designed to screen out the *génocidaires* (who would immediately go to the overcrowded prisons). For those who survived the gauntlet, there would be the inevitable encounter with a hostile and vengeful population wherever they went.

By the middle of April, the Hutu still refused to leave and the cordon was now so tight that human-rights workers said refugees were being forced to sleep in their own excrement. Lancaster wrote a report on his observations on the weekend of April 22 and 23: "Shortly before noon, a fierce lightning storm swept the camp. It seemed to ignite the boiling tensions inside and sparked a mass escape attempt. The RPA responded with machine-gun fire, rocket propelled grenades and mortars. The final body count remains a mystery but by 3 o'clock the human rights observer on site reported over my radio net that there appeared to be somewhere in the neighbourhood of 4,000 killed. By nightfall, that figure had doubled."

The following day, Lancaster attempted to guide some of the escapees to a sports stadium, where they could be protected. As he led one group of forty, mostly old men, very young children and women, he ran into trouble: "My heart sank. After nearly thirty years in uniform I can tell an ambush site pretty easily." Lancaster had witnessed the horrible organized slaughter of Tutsi, and now he was trying to prevent an act of revenge: "As we climbed the hill and entered the village, the stoning grew very heavy. Adolescent children ran in among my group slashing with sticks at everyone, regardless of age. They made great sport out of smashing the heads of babies being carried on their mothers' backs. My group began to panic and clambered on to the vehicle. Several mothers handed me their babies through the open window." By the end of the mayhem, Lancaster had lost about fifteen people.

Within days of the massacre at Kibeho, Lancaster decided he had had enough. He arranged to leave the country with a group of other Canadians who had been in Rwanda since the genocide. The killing would not stop, no matter how much goodwill they brought to the task. Unless the people responsible for the genocide could be brought to justice, the revenge attacks would continue. But those responsible, to the extent that anybody could be identified, were long gone. Those remaining would bear the weight of a nation's lust for vengeance.

In the refugee camps of Zaire, to which most of the Hutu population had moved, the ground was of volcanic rock and provided neither water nor material to absorb human waste. Conditions were appalling. The United Nations High Commissioner for Refugees (UNHCR) considers the flood of people out of Rwanda to be one of the greatest tragedies in its fifty-year history, the most rapid mass exodus UNHCR has ever faced. It quickly overwhelmed the international system. But worse, along with the filth and disease, the camps were also hotbeds of military organization.

Roméo Dallaire had offered to arrest the Hutu Power leaders as they fled the country—some with the assistance of the French soldiers in Operation Turquoise—but his superiors warned him that it wasn't his job to do so. In the camps, members of the former Rwandan armed forces, along with the ruthless militias of the Interahamwe, the *génocidaires* and the deposed political leaders, used the civilian population as a human shield. Every effort to separate the political-military machinery from the legitimate refugees created an uprising and reprisals against any Hutu who co-operated with the authorities. Fifty thousand people, mainly women and children, died of cholera in only a few weeks. The Hutu Power leaders consolidated their control and authority in the camps and would not allow aid workers to move the refugees to a more sanitary environment.

Principally, Hutu Power was preparing for another attack to finish the project that they had begun in the bloody spring of 1994: the killing of Tutsi. No one interviewed in these camps seemed to have any misgivings or remorse about what had happened in Rwanda. They had bought the line that they were simply acting to defend themselves from the advancing RPF. As long as they all spoke with one voice, no one could be singled out for punishment. As long as they all denied they had done anything wrong, the international community couldn't penetrate to the core of individual responsibility.

By April 1995, a year after the genocide began, the perpetrators had completely rebuilt their military structure in exile. In the words of Colonel Théoneste Bagosora of the former Rwandan government, they planned to "wage war that will be long and full of dead people until the minority Tutsi are finished and completely out of the country." Fed and protected in refugee camps supported by millions of dollars in international aid, the Hutu Power leaders were able to hold regular planning meetings and to recruit new members. Using hard currency stolen from government coffers before they fled, the Hutu leaders purchased arms on the open market; the Zairian dictator, Mobutu Sese Seko, turned a blind eye as their new weapons arrived in his country. All of this happened under the concerned, unblinking gaze of the international community.

While the Hutu Power army regrouped and rearmed itself in Zaire, the leading architects of the genocide moved on to hospitable foreign countries where they could live comfortably and organize their affairs without fear of punishment. Some of them simply wanted to escape Rwanda and disappear into obscurity, while others contemplated their return to power in Kigali. The countries that hosted the *génocidaires*-in-exile had no idea what to do with them and little understanding of their role in Rwanda. The world was far more transfixed by the two million Hutu refugees living in the squalid camps of Zaire and Tanzania. Justice was the last item on the agenda.

Bagosora — the chief military engineer of the Tutsi slaughter — moved to Cameroon, where he lived with dozens of other former leaders and organizers of Hutu Power. The prime minister of the interim government,

Jean Kambanda, went to Kenya, along with the minister of family and women's affairs, commanders of the former Rwandan army and a number of radio and newspaper propagandists. Some of the local leaders, who had been in charge of the communities where Tutsi populations were obliterated, went on to enjoy the bourgeois comforts of Belgium. Léon Mugesera, the former Laval University student whose inflammatory role in the early stages of the genocide marked him as one of its prime instigators, had safely returned to his alma mater in Quebec City.

If the world did not properly understand the guilt of Rwanda's political leaders, there was even less comprehension of the role that had been played by Rwanda's spiritual leaders. A Catholic priest, wanted for genocide, moved to Rome where he lived with impunity, surrounded by his religious brothers. Pastor Elizephan Ntakirutimana, of a Seventh Day Adventist parish in Rwanda (where, according to witnesses, he and his son had offered to shelter Tutsi and then had turned them over to the killers), decamped to the spacious Laredo, Texas, home of another son. The priest of Sainte Famille church in Kigali, who was wanted for torture, took up residence in France.

Not one of these leaders, nor any of the dozens of others living in exile throughout Africa, Europe and North America, had any concern for his safety. They all stoutly proclaimed their innocence, insisting that they were only trying to protect Rwanda from an invading force. There was no genocide, according to them, only a war. They are guilty of nothing but working for the legitimate interests of their people — defending themselves against the invading rebel force. And it seemed the world was ready to believe them, or at least ignore what they did. Dallaire's famous fax and the weak-kneed response from the United Nations had yet to surface in the periodicals and papers of Europe and America. The world still believed it had done its best. Few knew, or cared, about the appalling details of the wretched Rwanda "war."

The remarkable survival of those accused of directing the Rwanda genocide inspired a new phrase. They were enjoying the fruits of a new "culture of impunity" in the confused state of international justice.

2

BOSNIA

Tremble, thou wretch,
Thou hast within thee undivulgèd crimes
Unwhipped of justice. Hide thee, thou bloody hand,
Thou perjured, and thou similar of virtue
Thou art incestuous. Caitiff, to pieces shake,
That under covert and convenient seeming
Has practiced on man's life. Close pent-up guilts,
Rive your concealing continents and cry
Those dreadful summoners of grace. I am a man
More sinned against than sinning.
—William Shakespeare, *King Lear*

A spring morning in Sarajevo. The early light streams down over the surrounding mountain ranges, illuminating what's left of one of the prettiest towns in Europe. It is March 1996. The winter is over, and so is the war. Just months after the rulers of the former Yugoslavia signed the Dayton Peace Accords—a fragile agreement hammered together by the Americans in a desperate effort to give all sides some way to stop the madness—the guns have stopped. Bosnians are finally emerging from their bombed-out houses and apartments, taking stock, praying that this peace is the real thing.

The faces of the people you pass in the street still reflect the nearly four years of siege. They reveal the hundreds of sleepless nights as the hail of mortar shells marked and destroyed their buildings and their neighbourhoods, and shattered every pane of glass. They show the effects of the continuous fear and loathing of the snipers who used their children for target practice; the humiliation of lining up for water and skulking homeward with the precious plastic jugs, weak with fear of being shot. Now it's over. On a fresh spring day, you can walk through the parks and common areas, see where people have dug up green spaces to grow winter cabbages between the crudely marked graves, dodge the potholes and craters left by the shells, and still feel a sense of liberation.

In the midst of the rubble, a man is working in his garden, planting roses. He stops to talk to passersby. This can't be real. He tells others and himself the war will begin again at any time. Yet he turns towards his rose bushes.

Most Sarajevans with the chance to leave have done so. The ones who remain are the financially disadvantaged and the politically idealistic, those still loyal to the modern multi-ethnic Bosnia the Serb ultra-nationalists were trying to destroy. Sarajevo is filling up with outsiders. The numbers of white UN trucks have increased, and dozens of other aid organizations have joined in the service of Bosnia. They create communities of foreigners, smug in their control over the country and confident in their immunity from bombs and bullets as they drive through the pockmarked city. Sarajevo has gone from siege to a peculiar kind of occupation ... by the do-gooders and carpetbaggers who seem to descend on every post-war landscape.

There are Iranians who live here now claiming Islamic kinship for having offered Bosnia military support when the governments of other countries persuaded themselves they could help more by honouring a wrong-headed arms embargo. There are the war profiteers, salesmen from everywhere, hawking mine-detection equipment, building materials and passports to other countries. There are the peasants who came to Sarajevo because it was actually an improvement over life in rural Bosnia, where ethnic-cleansing campaigns had reduced the male populations and left thousands of female rape victims traumatized. Farm families too have taken up residence in the empty Austro-Hungarian-era apartment buildings. They plant potatoes on floors of living rooms. Occasionally, they keep livestock in the grand foyers.

Radovan Karadzic was astonishingly successful in achieving his ideological objectives. Many of these Sarajevans have come to believe that they can no longer live together in a multi-ethnic society. People of Serbian background fled their homes in the suburbs even after the war was over, fearing retribution. The principal danger wasn't from Muslims and Croats, but from Serb paramilitaries who were torching the homes of their own people if they tried to stay in a mixed community. In the final thrust of ethnic cleansing, hundreds of Sarajevan Serbs packed up their possessions and left, even digging up the graves of dead relatives to rebury them in the soil of their new Bosnian Serb territory—the Republika Srpska.

Republika Srpska is the ultimate payoff for Karadzic and his Pale Gang. The Dayton accords that finally ended the war partitioned Bosnia into a Muslim-Croat federation and a Serbian republic. The two entities rule jointly in a government that rarely reaches consensus. All political institutions are based on a defined ethnic composition. The division of Bosnia into Serbs, Croats and "Bosniacs" (the word now used to describe Bosnian Muslims) is enshrined in the document signed in Dayton, Ohio. The word "Bosnian," which once referred to a person of any nationality who lived in Bosnia (as Canadian means anyone living in Canada), has ceased to exist. Karadzic is victorious, even as he becomes an international pariah.

In the spring after the war, Sarajevans noticed for the first time large numbers of women on the street in hijab, their heads covered. Some people jokingly referred to them as M92s—people who have become conspicuously Muslim as a consequence of the war that started in 1992. The secular society of Sarajevo began to give way to a religious one as hardliners in President Izetbegovic's SDA party tried to purge the army and government of all non-Muslims. Izetbegovic attempted to stay the course while SDA extremists called for Muslim hegemony. Ethnic bitterness runs deep, even where there were sincere efforts to prevent communal friction before 1992. As one member of the party's most radical wing said: "The primary interest of the SDA is a state for Bosniacs, which will secure our survival, and not a common life, for which the other nationalities don't show any interest."

Despite the ominous changes in post-war Sarajevo, people, in the first peaceful spring after nearly four years of war, feel some hope. The new windows have arrived: UN plastic sheeting comes down, the clear panes of glass go up. Coffee shops fill up every night with chain-smoking Bosnians who talk of getting jobs or getting out. Anyone will tell you the war will start again any day now. But it doesn't. There's something in the human spirit that is taking over here, despite the wish for revenge. People essentially want to live normal lives.

That's what people desire in the northwest Bosnian town of Sanski Most too. In the early spring of 1996, as the frozen fields thaw and the snow retreats, Albassa Kurbegovic sits in her kitchen, drinking coffee, smoking cigarettes and crying. She has been in a state of despair for eighteen months, since the night paramilitary units under the authority of Arkan came to terrorize Muslims in her apartment building. That night was the last time she saw her husband. Husein was sixty-eight, but he was still considered to be of fighting age and therefore an enemy. Albassa could hear her husband crying out with pain in their living room while soldiers held her in the kitchen demanding that she give them more money, more valuables. They eventually found where the family had hidden their emergency cash. The cries stopped and everyone left—taking Husein Kurbegovic with them.

He is probably among the tangle of bodies buried hastily in an unmarked mass grave about twenty kilometres from Sanski Most. In 1996, it's a place journalists can get to only with difficulty, negotiating the military checkpoints of post-war Bosnia. By the side of the road is a pile of dirt with body parts protruding from it. A pale blue ski jacket covers an elbow, the sole of a boot pushes up out of the mud pile, which is unmarked except for the signs warning of the presence of land mines. Most mass graves are usually better concealed. But in the final days of war, as Muslim and Croat forces retook most of northwestern Bosnia from quickly retreating Serb forces, the so-called crisis committees—those in charge of ethnic cleansing and body disposal—couldn't work quickly enough to hide the evidence properly. In Sanski Most, they left behind one of the most complete accounts of systematic genocide in the country.

The courthouse in the centre of the town had served as a Serb military headquarters during the war, and it was where Bosnian investigators later found the lists of those who were to be rounded up and removed. Most of those people subsequently disappeared. Small metal tags, each numbered, are still piled on the table in the chief justice's office. Investigators suspect they were supposed to be attached to victims before burial so the Serbs could compile a final count—a plan that had to be abandoned as they rushed to finish their work before fleeing the area. Bodies were then bulldozed quickly into piles (no time even to dig a hole) or simply dumped into the Sana River. In early March, after the snow had melted and the swollen river receded, the corpses became tangled in the lower branches of trees along the riverbank, snagged along with bits of clothing, shoes and the other detritus from the grisly spring runoff.

At the edge of town, a new cemetery fills up; each grave is marked by a simple wooden stick bearing a number—the names are unknown. An old man who hovers at the edge of the graveyard, shivering and confused, repeats the same phrase over and over: "Kaput. Everything is kaput." Across the road from the cemetery is a small complex of garages and warehouse buildings, once used for storage but turned into jailhouses during the war.

Sanski Most's mayor lived here for almost a year of the war, sitting on a frozen concrete floor in an unheated garage with thirty other men. A single pump outside provided the only washing or drinking water, and the only exercise the men got was walking out to it. A single bucket inside each garage (there were three) served as a toilet. Even months after the end of the war, blood, vomit and excrement still stain the walls and floors. The men hid their family snapshots behind wallboards—a few of them are still there. Sometimes they ate their contraband money, fearing detection and the inevitable consequences. These men were lucky: they avoided the concentration camps at Omarska. And the paramilitaries whose task it was to kill the remaining non-Serbs in the final days of the war never got around to this particular garage complex.

Emir Erdemovic was one of the first people to return to Sanski Most after the Serbs had left. He was a prominent and respected judge before the war, and thus had been a prime candidate for elimination during the ethnic cleansing. Intellectuals, professionals, community leaders and writers were usually the first victims of these campaigns, following the familiar pattern of other killing regimes, whether it's Bagosora's, Pinochet's or Stalin's. The first threat that has to be removed is the one that thinks.

They came for Judge Erdemovic in the early days of war and brought him to one of the detention camps. But the camp lacked proper security, and with the help of Serbs who were horrified by what they were being asked to do to their neighbours and friends, he was able to escape. After many perilous weeks, the judge was able to join his refugee family in Germany.

He returned to a vastly altered Sanski Most. The charming little Balkan town, with its old stone bridges hunched over the Sana River ("most" means bridge in Serbo-Croatian), had been a popular draw for tourists before the war. People came to dine and drink in the many cafés lining the riverbank. By the spring of 1996, however, it had been beaten back into the Middle Ages: no phones or faxes; people hauling wood and supplies by horse-drawn wagons; only a few cars owned by relief workers and aid agencies; no functioning hospitals, food or running water. A few frightened people had managed to survive: Albassa Kurbegovic and a handful of other women, who remain in hopes of finding their husbands; orphaned children, who wander the streets begging for money or food.

The soldiers from the Bosnian Fifth Corps, who had miraculously managed to defend a large part of Bosnia and had retaken Sanski Most, held court in the ruins of their bombed-out headquarters each day, drinking a homemade plum brandy called *slivovitza* and hoping the war would start again, simply because there was nothing else to do but kill or be killed.

As a seasoned lawyer and magistrate, Erdemovic began gathering up the evidence of what had happened in Sanski Most and the surrounding area. He found a bonanza from a legal point of view: all the names of those on the crisis committee, their daily reports of ethnic cleansing, their lists of those incarcerated in makeshift jailhouses around town and the names of those to be killed. Albassa Kurbegovic and the other women come to him daily to ask if there's any news of their sons and husbands. Erdemovic is the right person to turn to: he also supervises local grave digging. As the bodies are exhumed, any objects buried with them, useful as evidence, are removed. Those corpses that can be identified are given a proper burial. The rest are marked simply by numbers; the people who could have recognized the remains are long gone.

Emir Erdemovic, Albassa Kurbegovic, the mayor of Sanski Most, the drunken officers of the Bosnian Fifth Corps, the Sarajevans drinking coffee, the man planting roses—all warily welcome the spring, even as they sniff the air for the scent of more war. It doesn't materialize. Now what they are missing is justice.

In the early months of 1996, Dr. Radovan Karadzic, reposing in his home just a half-hour's drive from Sarajevo, must find the idea of justice laughable. In the post-war Republika Srpska, the military operation is over but the self-appointed political wing of the Bosnian Serbs is still active. Here, Karadzic is making plans for his future, surrounded by a small personal army of thugs and thieves.

Karadzic has become a bona fide warlord.

As president of the SDS, Karadzic was in charge of the army as it lashed out at Sarajevo, destroying first its institutions, then its citizens. His party also organized the ethnic-cleansing campaigns—a prerequisite for a pure Bosnian state. And he is considered to be the driving force behind the events at Srebrenica. Karadzic is the embodiment of all that happened in Bosnia during the war.

But in spring 1996, instead of preparing his defence for a pending court appearance, Karadzic is confidently planning the campaign for his run at the presidency of the republic. Elections are called for in the American-forged Dayton peace agreement for both the RS and the Croat-Muslim federation. Karadzic should be in a jail cell, awaiting trial for some of the worst atrocities committed in Europe since the Second World War. Instead, he and his supporters are plastering the walls of the RS with campaign posters.

The bushy-browed psychiatrist is not the only indicted man enjoying the spring air. More than two dozen others on a United Nations wanted list live freely, visiting the cafés, communing with other Serb leaders and squandering the wealth amassed during four years of pillage. In addition to living off what they stole from ethnically-cleansed citizens, the warlords of Republika Srpska run mafia empires that trade in petrol, cigarettes, alcohol and hard currency. Ordinary Serbs, especially those who didn't support the SDS, live in fear. Others join their paramilitary armies, which, for the purposes of getting around the Dayton accords, they call police.

General Ratko Mladic has done less well in post-war Bosnia. Drinking heavily and apparently suffering from paranoia, he is rarely seen at his well-appointed Belgrade apartment. Instead, he haunts a rabbit warren of bunkers at Hans Pijesak, a refuge built by Tito that is now a part of the RS. Mladic's mentor, Slobodan Milosevic, distanced himself from the general, and from Karadzic, during the war. He wanted to curry favour with the foreign diplomats who would later toast him for signing the Dayton accords.

Ratko Mladic has become moody in the months following the war. According to friends in Belgrade, he unravelled after his daughter Ana committed suicide, apparently after she read in a Serb magazine that her father was responsible for genocide and crimes against humanity.

Zeljko Raznjatovic, better known as Arkan, the man whose paramilitary units had committed some of the war's most heinous acts, returned to his regular job as a kingpin among the elite racketeers in Serbia. He later ran for public office in Kosovo—a seat he won handily, since Kosovar Albanians (90 per cent of the population) boycotted the election. That Arkan was already wanted by Interpol for crimes he had committed in Western Europe before he became the darling of ultra-nationalists didn't figure among the election issues.

Besides General Mladic, the other military leaders considered responsible for the assault on Srebrenica had returned to their posts in Serbia, and many enjoyed promotions in recognition of their hard work. Those who ran the detention facilities at Omarska and Keraterm, close to where Albassa Kurbegovic's husband was last seen, lived in nearby Prijedor, where they ran black-market empires and tyrannized the local citizens.

The men who ran the most notorious rape camps of Bosnia, in the town of Foca, were frequently sighted in the same hangouts as the French NATO soldiers who serve now as peacekeepers. In Herzegovina, one journalist reported having breakfast a few tables away from a Croat paramilitary who was known to have killed dozens of Serbs and Muslims; all the while, NATO soldiers went about their business nearby.

By the time the first forensic investigators arrived in the country to begin work for a new judicial entity, clumsily called the International Criminal Tribunal for the Former Yugoslavia (ICTY), the people considered responsible for the war crimes were firmly in control. While preparing for elections, and profiting from their fiefdoms, the Bosnian Serbs under Radovan Karadzic were also positioned to ensure that no investigators could gain access to the massacre sites and the giant graves sown throughout the newly declared Republika Srpska. Though required by the Dayton agreement to reveal these sites, the RS leaders refused to comply, and NATO soldiers, who stumbled over the feet of relaxing war criminals daily, declared it would be "mission creep" to arrest these men or even help with the investigations.

The mass grave in the Republika Srpska that likely holds the body of Kurbegovic's husband is untouched; the witnesses who can identify the rapists of Foca are abandoned; the sniper victims in Sarajevo hear of wealth and glory heaped upon their assailants by the political thugs in Pale. Foreign leaders, along with NATO, turn their heads away, fearing any gesture that could disrupt the fragile peace.

Canada, December 1995. It is the dead of winter in Ontario, and an appeals court judge is called away from a hearing room in Kingston to take a very important phone call. Louise Arbour is presiding over an inquiry into events that took place at the city's federal prison for women months earlier. Some women inmates being held in isolation cells for disruptive behaviour had an encounter with male prison guards in full riot gear one evening: the guards came to teach the women a lesson. Over the course of a few hours, the women were stripped of their clothing. Officers cut off their slacks and underwear with scissors, examined them internally and externally—and dutifully recorded everything on videotape. Then the tape ended up broadcast on a national CBC television show.

Arbour is preparing to write a damning report about the Canadian corrections system. But what she hears in Kingston is no preparation for what she will hear in the coming months and years. The phone call is from the United Nations in New York City.

BOOK FOUR
The Eagle

1

IN THE SHADOW OF NUREMBERG

*The wrongs which we seek to condemn and punish have been
so calculated, so malignant and so devastating that
civilization cannot tolerate their being ignored, because it cannot
survive their being repeated.*
—Robert Jackson, the prosecution's opening speech at Nuremberg,
November 21, 1945

The Pale Gang was feeling no remorse in the aftermath of the Bosnian war. The regime in Belgrade brushed off even the suggestion of taking responsibility for the two million people displaced and 200,000 dead. In Africa, Théoneste Bagosora planned his return to power, while the new regime in Kigali did little to stop another wave of murder and terror. It was business as usual for the war criminals and *génocidaires* of the 1990s. They had no reason to suspect that the international community would respond to their behaviour any differently than it had throughout the Bosnian and Rwandan wars.

But some representatives in the United Nations—even in the Security Council—were decidedly uncomfortable with the moral ambiguity the UN had demonstrated during both crises. As early as the London conference in August 1992, some diplomats had staked out the principled position that even if they couldn't stop the murder and mayhem in Bosnia, at least the culprits responsible shouldn't think they were going to get away scot-free. It was a commendable stance, but one that was hard to take seriously, given that many of the culprits were sitting around the negotiating table with the people who were articulating the principle.

In the end, two wild cards—public opinion and private initiative—
would launch a genuine quest for justice.

The United Nations and the European Community had tried to justify the
inertia in Bosnia by inflating the significance of the Sarajevo airport relief
effort and the joint UN/EC peace talks, conducted by Cyrus Vance and
Lord David Owen. But the images of torture, rape and murder that blazed
out of TV screens daily presented an ongoing reality check that penetrated
the consciousness of even the most jaded viewers. The reassuring "Never
Again" of the post-war world was replaced by an accusatory "This Time
We Knew." The claims "We were doing all we could" and "The peace
process is unfolding as it should" didn't wash with the general public. Even
within the notoriously self-interested American administration and the
morally slack United Nations, people were becoming apprehensive. Something had to be done—or as the more savvy would put it, somebody was
going to have to create the appearance of something being done.

In the summer of 1992, the UN Security Council, pressed by the United
States, declared that people who committed violations of international
law in Yugoslavia "will be individually [held] responsible." By October, the
UN had appointed the Commission of Experts, an investigative body with
vague terms of reference that was to probe incidents of crimes against
humanity. The commission was modelled on a similar initiative established
in 1942 to investigate violations of the practices of war committed by the
Nazis. Starved for resources and with no staff, the 1942 commission accomplished very little. For those who wanted only the appearance of justice,
it was the perfect model for the United Nations' review of atrocities in
Bosnia in the nineties.

The first chairman of the newly constituted Commission of Experts
on war crimes in Yugoslavia was Fritz Kalshoven, a retired Dutch academic who, by his own admission, had no idea why he had been appointed,
except that he was available. Kalshoven was the only "expert" who actually banked a salary: all the other members received per diem expenses on
the rare occasions when they actually met. The UN loaned the commission
two staff members, but there was no money for field investigations or to
create any kind of database. The commission stumbled along, meeting
once a month in Geneva, not even sure what, specifically, it was supposed
to be talking about.

Michael Scharf, a U.S. State Department lawyer who was among a group of U.S. government bureaucrats pushing for the investigation of war crimes in Bosnia, chronicled the feeble early efforts made by the commission in his book *Balkan Justice*. He reports a fortuitous coincidence in December 1992, in which the Commission of Experts was meeting in a Geneva conference room while, in the next room, the acting U.S. secretary of state, Lawrence Eagleburger, was laying down the law in a speech to an international conference on the former Yugoslavia. Eagleburger delivered what would come to be called the "naming names" speech. Defying the Vance/Owen peace negotiations, Eagleburger identified ten people he believed should be immediately investigated for war crimes, a list that included the president of Yugoslavia, Slobodan Milosevic; the leader of the self-proclaimed Serbian republic, Radovan Karadzic; and his general, Ratko Mladic. The Eagleburger speech was not an accident, or a spontaneous gesture. Eagleburger had met with Elie Wiesel the night before. Wiesel, the Nazi concentration camp survivor and war crimes crusader, had told Eagleburger to light a fire under the Yugoslavian negotiators and get the war crimes process active.

Peacemaker Lord Owen described the gesture as "unhelpful." But Eagleburger had raised the stakes for the people who were supposed to be gathering evidence for the naming of names. In gambling terms, if the UN and the experts were bluffing, they would find it more difficult to continue doing so. The Eagleburger speech gave a much needed boost to the morale of a number of people who were quietly working behind the scenes to establish a system of international justice in the Balkans and it was a swift kick in the butt for the "experts commission."

There had been a number of significant high-level defections from the State Department during the first few years of the Bosnian war. The defectors joined NGOs and continued to be a thorn in the side of the American administration, speaking publicly (and angrily) and writing forceful op ed pieces in prominent U.S. newspapers. They condemned the government for failing to intervene with air strikes and for not demanding the lifting of the arms embargo, which they described as immoral. This chorus of dissent eventually had a profound effect on American decision-makers, not least among them the U.S. ambassador to the UN, Madeleine Albright.

While some members of the Clinton administration were keen to see justice done, Britain's Tory government under John Major still had difficulty accepting even the idea of a war crimes tribunal. Some of Major's ministers felt that the United Nations and, more significantly, the United States were anti-Serb, a bias that the British didn't share. The government, and many British war veterans, had fond memories of the Serbs as allies during the Second World War, and senior military men remembered how heroically the Serbs had fought the Nazis.

The Major government enjoyed close ties with Slobodan Milosevic and regarded the Yugoslavian leader as an ally. John Major, like Lord Owen, was incensed when Eagleburger said Milosevic should be investigated as a war criminal. In media interviews, Fritz Kalshoven let it be known that Lord Owen had actually warned him not to allow the Commission of Experts to get in the way of the peace process, and not to centre out any specific individuals in the report.

Owen quickly denied exerting any such pressure, as did the UN when it was suggested that Boutros Boutros-Ghali also pushed the commission not to interfere. But it was no secret that the secretary-general didn't want the war crimes issue to undermine the peace process. If peace required negotiating with mass murderers, it was important to find other ways of describing those mass murderers in public statements.

Notwithstanding semantic debates and diplomatic posturing, the commission limped along and, by February 1993, filed an interim report to the Security Council. And notwithstanding a great deal of private ambivalence among senior UN officials, the Security Council passed Resolution 827 in May, formally adopting a draft statute for an international war crimes tribunal.

It was a significant step in the right direction, and it might never have happened at all if people like Michael Scharf and others in the U.S. State Department—in concert with the dissidents and the NGOs on the outside —hadn't nudged the process along. But the high-level resistance was still strong and Fritz Kalshoven finally resigned in September 1993, citing health reasons and the fact that there wasn't enough money for the commission to accomplish anything further.

On November 17, 1993, the first international war crimes tribunal since Nuremberg and Tokyo met in The Hague for preliminary discussions. The chosen judges, under the leadership of an outspoken Italian law professor, Antonio Cassese, assembled in a room that had been booked for only two weeks. There were no staff, no budget and no offices. Worse, there were no cases to judge and no prosecutor who could bring cases before them.

Whether they would ever find any useful work to do would depend on the efforts of an extraordinary American lawyer.

Cherif Bassiouni is an Egyptian-born American law professor and an authority on international criminal jurisprudence. He had been a member of the original Commission of Experts, but an energetic one who took an activist approach to the commission's work. When Kalshoven resigned as chairman, Bassiouni took over. He publicly denounced what he saw as political interference from Lord Owen and others. And when the UN declared that there would be no more money for investigations, Bassiouni assembled a force of fifty lawyers and students from across the U.S., at the De Paul University Human Rights Law Institute in Chicago, all of them willing to work gratis. With us$800,000 in grants from billionaire/philanthropist George Soros's Open Society Fund and the MacArthur Foundation, Bassiouni set to work.

Throughout the winter, the Chicago offices of the FBI kept a close watch on the security of Bassiouni's operation, acutely conscious of its sensitive nature. Commission members, including the Canadian lawyer Bill Fenrick (on loan from the Department of National Defence in Ottawa), and Bassiouni's army of volunteers put together an extraordinary database. Fenrick became rapporteur for on-site investigations, and as such organized thirty-four field studies in Yugoslavia with the help of a half-dozen Canadian lawyers and police workers and more than a million dollars in donations. Christine Cleiven, a Dutch law professor, began the first comprehensive research on rape as a war crime; she and a contingent of female lawyers interviewed 230 women who claimed to have been victims. Bassiouni established a separate Prijedor Project to specifically investigate the POW camps in northern Bosnia. The De Paul University research group restored some real hope that there might still be effective war crimes prosecutions after all, in spite of suspicions that the United Nations really wanted to prevent it.

Bassiouni received a letter from the UN in December 1993, informing him that the Commission of Experts would have to wrap up its work by the end of April 1994. The instruction was, at best, optimistic, especially in view of the fact that the war would go on for a year and a half past that deadline. People who were doing the work argued that there were still hundreds of interviews to complete and the most important excavation site — at Vukovar — had yet to be exhumed by Fenrick and his people. The UN countered that the commission had more than fulfilled its purpose.

But Bassiouni himself was satisfied that the commission had at least made headway and laid the groundwork for some real accountability. He told his colleagues at the U.S. State Department that he had most of what he wanted. Because the Security Council had already established a war crimes tribunal—albeit a still toothless one—it would be next to impossible to ignore the evidence Bassiouni and his team had amassed. The Commission of Experts' final report, submitted in April 1994, was the size of five Chicago telephone directories. The team of lawyers had prepared sixty-five thousand pages of documents, as well as three hundred hours of videotape that included hundreds of interviews. It recorded 150 mass grave sites, each containing between 5 and 350 corpses; it had identified 900 prison camps and 90 paramilitary groups, Arkan's Tigers being only the most organized and conspicuous.

The first employees of the new war crimes tribunal arrived at their jobs in November 1993, excited by a sense of historical continuity with Nuremberg—the world's first successful attempt to determine what is "legal" in warfare and what is criminal—and to have it tested in a court of law. The Nuremberg trials took place just after the end of the Second World War. The legal minds behind Nuremberg determined that there would undoubtedly be other wars, but that warriors had to abide by universal norms of justice. Nuremberg set out to establish that soldiers could never again justify criminal behaviour by claiming they were "just following orders." It also recognized a new category of culpability: the crime against humanity. Any criminal act committed against the citizens of any country—even if the perpetrator was the government—would be regarded, in law, as an act committed against the entire human race.

Nuremberg had been a unique legal event: what is called victor's justice. Those who won the war were clearly in a position to prosecute those who had lost. The staggering atrocities perpetrated by the Nazis during the Second World War might have gone unpunished if not for the complete victory of the Allied forces, which successfully occupied Germany and seized exclusive control over the territories where the death camps had been located. American and British investigators found mountains of incriminating documents—the same type of reports later linked to the "crisis committees" in Bosnia (though Bosnia's were on a much smaller scale).

More damning, the victors discovered the blueprint for the Nazis' so-called final solution: the plan to swiftly murder and dispose of the millions of men, women and children they'd been holding in their concentration camps.

In 1945, twenty-two top Nazi leaders, including Hermann Goering, Julius Streicher and Rudolf Hess, all held in captivity since the end of the war, went on trial in a Nuremberg courtroom. For purposes of the prosecution, lawyers crafted a set of new statutes based on the Nuremberg prosecutions, which later became a part of the Geneva Convention. They tried all the accused at the same time for their crimes of war. Nuremberg had one hundred prosecutors working full time with a staff of two thousand people. The trial lasted 284 days. All but three accused were found guilty as charged. Twelve were sentenced to hang.

The new Hague tribunal borrowed its jurisprudence from Nuremberg, but it could never reproduce the controlled conditions that had allowed the 1945 trials to function so successfully. There was only a handful of people in the UN and the powerful U.S. State Department who even wanted the newly hatched tribunal to succeed at all. The court was not operating out of "victor's justice" but out of UN Security Council resolutions. The only material the court had to work with was the massive and tantalizing databank from Bassiouni and his commission, the product of an independently funded initiative. Without the Commission of Experts' report and the supporting database to spur the process, the tribunal would probably have expired from inertia.

One symptom of that inertia: the United Nations couldn't decide on a chief prosecutor for The Hague tribunal, and the haggling soon opened a conspicuous rift between those who actually wanted the tribunal to do something and those who didn't. Cherif Bassiouni—who was a leading expert on international law even before he compiled his Balkan databank during the winter of 1993–94—was the logical choice for the position, but the British were quick to reject him. They pointed out that he had never been a prosecutor. Their opposition came as no surprise to Bassiouni, who knew he'd already upset the Major government by calling Karadzic and Mladic war crimes suspects during peace talks. *The New York Times* and other leading international news agencies reported that Britain did not want a Muslim in charge of prosecuting cases where Muslims were the chief victims, and rejected Bassiouni.

A dozen other names emerged, including that of a Canadian,

Christopher Amerasinghe from the federal justice department, but the Russians vetoed him and anybody else from a NATO country. Russia was determined to look out for the interests of its fellow Slavs in Belgrade. China, possibly with fresh memories of Tiananmen Square in mind, was uneasy with the prospect of any tribunal having wide powers. It feared a precedent that might one day drag its own leaders into a courtroom. The Americans were, as usual, of two minds.

The Security Council debated names of possible candidates for months, and the judges and other employees of the fledgling tribunal extended their short-term lease on the rented office in The Hague. UN watchers say that even in United Nations terms, the job search was absurdly long. Fourteen months after it had established the tribunal, the Security Council still had found no one acceptable to act as prosecutor. And of course, by the spring and early summer of 1994, the UN was also somewhat distracted by events in Rwanda that, for human savagery, were quickly pushing Bosnia into the background.

Finally, as the paralysis approached a permanent state of bureaucratic stasis, one name surfaced that nobody could find specific reasons to shoot down: Richard Goldstone. He was a South African, and South Africa was, by then, redeemed in the world community. He was not from a NATO country. He was Jewish, which presumably invested him with a mystical mandate for the prosecution of war crimes. Nobody seemed to know who he was, which was a good thing—he carried no political baggage. And most important, he was probably available. He had no experience as a prosecutor either, but that no longer seemed to matter to the British. In July 1994, an unsuspecting Richard Goldstone in far-off Johannesburg got an urgent fax from the ICTY.

Richard Goldstone had been active in the anti-apartheid movement since he was a student in the 1950s. As a white lawyer of British ancestry who practised commercial law, and then a judge, Goldstone kept his distance from the odious regime that ran his country, and he became celebrated for a number of controversial, and fair, judgments. He once ruled in favour of an Asian woman who was about to be evicted from a "whites only" neighbourhood. Later, he was appointed to investigate the mysterious death of Winnie Mandela's daughter's boyfriend. In a politically charged environment, where the black community claimed it was murder, Goldstone declared it suicide.

But Goldstone was best known for his work on a commission established to investigate political violence in South Africa after the release of Nelson Mandela from prison and the breakdown of apartheid. Called the Goldstone Commission after its chairman, the three-year probe revealed the violent conspiracy on the part of right-wing white South Africans to stop political reform in the country. The final report was widely celebrated and it is undoubtedly that work that brought Goldstone to the attention of those searching for a chief prosecutor for The Hague.

Goldstone's judgments challenged preconceptions on both sides of the racial divide, and he was paying a price in his own country. He and his family required full-time bodyguards plus an elaborate security system. When the fax came from the tribunal, Goldstone saw the job as a possible respite from the turmoil and a welcome break in his routine. He accepted, not knowing that within the year, he would long to be back on the judicial hot seat in his own troubled country.

Goldstone was installed at The Hague, as chief prosecutor for war crimes in the former Yugoslavia, in August 1994. He was on loan to the United Nations from the newly constituted South African Constitutional Court for a two-year period, at the end of which he was expected to return. Goldstone hinted to his new masters that he'd be willing to make the appointment longer if there was real work to do—something as important, say, as the Nuremberg trials. Goldstone was told it would all depend on resources. The tribunal's budget would be decided as the investigations went along.

Within months of his arrival in The Hague—with all the attendant hopes that the court would now bring perpetrators to justice—Goldstone watched the tribunal enter into what internal reports quaintly referred to as the Period of Impatience. All the people who had been trying to keep some momentum going, and to prevent the war crimes process from dying before it ever started, began to seriously doubt it would ever work. British papers described the International Criminal Tribunal for the Former Yugoslavia (ICTY) as a "fig leaf for inaction" and judged that it could have no practical effectiveness. *The Economist* asked: "Will it be Nuremberg or Leipzig?"—a reference to the failed attempt at war crimes prosecutions following the First World War. The coverage was depressing, especially in an environment where media approval was often a precondition for political survival.

Cherif Bassiouni flew to The Hague and met with Goldstone soon after he was installed as the chief prosecutor. Bassiouni recalls a surreal scene: "I found Goldstone sitting alone in a white room, they had painted everything white; the chairs, the desk, the walls. He was all alone with nothing to do. He didn't have a map and didn't seem at all familiar with the sad history of Yugoslavia."

But in 1995, with the war still raging, Goldstone continued with on-site investigations and by February, he was willing to make a giant leap into legal history. Goldstone indicted the entire leadership of the military unit that ran Omarska camp, the wretched detention facility that had generated some of the most horrifying accounts of brutality during the war. The media suddenly became interested in the Hague tribunal. But it didn't last for very long. There was no trial and the indictment just sat on a shelf, collecting dust. Reporters returned to covering events their editors considered more important—like the saga of the O.J. Simpson trial.

Six months after the Omarska charges, Goldstone issued more indictments—for twenty-one of the Serbs who ran the Keraterm detention centre, the second most notorious camp. Then, on July 24, 1995, he indicted Radovan Karadzic and General Ratko Mladic for crimes against humanity and genocide. It was the audacious gambit everyone had been waiting for, and the media responded with enthusiasm. Here was the prospect of a trial to watch—if not Nuremberg, at least as thrilling as the O. J. spectacle. Television crews and newspaper columnists around the world prepared for what they thought would be the courtroom drama of the decade. There was only one problem, and it would gradually translate into a provocative question: Which decade?

The tribunal discovered there was no practical way to serve the indicted people with arrest warrants. The authorities in Pale and Belgrade certainly would have nothing to do with enforcing the court orders, and no foreign power was prepared to upset the political apple cart by conducting a military raid on the bunkers of the Pale Gang. The war in Bosnia was still raging and Mladic had no shortage of hostages within his grasp, including the entire contingent of UN peacekeepers; he made menacing gestures in their direction every time there was even the suggestion of outside intervention in the war. Goldstone could issue indictments to his heart's content, but he lacked the muscle to arrest anyone.

The statutes for the tribunal specified that the country hosting the indicted individuals had the duty to arrest them. Fat chance that this would happen on turf controlled by the former Yugoslavia. Goldstone turned to the United Nations for help, but predictably, he got nowhere. His contacts in the UN reminded him that it was nothing short of miraculous that the tribunal existed at all. Goldstone sent out petitions for help to anyone who'd listen, from Washington to Bonn, to no avail. But he also turned his attention towards the one case he might realistically hope to prosecute.

Bosnians fleeing the war poured into neighbouring countries—Germany was a principal destination. Once safe, however, the refugees quickly turned on anyone within their ranks who might more properly be defined as a fugitive from justice than a fugitive from war. Dusan "Dusko" Tadic, better known to those who had been held as prisoners of war as the Butcher of Prijedor, wasn't hard to spot or, from Goldstone's point of view, hard to catch. A television crew took clandestine pictures of Tadic in Germany and confirmed his identity. German authorities arrested him, and by the spring of 1995, the tribunal had a real-life war crimes suspect in custody.

Tadic had been a policeman and an army reservist, as well as a karate instructor and the owner of a café (no Muslims allowed), before becoming a refugee in Germany. But witnesses, and there were many, knew there was more to his resumé than that. Tadic had been a guard at the Omarska camp and also a regular at the nearby Keraterm and Trnoplje detention centres. According to his indictment, he'd used truncheons, iron bars, rifle butts, wire cables and knives to torture detainees before killing them. In some cases, he was reported to have jumped on the victim's back as a grand finale to his torments. Tadic had reportedly discharged the contents of a fire extinguisher into a prisoner's mouth.

Many of the men in those camps died, and the majority of non-Serbs who had lived in Kosarac, Tadic's hometown, disappeared. Witnesses who testified against Tadic stated that the worst act of sadism took place on June 18, 1992. Hari Harambasic, a Muslim police officer, was badly beaten by Serb paramilitaries under the leadership of Tadic. As the popular Muslim song "Let Me Live, Don't Take My Happiness Away" played in the background, the Serb soldiers ordered another prisoner to bite off the testicles of Harambasic. "Bite harder, harder," they ordered as the song played and Harambasic screamed. He was dead by morning.

Tadic was the first man in almost fifty years to appear before an international war crimes court, and the media were there en masse. The Dutch press reported, "The Paper Tiger Roars." The opening proceedings went out live on the U.S.-based cable channel, Court TV. The tribunal counted

134 news reports on the trial. It was a heady time, but it was only one trial, not enough to keep the world's attention riveted on The Hague, which was what Goldstone really wanted.

Tadic's lawyer, Michail Wladimiroff, claimed the tribunal had arrested the wrong Dusko Tadic. This was new. Whatever other defences the Nazis at Nuremberg might have argued, they'd never tried mistaken identity. The lawyer for Tadic also complained that he could not properly defend a client when all the evidence he needed was inside a war zone. Wladimiroff said he had no money for the trial (the tribunal paid for defence council of those who couldn't pay themselves, but those expenses were subject to the same drastic financial restrictions as everything else at the UN), and the Bosnian Serbs, Tadic's own people, wouldn't assist in his defence (even if he was a fellow soldier) because Belgrade and Pale had declared the tribunal illegal.

The trial didn't get under way for another year after Tadic's preliminary appearance. Public interest diminished sharply. But Goldstone soon had another alleged perpetrator in court.

Drazen Erdemovic was a twenty-five-year-old Bosnian Croat, a conscript to the Serbian republic's army. He'd confessed to a newspaper reporter that he killed seventy people during the slaughter of seven thousand men and boys at Srebrenica. He was arrested in March 1996 and spirited away to The Hague. Erdemovic's confession fascinated the world —briefly. He too was just a foot soldier. As compelling as these cases may have been to the tribunal staff, for a jaded international press corps, these were not the promised Nuremberg II.

By the summer of 1996, Goldstone had issued fifty-two indictments of Croats, Serbs and Muslims, and had plastered wanted posters on poles and walls all over Europe. He had petitioned NATO peacekeepers to arrest suspects (NATO took over peacekeeping responsibilities from the UN after the war ended). NATO promised that it would—if its peacekeepers saw any of them, which of course they never did.

In another piece of theatre designed to focus public attention on the tribunal—and to keep the world's most wanted men in the spotlight— Goldstone took advantage of one of the court's more controversial rules and held a "hearing" on the charges against Mladic and Karadzic. The tribunal was not allowed to hold trials in absentia, but its Rule 61 allowed for a review of the reasons why the accused weren't in court and to reveal the strength of the prosecution case.

The Rule 61 hearing was high profile. Karadzic had a lawyer present, the California attorney Edward Medvene, who was also working on the O. J. Simpson civil trial in Hollywood. His assistant, Tom O'Hanley, was an associate of a generous and eccentric Hollywood plastic surgeon, Borko Djordjevic, a personal friend of Karadzic's who had tried to persuade the doctor to show up at The Hague in person.

The attorneys argued that the court had no legitimacy, which raised the intriguing question: If the court was not legitimate, why were they there? Though the testimonies were valuable, nothing conclusive came from the hearing. It served mostly as a preview for the main event, the big show that would justify the tribunal's existence — the arrest and trial of "the big fish."

In November 1994, while he was struggling to bring the international criminal process to life, Goldstone found himself saddled with another, perhaps more onerous, task. The United Nations had realized that it could no longer dither over what had clearly been a genocide in Rwanda. And so, as Phil Lancaster and other personnel from UNAMIR II were busy fishing cadavers out of Rwandan rivers, the Security Council resolved that the situation also called for a war crimes tribunal. But rather than start from scratch — a process that might take years — the SC decided to fold Rwanda into the responsibilities of the Yugoslav tribunal. The two courts would share the same chief prosecutor and the same appeals chamber, but would be otherwise separate entities. The International Criminal Tribunal for Rwanda (ICTR) would sit in Arusha, Tanzania, next door to Rwanda. Goldstone's second prosecution office would be based in Kigali, Rwanda's capital.

The UN presumed Goldstone's familiarity with Africa would be useful, and it was. He knew exactly how complex the Great Lakes region was and how massive the task that had been assigned to him. He was also becoming painfully aware of how difficult it was to accomplish anything within the giant bureaucracy of the UN. He had no deputy prosecutor for Rwanda and no office staff in the country. It would take a year of wrangling to get a budget for the Rwanda tribunal. It would take even longer to get a single indictment issued, even in the face of what was obviously a massive crime.

From his first visit to Kigali, Goldstone could easily see the obstacles. First of all, he didn't speak French and was able to communicate with some of his staff only through an interpreter. When he finally got a budget, it was initially for US$13 million, hardly enough to investigate the deaths of nearly a million people with the suspects scattered all over the world. From the earliest days, Goldstone suspected the International Criminal Tribunal for Rwanda was going to be the poor cousin to The Hague, and he was right.

The Americans, principally a diplomatic bulldozer named Richard Holbrooke, took over the peace process in the former Yugoslavia in 1995, having concluded that the Europeans were incapable of cleaning up the mess in their own backyard. The Clinton administration had provided the impetus behind the final NATO bombing campaign, and now Holbrooke's tough diplomacy was pushing the parties close to a resolution. Goldstone learned that part of the peace deal might be an amnesty for all the war crimes suspects—including Karadzic and Mladic—and he was furious. He threatened to resign and to take half the staff with him.

In February 1996, with Holbrooke trying to implement the precious Dayton Peace Accords, two Serb officers made a wrong turn on a road just outside Sarajevo. Bosnian military forces promptly surrounded and captured them. Holbrooke was alarmed by the possibility of repercussions, and President Izetbegovic might have been persuaded to simply let the men go in the interests of the peace process. But Richard Goldstone had already indicted one of the men, and another was wanted as a witness. He demanded they be brought to The Hague.

For Goldstone it was a chance to fire a warning shot across the bow of the American negotiators who were threatening to backslide on the issue of war crimes. Goldstone would not go along with any offer of amnesty for war criminals. He demanded that the men be turned over to the tribunal, and Holbrooke had no choice but to comply. Goldstone had become an effective player on the world media stage, and it would have been perilous to confront him on an issue like this one. An elite squad of specially trained French commandos plucked the two officers out of a Bosnian jail and whisked them to Holland on American helicopters on the night of February 11.

Because of the arrests, Milosevic and the Bosnian Serb leaders announced they were pulling out of the Dayton process, and the whole house of cards, carefully constructed over six months, began to totter. Holbrooke was furious with Goldstone. He wasn't entirely opposed to the tribunal (he'd actually wanted NATO to arrest Karadzic to get him out of the way during the Dayton peace process), but he wanted it to work in lock-step with what he was attempting to do. Goldstone insisted that a court could not become a tool for politicians and diplomats. And he was right. War criminals were not chattels to be traded for peace. But the ongoing struggle to maintain the integrity and the usefulness of the court was taking a toll on the South African judge.

As Goldstone's two-year contract came to a close, people in the State Department were begging him to stay on. Holbrooke wasn't among them, but the U.S. ambassador to the United Nations, Madeleine Albright, was one of Goldstone's fans. The man who had become prosecutor mostly because nobody could think of a reason to object to him suddenly seemed indispensable. Goldstone's media savvy and his ability to make the tribunal appear as though it had a historical mission had kept it alive. But now Goldstone just wanted to go home, to a place where he thought he really could make a difference. Nelson Mandela was insisting he return to help with the country's difficult transition from apartheid to unity.

What the tribunal's supporters feared most was an outbreak of wrangling and internecine warfare at the Security Council that would mar the search for a new prosecutor. It had taken fourteen months to find Goldstone, and the fledgling tribunals would surely be dead if it had to go through another significant delay before he was replaced. Goldstone declared, as a final assignment, he would take on the task of finding his own successor.

Sometimes a chance encounter between two people can turn a life upside down. Richard Goldstone had first met Louise Arbour at a legal conference at Wittwaterstrand University, in Cape Town, in 1990. Arbour was in South Africa by happenstance — another judge had backed out of the conference at the last moment. "She made quite an impression on people at that conference," recalls Goldstone. South Africa was wrestling with constitutional matters at the time, contemplating how a white minority could legally act as a distinct society within the larger society. It was oddly similar to an issue Canada was in the midst of debating: the Meech Lake Accord was an attempt to find a way for Quebec to survive as a distinct society within the Canadian federation. As a French-Canadian jurist, Arbour had a lot of insights into the pleasures and perils of such laws, and the South Africans were fascinated.

A year later, she returned to South Africa for another conference, this time with her common-law spouse, Larry Taman, and a strong friend-ship developed between Arbour and Goldstone. He remembers a walk with her in the mountains where they talked for hours. He got the impres-sion that their sensibilities were somehow pitched in the same key.

After he told Madeleine Albright he would find his successor, he turned to his wife, Noleen, for advice: "She asked me, 'What qualities are you looking for?' And I said, 'It has to be a woman.'" Goldstone was ter-ribly concerned that the rape cases compiled by the Bassiouni investigators were not a priority at the tribunal, and he thought a woman would push that agenda. "'And it's absolutely essential that she be fully bilingual.' The words were hardly out of my mouth before I thought of Louise Arbour."

Goldstone didn't know for sure if Arbour was suited for the work, but he knew by then that he wasn't. "I had never worked in a big organization in my life, and I found it extremely irritating. For me the fight [with the bureaucracy] was far more frustrating than the big things like the non-arrests. The thing that kept me awake at night was the UN bureaucracy."

Before the end of his term at The Hague, Goldstone travelled to Canada on personal business and had dinner with Arbour and Larry Taman in Ottawa's Claire du Lune restaurant. That's where he made his pitch: he wanted to submit her name as a candidate for the job of chief prosecutor of the Yugoslav and Rwandan tribunals. Arbour was startled, then excited and finally doubtful. She told him she had no experience that would qual-ify her for such a position. But Arbour's lack of expertise as a prosecutor wasn't what Goldstone worried about (he had had none, either). He was reasonably confident that she could get the red-eyed devils indicted for their war crimes. It was the papier-mâché devils in the United Nations bureaucracy that bothered him: he wasn't sure that anyone could get around them.

2

EDUCATION OF A CONVENT GIRL

There's no going back. [The tribunal] has to move forward.
Otherwise we would have been better off never rekindling the Nuremberg dream
of having justice contribute to peace. We would, in fact, have very seriously
aggravated the situation by confirming that impunity is an absolute guarantee,
because we would have tried and failed. Never—I think certainly in our
generation—would we be able to credibly launch it again.
—Louise Arbour, February 1997

The note dropped on Louise Arbour's desk in that Kingston hearing room on a December morning in 1995 said that the Canadian ambassador to the United Nations was on the phone. Arbour had never met Ambassador Robert Fowler, and he knew nothing about her. Fowler told her that he had been asked to arrange a highly confidential phone call between her and the UN secretary-general, Boutros Boutros-Ghali. "Do you know what this is about?" Fowler asked tentatively. "I just have a little idea," she answered, remembering her last conversation with Richard Goldstone at dinner in Ottawa. "It must be extremely confidential," said Fowler, ever conscious of protocol, "because he didn't even go through his own office when he made the call. He went straight to me."

At two o'clock that afternoon, Boutros-Ghali called Arbour to tell her he wanted to put her name forward as a candidate for the job of chief prosecutor for international war crimes. "You have to tell me right now, if I make this happen, you will take this," said Boutros-Ghali. "Because I can't take this any further if I don't have you on side."

Arbour's first concerns were with the federal government in Ottawa. She had no idea what would happen to her position as a judge—there were few—if any—precedents in the Canadian judiciary for temporary foreign appointments. And she didn't know if this was something Ottawa would even want. "I told him the Canadian government may have ambitions for other people, someone they want to promote. I can't make a commitment to you without knowing how the Canadian government would react." Boutros-Ghali said coolly, "Leave all that with me." In fact, he was calling Arbour from Ottawa. "But you must not speak about this with anyone. This is absolutely critical. If this starts leaking, people will know Goldstone is leaving and there will be all kinds of campaigning." She would know, he said, by the end of January.

For Arbour, the prospect of going to The Hague was fascinating. She knew little about the wars that had produced the need for such a court, other than what she had read in the newspapers. Goldstone had told her it wouldn't take long to catch up—there were many books available. He had been more concerned with the complexity of the UN than the elusiveness of the Pale Gang. Goldstone was known to be a wizard at getting around bureaucracies, and if he found the task daunting, what could she expect?

The prize was irresistible. Here was a chance to put her stamp on history, to pave the way for a permanent international criminal court that would bring down the world's tyrants and establish a legal landmark as important as English common law. Arbour was ambitious, and this was a job that was as large as her dreams. It was risky, but she also enjoyed taking risks.

She was born in Montreal on February 10, 1947. Her parents, Rose and Bernard Arbour, had a stormy, unhappy marriage. In the final years they were together, Bernard Arbour managed two motels in rural Quebec, and the family lived in them from time to time. Home life was often bleak. Louise Arbour says John Irving's novel *The World According to Garp* comes close to describing her own childhood, a dysfunctional and unhappy period of her life.

At ten, she entered the cloistered world of a convent school, an experience that had a profound effect on her. The Collège Regina Assumpta offered its girls a rigorous classical education while it protected them from the realities of the contemporary world. Arbour's parents finally separated while she boarded at the convent, and she didn't see her father again for many years. Rose Arbour raised Louise and her brother, André, on an income from a women's clothing boutique she opened in Montreal.

Growing up, Arbour had no significant contact with people who did not share her religion, language, culture and gender. It was only after she graduated from the convent college in 1967 and went on to Université de Montréal law school that she began to experience the real world. She was shocked to discover that most of her textbooks were in English (Arbour recalls asking the clerk at the law school bookstore to direct her to where the French textbooks were, much to everyone's amusement). Law school was the first time she truly realized that she was a member of an ethnic minority, and that the laws of her country—Canada—were all in English, a language she could not speak.

Her first exposure to the wide world came through Montreal's Expo '67, as it did for so many young people in Quebec at the time. Arbour applied for one of the coveted hostess jobs. She expected to get a nifty uniform and a chance to tour people around, but she quickly found herself answering phones. "I worked with all the other rejects who weren't tall enough or pretty enough," says Arbour. But she had a free pass to all the pavilions and a chance to practise speaking English. The exposure convinced her that there was much more going on out in the world than the nuns had ever told her, and that she was missing out on it.

University life proved to be almost as cloistered as convent school, except for the presence of men. In spite of the workload, Arbour learned to smoke, play poker and dance in the clubs. She fancied herself a Quebec nationalist. She had little time for active politics, but no socially conscious young francophone in Quebec in the late sixties could be anything but a nationalist. "It was all about claims of entitlement that I thought were extremely well founded. About being master in your own house, working in your own language. But what I had then was an extremely romantic view of nationalism."

October 1970 was an eye-opener. That was when the Canadian army took over the streets of Montreal and the police began arresting people suspected of conspiracy and terrorism, often without the formality of laying charges. For Arbour, the War Measures Act, the suspension of civil law in Canada, was a shocking violation of human rights, and it was especially alarming to a law student. But unlike some of her more nationalistic friends, she was able to see some validity in the government's action: "People were also turning up dead in the trunks of cars," says Arbour, referring to Pierre Laporte, the Quebec politician who was kidnapped and murdered by the Front de Libération du Québec (FLQ). The events of 1970

shook her romantic view of self-determination at a time when it was confirming the nationalist and separatist opinions of a number of her colleagues in the university law faculty.

The heavy-handed federal response to the crisis didn't stop her from
recognizing that Ottawa was the centre of the universe for a Canadian law
student, and she eventually went there to look for work as a law clerk. "I
borrowed a car, got out a map, found Ottawa," she recalls. "There were the
Parliament Buildings, so the next one must be the Supreme Court."
Arbour asked Justice Philippe Pigeon for a job. When he asked her if she
could speak English, she said of course she could. Kind of. After twenty
minutes, he hired her.

The drive to Ottawa that day was a calculated risk that paid off, and
Arbour says it's the only event in her past experience that is comparable
with her later move to the war crimes tribunal. She had the same heady
sense of flying into the unknown, a foreign territory about which she had
minimal knowledge. She didn't know the language and she didn't know
the culture. Anything could happen. Friends say there are few examples of
such audacity in her life. Her childhood was a study in contrasts, the concrete certainties of convent life measured against the organic frailty of her
unhappy home. It made her cautious about taking chances when she
became an adult. But when she did take a risk it almost always paid off.

In Ottawa, working at the Supreme Court, she met a lawyer named
Larry Taman. He was an anglo from Ontario, and at first the law was all
they had in common. "Larry Taman was the smartest person I had ever
met," recalls Arbour. Their romance was as much an education as a court-
ship. "He was very much a social activist. In Quebec, I had been part of
the intense preoccupation with the national question. Larry introduced me
to the larger world of social consciousness. I discovered the North American feminist movement really for the first time. There were few great feminist thinkers in Quebec at the time." But despite Taman's social activism,
Arbour never became part of any movement. "I'm not a joiner," she says.
Her fidelity was to the law, not the cause. When she and Taman finished
their apprenticeships, they moved to Toronto and settled into a large, ram-
bling Rosedale house.

Arbour had led a sequestered life, in a society sheltered by its own
history and language and determination to be different from the rest of
North America. Now suddenly she was becoming a matron of the anglo
elite: living in a stereotypical anglo neighbourhood; weekending in the

Orange heartland of Hockley Valley, where she hosted sparkling social functions; teaching at the bastion of the Canadian anglo legal establishment, Osgoode Hall law school. And then there were three children: Emilie, Patrick and Catherine.

Her career arced steadily upward: law professor, associate dean, justice of the Ontario Supreme Court. And then she was appointed to the Ontario Court of Appeals. The judges and the lawyers who appeared before her soon came to regard her as capable and efficient. She was petite and pretty, with a quick wit; she was a refreshing change in the stuffy backrooms of the Ontario justice system.

Gradually, and not surprisingly, she acquired a reputation for cautious and conservative judgments. Arbour loves the law, and she believes that fidelity to its intricate codes and precedents will yield priceless and sometimes surprising benefits in a democracy. Though a conservative thinker, she is a legal idealist.

In 1987, as vice-president of the Canadian Civil Liberties Association (Alan Borovoy was president), Arbour argued for overturning a law that protected the personal history of rape victims. The rape shield law was the end result of a ten-year struggle on the part of Canadian feminists to stop unscrupulous attorneys from using the past sexual history of a rape victim as part of their client's defence. When the law entered the criminal code in 1983, it severely limited the ability of lawyers to cross-examine victims. The problem was, Arbour now argued, the rape shield law was unconstitutional.

To the chagrin of feminists who had fought the battle, she argued successfully that there was "nothing to gain in protecting women if innocent men are convicted." Though Borovoy, a Canadian icon in the field of civil rights, was actually the client in the CCLA case, Arbour took much of the criticism. She was the legal counsel and also she was a woman. She wasn't known as a feminist or any other kind of -ist, but she argued that principled feminists should accept that "it will take only one wrongful conviction for all the gains that women have made in this area to be lost."

It was shortly after that controversial case that she was appointed to the bench of the Ontario Supreme Court, and in 1990, she went to the appeals division. Her judgments were consistent in their high regard for the rights of accused people. In 1992, Arbour was part of a panel that gave prisoners the right to vote (they can read newspapers and follow developments on television, argued the judgment, so certainly they're qualified to help determine the country's leadership). In a far more controversial case, Arbour was part of the three-person decision to acquit a Hungarian immigrant, Imre Finta, who had been accused of war crimes. The charges against Finta alleged that he sent 8,716 Jews to their deaths in the Second World War. The 1992 ruling, which Arbour helped to write, determined that "by definition [Nazi war crimes] do not meet stringent domestic evidence rules."

For decades, Jewish Canadians had lobbied Ottawa for action against the many suspected Nazis who had come to Canada following the defeat of the Third Reich. Irving Abella had co-authored a seminal book, *None Is Too Many*, on Canada's horrendous policy of allowing in German immigrants while returning boatloads of Jewish refugees to their deaths during the war. Among the Germans, Canada eventually admitted, were numbers of middle-ranking Nazis — camp commanders and members of death squads. It took years to force Ottawa to prosecute a handful of known cases. By then, most of the accused war criminals were old, doddering men. The memories of their accusers and the witnesses to their deeds had faded. Finta, however, was considered to be a solid case, and an important test run for future prosecutions.

Finta had been a gendarme captain in Hungary during the war, and he never denied that he was responsible for arranging to transport thousands of Jews to Auschwitz. But he claimed he was just following orders. A jury found Finta not guilty of war crimes, and the Ontario Supreme Court upheld that decision. It proceeded to the appeals court, where the judges, including Arbour, upheld it as well. Ultimately, a narrow majority of the Supreme Court of Canada justices agreed. Not only was the first war crimes prosecution under Canadian law now defeated, but the rulings left a trail of precedent that made it almost impossible to ever prosecute a suspected war criminal in Canada again. Canada, the judges pronounced, did not have domestic jurisprudence that allowed for such prosecutions. The "crime" had been committed on foreign territory by a man operating under the authority of a sovereign government. The man believed what he was doing was legal.

Arbour's opinion was consistent with that of the majority of judges in the high courts of Ontario and the federal system. But human-rights activists argued that they had all interpreted Canadian law far too narrowly and had lost a historic opportunity to join with enlightened countries that support such prosecutions. Over the years, Louise Arbour would continue to be singled out for criticism over the controversial ruling.

In April 1995, Arbour was appointed by Order-in-Council to conduct an inquiry into events at the Prison for Women in Kingston. She listened to shocking evidence of brutality towards female inmates by their male guards, but it was soon obvious to her that the particular incidents at the P4W were symptomatic of larger problems in the Canadian corrections system. Arbour wrote a blistering report, condemning Correctional Services Canada for an utter disregard for human rights and for the rule of law. Six women prisoners had suffered "cruel, inhuman and degrading treatment," wrote Arbour, when they were strip-searched by a male riot squad, shackled and left nude for twelve hours on a concrete floor in the solitary confinement cells of Kingston's grisly old prison.

Arbour wrote eloquently on the historical and contemporary plight of women prisoners—many of whom were the products of abusive situations in their childhood and adult lives, and who ended up in penal institutions with no understanding of the lives they had lived. Following Arbour's report, the head of the federal corrections system resigned and Solicitor General Herb Gray issued a "heartfelt apology" to the women involved in the P4W incident.

The female convicts were satisfied with a process they described as fair and sympathetic, especially since Arbour's report demanded financial compensation be paid to the women. But Arbour was criticized by the feminist community, and also by some prisoners' rights activists, for not naming names. Arbour's condemnation of the system was brutal, but she failed to hold individuals accountable. Arbour replied that she'd been given a deadline of March 31, 1996, and that she'd never have met it if she'd gone into such detail. In any case, it was the job of the federal government to allocate personal blame. It never did.

The phone call from Boutros-Ghali came in the midst of her P4W inquiry and Arbour heard nothing further after that, at least not from the United Nations. But the rumour mills at the UN were already busy. Goldstone was leaving the tribunal and was about to write it off as a lost cause. He was recommending a Canadian judge as his replacement.

After four years of trying to keep the war crimes tribunals alive and viable, supporters in the U.S. State Department and a number of powerful representatives from NGOs were more than a little alarmed. The prospect of seeing a complete nobody appointed as chief prosecutor revived their first and worst suspicions—this organization was just window dressing. No one had heard of Louise Arbour, and very few appointments are made at that level unless from a pool of well-known and carefully screened candidates. To say the least, there was no groundswell of support for her appointment in any government or non-government circles.

A call went out into the legal and NGO communities for all interested parties to discover whatever they could about the mysterious Louise Arbour. Canada was the only country where people knew who she was, and the reaction there was quick and critical. The Canadian Jewish community—principally through the Canadian Jewish Congress (CJC)—reported that Arbour had played a seminal role in making Canada a safe place for Nazis. The CJC argued that someone who had acquitted the likes of Imre Finta couldn't be trusted to prosecute war crimes from any era, anywhere. Arbour argued that she was hardly alone in the Finta decision— a jury and three other courts had agreed—and that the ruling only illustrated the need for international courts for prosecuting such crimes. Canada lacked jurisdiction and it, perhaps, should amend its laws rather than blame the courts. But her arguments didn't wash. Arbour was considered to be soft on war criminals.

Canadian feminists, particularly members of the feminist Legal Education and Action Fund (LEAF), insisted that anyone, especially a woman, who had opposed the rape shield law couldn't be trusted with the important task of proving that rape had been a chief weapon of war in either Rwanda or Yugoslavia. And activists representing prisoners' rights warned that someone who had failed to call the violators of human rights in the Kingston prison by name was not someone who would understand the importance of nailing individuals for their participation in atrocities committed collectively.

Most of the Canadians who knew about the prospective appointment answered the "Who is she?" question with a loud "You don't want her!" A flurry of faxes to New York explained why Arbour was an enemy of human rights and unworthy of the position. American agencies reacted quickly with a campaign to stop the appointment. The Working Group on Human Rights of Women sent out a fax, asking anyone who cared to tell the powers that be to hold off on the Arbour appointment. In Canada, the campaign became personal. Selected journalists were taken aside and told the "real" story behind the proposed appointment—Louise Arbour and Richard Goldstone were secret lovers. In interviews, both Arbour and Goldstone dismiss the charge as offensive and wrong. And, indeed, it was a low blow in a campaign against the appointment that relied on feminist

issues to make its case. What could be more anti-feminist than the suggestion that a woman was awarded a plum position as a consequence of her
work in the bedroom?

Off the record, reporters also heard that Arbour was an anti-Semite.
This was based entirely on her role in the Finta decision. If the UN wanted
a Canadian woman, Arbour's detractors said, there were better prospects
available. One of them was Rosalie Abella, also a judge on the Ontario
Appeals Court bench. Abella had sterling credentials as a political activist
though she never gave any indication that she wanted the job.

Arbour says she was deeply offended by the gossipy quality of the
opposition, but not enough to withdraw her name. It was, after all, what
she had expected from the small, closed world of the Canadian legal community, rife as it is with petty jealousies. Arbour dismissed the attacks and
told friends it reminded her of the story of the woman in the seafood
store: "Some lobsters in the tank were getting dangerously close to the top
and snapping at customers. The woman asks the clerk, 'What if one of
those lobsters climbs out and hurts someone?' The clerk answers, 'Oh, no,
madam. It is impossible. They are Canadian lobsters. If one gets too close
to the top, the others will pull it back down.'"

At the United Nations, Boutros-Ghali tried to fast-track the appointment
as soon as Goldstone declared he was leaving. The secretary-general had no
stomach for the kind of politicking and infighting this appointment was
likely to create. He wanted it over quickly. But there would be no appointment to the war crimes tribunal without the support of the most powerful female politician in the U.S. — someone who was trying to become the
unofficial guardian angel of the tribunal.

As the American ambassador to the United Nations, Madeleine
Albright had been determined to put her personal stamp on foreign policy. She was born in Prague in 1937 but escaped to London with her
family when Hitler invaded Czechoslovakia two years later. The family
returned after the war but fled again in 1948 when a Stalinist government
took over. This time they moved to the United States. Albright was raised
a Roman Catholic and learned only while in office at the United Nations
that she was really Jewish. Her parents had kept it a secret. They went to
their graves without telling her that three of her grandparents had died
in Nazi concentration camps. The belated discovery that she had been a
member of an oppressed minority had a profound effect on her.

At the UN, Albright led the U.S. push for armed intervention in Bosnia in the summer of 1995. She was a contributor to the stiffened international resolve that helped bring the war to an end. Heeding the activists within the U.S. State Department, she had subsequently taken on the fight to ensure the tribunal did not die the cruel death that its detractors had planned for it since day one. She had told Slobodan Milosevic there could be no real peace unless he turned over the criminals he had been harbouring in Serbia, and she told the Croatian government she was "disgusted" by the country's treatment of Serbian refugees. Albright would also be instrumental in ending Boutros Boutros-Ghali's career at the UN. Her actions so traumatized the usually circumspect secretary-general that he ultimately wrote a tell-all book about his troubled relationship with the American administration.

The Security Council has a rotating chairmanship, and when Goldstone let it be known that he was leaving, Madeleine Albright was at the helm. She had never heard of Louise Arbour, and the warning signals from American NGOs were coming in loud and clear. Albright called Robert Fowler, her counterpart at the Canadian mission, and told him to bring this woman around to her office so the Americans could check her out.

Drawing on his experience in these diplomatic affairs, Fowler said he would not bring Arbour around, but he would happily arrange a meeting between Ambassador Albright and Louise Arbour at the Canadian mission. Though Fowler didn't know that much about Arbour, now he was riding shotgun for her in the Byzantine world of UN politics. "We diplomats worry about little protocol things. There was no reason for Madame Arbour to call on Madeleine Albright. Particularly, we wanted to make damn sure it wasn't interpreted as some kind of vetting. And I thought the best way was for Madeleine Albright to come around for a cup of coffee."

That, in diplomatic language, was Canada showing some muscle, which was about all it could show. Ottawa's foreign affairs department didn't even know who Louise Arbour was when the idea first floated to the surface. In fact, the Russians were the first to inform the Canadians that one of their own judges was being considered for the job. Albright arrived at the Canadian mission for her cup of coffee with full imperial entourage. "I'm used to this kind of style now," says Arbour when she reflects on the extraordinary court-of-Versailles quality of those days in January 1996. "It's always a lot of them and not many of me. But I wasn't used to it then, these people who move with bodyguards and note takers — it moves a lot of air as they go around."

Madeleine Albright had a half-dozen top-level people with her from the U.S. State Department. She insisted that she first wanted to meet Arbour alone, which Fowler found highly unusual, considering the power players who had come along for his little coffee party. But sure enough, Albright took Arbour into Fowler's office and shut the door behind them.

Albright had a reputation for championing women in high office, and she was personally intrigued with the idea of having a Canadian female take over the chief prosecutor's job at The Hague. She would have also been struck by the uncanny similarity in appearance and manner between her and Louise Arbour. Both are just about five feet tall in heels; both had been academics, and both were bilingual and ambitious. They both had three children. (Albright was exactly ten years Arbour's senior, and she had already seen her husband walk out for another woman. Arbour would experience the same ordeal before long.) Sitting on opposite couches in their trim blue power suits, the women hit it off immediately. "I liked her very much," recalls Arbour. She can remember only one thing the U.S. ambassador said to her that day: "'If you are to do this job, you'll have to be very tough. A lot tougher than anyone can imagine.' She has since reminded me of that conversation."

After the two women had sniffed each other out, they retired to the bigger room for the bigger sniff. It didn't last long, but it was a tough cross-examination, not unlike a U.S. congressional confirmation hearing. The group consisted of many of the tribunal's strongest American supporters, including John Shattuck, who held the human-rights portfolio at the State Department. No one was too interested in knowing if Arbour could distinguish a Croat from a Bosnian or a Hutu from a Tutsi, but they all wanted to know a great deal about her decisions as a judge and why she had made them, from Imre Finta on down. They had done their homework — and it was her first opportunity to reveal the potential to be "a lot tougher than anyone can imagine." She told her inquisitors that she didn't much like their line of questioning. Canadian courts are different from American ones. Canadian judges don't have to explain their decisions or win elections to serve on the bench. And she certainly didn't feel obliged to explain her reasons for decisions she had made along with the other appellate judges on the bench.

Arbour is an attractive and very soignée Québécoise who combines a quick, sharp mind with a face able to convey an array of emotions worthy of an Edith Piaf. The combination can quickly throw detractors off their game, and it didn't fail her on this day. But both Arbour and Fowler had the overwhelming impression that the decision had already been made, that the fifteen minutes of female power play in the other room had been all that really counted.

Albright said almost nothing; she just watched the others pepper Arbour with questions and the Canadian judge toss them back. It was all very detached and almost by rote, except for one zinger Arbour wasn't prepared for. Someone asked: "Is there anything we should know about your past that could be a cause for concern?" Arbour burst out laughing. "I said, 'Listen, I don't know how far you want to go back, but I've been a judge for the past ten years, and so I can tell you [that] at least for the past ten years, I've had a rather subdued existence.'" The question was withdrawn and the meeting came to an end. Albright had her woman.

It was now on to the recalcitrant Russians. Fowler arranged a meeting. "The Russians were very worried about anti-Serb biases," recalls Arbour. "I had no biases. The Russians believed there were too many Americans working at the tribunal. I came from Canada, where we knew all about American imperialism. It was a good lunch." The Russians were also much encouraged by Arbour's legal record. Unlike the NGOs and the legal experts who thought Arbour might be too soft on rapists and war criminals, the Russians liked her record of supporting the rights of the accused, something they felt had been lacking in the Goldstone era.

Arbour charmed the Russians, especially when she hinted she would want a full-time Russian adviser on her staff (something that infuriated the Americans). Moscow quickly dropped its prerequisite that the chief prosecutor *not* come from a NATO country and supported the Canadian. Other members of the Security Council had even fewer problems: France wanted the appointee to be a native French-speaker. The British were happy the candidate was not the American troublemaker Cherif Bassiouni. The Chinese were keeping their powder dry for a later fight against plans for a permanent international criminal court. And so the appointment progressed through all the diplomatic channels at the Security Council, under the careful supervision of Ambassador Fowler, who was as intrigued by Arbour as all the foreigners.

Aside from Fowler, Ottawa had almost nothing to do with the Arbour appointment; it had not even prepared her exit from the Canadian judiciary, which would eventually lead to a parliamentary dust-up. There was almost no lobbying for Arbour; if the appointment carried, it would be almost exclusively because of Madeleine Albright. Fowler would be the one to lead Arbour along her rapid learning curve: "She wanted to know everything. Who did what to whom, who advised whom, where were the mines buried on this one. She wanted to know what degree of support there was from the Security Council, who was supportive, who was less support-ive." Swiftly, Fowler realized that Arbour had an acute instinct for spotting court intrigue. She would need it.

Madeleine Albright had until the last day of February to get this appointment through before she lost the chair of the Security Council. The complaints about Arbour kept coming in, but Albright was prepared to ignore them. In fact, it was precisely because Arbour had no history of activism that she was attractive to Albright. Arbour represented no cause. She might actually win unanimous approval by the Security Council.

On February 29, 1996, Madeleine Albright led the vote that approved the appointment of Madam Justice Louise Arbour to be the next chief prose-cutor for the international criminal tribunals for the former Yugoslavia and Rwanda.

For Albright it was time to pop the champagne corks, but the anti-Arbour campaign, in some circles, actually became more strenuous after the appointment. An article in *Ms.* magazine by the Toronto writer Alice Klein asked in a headline: "Is War Crimes Prosecution in the Right Hands?" It went on to argue that Arbour was no friend of women and the last person who would ever pursue rape as a war crime. In Ottawa, Senator Anne Cools called for the Ontario Court of Appeals to fire Arbour for abandoning her post, arguing that a sitting justice can't take on other work. The Liberal government had to amend regulations under the Canadian Judges Act to allow for Arbour to go. None of this was of much concern to the State Department or the UN. The tribunals had, once again, been pulled back from the brink of the abyss.

Arbour had expected to depart for The Hague in the spring of 1996, as soon as she had completed the P4W commission. But the UN told her the appointment would not take effect until October 1. As surprising as this long delay was, it could have been even worse. The American ad-ministration wanted to postpone the appointment for almost a year—until February 1997.

Even though the State Department was confident it had found the right replacement for Justice Goldstone, no one was quite sure what Arbour would do. It was a U.S. election year and Bill Clinton had made it clear he wanted all departments to avoid any dust-ups. Goldstone, it was believed, was on-side with the U.S. administration. People from the State Department were on his staff. Arbour was an unknown.

Clinton called President Nelson Mandela personally to ask for an extension of the Goldstone appointment. The only compromise possible was that Goldstone would "overlap" the Arbour appointment until October. That might at least cover for the presidential election campaign.

Arbour was furious with the delay, but it actually gave her a chance to learn the ropes before Goldstone departed. It also allowed time for the tribunal-watchers to get to know her.

American NGOs and human-rights groups soon found that Arbour was not the right-wing reactionary they had feared. She was something of a blank slate for them: she had few preconceptions, and they were able to advise her freely. Besides being a quick student, Arbour was a voracious reader. The first book she read on Yugoslavia was an early twentieth-century classic: Rebecca West's *Black Lamb and Grey Falcon*. Then she decided to jump ahead a few years. "I have to get to the war faster than this," she told friends. She watched the encyclopedic documentary *The Death of Yugoslavia* several times and read all the Bosnian war literature; she was profoundly influenced by the work of David Rieff and Roy Gutman. Alison Des Forges, the most knowledgeable of all the human-rights workers in Rwanda, briefed her at length.

The Washington Post reporter Charles Trueheart wrote one of the first American profiles of Arbour, and it was a glowing one. But he included one personal detail that caused a sudden anxiety attack in the U.S. State Department and in New York. It seemed none of the suits in Foggy Bottom had thought to ask her about her marital status. Now, it seemed, Arbour was unmarried. She had three children from her twenty-eight-year common-law relationship with Larry Taman. It had never occurred to Arbour that this could be a problem, or that there was anyone who didn't know. She had been appointed a judge after her third child was born, and her marital status had never caused a ripple in Canada.

Moral ambiguity in foreign policy is central to Washington's role in world affairs. But ambiguity in personal or domestic matters is another story. No one in Washington (or at the UN, where many people also heard the news for the first time) could figure out how this was going to play. The statutes for the tribunal spell out that the chief prosecutor must be of "high moral character." Tribunal watchers held their breath and waited for the fallout from *The Washington Post*'s disclosure. There was none.

The two international courts now had a new chief prosecutor. No one was sure if Arbour was the right person, but they were fairly certain she wasn't the wrong one.

3

CULTURE OF IMPUNITY

The real culprits in this long list of executions, assassinations,
drownings, burnings, massacres and atrocities furnished by this report are
not — we repeat — the Balkan peoples.... The true culprits are
those who mislead public opinion and take advantage of the people's
ignorance to raise disquieting rumours and sound the alarm bell,
inciting their country and consequently other countries into enmity.
The real culprits are those who by interest or inclination, declaring
constantly that war is inevitable, end by making it so, asserting
they are powerless to prevent it. The real culprits are those who sacrifice
the general interest to their own personal interest, which they
so little understand, and hold up their countries to a sterile policy
of conflict and reprisals.
— Baron d'Estournelles de Constant, International Commission
to Inquire into the Causes of the Balkan Wars, 1914

The Hague is a dour, overcast city on the Dutch coast, chilled for much of the year by a cold wind that blows in from the North Sea. It is a fitting place to install a war crimes tribunal: both war and justice have played a key role in the history of the place. Armies fought over religion during the Reformation, the Counter-Reformation and, later, the Thirty Years War. Napoleon and Hitler both sent their legions through the city. The name of this bleak place, however, is most associated with numerous international treaties and peace arrangements signed over the past four hundred years, including The Hague Conferences of the turn of the century, which established the rules of modern warfare and furnished a model for the future League of Nations and the UN.

The Hague is the administrative centre of the Netherlands and the home of the International Court of Justice, where world governments go to argue over breaches of international treaties and conventions. It's also a hub of cultural enlightenment: past residents include Erasmus, Galileo and Johannes Kepler. Jan Vermeer of Delft painted some of his extraordinarily lucid oil paintings here, giving the world its first intimate impressions of the genteel lifestyle of the seventeenth-century Dutch bourgeoisie.

Near the centre of town, a modern structure with a fifties-vintage white-granite façade is conspicuous mostly for a particularly ugly display of public art that has been installed on its front lawn. The building was originally the offices of a Dutch insurance and securities company. It became the headquarters for the International Criminal Tribunal for the Former Yugoslavia mostly because it was available and needed only a few modifications to meet the high-security specifications of a modern war crimes court.

Visitors no longer enter by the original stone steps, which lead to the giant wooden front doors. There is now a special entrance, a glass-and-steel bunker attached like a burr to the side of the old building, where UN security personnel carefully scrutinize visitors' identification. Makeshift partitions clog the pretentious neo-Roman revival entrance hallway and much of the first floor, providing workspace for members of the media. The actual courtrooms are at the top of a sweeping circular staircase, past more guards, metal detectors and a high-tech security bubble.

No one who comes to the tribunal fails to be impressed by the courtroom: it is, at once, absurd and awesome. A wall of bulletproof glass, from floor to ceiling, divides it into a public seating area and the segregated court. When there is particularly sensitive material to be presented before the court, a massive venetian blind descends to block the view from the spectators' gallery. From the public side of the glass, the courtroom has the appearance of a clinic; one expects to watch an experiment of sorts. The impression is not entirely inappropriate.

Beyond the courtroom, in three floors of offices and meeting rooms, scores of lawyers, investigators, forensic experts and administrators pore over the evidence that arrives each day from the tribunal's field workers. Louise Arbour inherited an impressive body of data from Bassiouni and Goldstone: records of 150 mass graves, 900 prison camps and 90 paramilitary groups. Some of the world's best legal minds worked at verifying and organizing this information. They came here on secondment from jobs in Europe and North America, labouring under the uncommon belief that they could make a difference, that their work could help make amends for the years of madness that consumed the former Yugoslavia.

The rabbit warren of little offices, the surreal bulletproof courtroom, the pretentious marble entrance hallway, with its chandeliers and checker-board linoleum floor, seemed unreal to Arbour when she arrived for the first time. The cold and clinical atmosphere made her feel that she would be more appropriately dressed in a white lab coat. But what encouraged her was a visit to the steel-lined vault in the building's basement, where the files and evidence were carefully stored. Here she found the material from Bassiouni and his commission of experts now supplemented and sub-stantiated by a team of prosecutors and investigators. She had the raw evidence from the field workers, even bits of material from graves. There was the personal testimony from Sarajevo: descriptions of mortar and sniper attacks, the breadline massacre, the intercepted conversations in which General Mladic told his men to "bomb them to the edge of madness." There were hundreds of hours of taped interviews with victims and per-petrators, as well as boxes of papers from concentration camps and "depor-tation" bureaus, where people were forced to sign over all their property before boarding buses that would take them away from their homes, in many cases, forever. There were the statements of people who were com-pelled to torture friends and neighbours; forensic reports on mass graves that were carefully excavated over weeks and months to reconstruct events that had taken only hours to consummate; reports about the babies born to women who were raped as part of a campaign to damage a people so com-pletely that they would never want to return to their homes; the testimony of Albassa Kurbegovic, who grieved for a lost future.

It was the evidentiary account of three Balkan wars over a span of five years. No single element could tell the story. But collectively, these files and scraps of evidence offered a record of what had happened to the for-mer Yugoslavia. It was all neatly filed and stored in acid-free containers, awaiting the extraordinary effort that would be required to organize it in support of an unprecedented quest for justice a thousand kilometres away from where the crimes took place.

The indictments were impressive — for seventy-four people in all, including leaders of the Serb, Bosnian and Croat militias. It might have made the seasoned jurist's heart swell in anticipation of the days to come, except that there were only seven people in custody and none was very important in the scheme of things.

The tribunal's jail is a specially built compound in the heart of an old Dutch prison. Dusan Tadic was in custody there, along with three Muslim military leaders accused of war crimes and hastily handed over to The Hague by the Bosnian government of Sarajevo. The Bosnians hoped that their efforts to co-operate would be rewarded with the swift prosecution of those they believed were mainly responsible for what had happened.

Arbour arrived in The Hague in August 1996, well before her official appointment, in order to overlap with Goldstone. It didn't work out that way: The tribunal's first chief prosecutor already had one foot out the door. Goldstone knew that Boutros-Ghali wanted him gone — the secretary-general thought Goldstone was too tight with the State Department — and Goldstone had grown weary of the whole lot of them anyway. Arbour discovered she'd be on her own during the sorting out of her new job. And she knew that a thousand kilometres away, the Pale Gang, the perpetrators of the events that would consume her life for the next three years, were also being left on their own.

The men in the motorcade gliding along the main highway that runs through Republika Srpska offered no more than a nod to the French soldiers at the checkpoint. The fact that some of the men in the cars were charged with unimaginable crimes seemed to be the last thing on their minds as they came and went with apparent impunity. Among them was Radovan Karadzic, commuting from his large white house — newly built — to his office near Pale. The former psychiatrist and self-styled poet with the familiar mop of thick grey hair and the signature white ascot commanded a perverse kind of respect from the foreign soldiers who guarded the checkpoints.

At one time, the soldiers would salute his military chief, General Ratko Mladic, but in the summer of 1996 no one saw much of the general. Mladic was spending his time in a bunker halfway between the American peacekeeping troops and the French contingent (when he wasn't relaxing on the beaches of Montenegro), though from time to time they'd see him as he crossed the border into Belgrade to catch a basketball game.

No one saw the popular Nicole Koljevic at all. He was the former Shakespeare scholar who had found a new calling and a new passion for killing people during the Bosnian war. His relationship with the international peacekeepers was sufficiently well developed in those days that when he wasn't sure what to do with his UN hostages in 1995, he called General Lewis MacKenzie's cellphone to get advice. Koljevic killed himself shortly after the war ended.

Under the Dayton accords, the capital and the government apparatus of the new Republika Srpska were located in the northwestern Bosnian city of Banja Luka. Foreign negotiators wanted to put some demonstrable distance between the politicians and the warlords in Pale. But few were fooled by the logistical game. Almost everyone, including the NATO soldiers, knew that the old Pale Gang still ran things, even though many of them, including Karadzic, were wanted men.

In Karadzic's case, he'd been indicted for crimes ranging from kidnapping to genocide. But what did he care? It was clear nobody had the gumption to interfere with his movements, and as a matter of fact, some of the foreign soldiers—mostly the French—would occasionally warn him to lie low when there was potential for trouble. After all, their mandate was to keep the peace, not rock the boat. Karadzic's security was in no small way linked directly to theirs.

It became a popular media sport for journalists to stand near NATO checkpoints and take notes and pictures of the indicted criminals passing through. Some of the NATO soldiers—called IFOR for Intervention Force— had been observed on camera drinking in the same bars or hanging out in the same clubs as the accused. By 1996, after a few such media incidents, the soldiers were trying to be more careful. When they saw "wanted" men at events—like press conferences—they carefully stepped out of the way lest an enterprising reporter catch them in the same frame as someone indicted for rape and murder. It was often tricky. In interviews, the accused men bragged about how many times a day they passed NATO troops without interference. The best stories were the ones they told about IFOR soldiers checking their identification documents and then waving them on. Stories like those could end up on the front pages of U.S. newspapers.

In the summer of 1996, NATO still claimed it didn't know the names of any criminals and didn't have enough information about them to make arrests. The war crimes tribunal supplied them with large wanted posters —complete with the names and grainy photographs of dozens of indicted men. These posters were backed with blue cardboard and could easily be mounted on a wall. The photos weren't very good, but the subjects hadn't changed much. They didn't go in for disguises. Why bother? They lived in the same houses they had occupied during the war (except for those who stole enough money to build new ones), and reporters called them up using their old phone numbers. One of the most notorious of the wanted men, Milan Martic, lived one hundred metres away from a British post in the Prijedor district of Bosnia. But it was convenient for NATO officers to remain wilfully in the dark. It made life less complex and perilous.

NATO had promised repeatedly to begin arresting these men—if its soldiers ever saw any of them and could make the arrests safely. Somehow they never did see any. This charade was easy to sustain, since the architects of the Dayton accords had left the provisions for arresting war criminals deliberately vague. They didn't want war crimes prosecutors or NATO soldiers to do anything that might provoke the Serbs to reject the peace document and embarrass Bill Clinton in an election year. The Dayton deal did specify that NATO had the *authority* to arrest people, but it never said it had an *obligation* to do so.

Just as Louise Arbour was trying to make sense of all of this, anonymous individuals inside IFOR leaked documents to Human Rights Watch indicating that Karadzic was at the head of a sophisticated paramilitary network. His objective, as the whistle-blowers explained it, was "to de-stabilize the peace process and create opposition to IFOR."

Karadzic had been forced out of power by the Dayton peace-brokers, who informed Milosevic that the Bosnian Serb leader was to be barred from running in any future elections. It was forbidden even to use his image in campaign material or to broadcast his statements. Any posters that his supporters had already installed around the RS had to be removed. But everyone knew he was still boss. His former deputy, Biljana Plavsic, actually complained to the Organization for Security and Co-operation in Europe (OSCE) about Karadzic's extortionist black-market dealing in petrol and alcohol. He had her arrested. Plavsic finally realized that among all the fascist ideologues, she stood alone in her purity of purpose. The others were just criminals and warlords.

The leak from IFOR to Human Rights Watch was the first indication that some of the NATO soldiers were actually fed up with acting like blind monkeys. NATO bosses in Brussels had argued that the mission would quickly unravel if they took on the task of arresting the indictees. But those on the ground realized they would never have any real control over the situation as long as pariahs and gangland thugs were running the country with support from their private armies.

Peace-brokers like Richard Holbrooke had once been ambivalent about the war crimes tribunal. But now, they too could see that peace was impossible as long as the country was still effectively under the control of the White Eagles and Arkan's Tigers. Finally, Robert Frowick, the ambassador to the OSCE, announced that the whole peace process depended on apprehension. And Holbrooke ultimately declared his new-found certainty that "Karadzic at large means Dayton denied." But it would take a while before the new belligerence translated into a change in purpose for the peacekeepers on the ground.

Arbour took advantage of the lag between the announcement of her appointment and its official starting date to visit one of the grave exhumations. In late August 1996, she went to Vukovar, Croatia, to see what the tribunal was doing in the field. She found it shocking: "In Vukovar, I was blown away. It was like a B movie from World War II. I remember it as though it were in black and white." It was only the first shock of many.

Arbour officially visited the Balkans as the chief prosecutor in early 1997, and she quickly got a measure of the scale of the problems she was facing. She had dozens of indictments — and possibly enough evidence to obtain convictions — but she had no police force to round up the people she wanted to put on trial. The UN had said that the indicted people were to be arrested by the countries that hosted them. From her first conversations in the capitals of the former Yugoslavia, she could see that this declaration was some kind of cruel joke.

Arbour started to seriously ask herself why she had ever consented to take on the job. In interviews, she hinted at her profound disappointment at being unable to persuade NATO to help her. Years later, she would describe these frightening years as chief prosecutor: "It was like driving around at top speed in a Grand Prix racing car made out of porcelain. You had to maintain the speed, but if you even so much as touched or bumped anything, you would shatter into a million pieces." Failure could mean sudden death, for people and for the prospects of international justice.

Unlike a judicial system in a democratic country, where there is a sense of permanence and history, and a functioning apparatus to give the law practical relevance, the ICTY was really based on nothing more than a set of laws that had not been used in forty-five years. The tribunal had to be perceived to be doing something, or the UN might just dismantle it. Arbour's fear of failure was palpable. And yet she lacked some of the basic tools she needed.

In Belgrade during the winter of Arbour's first visit, tens of thousands of people took to the streets to protest the leadership of Slobodan Milosevic. For the first time since the end of the Cold War, a bona fide political opposition had emerged in the former Yugoslavia, possibly with enough momentum to oust the president. But the people in the streets, blaring horns and blowing whistles, were protesting against Milosevic only because his wars had brought so much hardship to people in Serbia, not because of the death toll in Bosnia. The people in what was left of Yugoslavia — Serbia (including the province of Kosovo) and Montenegro — were facing a series of economic sanctions from the international community, a large world they believed simply did not understand Serbs or the security imperatives of Greater Serbia. There would be no co-operation from Belgrade, a regime that had declared the war crimes tribunal a kangaroo court.

Conditions were even worse in Republika Srpska, a beaten, battered and criminalized society with a 90 per cent unemployment rate. The most promising job prospects were in the service of one of the bosses who ran the place, as a bodyguard or a member of the "police," meaning one of the private armies financed from black-market profits. Consumer prices were outrageously high. The warlords told people it was because of the economic sanctions imposed by the West, which was partly true, but the ultranationalists who had run the military campaign were now controlling the prices and extorting as much money from people as they possibly could.

The Rhine Maiden of Serbia — Biljana Plavsic — had been "elected" as the post-war president of RS through the careful machinations of the OSCE, and she had taken her position in the parliament in Banja Luka. She indicated she was willing to work with the international representatives of the Dayton peace process and she had not been a target of The Hague indictments. But Karadzic had already demonstrated who was boss when he had had her arrested. Whenever Plavsic kicked up a fuss, she could expect a gang of locals to retaliate by shooting up her office. This was hardly a place where Arbour could expect to find much help. The indicted criminals were running the show.

In Zagreb, Arbour found the Croatian government to be only slightly more helpful. The wily president, Franjo Tudjman, had managed to come out of the wars in Yugoslavia with a squeaky clean image at home and abroad, and his new nation-state was enjoying a lot of support from the international community. He offered to hand over a few of the people

Arbour was looking for as a kind of goodwill gesture, but he would not allow her forensic teams to come into the country for specific investigations unless they involved Croat victims.

Arbour complained publicly about Tudjman's intransigence, but it didn't do any good. The UN wasn't about to put any pressure on him. It didn't matter that he had directed wars and ethnic-cleansing campaigns against Muslims and Serbs that were a little less bloody and atrocious than those of Slobodan Milosevic only because they were shorter and the enemy was better defended. Tudjman was co-operating with the UN and, many would say, getting away with murder. By paying lip service to the right people while refusing to co-operate in any meaningful way with Arbour and the tribunal, Croatia was invited to join the Council of Europe, the oldest and one of the most prestigious pan-European organizations, dedicated to human rights and the rule of law. Arbour complained loudly about the invitation but to no avail.

In Sarajevo, she found the only flicker of real encouragement that she would encounter in the Balkans in those early days. Izetbegovic surrendered all the indicted Bosnians known to be in his territory, which was all that he could do. The rest was up to Arbour and her team at The Hague, and she needed a police force. The only one available, NATO, wasn't co-operating.

Arbour met the NATO peacekeeping commanders in the field and petitioned them to help her. But authority was really with the leadership in Brussels. After her tour of the crime scene — the former Yugoslavia — Arbour went to see NATO's top command with high hopes that she could reason with them and, if necessary, shame them into action. She had a straightforward analysis of the situation: Bosnia didn't have peace, it had an elaborate ceasefire. NATO wasn't preventing the resumption of war, it was only perpetuating conditions that allowed the Balkan mafia to conduct a roaring business. The analysis made sense, to her.

The journey to Brussels from The Hague isn't a long one, and Arbour had to make the trip often. Sitting in a room full of men with rows of ribbons on their chests, their padded shoulders as wide as she was tall, Arbour made her case for apprehending the criminals. The generals had heard it all before, though just to be polite they assured her that arrests might happen in the future, when they were sure the peace had taken root. But not now. It would be premature and too risky. Arbour told them: "Gentlemen, it seems to me arresting war criminals is a bit like getting pregnant. It's never the right time. But eventually you just do it." The analogy might have been apt, but the audience was all wrong.

Arbour didn't entirely blame the generals. "Everybody buys into the long-term ideals of justice," she reflected after the meeting. "But not everyone's prepared to face the reality that criminal justice is a very coercive process—a disturbing process." The "non-arrests issue," as it was delicately called at the UN, was also becoming expensive for the tribunal. Once Arbour had found out where her suspects lived, she had to keep them under surveillance. "Keeping track of the people we indict is very taxing for our resources," she complained to the UN, without any apparent effect.

Staffers at the tribunal were accustomed to Goldstone's bombastic style. He had been a fierce public fighter. Once he even threatened to resign and take half the staff with him. Their new chief prosecutor was telling them that there was no point in public demonstrations of frustration. "No one owes us anything," she told her staff. "We're a new organization and we have no entitlement. If we want something to happen, we'll have to make it happen."

Inside the tribunal, and among the outside NGOs, a lot of people were suspicious of Arbour. Maybe what they had heard—that she was appointed only to keep the tribunal out of the way of diplomats and politicians— was true. The European press published the same profiles as the North American media, stories about Arbour and the rape shield law and the Imre Finta decision, stories suggesting that she was soft on criminals and lacked the scrappy instincts required to bring down the bad guys.

Arbour had a lot to learn about the mysterious ways of NATO and the UN, and there was little in her experience to fall back on when she met such determined intransigence. Arbour told her staff: "You have to play the hand you've been dealt." That disappointed many of them, who didn't understand that she was developing a strategy of her own. "I love gamesmanship," she confessed in an interview. "I love to play all kinds of games: cards, board games, whatever. Games of strategy where you have to plot the next seventeen moves. I think, If I do this, he'll do that. [That] kind of thing." It was the same at the tribunal: "I calculated my moves in so many ways." Behind her apparent early despair, her survival instincts were kicking in. Soon Arbour had a plan.

One of the problems NATO had with making arrests was rooted in the glaring transparency of the justice process up to that point. Everyone knew who had been indicted and who was vulnerable. Bodyguards for the accused men were often better armed than the combat-ready IFOR soldiers, and they looked out for each other. The chances of a surprise arrest were non-existent and the possibilities for casualties numerous. And the media were never far away from the wanted men. If something went wrong, it would be on television in the blink of an eye, bringing IFOR into disrepute and possibly even inciting attacks on NATO soldiers.

Goldstone had issued his very public indictments more to make a point than to build a caseload; he had to keep the tribunal alive and funds flowing. When Arbour's office had completed a number of new cases and she was ready to issue new indictments, she tried a different approach. Instead of distributing large wanted posters with details of the alleged crimes on the tribunal's Web site, Arbour sealed the indictments and kept them a secret from all but the handful of people working on each case.

Among the secret indictments was one for Slavko Dokmanovic, a Serb who had acted as president of the municipality of Vukovar during the Croatian conflict, the war many regarded as a dress rehearsal for Bosnia. Shortly after Croatia claimed independence in 1991, Serbian paramilitaries declared the Croatian area known as the Krajina to be Serbian territory. Led by Arkan's Tigers, the soldiers began to sweep the area of all Muslims and Croats. The campaign in the Krajina was particularly gory, and it was difficult to know who had really been in charge of it. But one event stood out as a particularly well-planned and ruthless operation.

Serb soldiers entered the town of Vukovar on November 20, 1991, to expel and kill the non-Serbs. Knowing what was probably about to happen, many people, particularly the men, had gone to the local hospital, hoping to hide among the patients there. In these early days of the war, nobody knew just how vicious the paramilitaries could be. To be sick or wounded, or a woman or a child, offered no protection. And so when the Serbs arrived in Vukovar, they took 280 people out of the hospital, piled them onto trucks and drove them to a farm—a place called Ovcara.

The forensic team that investigated Ovcara—the site Arbour had visited in September—issued its final report in October 1996. They had found the corpses of 198 men and two women piled into mass graves. (Bodies of another eighty missing people have never been found.) Forensic evidence supported what a few eyewitnesses, those who had managed to escape from the trucks, had described: the Serbs forced hospital patients to walk out into a field with the men who had tried to hide among them.

They were beaten, some with their own crutches, then killed. Many bodies, still in their pyjamas, were found tangled together (some of them fused in an embrace, indicating they hadn't died instantly), some with bandages, broken crutches and, in one case, catheter tube still attached. As the civilian in charge, Slavko Dokmanovic was (secretly) indicted for aiding and abetting this mass murder.

On June 27, 1997, Dokmanovic made a short trip to visit property he owned in eastern Slavonia, now under the control of Croatia. He didn't know about the sealed indictment alleging that he was guilty of crimes against humanity. The call he received advising him to go and check his property was possibly a set-up. In eastern Slavonia, the United Nations, not NATO, ran the peacekeeping mission. UN soldiers nabbed the unarmed and unsuspecting Dokmanovic, handcuffed him, read out his charges and whisked him by helicopter to the jail in The Hague. It was the first arrest by a foreign team in a jurisdiction that had once been part of the Yugoslav union. It went without a hitch, but it was only a test run.

In 1997, NATO was going through a period of major change. Plans to enlarge membership of the organization were moving forward and injecting NATO with new blood. There would soon be a new supreme allied commander for Europe with a very different sense of NATO's role from his predecessor. General Wesley Clark was a thirty-six-year-old West Point graduate with a military crewcut and the ability to make quick and, if necessary, brutal decisions.

Before the end of the decade Clark would lead NATO in an unprecedented bombing attack directed against Milosevic, for whom Clark eventually developed a personal loathing. Fortuitously for Arbour, Clark had also been on the negotiating team at Dayton—and had specific interest in its military aspects. Anyone who had participated in bringing about the peace agreement had his reputation on the line, and a direct stake in its successful implementation. That included the young hotshot from the Pentagon.

Wesley Clark knew the agreement would never succeed as long as the other side had more guns than the peacekeepers did, and as long as the indicted men were free to travel the region under the auspices of warlords and criminals. Arbour quickly realized that Clark would be a crucial ally—someone who might be able to appreciate the importance of involving NATO in the justice process, and had the guts to act. She was right.

The summer of 1997 was a turning point. There was no single development that directly explains how the climate changed in that crucial
period, but it is clear in retrospect that there was a fundamental shift in
thinking at the top levels of political and military decision making. In addition to the changes at NATO, Great Britain had a new government. Prime
Minister John Major had strenuously opposed intervention in Bosnia, and
his Tory party had supported the Vance-Owen peace plan. The British
hadn't been particularly happy when the Americans took charge of the
process in Dayton, since there was a strong historic bond between the
Serbs and the United Kingdom, and Milosevic's party had quietly contributed to the campaign war chests of select Conservative candidates. Of
course, none of this mattered to Britain's new PM, Tony Blair.

Blair was a new phenomenon in British politics, and he was anxious
to show that his Labour-with-a-capitalist-face government was going to
make a clean break with the past. Bosnia offered a clear-cut opportunity to
do so. Arbour began to petition the British government for help almost as
soon as Blair was elected.

British troops patrolled the southwest division—more than a third
of Bosnia and much of Republika Srpska. This was where many of the
most notorious wanted men lived, including the sadists who had been
responsible for the prisoner-of-war camps. Arbour's secret indictments
identified a number of suspects in the British sector, among them Milan
Kovacevic.

Kovacevic had been well known to foreign reporters since 1992, when
they broke the story about the Omarska and Keraterm camps. He was the
man who decided which journalists could enter the gates of hell and report
on the conditions there. First, he would brief the foreign media on the
tragic history of the Serbian people, going back six hundred years to
outline their legacy of abuse and victimization at the hands of Croats and
Turks. Kovacevic required journalists to watch videotapes allegedly showing Serb children being murdered by Croatian Ustashe forces during the
Second World War—the same pictures and reports that Serbian TV fed to
the population on the evening news with the intention of keeping fear of
the enemy pumping in their veins.

Kovacevic denied that the Serb paramilitaries in the area were evict-
ing innocent Muslim and Croat women and children. He told visiting
reporters that the men they were incarcerating in the Omarska and Kera-

term camps just outside Prijedor were the true villains. He and the other Serbs were only defending themselves and their people against degenerates who would kill them first if given an opportunity.

The Serbs were forced to close the camps after their existence was reported in the international media, though the mass murders and the forced deportations of people continued for another three years. After the war was over, Kovacevic and his comrades lived comfortably on the proceeds of what they had stolen and extorted. But both reporters who returned to the area and local people who knew Kovacevic said that he often seemed remorseful and uncertain about some of the events of those days of murder and mayhem.

On July 10, 1997, British troops under NATO command literally dropped in on the city of Prijedor. The Special Air Service (SAS) is famous for its lightning-like small SWAT missions. The commandos were decked out like Rambo, but the job was fairly straightforward—to serve arrest warrants on two men, neither of whom knew he had been indicted: Kovacevic and his brother-in-law, Simo Drijaca, the former chief of police. The British soldiers nabbed Kovacevic and whisked him off to The Hague; Drijaca unwisely tried to make a run for it and was killed in a shootout. The whole event was over in a matter of hours. For the first time, NATO troops had arrested an indicted criminal in the former Yugoslavia without the permission of the local authorities. There were no injuries to the British soldiers, and Tony Blair's new government basked in loud praise for the daring feat. Arbour will not say what influence she had on the British decision to act, or what role Wesley Clark played in these developments. But it couldn't have been closer to her heart's desire if she had planned and executed the raid herself. She was on a roll.

Within months of those SAS arrests, ten Croats indicted by Richard Goldstone—men whose indictments had been widely publicized—surrendered themselves to the tribunal. A Dutch Hercules aircraft picked them up in Zagreb and flew them to their new accommodations in Holland, the special jail run by the United Nations in the heart of the old red-brick prison at The Hague. They pleaded not guilty. Arbour had told her staff that after the raids she expected people to give themselves up, and now she said they should expect more of the same.

But Arbour wasn't about to rely on the inclination of war criminals to surrender; she actively encouraged Wesley Clark and NATO to continue making arrests. Another daring, almost bungled, arrest by Dutch marines backed up by British forces brought in two more publicly indicted Croats. But to everyone's amazement, the day after the raid, Arbour announced she was dropping the charges against three of the Croats who had turned themselves in.

Arbour had never properly reviewed their indictments and on close inspection, she discovered that the evidence was thin. She doubted she could win the cases. Arbour decided she had better check out the rest of the indictments on her shelf, and she eventually judged that a lot of the supporting material was disappointing. With her limited resources and only one courtroom, she decided she had to pick her fights carefully.

Arbour insists she didn't release the men because she was convinced of their innocence. But within her understanding of the norms of justice, she wasn't satisfied that the evidence against them added up to proof. The gesture — which was not inconsistent with the conservative approach she displayed in Canada — brought her a lot of goodwill in Europe, augmenting her reputation for fairness. One of the indicted men broke down and cried when he was told he was a free man. But Arbour made it clear that dropping cases wouldn't stop her from charging the suspects again later, if better evidence emerged.

The NATO bosses didn't entirely share the general European enthusiasm for Arbour's sense of justice. At a NATO conference a few weeks after she released the Croats, some of the generals wondered out loud why they should bother risking their lives to arrest people if Arbour might let them go afterwards. But the favourable publicity, which emphasized the drama of the arrests as well as the quality of the justice process, was good politics, and the Dutch and British governments continued to support the arrest missions. The French saw matters in a different light.

For purposes of SFOR peacekeeping (IFOR became SFOR — Security Force — six months after Arbour arrived), Bosnia had been divided into three sectors: the southwest, which was in the hands of British troops, with support from a multinational force that included Canadian soldiers; the north sector, which was under control of the Americans; and the southeast division, run by the French.

Many of the hot spots were under French authority, including Mostar, where Bosnian and Croat units were still fighting. The French also had responsibility for Sarajevo, where there was an uncertain peace after so many Serbs had been forced to leave. But the most contentious turf included Pale, where the Bosnian Serb mafia had its unofficial headquarters and where Radovan Karadzic continued to wax prosperous in his black-market businesses.

The French were doing a pretty good job of ignoring indicted war criminals in their sector. Next to the Pale Gang, the most notorious suspects lived in the town of Foca, the scene of the worst reported examples of organized rape and of the internment of women and girls during the Bosnian war. The men were accused of atrocities in a document known as the Foca Indictment.

French TV broadcast video showing SFOR soldiers drinking in a bar while Janko Janic — one of the men named in the indictment — talked to a reporter. Janic said he was prepared to describe how he slit throats and gouged out eyes if the reporter would pay him five thousand Deutschmarks.

The conversation was being secretly taped, though not to get Janic on the record with stories that every reporter had already heard in numbing detail. The point of the clandestine video was to show how comfortable the French soldiers were around people like Janic. He was charged with "gang rape, systematic rape, sexual assault, torture, enslavement of Muslim women, some as young as 12." His indictment was not a secret. Janic didn't hide from anyone, including SFOR. The French TV broadcast was picked up by news agencies around the world as evidence that French NATO troops were harbouring fugitives. But the French military leaders tossed off the criticism.

Louise Arbour decided to pay a visit to the government of France in December 1997. To attempt to shame a government into action is a complex and risky gamble. Arbour had never tried it before, and she knew from the start that the Quai d'Orsay was notoriously hard to shame. Just days before she was to leave for Paris, the French minister of defence, Alain Richard, told the French media that, under no circumstances would his military personnel ever be allowed to testify before the international tribunal. Richard dismissed the work of the ICTY as "justice spectacle" — a kind of theatre of law with no real legitimacy.

Arbour arrived in Paris three days before her scheduled meeting with the government in order to attend a conference on Rwanda. The French media pounced on her to give some reactions to the defence minister's charges.

The Canadian judge was just learning how to get a message across through the media and finding that nothing works better than eloquent moral outrage. Arbour told the media how disappointed she was by the indifference of a country that helped to create the tribunal by its presence on the Security Council, a country whose intellectuals had contributed so much to the development of human rights and the dignity of man over several centuries.

Arbour awoke the next morning to find her critique of French moral weakness plastered over the front page of *Le Monde*. By the end of the next day, she was interviewed on every important media outlet in the country. She sustained her outrage through them all.

By the time she arrived for her scheduled appointment with Hubert Vedrine, the minister of foreign affairs, he was livid. He normally included many minions in his meetings, but on this Monday morning he brought no one. "He was furious," recalls Arbour. "But so was I."

She complained about the "total inertia" of the French NATO forces in the former Yugoslavia and accused the French of making the south-west sector of Bosnia a place where the most notorious of wanted men "feel totally safe." The French foreign ministry called a press conference to denounce the little upstart from The Hague: "We are shocked by her scandalous allegations." NATO, scrambling to patch up relations with Paris, issued a glowing defence from Brussels headquarters, publicly commending France for its "outstanding job" in Bosnia. But Arbour had hit a soft spot in the French self-image. Her rigorous classical education had paid off.

Arbour also discovered that the French government and its military were not all singing the same tune. French president Jacques Chirac had been a prime mover behind the Dayton accords, and he was on the record declaring that as long as Radovan Karadzic and Ratko Mladic walked the streets of Bosnia, there would be trouble. Chirac's view of Serb culpability wasn't necessarily shared by the leadership or the rank and file of the French armed forces, who, like Allied soldiers everywhere, remembered Serb fighters as stalwart allies in the Second World War. Nevertheless, Chirac's discomfort led to secret moves that might well have put Karadzic to a much rougher form of justice than anything envisaged by Louise Arbour.

According to an investigative report published in August 1998 by *Time*, French and American intelligence agents had recommended to their political leaders as early as the fall of 1995 that the best way to deal with Karadzic and Mladic was simply to assassinate them. Jacques Chirac and Bill Clinton had declined to give NATO the go-ahead for such a mission (the *Time* report suggests that Clinton resisted because it was against the laws of the United States, though Chirac was under no such restraint).

In any case, the two countries agreed that they needed each other's support for whatever action they were going to take against the former Bosnian Serb leaders, and they finally settled on a joint commando raid to arrest Karadzic. If he happened to be killed in the process, well then... *tant pis!* It was a high-risk operation, and it wasn't clear whether the U.S. was going to cover for the French as they moved in on the famous fugitive or vice versa. But they never had a chance to execute the plan.

Neither Paris nor Washington has ever fully disclosed what went wrong, but it seems a French intelligence officer by the name of Hervé Gourmelon was called back to Paris from Bosnia shortly before Louise Arbour's visit there in December 1997. According to leaked reports out of Washington, Gourmelon had taken it upon himself to warn Karadzic of the impending raid. Wesley Clark immediately put the plans on ice. It was a major setback. It undermined American confidence in the French, and it extinguished any hope Arbour had nurtured that she'd one day face Karadzic in court.

After the bungled arrest scheme, his slick black cars no longer whisked past the checkpoints en route to the office. The doctor retreated to a series of hideouts and safe houses, never staying more than a single night in any one place, effectively disappearing from view.

A number of his friends, including his Hollywood lawyers and the plastic surgeon, Borko Djordjevic, tried to talk Karadzic into surrendering himself before something nasty happened to him. "He became very depressed after he went underground," says Djordjevic. "I think he really wanted to go to The Hague and clear his name." A number of Belgrade lawyers joined forces to try to build a case for Karadzic's innocence, and they insisted the doctor could never get a fair trial after years of negative publicity. Karadzic was apparently torn between two groups of supporters — one urging him to turn himself in and the other opposed to it.

In the end, Karadzic believed (and told his friends) that Milosevic would probably have him killed if he attempted to surrender to The Hague. He decided to stay put. He knew too much and he could implicate too many people, possibly including Milosevic himself, if he ever got to court. As a kind of survival insurance, he deposited files and "evidence" with various trustees around the world, with instructions to send it all to The Hague if anything should happen to him. For the rest of the

1990s, Karadzic stayed close to his aging and ailing mother, who still lived in Montenegro, near the ancestral village of the family clan. SFOR always knew where he was, even as he changed his hiding places, but nobody bothered him. Eventually he resumed his business activities, though never again as conspicuously as when he considered himself immune from arrest and assassination.

Arbour continued to demand at every possible opportunity that the French soldiers of NATO arrest Karadzic, but nothing came of it. "I can't tell you why he was never arrested," Arbour admitted after she left the war crimes tribunal. "I was told a number of reasons [by NATO], but I didn't believe any of it. Perhaps there was a deal. A gentleman's agreement that he would not be arrested. People—men—never go back on their word, and Karadzic had a lot of friends."

Without Karadzic and Mladic (Mladic was even easier to track: he travelled with a mobile radio in his car and SFOR monitored his movements,) it seemed Arbour would have to settle for whomever she could sweep up. But she really didn't want a dozen little Tadic trials (Dusko Tadic had been sentenced on July 14, 1997, to twenty years). She promptly dropped charges against fourteen people indicted for their relatively minor roles in the Keraterm and Omarska camps. Members of the Bosnian Serb leadership went to The Hague and took Arbour to dinner. It was an embarrassing gesture. She went along with it only because she thought they wanted to discuss future arrests, but they really wanted to thank her for finally seeing the light. When she realized the true purpose of dinner, she told them what she really thought—that the men were guilty as charged, but that she just didn't have the resources to try perpetrators at their level. "I told the Bosnian Serb leaders that they should be trying the Omarska people in their own courts." They looked at her in disbelief.

Arbour was more enthusiastic about the trials that came about as a result of her secret indictments and the SWAT arrests by the NATO commandos. "The arrest in Prijedor was a turning point," says Arbour of that historic moment. "Ever since I came here, there was a perception of impotence, that this tribunal was not sufficiently established. The arrest in Prijedor changed that."

Slavko Dokmanovic, the former Vukovar mayor who had been arrested in eastern Slavonia, seemed a sure bet for a conviction. There was a year-long trial involving the painstaking reconstruction of the mass murder in Vukovar. Tribunal investigators recovered evidence from the grave of the hospital patients. The case, it seemed to the prosecution team, was airtight. Then, on June 29, 1998, four days after his trial ended and before the court could issue a verdict, Dokmanovic killed himself. His jailers found him hanging by the neck behind the door of his prison cell.

Milan Kovacevic, the man arrested in Prijedor, escaped through the same exit. Kovacevic died in his cell of a heart attack just as his trial was coming to an end. Arbour had looked forward to hearing the first guilty verdict in a trial for genocide in the former Yugoslavia; it would have set the precedent for cases to follow. But since his dramatic arrest by British SAS forces the year before, Kovacevic had been suffering from severe hypertension and heart trouble. His prognosis was poor. His lawyers had asked that he be released on bail to await trial in Bosnia, but the court refused. Jail authorities insisted his health was monitored closely, but his supporters say he never got proper treatment. Arbour was on a holiday in Canada when she got the news that he was dead.

The two deaths, both in the summer of 1998, gave Milosevic and the Serb nationalist leaders ammunition to argue that The Hague was a dangerous place where people were being killed or driven to suicide. There were allegations that prisoners were drugged so their jailers could extract confessions from them. Then there was a dramatic rebuttal—from the detainees themselves. In an open letter to the president of the ICTY, twenty-six prisoners stated: "We have become aware of recent reports in the media picturing us among other things as depressed and preparing for riots. These reports do not have any substance: we are in a better position than anyone to say that reports of this kind are complete nonsense and lies.... The deaths of Mr. Dokmanovic and Mr. Kovacevic have had a heavy impact on all of us. Every one of us has reacted to these tragic events in his own way. But they have also brought us something positive: we have become closer to each other."

The image of these prisoners, who were accused of committing heinous acts of cruelty on their neighbours, involved in a kind of group hug is bizarre. The men included Goran Jelisic, who called himself Serb Adolf, and also some of those accused in the Foca Indictment, who had recently been arrested. But it was nevertheless an irrefutable message that the tribunal was not as sinister as the Pale Gang and the ministry of information in Belgrade painted it.

When Arbour took stock in the fall of 1998, she had to admit that she hadn't yet had an unmitigated success. Karadzic and Mladic were still at large. Her two best cases were dead. But many previous sceptics were beginning to take the court and the chief prosecutor seriously. If Arbour had biases, she never revealed them. Karadzic might have been depicted as "the one who got away," but not before he was demonized in the eyes of the world and driven into an existence of frightened isolation. Arbour's court, on the other hand, had won credibility where it counted—in the inner circles of the world's most powerful organizations and within the leadership of NATO.

There would be many more arrests. The United Nations constructed two more hearing rooms to accommodate the trials. The court's first budget in 1993 had been a paltry US$276,000; that had grown to US$35 million when Arbour took over as chief prosecutor. By 1998, the tribunal's budget had expanded again, to US$64 million, and it employed five hundred people. Arbour was travelling around the world, persuading governments to give her more money, particularly for exhuming graves. It cost a million dollars to open the graves of Srebrenica; the forensic team consisted of international scientists who had investigated the Estonian ferry disaster in 1994. Other forensic experts came from the police forces of the world. Like participants in a lurid foster child program, countries "adopted" specific gravesites and gave generous donations for forensic research. With dozens of exhumations completed throughout the former Yugoslavia (including the grave holding Albassa Kurbegovic's husband), with every jail cell full and more being built, with three courtrooms fully occupied, the future of the ICTY no longer seemed in doubt.

Rwanda was a different story.

4

LE COUSIN PAUVRE

My conscience hath a thousand several tongues,
And every tongue brings in a several tale,
And every tale condemns me for a villain.
Perjury, perjury, in the highest degree,
Murder, stern murder, in the direst degree,
All several sins, all used in each degree,
Throng to the bar, crying all, "Guilty! Guilty!"
I shall despair. There is no creature loves me;
And if I die no soul will pity me.
—William Shakespeare, *Richard III*

Louise Arbour went to Africa to take stock of what she had inherited in the fall of 1996. She was overwhelmed. She had thought her job was to investigate a travesty of war, but she found she had a travesty of bureaucracy: "People were slipping brown-paper envelopes under my door alleging fraud and conspiracy. It was a mess." Over the next two and a half years, her visits would rarely be more encouraging.

Like the Yugoslavian court, the International Criminal Tribunal for Rwanda (ICTR) is structured around three departments: the Office of the Prosecutor (OTP) conducts investigations; the registrar runs the administration; and the trial judges preside over the cases that come before the court. Yugoslavia and Rwanda share both the chief prosecutor and a court of appeal. But that's where the similarities between the two institutions end.

Arbour's prosecution office was in Kigali, Rwanda—at the heart of the crime scene—but the rest of the organization (the registrar and the court) operated out of neighbouring Arusha, Tanzania. Arusha is a sleepy little tourist town whose citizens know and care little about the goings-on at the tribunal. The ICTR is housed at the Arusha conference centre, an immense concrete bunker close to the centre of the city. The building has all the trappings of a security system—blue-shirted UN police ask for your ID at the door, just as they do in The Hague—but those who work in the bunker have noted that just about anyone can walk in.

There are three courtrooms inside, where electricity works only part of the time. When it does, large fans beat ineffectually at the thick, humid air. The courtrooms, as in The Hague, have a wall of bulletproof glass separating the proceedings from the spectators, but the Rwanda court lacks the sterility of the ICTY.

Arbour had been warned that the ICTR was a shambles, but nothing prepared her for the conditions she found. There were few working phones, no computers, few competent staff—the most frequent complaint was a lack of paper and pencils. As UN officials talked proudly about the spirit of Nuremberg being rekindled in the heart of Africa, Arbour was learning about reality there.

The root of the problem seemed to be not a lack of money, but how the money was being spent. For example, of the twenty-seven vehicles purchased in Arusha, most had been allocated to the various chiefs of administration. The deputy prosecutor, whose role had yet to be determined, had two cars. His secretary had one. Another car was reserved for the chief prosecutor whenever she happened to be visiting Arusha. But on the weekends, most of the cars simply disappeared for a few days as people headed out of town. It wasn't clear who, specifically, might be abusing the system, since the court administration at Arusha had little interest and less apparent skill in keeping records.

There was no road system between Arusha and Kigali. The only real connection between the two cities is by air. There were no regular flights, but the Danish government had supplied a plane for ICTR staff. Arbour learned it was rarely used for real tribunal work. Records of the flight's passengers, filed at the United Nations, indicate that the plane was mostly engaged to transport members of the Arusha administration, along with members of their families, on what appeared to be private business.

The office in Kigali was even worse than Arusha. Arbour's investigators were barely able to function. One of them, Luc Coté, a big bear of a man who had spent eleven years as a public defender in Montreal before coming to Rwanda to help redress one of the biggest crimes of the century, found himself twiddling his thumbs. He told Arbour: "We don't have pens, but there's $40 million voted somewhere," referring to the ICTR budget, which had been approved by the United Nations. "We have three photocopiers and not one of them is working. We have no computers, and computers are essential to compile testimonies and statements." The staff had removed the doors of their offices and mounted them on crates to make desks. They used wooden boxes for chairs.

In a dense country of rough terrain traversed by roads that wind around and struggle over a thousand hills, the investigators were expected to determine criminal responsibility for the murder of about 800,000 people. The vehicles they had were unreliable. The one usually dependable car was in the repair shop, but they couldn't get it out because tribunal bean-counters in the registrar's office wouldn't pay the bill. It was the same with the phones. When they were functioning, it wasn't unusual for a conversation to be cut off because someone had neglected to pay a phone bill.

The source of the problem seemed to be the tribunal's registrar in Arusha. A similar office serves as the administrative hub of any court; it's responsible for sending out the indictments, protecting witnesses, supplying defendants with legal counsel and making sure people get paid. It's supposed to grease the wheels of justice, but in Arusha, as Arbour discovered, it had become the wheels: a self-propelling bureaucracy that had little or nothing to do with justice. The registrar was a Cameroonian, named Andronico Adede, who ran the tribunal as his own private fiefdom; he made all the big decisions—who would be paid and how much, who would be hired and who would be prosecuted. No one complained about Adede because he controlled the purse strings and had a kind of absolute power.

It was an absurd arrangement made all the more unworkable since Adede was "travelling on business," according to UN records, almost all of the time, and thus was often unreachable. The UN later discovered that Adede operated with a petty-cash float that at one time reached US$600,000. He travelled frequently on the tribunal's plane, often carrying with him thousands of dollars to be spent on tribunal business, and disappearing for weeks at a time. It seemed the registrar was accountable to no one. Everyone who wanted to get some work done turned to Arbour in hope she could fix the ICTR before it ceased to exist.

In October 1996, Arbour went to the UN legal office in New York to report what she had learned in Arusha and Kigali; the picture she painted wasn't a pretty one. She backed up her claims of incompetence and possible corruption with an armload of letters and memos from people who were paralyzed because of the way the registry was being run. Her complaints were forcefully made—the UN had already heard many of them—and she assumed the situation would be corrected.

Arbour wanted to get beyond this bureaucratic tangle and start the job she'd been hired for. There was compelling evidence that the Rwandan war could break out again at any moment, since the perpetrators of the genocide were living just over the border in neighbouring Zaire. Paul Kagame's government in Kigali claimed to be committed to a peace process but had many old scores to settle. Reprisal killings—both Hutu and Tutsi—were daily occurrences throughout the country. Arbour felt it was imperative to get indictments out and mobilize an authentic judicial process, if only to make it clear to both sides, the Hutu Power militias and Kagame's RPF, that there would be legal consequences for murder. Her Rwanda office remained unworkable and her people there were ready to quit out of frustration.

When she went to New York, the war in Rwanda had been over for three years. There still had not been a single war crimes trial in Arusha, and there was no prospect of having one in the near future. Because the Hutu Power leaders had taken much of the paper evidence of genocide with them when they fled, the ICTR had to rely on eyewitnesses for evidence. But there was no functioning witness protection program. Arbour later learned that the registrar's office had been careless with the names of people who were prepared to testify, putting many of them at risk. A crucial tool of the prosecution—credible witnesses—had been gravely compromised.

There was a "witness clothing program," whereby witnesses from rural areas who were willing to testify could be supplied with proper clothing and footwear to appear in court. But the program only had $5,000 in the kitty. Arbour told her bosses in New York that if they were serious about bringing justice to Rwanda and seeing an end to the cycle of violence, they were going to have to do something drastic to repair the system they'd created to achieve those noble ends. The UN told Arbour it was already on top of the situation. The Office of Internal Oversight (the UN's audit department) had ordered a complete review of the ICTR and its practices.

Arbour told her staff there was nothing more she could do but sit back and wait until the audit was done, even though their phones were disconnected and their paycheques were in arrears. She asked her investigators and prosecutors to be patient. This was hard to swallow since they knew that back at The Hague, Arbour had the services of some of the best forensic experts and lawyers in the world. Rwanda was quite a different scene. The ICTR was *le cousin pauvre* of the system. "While the ICTY people were travelling first class, we were in the luggage compartment," Luc Coté complained.

The UN investigation of the Rwanda tribunal lasted for months. Finally, in February 1997, Karl Paschke, the undersecretary-general for Internal Oversight, issued his report. It was blunt. Paschke declared that "not a single administrative area functioned effectively." He stopped short of alleging fraud and corruption, but only because he lacked detailed records of where all the money had gone, and to whom. Paschke pointed out the obvious problems: dead phones, lack of basics like paper and pencils, no computers, nepotism in hiring practices. He wrote: "It would seem axiomatic that the most important criminal trials since Nuremberg would require a high degree of expertise in criminal law." A lot of the people working at the tribunal, including those in the prosecutor's office, were there because they were the friends or relatives of those doing the hiring.

Paschke reported that Arbour's investigators were often threatened by local people, who still lived with bitter memories of how the UN had abandoned them during the genocide. Staff members from the prosecutor's office were even assaulted. (U.S. citizens with the tribunal were warned that there had been death sentences issued against them.) There was no security for investigators, who often had to hitch rides into the regions they were investigating.

Paschke confirmed much of what Arbour had been told and he assigned the blame chiefly to people in New York, who, Paschke concluded, had demonstrated a total disregard for what was happening in Arusha. Bureaucrats at the UN denied responsibility, arguing that the Rwanda tribunal was supposed to be independent. Such excuses didn't wash with the auditor, however, who pointed out that the UN legal office had been intimately involved with the Yugoslav tribunal but had virtually ignored Rwanda. The folks in Arusha had been handed a large wad of cash and set adrift in a rowboat that had no oars. Yet Paschke stopped there. He recommended a variety of minor penalties, but he wouldn't go so far as to suggest that people in New York should actually lose their jobs.

It was different in Africa. For Arbour, the auditor's report gave the

UN the authority for a major housecleaning in Arusha and Kigali. By the spring of 1997, the tribunal had a new registrar, Agwu Ukiwe Okali, a Nigerian with a law degree from Harvard. The UN assured Arbour that he'd do a more honest and competent job of managing money and supervising people. She hoped they were right.

Arbour flew to Africa in May 1997 for her first meeting with the new staff, including her new deputy prosecutor. Bernard Muna is tall and rotund, a Cameroonian whom Arbour believed was both competent and useful. "Muna was comfortable on the whole continent of Africa," declares Arbour. He could speak French and English and he had connections everywhere. Arbour and her new deputy were determined to arrest the Hutu Power leaders who now lived all over Africa, Europe and North America.

As she had done in Yugoslavia, Arbour was plotting a series of moves that she hoped would bring the ICTR some desperately needed credibility. One of her first requirements was a media success story. Paschke's report had criticized the prosecutor's office for lacking a strategy, and it was time to do something about that. People at the Rwandan tribunal knew they were lagging so far behind The Hague court that it was almost a source of jokes. Now that things were changing in the African set-up, there was a spirit of competition in the air between the rich and the poor cousins. Arbour thought she could take advantage of that.

At the May meeting, held in Dar es Salaam, Arbour told her staff the only possible route to success would be to devise a strategy like the one she'd crafted for Yugoslavia. To date, the ICTR had indicted many people, but there was no coherence in those indictments: they were from isolated incidents in the genocide. Arbour didn't want the Tadic syndrome to engulf the process in Rwanda, bogging the court down with countless and endless trials of small fish. She told her staff, and they agreed, that the plan was now to aggressively go after the highest-level suspects and throw the book at them.

This first meeting of the new prosecution staff (Arbour also brought in people from The Hague to help out) would be the most important in the Rwandan tribunal's history. The ICTR was in a "do or die" position and everyone knew it.

A number of Canadians — including officers from the Royal Canadian Mounted Police (RCMP), on loan to the ICTR, helped to plan what would be the Rwandan office's first big raid. Luc Coté was the brains behind the plot to move in on the Hutu Power brokers in Kenya. Nairobi was awash with suspects and the Mounties at the meeting, Alphonse Breau and Gilbert Morrisette, were pretty sure they could find them.

The snag was the government of Kenya. President Daniel Arap Moi had been good friends with Juvénal Habyarimana and he remained protective of the Hutu Power brokers living in Kenya. Moi had declared he would arrest anyone caught sniffing around his Rwandan refugees, even if they were from the ICTR.

The Kenyan exiles were of a very high order—Hutu politicians, professors from the National University, businessmen—and could afford expensive hotels and apartments. They drove Mercedes-Benzes and Japanese-made recreational vehicles. According to hotel staff, they made long, expensive phone calls to their colleagues in Brussels. They told visiting reporters they had nothing to fear.

It took some delicate diplomacy, but Arbour's people, working with the Canadian Embassy in Nairobi, managed to convince Moi it was in his best interest to allow the tribunal to make some arrests. It was just before an election in his own country and Moi needed foreign support to hold on to power. The Hutu Power leaders were completely unprepared for the president's change of heart.

On July 18, 1997, just a week after the British Special Air Service had made the high-profile bust in Prijedor, members of the Rwandan prosecutor's office, working with the Kenyan authorities, swept Nairobi in a well-organized and efficiently executed SWAT-style operation. Breau and Coté were among the twenty people from Arbour's staff who conducted the raid. "We must have rented every vehicle in Nairobi to do this," says Coté. At 7:00 a.m., they struck at the heart of the Hutu Power leadership in exile, rousing them from bed and packing them off to jail in Arusha. They were able to collar seven people, including Jean Kambanda, the former prime minister of Rwanda; Hassan Ngeze, the chief editor of *Kangura* newspaper, which had disseminated stories inciting hatred of the Tutsi people and giving instructions for their extermination; the minister of family and women's affairs, Pauline Nyiramasuhuko (the first woman to be indicted by any international criminal tribunal, including Nuremberg), and her son, who was accused of helping his mother catch and murder her Tutsi victims. It was a coup. For all its functional efficiency, The Hague tribunal had never come close to this level of arrests. It was a bases-loaded home run for the people in the demoralized African office, and Louise Arbour was the hero of the moment.

According to Muna, Operation Naki, as they called it (joining *Na*irobi with *Ki*gali) was more than just an arrest-sweep: it was a deliberate effort to boost morale at the Rwandan tribunal. Muna says they planned the timing of the operation and then persuaded their contacts in the Kenyan government that it was in their interest to help with the arrests.

It created quite a buzz around Rwanda and New York, and the ICTR was taken seriously for the first time. But it didn't generate much international news coverage. If something like Operation Naki had occurred in Yugoslavia, sweeping up Karadzic and Mladic and assorted other high-level suspects, it would have generated headlines around the world. On the other hand, if it *had* been in Europe, it would have been more closely scrutinized for possible violations of the rights of the accused.

Only two of the people caught in the dragnet had actually been indicted before they were arrested. It was a case of shoot first and ask questions later. After the arrests, Muna had to spend months gathering the evidence he needed to build cases against the people he'd already brought into custody. Arbour argues that the ICTR was required to operate somewhat differently from other courts and needed the flexibility to hold suspects without charges. Due process, as understood in North America and Europe, would have made it almost impossible to arrest the prime suspects. Eventually, all the people arrested in Operation Naki were indicted, except one—a young man who fell victim to a classic case of mistaken identity.

His name was Esdres Twagirimana; he was a twenty-two-year-old husband and father who had fled Rwanda with all the other refugees as the RPF blazed its trail of liberation and vengeance through the country in the wake of the genocide. Arbour's staffers thought they had arrested the son of the minister of families and women, Shalom Ntahobali—one of only two people actually indicted before the raid. But the individual they picked up turned out to be someone who had simply been in the wrong place at the wrong time.

When the ICTR was finally convinced they had the wrong guy (the minister of women's affairs, supposedly his mother, insisted she had never seen him before), they proposed simply sending him back to Kenya. Of course, that would have been the same as a death sentence. Twagirimana had been in Kenya illegally, like most other refugees, and he lacked high-level connections. The Kenyan authorities would ship him back to Rwanda, where he'd meet a summary form of justice at the hands of surviving Tutsi. Most of his family had already been murdered in reprisal killings.

Twagirimana remained in custody for two months without ever seeing a lawyer. He really didn't need one, the new registrar reasoned, since he wasn't charged with anything. The UN High Commissioner for Refugees (UNHCR) tried to negotiate refugee status for Twagirimana in Kenya. Gradually, a case of mistaken identity and false arrest spiralled into a Kafkaesque nightmare. When Twagirimana eventually returned to Kenya, under the impression that the UNHCR had won refugee status for him, the Kenyans promptly arrested him and seized the $1,500 he'd received in compensation from the war crimes tribunal. Eventually, he simply vanished into the kind of refugee hell experienced by people who have no homes to take them back and nowhere else where they are welcome. His miserable story would leave a stain on the record of the ICTR and dampen the excited reaction to its aggressive new style.

Amnesty International took up Twagirimana's case, accusing the tribunal of wrongful detention and false arrest. The registrar brushed the criticism aside. It was an honest mistake, he insisted. Amnesty's criticism was declared a white, Eurocentric value judgment made against a sincere African attempt to pursue justice. The tribunal's media office, sensing a moral soft spot in the Amnesty stance, accused the organization of being condescending: "It is fashionable in some quarters to denigrate and distort the efforts of the International Criminal Tribunal for Rwanda, to willfully suppress the achievements it has created." The tribunal's spin doctors took issue with "invidious comparisons with...the Yugoslavia Tribunal in The Hague," since Amnesty had suggested that things were handled differently (and better) at the ICTY.

Arbour and her staff soldiered on, content that at least the other cases were shaping up well, especially the indictment of the biggest fish of them all, Jean Kambanda. Kambanda's indictment was filed in court in October 1997. He was charged with genocide.

After the president's plane was shot down, the military leaders of the Rwandan armed forces sent soldiers out to look for Jean Kambanda. He thought they had come to kill him. When it turned out they wanted to crown him instead—as head of the interim civilian government, a position he had long coveted—he accepted and before long was in charge of the killing campaign against the Tutsi population and members of the moderate Hutu minority, many of whom he knew personally.

When the RPF took over, Kambanda had fled to Kenya; he lived there until his arrest during Operation Naki. From the moment he was detained, he was anxious to co-operate with the tribunal, in exchange for protection for his wife and young children and their relocation to a safe country. Kambanda never went to the jail with the other detainees but instead was held in a secret safe house where, it was reported to the court, he began negotiating the terms on which he'd tender his confession.

Defence lawyers who worked at the Arusha tribunal gradually became suspicious about the unusual activity around the former prime minister. If he was under arrest, why didn't he have a lawyer? The registrar, who was responsible for supplying legal counsel to defendants who had none of their own, told them Kambanda didn't want one. Only three weeks before he was to appear in court, and almost nine months after he was taken into custody, the former prime minister was finally assigned legal counsel, a result of pressure from defence lawyers and the ever-vigilant Amnesty International. But his lawyer was a family friend of the deputy prosecutor, Bernard Muna, the lobbyists noted darkly.

The lawyer seemed hardly necessary. Kambanda's trial began on May 1, 1998, a rainy day. The courtroom was warm and humid. Kambanda, in a dark suit and with his characteristic large spectacles, stood for his plea. The registrar read out the first charge—that Kambanda had "incited, aided and abetted the prefect, burgomasters and members of the population to commit massacres and killing of civilians, in particular Tutsis and moderate Hutus"—and the accused man's voice rang out in the court: "I plead guilty, your honour."

The spectators' gallery was crammed with Rwandans focused intently on the former prime minister. History was happening before their eyes. Jean Kambanda had become the first person in history to confess and to be found guilty of genocide. (The Nazis at Nuremberg were charged with lesser crimes, as there was no formal or legal definition of genocide before that court.) The normally cool and disinterested *Ubutebera*, the in-house (but independent) tribunal newsletter, described the reaction in the courtroom: "The word was finally uttered, and would be repeated five more times. At the fourth indictment his voice was weaker, almost inaudible. Far from diminishing, the tension in court thickened as the minutes passed. Nine minutes of truth, nine minutes to change the life of a man, and nine minutes to try [to] make peace with others and with oneself. At the sixth indictment, after guilt was acknowledged for the last time, some faces visibly lit up while others seemed to shut down."

It may have been nine minutes of truth and reconciliation for the Rwandans who sat in the courtroom, and for those who heard about the trial on radio back home, but it was a devastating setback for the tribunal's defence attorneys. It was a setback not just because the head of the former government had confessed to leading a murderous regime, but also because he had agreed to testify against the other defendants... their clients. He would be a powerful witness whose testimony would be difficult to refute. There was a need for damage control, and the first place to look for flaws in the prosecution's position was in the Kambanda confession itself. When they found irregularities there, they went after Louise Arbour with a vengeance.

The Rwandan tribunal had not attracted a lot of seasoned legal talent. But owing to the bilingual nature of the ICTR—it was conducted in both French and English—it had attracted a lot of quality Canadians to both sides of the courtroom, defence and prosecution. There were more defence lawyers from Canada than from any other country, including African ones. Among them was a young, sharp-witted Québécoise named Tiphaine Dickson who was trying to make a name for herself in international criminal law. Attractive and outspoken, she cut a swath: everyone involved soon came to know who she was, and she quickly got to know anyone who mattered. So it surprised her one day to see at the tribunal a man whom she recognized but couldn't exactly place. "I know you," Dickson said to him, and he laughed. "Tell Girouard I said 'hi,'" he replied enigmatically. He was referring to her law partner back in Montreal. And then it hit her: the man was Pierre Duclos, a former Sûreté du Québec (SQ) police officer. Dickson's partner had been one of the defence attorneys at a high-level drug-smuggling trial in Montreal involving Duclos.

It was called the Matticks Affair. Officers of the Sûreté du Québec had been trying to nail members of the Matticks family for years, suspecting they were behind the large, lucrative drug-smuggling trade at the Montreal waterfront. Eventually the police seized twenty-six tonnes of hashish and arrested the brothers. It seemed to be a major victory in the relentless war against drug traffickers, but a Quebec judge with a quick eye noticed something highly suspicious about one document in the pile of incriminating paper evidence. It was a bill of lading that had allegedly come from the Matticks' office. But the return address at the top revealed that it had actually come from a fax machine in Canada Customs. Judge Michelin Corbeil-Laramée threw the case out of court, and suddenly the four investigating officers were facing criminal charges themselves. One of them was Pierre Duclos, charged, along with the other officers, with fabricating evidence, obstructing justice, perjury and conspiracy.

In June 1996, a jury acquitted the officers of all criminal charges, but they weren't entirely off the hook. The Matticks Affair shook the Quebec law-enforcement world to the core. It spurred two provincial probes into police wrongdoing. The first was shut down, but the second, the Poitras Commission, followed a trail of official corruption all the way back to the days of Maurice Duplessis. The Poitras Commission also examined the charges against the Matticks Affair officers, and investigated whether or not Duclos had intimidated his witnesses. The prosecutor, Pierre Lapointe, accused Duclos of pressuring his fellow officers to lie. When Duclos turned up in Arusha as an investigator for the Rwandan tribunal's prosecution office, he and the original officers whose conduct in the Matticks case sparked the investigation were still facing a disciplinary hearing.

Duclos had applied to the UN for work just after his acquittal and before the broader inquiry was finished. Arbour was desperate for the services of competent police investigators, and Duclos lived up to her expectations. He quickly gained a reputation in Rwanda and Arusha as a hard-working cop who got things done. When Jean Kambanda went to a secret safe house, he was accompanied by Pierre Duclos.

It's impossible to determine just how much time they spent together during the nine months of Kambanda's confinement, or how much of the prime minister's confession might be attributed to the skills of Pierre Duclos. There is little doubt that the Montreal policeman played a prominent role in the process of "debriefing" Kambanda, and that he was in on the crafting of his eventual guilty plea. That was enough to convince Tiphaine Dickson and other defence team members that there were grounds to challenge the Kambanda confession.

Louise Arbour dismissed the lawyers' complaints against Duclos and defended her decision to hire him: "He was good. And he needed the job," she says. As far as she was concerned, Duclos had been acquitted of evidence tampering and perjury, and she was satisfied. Also, he had delivered the goods in what was perhaps the most important case in the tribunal's history. Arbour maintained that the defence was acting out of desperation, trying to deflect attention away from the crimes of the accused.

Duclos was well liked by his colleagues at the OTP, and they were still savouring the achievement of having beaten The Hague to the honour of winning history's first genocide conviction. One senior member of Arbour's office, though, admits that the victory was flawed because of Duclos's record in police circles back home in Quebec. "There was nothing irregular about the Kambanda case," says the staffer. "But admittedly, Duclos's past made him vulnerable." And that left the case wide open to criticism.

Dickson and a group of lawyers, including the vice-president of the Association of Defence Attorneys for the ICTR, issued a press release: "Given the fact that Kambanda's detention without an initial appearance lasted nine and a half months, that he was without a defence counsel almost nine months in a secret place of detention and that he was apparently in the custody of an ICTR investigator and former Quebec provincial police officer, Mr. Pierre Duclos, presently the object of a commission of inquiry into allegations of fabrication of evidence, perjury, suborning perjury and obstruction of justice, the defence attorneys believe that there are legitimate grounds to question the voluntariness of Mr. Kambanda's guilty plea."

But the Rwandan legal dust-up failed to impress the outside world. Beyond the immediate perimeters of Kigali and Arusha, the media were reporting only that the prime minister of Rwanda had confessed to genocide. The tribunal's paymasters in New York were happy to see the ICTR get some positive media coverage and create a little buzz. *The New Yorker* had just published General Dallaire's Cassandra-like message to the UN, and Kofi Annan, now secretary-general, needed all the help he could get to counter this damning evidence of his moral ambivalence. The publicity surrounding Kambanda's conviction was a timely astringent, no matter what might have happened behind the scenes.

A few days after Kambanda's guilty plea, the secretary-general took advantage of the political capital afforded by the prosecution and turned up in Arusha to give the court his personal expression of gratitude. Few failed to note the irony. Annan had been one of a handful of people in a position to stop the madness that resulted in the tribunal in the first place.

Ubutebera's description of Annan's visit dripped with sarcasm as it reported the ostentatious display of pomp. "Never mind the red carpet adorning the entrance hall, for everyone knows the great and powerful of this world love walking on crimson. But the freshly painted walls? Carefully varnished wood and cargoes of furniture appearing as if by magic? And what of the hastily prepared exhibition of photographs? [The tribunal had mounted a display of photographs of handcuffed suspects.] Clearly a secretary-general should never be expected to cast his eye over the dismal dusty interiors which for the last three years have been the daily decor of tribunal staff?"

A few unappreciative people turned up to protest the visit, including one staffer who had recently spent three weeks trying to acquire a filing tray. *Ubutebera* reported that Annan received more international media coverage for his visit than Kambanda had at his court appearance a few days earlier.

Despite such institutional pathologies, the tribunal proceeded with more arrests and more trials. Defence attorneys continued to voice their complaints, accusing the judges of being biased in favour of the prosecutors. Phil Taylor, a crusty former U.S. Marine who worked for the defence lawyers, kept track of how many times the bench deferred to the prosecution and how dismissive judges were to defence interventions. Taylor maintained that the staff of the ICTR suffered from an inferiority complex and often tried to characterize their work in grand historic terms. He reported to the NGO Africa Direct Conference that during his seven months sitting in the courtroom, "I heard the word 'history' so many times I almost got a rash."

Tiphaine Dickson also gained a reputation for her sharp criticisms, including at one point a complaint that the court was so eager to deliver guilty verdicts, she expected it to start issuing trading cards with pictures of the judges and their statistics on the back. The media were criticizing the tribunal for taking too much time to show results, but the dozens of defence lawyers who worked there were complaining that the ICTR was a court in a hurry.

Shevengen prison in The Hague has a hundred years of history, but few of the criminals it has housed have had the status of Jean Kambanda, former prime minister of Rwanda, the world's first internationally recognized *génocidaire*. The state-of-the-art UN-controlled jail cells are separated from those of ordinary thieves and perverts, the inner compound remodelled exclusively for prisoners from the former Yugoslavia. The court transferred Kambanda to Holland from Tanzania for safekeeping as he awaited his final sentence. It was a strange time to be in Shevengen: shortly after Kambanda arrived, Slavko Dokmanovic and Milan Kovacevic would both be dead.

On September 4, 1998, Kambanda made one last trip to Arusha, where he was sentenced to life imprisonment for genocide and crimes against humanity. He had expected the tribunal to consider his guilty plea and his co-operation with the court as mitigating circumstances, but the crimes were too serious to justify leniency. Kambanda went back to prison in Holland to await word on where he would be incarcerated.

According to the accounts of people who know him, Kambanda felt remorse for what happened in Rwanda. But he was also starting to suspect he'd been hoodwinked by the tribunal's prosecutors into taking too much of the blame. And he was beginning to learn a lot more about Duclos, the friendly cop from Quebec with whom he had spent so much time.

In a September 11 letter to the registrar in Arusha, Kambanda was polite and deferential, but he wanted to draw the attention of the court to many irregularities in his case, and to "put into doubt certain practices surrounding my trial." First, he learned only after the trial was over that he hadn't been obliged to accept Oliver Michael Inglis, the unilingual, English-speaking lawyer he'd been given, a man with whom he hadn't been able to communicate directly. He could have had a French-speaking co-counsel. To make matters worse, he felt Inglis was indifferent to his case and was extremely hard to reach. Kambanda had been told that his wife and children would be moved to a safe country, but they were still in Kenya, receiving no protection. Phone calls he made to Inglis from The Hague went unreturned.

In five pages of complaints, written in careful and polite French, Kambanda suggested that Inglis was working for the prosecutor's office. Inglis had once given him a calendar listing the work that needed to be done to prepare for the final decision, and there was a plan for almost daily contact. But after that discussion, Kambanda wrote, he never heard from Inglis again until just before the court date. Forty-eight hours before sentencing, Kambanda asked for a postponement and his lawyer sent the deputy prosecutor, Bernard Muna, to see him, along with a legal adviser "whose mission was to convince me to accept the unacceptable." Kambanda has since retained legal counsel in Holland. He has filed an appeal to challenge the fairness of his trial and the legality of his own confession.

5

JUSTICE DELAYED

*My daughter, my sister-in-law and I were not only raped.
We were raped and beaten almost every day for a month. They put about thirty
women and girls in a house. They beat up the other women so badly
that they all died. Since the men doing this were people we knew, I suppose
they spared my family so as to embarrass us.*
—Maria Gorette, from an interview in "Rwanda: Death, Despair and
Defiance," African Rights

NO matter how serious the fallout or how outraged the reaction of defence lawyers, the Kambanda trial was a success story for Louise Arbour. It showed her to be a master of the games she loved—mental contests that required forward thinking and anticipation. She and her people had been in control from the inception of Operation Naki right down to Kambanda's historic nine-minute confession in court. The trial had generated an unprecedented amount of positive publicity for the ICTR, and had created at least the appearance of momentum.

There were more SWAT-style arrests in other cities and countries (though none quite as spectacular as those in Kenya), and by the summer of 1998, Arbour had thirty-one people in custody. Five of the prisoners had not been indicted but were only "suspects" snatched from hideouts across Africa and Europe. Authorities in the United States had finally picked up Pastor Elizephan Ntakirutimana, who had been living with his son in a wealthy suburb of Laredo, Texas. Bagosora had been arrested in Cameroon and transferred to Arusha in January 1997. There no longer seemed to be any safe place to hide, and the "culture of impunity" appeared to be broken.

There were other "firsts" at the tribunal, and they generated more favourable publicity: after the first conviction for genocide came the first conviction in history for rape as a war crime. Jean-Paul Akayesu, former mayor of Taba, was found guilty of both crimes. During the lengthy trial, witnesses told of how Akayesu had supervised both the killing and the sexual assault of Taba's citizens. A witness recounted Akayesu's order to burn the homes of Tutsi and steal their cattle, but the most damning evidence involved his direction of a rape camp at Taba's cultural centre. A witness testified that Akayesu instructed the militiamen of the Interahamwe who had been raping the women there: "Never ask me again what a Tutsi woman tastes like. Tomorrow they will be killed." All the women incarcerated at the centre were dead the next day.

The Akayesu trial was sensational. It represented an enormous victory for women's groups, which had argued strenuously that the tribunals for both Yugoslavia and Rwanda should treat systematic sexual assault as a crime against humanity. The lobbyists now had a legal precedent that would apply to both courts. The feminist scepticism about Arbour diminished, at least temporarily. The United Nations in New York put out a press release: "These two landmark decisions will also for the first time bring to practical life the lofty ideals of the Geneva Convention." Arbour added rape charges to some of the other indictments, including that of Pauline Nyiramasuhuko, the minister of women and family affairs and the first female defendant to be charged by the international criminal courts.

These were impressive accomplishments for an institution many had written off as ineffectual only a year earlier. The tribunal appeared to be functioning, but Arbour had a secret. She knew the court was still a long way from achieving the concrete results for which she longed. It was, as she would later come to characterize it, "a by-product of shame"—the world's way of compensating for its failure to protect the Rwandan people during the bloody spring and summer of 1994. Arbour herself now admits that she was profoundly concerned that as a meaningful exercise in justice and accountability, the ICTR was going to fail: "There were too many fault lines in the Rwandan tribunal."

First, the administrative problems hadn't been entirely dealt with. It had been difficult to find qualified people for the complex and dangerous investigations and legal research. "The talent pool was very uneven," says Arbour. Often she decided to drop a case rather than try to take it forward on the strength of flimsy evidence gathered by an inexperienced investigating team. She tried to find better people, but her efforts were often thwarted by officials in the registry, who managed to control much of the hiring. "There were seventeen positions in my department filled without [anyone] even consulting me," says Arbour.

The new registrar had improved a number of operational features, and there was more accountability, but Karl Paschke filed a second auditor's report that suggested that many of the problems he'd highlighted in his first review — particularly personnel problems — were still apparent in the tribunal's administrative operations. The tribunal was chronically understaffed, particularly at the prosecutors' level. And nepotism was rampant.

NGOs who closely watched the tribunal had other, and more ominous, concerns. The Montreal-based International Centre for Human Rights and Democratic Development issued a damning report. Using testimony from Rwandan women who had been victims of rape or witnesses to it, the report chastised the tribunal for its dismal failure to protect them or shield their identities. In the words of one survivor: "I told the ICTR staff of the continued security concerns that I have, but nothing was done.... Since I have come back from testifying in Arusha, life has been particularly hard. I was chased from the house I was renting. Because I had to move, I was unable to continue to run the small shop I had. I used to be able to make a living, but this is no longer possible. I cannot survive. I feel like the ICTR is just bringing us problems for nothing." The report pointed out that among the people who mattered most — the victims of horrendous crimes — the ICTR's credibility in Rwanda was at an all-time low. The prosecutor's office was in serious danger of losing its most important source of evidence: the testimony of survivors.

Another fault line for Arbour was the tribunal's jurisdictional limits. Unlike the Yugoslavian tribunal, which has no restrictions in its mandate, the Rwandan prosecutor's office could indict people only for crimes committed in a single calendar year, 1994. The government of Paul Kagame had protested the time limit, since it meant the court could not prosecute the people who had incited Hutu to murder Tutsi in the years leading up to the genocide, which meant impunity for people like Léon Mugesera, who was safely living in Quebec City when the real horror was under way.

But for Arbour, there was an even darker and more frustrating aspect to the narrow window that reflected on the integrity of the entire undertaking. Kagame might have been publicly complaining, but he had private reasons to feel relief about the time frame. It meant that Arbour had to ignore the many atrocities committed by his own regime, starting before the Arusha Accords and continuing into 1995 and even later. The massacre of Hutu refugees at the Kibeho camp in Gikongoro, as described by Phil Lancaster, could not be examined because it occurred after the cut-off date. Lancaster had witnessed some unspeakable horrors—frantic women thrusting their babies at him through his car window as they were being beaten by Tutsi attackers, thousands of refugees massacred—but the Rwandan tribunal was powerless to do anything about it. Arbour might have been tempted to argue for an expansion of the narrow time frame, but she knew she wouldn't get very far. Though the RPF seemed to want unlimited prosecutions of their enemies, they were proving to be less receptive to any suggestion that they should be held accountable for their own violence.

Robert Gersony of the UNHCR had privately estimated that the RPF might have killed as many as thirty thousand Hutu between July and September in 1994, well within the tribunal's time frame. But without some solid backing from UN headquarters, Arbour felt powerless to act on the information. "How could we investigate and prosecute the RPF while we were based in that country? It was never going to happen. They would shut us down."

The government was already making it clear that it wouldn't hesitate to use its power against the prosecutor's Kigali operation if it felt threatened. When the tribunal's appeals chamber in Arusha ordered the immediate release of Rwanda's former minister of foreign affairs, Jean-Bosco Barayagwiza, the outraged RPF government practically shut down the prosecution office. The judges ruled that his fundamental right to a fair and swift trial had been repeatedly violated, but Kagame wasn't interested in the fine points of the law and, for a period, his officials made it impossible for ICTR prosecutors to enter the country.

And there were more sinister signs of Kagame's attempts to assert control over the ICTR. "The Rwandan government was reading my mail," recalls Arbour. "We were infiltrated. They knew what I was doing. So if I sent someone off to do an investigation of the RPF, they might be killed. I wouldn't do it." Her fears must have deepened when a former Kagame cabinet minister, Seth Sendeshonga, who had resigned because of the unchecked reprisal killings, was assassinated.

Arbour complained often to the United Nations about the arbitrary limits imposed on the justice process, and about the fact that being based in Kigali made her team vulnerable to political interference. But UN officials had made the decision to put the prosecutor's office in Rwanda for political reasons. They somehow wanted to make amends for their moral failure in Rwanda during the genocide. Basing the prosecution there had symbolic significance, and it was going to remain there even if it meant limiting the prosecutor's work. Kagame would remain immune from prosecution no matter how many skeletons were rattling in his closet.

The tribunal looking into war crimes in the former Yugoslavia faced no such restraint. Its agenda stemmed largely from crimes either sponsored by or committed by Serbs, but it would one day feel free to investigate murder and other acts of retaliation against Serbs in Kosovo. Soldiers of the Kosovo Liberation Army (KLA) terrorized Serb civilians and drove 100,000 of them from their homes after Slobodan Milosevic was forced to withdraw his troops from the territory. These were considered indictable crimes for the ICTY. But then, the KLA lacked the kind of political and systemic clout in Kosovo that the RPF held in Rwanda.

The most significant fault line was the startling difference between what was happening to the thirty-odd prisoners and indictees in Arusha and to the 130,000 suspects incarcerated in Rwandan prisons. Arbour's jail in Arusha, with its sanitary toilets and access to telephones, was reserved for the kingpins in the genocide. The minions and flunkies who betrayed their Tutsi neighbours, who manned the roadblocks, who rounded up the Tutsi citizenry and slaughtered young and old, men, women and children, faced an entirely different judicial process and a completely different kind of incarceration in filthy prisons that were so crowded there were four people for every square metre of space. While Jean Kambanda complained about conditions in The Hague, there were 130,000 of his former fellow countrymen — once his faithful followers — who would have happily traded places with him.

Kagame's government had announced soon after it took power that it intended to prosecute everyone it considered responsible for the killings. This was an ambitious undertaking. The former government had stolen much of the country's cash reserves. Officials took computers, fax machines, telephones and even furniture. The killings and the terror also stripped the country of its intellectual capital. Qualified judges and lawyers had gone into exile or been murdered. After the genocide, the country could muster only thirty-six magistrates and fourteen prosecutors. The shattered legal system needed about seven hundred new judges and prosecutors if there was to be a process that in any way functioned according to acceptable norms. The government in Kigali was publicly committed to fair trials, but there was no justice system or much support for notions of fairness and reconciliation among the surviving citizens of the shell-shocked nation.

Canada and Belgium took the lead in a wildly ambitious plan to rebuild the justice system in Rwanda. The Canadian International Development Agency (CIDA), working with the University of Ottawa, put together a $4.5-million program to help train judges and prosecutors. William Schabas, the Quebec lawyer who was representing the Tutsi refugees in Canada who were trying to sue Roméo Dallaire and UNAMIR for failing to stop the massacre, joined with an American organization in an effort to develop qualified staff. The international agencies placed an advertisement on Rwandan radio, asking interested citizens to sign up for training to be judges and lawyers.

By Western standards, the qualifications were less than stringent. The applicants had to be free of any criminal record, twenty-five years of age or older and have a secondary-school diploma. They had to be able to answer a few skill-testing questions, for example: What is the capital of Canada? Jean-Paul Sartre is the author of (a) *The Second Sex* (b) *The Outsider* (c) *Being and Nothingness*. The author of *The Republic* is (a) Plato (b) Aristotle (c) Euripides.

Anyone who could pass the one-hour test qualified for a fast-track training program that lasted anywhere from one to five months. At the end of it, successful candidates were declared to be qualified prosecutors, investigators and judges. Formal education had never really been an issue in Rwanda, where only one in fifty judges of the pre-war judiciary had a degree in law.

By 1996, the program had turned out a large number of people who were considered qualified to investigate and preside over cases. They were poorly paid and their working conditions were difficult, to say the least. Many of the newly minted judges were realistically afraid of the consequences of rendering any verdict other than guilty. They knew that the "legal" response expected of them fell closer to revenge than to justice. When one judge ordered forty suspects freed for lack of evidence, the people were promptly re-arrested and the judge disappeared. Human Rights Watch presumes the judge was killed. Many of the new judges gave up soon after beginning the difficult assignment, and it gradually became harder to find people who were willing to take on the job.

In September 1996, Rwanda held its first trials since the genocide. There was an atmosphere of near hysteria leading up to the events: large crowds jostled to see the defendants. NGOs reported that the courts imposed heavy sentences and demonstrated an utter disregard for the rights of the accused. Testimony was crucial; people working for NGOs reported that witnesses could be bought. Even without bribes, witnesses would produce incriminating testimony out of fear of what might happen to them when they went home. Many judges were unwilling or afraid to call people for the defence, and many of the people who were on trial had no lawyers to compel them to do so.

But as the courtroom spectacles became more commonplace, people relaxed and the hearings developed their own rhythms and routines. Many of the new judges grew in confidence and learned to ask sober, reflective questions. Trials would sometimes last for several hours. Half the people appearing in these proceedings were, according to observers' estimates, probably innocent of any real crime. Given the enormity of the genocide and the mood of the country, it was miraculous that 17 per cent of the defendants in these courts were actually acquitted.

The courts operated under a new law, established with assistance from many of the same foreign agencies who developed the judiciary. It was called "*une loi organique*": "The Organic Law on the Organization of Prosecutions for Offences Constituting the Crime of Genocide or Crimes Against Humanity since October 1, 1990."

The law had four categories of crime. Category one was reserved for the leaders and organizers of the genocide and anyone who committed particularly heinous acts of murder or sexual torture, such as running a rape centre. Ordinary murderers fell into category two; category three included those who had committed grave assault without death. Category four was for property crimes.

Those found guilty under category one received the death penalty. All other category suspects could bargain for a reduced sentence by confessing to the crime and revealing the names of other perpetrators. Those found guilty—or those who pled guilty—had to apologize to the family of the victims.

Countries like Canada, which had helped structure and instruct the new system, were criticized for supporting a legal process that carried the death penalty as its maximum punishment. Rwanda wanted the ICTR in Arusha to impose the death penalty for genocide, but the UN refused. The maximum sentence at both the Yugoslavian and Rwandan tribunals is life imprisonment. The United States, for obvious reasons, had no problem with the death penalty, and Canada simply decided to hold its nose while agencies like CIDA continued to help the Rwandans rebuild their justice system. Twenty-two people went before firing squads in Rwanda in 1998, and many more convicted criminals are awaiting execution.

All in all, Rwanda's new system, crude and amateur as it is, works in its own rough way. The first trial was in September 1996 and within six months nine thousand people had confessed to their crimes to take advantage of the plea-bargaining arrangement. Proceedings, including executions, have been open to the public and, in many cases, broadcast live on radio. In contrast to Arusha, where trials are conducted in French and English (with simultaneous translation), the language of justice in Rwanda is the one everybody speaks—Kinyarwandan.

Human-rights groups have mixed feelings about the system. Avocats Sans Frontières (Lawyers Without Borders) has recruited defence attorneys for some of the accused prisoners. The highly respected International Crisis Group (ICG) has reported that "over 900 people have been tried for genocide and crimes against humanity in proceedings that were generally found to be satisfactory. The number of trials rose from 300 in 1997 to 600 in 1998."

At the same time, the ICG had to concede that given the scale of the assignment, it would take 160 years to bring all detainees to trial.

People at the United Nations originally hoped the ICTR and Rwanda's homegrown courts would complement each other. But Louise Arbour found there were few points of intersection between the two systems of justice. A number of critics (both Rwandan political leaders and outsiders) commented that the survivors of the genocide might have had less zeal to prosecute all the lower-level perpetrators if they had been able to pursue the Hutu Power leaders. A swift death penalty for a few dozen cadres could have quelled the lust for vengeance and perhaps allowed for an amnesty for those remaining. The fact that the "big fish" lived in comfortable prisons while the "little fish" rotted in filthy hellholes wasn't lost on local people.

But there is one important area where Arbour and her prosecutor's office could have complemented the Rwandan courts: that was in the area of rape and sexual assault as a war crime.

Survivors' accounts in both Yugoslavia and Rwanda reveal sickening similarities. Their tormentors would first single out men and boys, then either slaughter them on the spot or remove them to some other place for killing. The women would be terrorized, then forced to watch the murder or the removal of their sons and brothers, fathers and husbands. They'd be harangued about their ethnic inferiority and told that they were being spared to live in shame and pain. Sexual assault victims described unimaginable degradation, of being raped with guns and sharp objects, of watching their daughters violated while soldiers claimed to be deliberately trying to impregnate them to perpetuate the agony. The parallels in the stories from victims in the two countries, presumably worlds apart in time, space and culture, were uncanny, and should have eliminated any doubt that rape is a true instrument of genocide and one of the most brutal and sordid of the crimes against humanity. The estimated number of rape victims in Yugoslavia ran between 12,000 and 20,000; in Rwanda, the number was 250,000. Rwanda and the former Yugoslavia should, and could, have become testing grounds for crucial jurisprudence in this dark and largely unexplored legal field.

But the indigenous Rwandan courts rarely dealt with it. The crime was too widespread and involved too many cultural taboos. Sexual-assault victims in Rwanda are so stigmatized that public complaints are unusual and witness testimony is almost impossible to find. With some determined effort and a proper witness-protection policy, Arbour's court might have changed that.

Arbour obviously wanted to break some new ground; she established a sexual assault committee to focus on the rape cases in Rwanda. In Yugoslavia, she created a similar team to pursue many of the cases first established by Bassiouni's research committee. But she could sustain neither initiative. In Rwanda, the massive scale of the problem—and the difficulty of prosecuting the cases—eventually overwhelmed her enthusiasm for an historic attack on a war crime that is as old as war itself.

The human-rights groups that had pushed the UN tribunals to recognize rape as a crime against humanity became discouraged. "It was a mistake on our part to assume we had made permanent gains in recognition of rape as an international war crime," says Binaifer Nowrojee, a lawyer with Human Rights Watch. There were insurmountable problems with getting women to admit to some of the things that happened to them; they were reluctant to testify in court in the absence of an effective witness-protection program and resettlement plans for after a trial.

Nowrojee says the Rwandan tribunal itself was always uncomfortable with the challenge of investigating rape as a war crime. The first deputy prosecutor told her, "It is a waste of time to investigate rape charges in Rwanda because African women don't like to talk about rape. We haven't received any real complaints." But Nowrojee also suspects that the prosecutor's investigators often didn't ask about rape. During one genocide trial, a woman told of hiding in a tree for days as Interahamwe members slaughtered her family. The only survivor was her six-year-old daughter. She and the child eventually tried to escape, but they were caught and she was forced to watch as three men raped the little girl.

One judge who heard her story, Navanethem Pillay, a South African and the only woman among the ICTR justices, was outraged. The incident wasn't included as part of the indictment against the accused person. The woman's horrifying story was merely a sidebar to the genocide case, and Pillay could only listen impotently. "I'm extremely dismayed we're hearing evidence of rape and sexual violence against women and children, yet it is not in the indictment because the witnesses were never asked about it," she fumed.

Arbour explained the problem in an interview near the end of her tenure at the international tribunals. "I think part of the difficulty is that up to this point, we have not been able to substantiate [stories of rape] with the kind of evidence you need to prove a criminal case." This was particularly true in Bosnia. "The evidence is just not there for us to be able to use it in any fashion whatsoever. I don't know why that is. It is also possible that the numbers have been overestimated."

She claims she wanted to pursue rape cases more aggressively, but it isn't clear that her Rwandan deputy shared her interest in the subject. In an interview, Bernard Muna confirmed this. He dismissed sexual assault as very much a side issue for the prosecutor's office. "All that stuff about sexual harassment is for the politically correct people," said Muna, referring to the NGOs who pressured the tribunal to prosecute rape. Muna was much more interested in genocide.

The many human rights and women's groups that had pursued the issue of rape as a war crime weren't prepared to lose the opportunity to change things. In March 1997, Hillary Rodham Clinton went to Africa where she took up the cause and began lobbying for rape charges at the ICTR. Following a round-table meeting with a number of Rwandan women, Clinton said, "The United States is aware that the tribunal has had administrative problems and has been rightly criticized as being ineffective." In a more condescending part of her address, Hillary Clinton suggested she had fixed the problems: "I had a long meeting with Justice Arbour, who has been appointed to work on behalf of the tribunal. I am hoping that the critical work of the tribunal will now go forward more effectively and that you will be able to see the differences." Hillary Clinton also helped to "fix" the problem with a healthy donation—US$650,000—to investigate crimes against Rwandan women and children.

In the following months, a number of women's groups turned up the heat on Louise Arbour with some results. By June 1997, Arbour had added rape to the charges against Jean-Paul Akayesu and in the coming months her prosecutors would add rape to a number of other genocide and crimes against humanity cases. The ICTR judges, as well as defence counsel, complained that the charges seemed too much like an afterthought. Nonetheless, soon after, the ICTR saw the first prosecutions in history for rape as a crime of war. Women's groups claimed victory but Arbour says she yielded to no one's pressure but her own. The rape indictments were all planned, she says, and she fiercely defends her record on sexual violence prosecutions. "It's absurd to say we didn't want to do it," she argues. "But trying to find command responsibility in rape is very hard."

Arbour says it's difficult to persuade investigators to pursue the sexual violence crimes. "When you arrive at a scene where 10,000 people have been killed—as we did in Rwanda—it may seem secondary to then gather testimony from one hundred rape victims," she says. Trying to deal with sexual assault with specially assigned teams also failed to work: "Then the investigators pursuing the genocide prosecutions think it isn't their job to pursue the rape cases."

Louise Arbour made history in her time at the international tribunals, but not for breaking new ground in the prosecution of wartime rape cases. Her legacy would be, perhaps, more controversial: the indictment for crimes against humanity of a head of state while he was still in office.

6

IN THE FIELD OF BLACK BIRDS

Serbs in their history have never conquered or exploited others.
Through two world wars, they liberated themselves, and when they could, they
also helped others to liberate themselves. The Kosovo heroism does not
allow us to forget that at one time we were brave and dignified and one of the few
who went into battle undefeated. Six centuries later, again we are in
battles and quarrels. They are not armed battles, though such things should
not be excluded yet.
—Slobodan Milosevic, June 28, 1989, during a speech
delivered in the Field of Black Birds, Kosovo

IT plays like the rerun of a melodramatic war movie. It is the autumn of 1998. You drive through the broken Balkan villages, pummelled to rubble by heavy guns. The images are resonant of other places. Prijedor. Srebrenica. Sarajevo. But this is not Bosnia. This is Kosovo.

Buildings that survived the shelling have been burned. Slaughtered cattle rot in the fields, and the stench, even on a cool morning, is familiar to those who have seen all this before. The villagers return to their homes when they believe it is safe to do so, picking through the destruction, looking for lost fragments of their lives. TVs and radios have been stolen, along with cars and tools. Their wells are poisoned, and their crops are burned; a beekeeper discovers his beehives have been destroyed, gasoline poured over them and set alight. The villagers know there's no point trying to rebuild —it will happen again. They are lucky to be alive, but if they stay here, that too could change. The Serbian special police will undoubtedly be back, looking for "terrorists"—or so they claim—burning, bombing and looting villages and farms as they go. Most of the Kosovo Albanians are hiding deep in the frigid forests that cloak the flanks of the surrounding hills, crouched in their plastic shelters.

The scene is so familiar because it is the common backdrop for the story of the former Yugoslavia as it played out over the final decade of the twentieth century. The Kosovo Albanians are hiding from the same murderous regime that had already destroyed so much of the Balkans, murdered hundreds of thousands of former Yugoslavians and reduced a nation to poverty — all in the name of Greater Serbia. And there was more to come.

Slobodan Milosevic, like many of history's villains, is a classic product of a childhood filled with tragedy. His father, a theology student and a teacher in Montenegro, committed suicide when Slobodan was a boy. His mother was a dedicated Communist who committed suicide a decade after her husband did. Milosevic had few friends in life, with the exception of Mirjana Markovic, his girlfriend from school days. She would become his wife and the one person in his life whom he would trust implicitly.

It was his ambitious wife who spurred him on through the eighties as he rose through the ranks of the Communist establishment, eventually becoming head of the League of Communists in Serbia. The Byzantine politics helped him hone the powers of deception and intrigue that would serve him well on the international stage during the 1990s. Even as he directed the brutal wars in the breakaway Yugoslav republics, Milosevic had a remarkable ability to persuade foreigners that he was actually a man of peace trying to keep his federation together. While he shuttled around the capitals of Europe as a statesman, he consolidated power by winning absolute control of the army and the police, whose leaders he rewarded for their loyalty.

American ambassador Warren Zimmerman had proven himself an able student of character in the former Yugoslavia. But even after spending many hours with Milosevic, he could not understand the man. One moment Milosevic was a bully, the next a diplomat, Zimmerman wrote in his memoir on Yugoslavia, *Origins of a Catastrophe.* "There were really two Milosevics. Milosevic One was hard-line, authoritarian, belligerent, bent on chaos, and wedded to the use of force to create Greater Serbia.... Milosevic Two was polite, affable and cooperative." Both the hard-liner and the diplomat had in common a deep hatred for Albanians and the belief that there was an active world conspiracy against Serbs. Zimmerman says that Milosevic Two "would often be summoned to repair the horrendous damage caused to Serbia's reputation by Milosevic One, who would be sent back to the locker room. There his handlers would salve his wounds and get him ready for the next round. The one sure thing I concluded, Milosevic One would always be back."

Milosevic began his campaign for Greater Serbia in the late 1980s, in the power vacuum left behind by Tito's death. He consolidated his control over the crumbling federation by rekindling the passionate flames of Serbian nationalism that Tito had managed to suppress. Ethnicity had always defined the deep political divisions that made "Balkan" synonymous with "instability." But Tito had successfully united his fractured population in a common commitment to the larger goals of a united Communist federation ("the union of south Slavs"). Milosevic, hungry for absolute power and control of Yugoslavia, but with none of the vision or imagination of Tito, found a way to manipulate the country's largest ethnic group.

Tito's biggest challenge had always been in Kosovo, the only territory in which the people were not predominantly Slavs but ethnic Albanians. Tito gave the Kosovo Albanians political autonomy, through which they had developed their own schools, hospitals and government. They freely conducted their affairs, private and public, in their own language. The Albanians weren't so generous to their Serb minority (10 per cent of the region's population of 1.9 million). But discrimination against the Serbs would hardly justify the price the Albanians would eventually pay.

Kosovo has huge iconic significance in the Serbian communal memory. It is the symbolic heartland of Serbian history (or perhaps more accurately, historic mythology). In 1389, at a place called the Field of Black Birds, the Ottoman Turks defeated the Serbians and their legendary hero, Prince Lazar. That disaster marked the start of five hundred years of Turkish domination. The conquest would never cease to be a reference point in the Serbian memory, or fuel for the Serbian imagination. Heroic images of the battle hang on the walls of Serb homes and offices, stirring reminders of martyrdom and victimhood. It was on an anniversary of the defeat on the Field of Black Birds, in June 1914, that the Serb nationalist Gavrilo Princip assassinated Austrian archduke Franz Ferdinand on a street in Sarajevo. The incident started a chain of events that would lead to the First World War, which arguably set the stage for much of the horrifying violence that marked the twentieth century.

Exactly six hundred years after Prince Lazar's defeat, Slobodan Milo-sevic stood in the Field of Black Birds and delivered a speech that was intended to stir the nationalist pot that had simmered and stewed for cen-turies. The Soviet empire, which had overshadowed Yugoslavia for decades, was finished. Change was sweeping Central and Eastern Europe. In order to consolidate his power, Milosevic turned up the heat under the brew of ethnic hostility that had kept the Serbian nation alive in the popular imag-ination. More than a million Serbs responded, returning like pilgrims to the Field of Black Birds to declare Milosevic the modern-day father of Serbian destiny. That day, June 28, 1989, is recorded in modern history as the day Yugoslavia began its descent into war. Milosevic mobilized the ghosts that still tormented the Serbs and turned them against the contem-porary embodiment of the long-dead Turkish empire: the Muslims of Kosovo and Bosnia.

Throughout the 1990s, as the world watched the nationalist jugger-naut move through Slavonia, Croatia and then Bosnia, few noted that Milosevic was waging a less aggressive war in Kosovo. First, he withdrew the autonomy that Tito had awarded the Albanian majority and imposed a Balkan version of apartheid. Schools were partitioned, with Albanian children packed into rooms on one side, Serbian children on the other. Albanian doctors who tried to serve their patients in their own language were fired from most public institutions and forced to set up their own self-financed clinics in abandoned buildings. Anyone who protested the changes found himself in jail or he simply disappeared. The International Federation of Library Associations estimates that the Serb-controlled gov-ernment in Kosovo destroyed 100,000 Albanian-language books between 1991 and 1995.

Inevitably, there was resentment, and as it grew, there developed among the angry young men of the region a small, fierce guerrilla force, which became the Kosovo Liberation Army (KLA). Its members terrorized Serb police units with quick, brutal assassinations. In retaliation, the armed forces levelled entire villages. The KLA would strike again, kill another policeman and another village would be destroyed. As with all liberation armies, the ham-fisted retaliation only drove more volunteers to the KLA.

Milosevic eventually became impatient with the low-grade war against the Albanians and the annoying KLA. Throughout the 1990s, his political sidekick, Vojeslev Seselj, a man Warren Zimmerman publicly called a psy-chopath, and who was second only to the warlord Arkan in his ethnic-cleansing activity, was making plans for the complete removal of the Albanians from Kosovo. Seselj suggested the police would be more inclined to get rid of the Albanians if they were allowed to keep the land and chattels they seized during raids. Belgrade would then arrange to repopulate Kosovo with the thousands of Serbs who had been displaced by the wars in Bosnia and Croatia. Seselj's plans for removing the Albanian population have been documented and might have made a Nazi blush.

He wrote that the rights of the "Shiptars"—a Serbian term of derision for the Albanians—should be revoked and the Shiptars eventually removed from the territory, where they did not belong. Seselj was reported by local media to have suggested that the most expedient way to deal with the Albanian problem was to infect the entire population with AIDS.

After the war in Bosnia, Milosevic faced the criticism of a growing opposition movement in Belgrade. In the winter of 1996–97, opposition leaders actually attempted to overthrow his government. Many people in Serbia were angry with Milosevic's war efforts, not because he was aggressive and unjust, but because he hadn't won. People were now alarmed that having started trouble in Kosovo, he could lose the entire province to the ragtag KLA. Even some moderate Serbs, who opposed what had happened in Bosnia, supported a campaign to recover control of Kosovo, which was so important to the Serb mythology. Milosevic saw an opportunity to turn up the nationalist heat once again and recover his flagging popularity. His plan was called Operation Horseshoe.

At 6:30 a.m. on January 15, 1999, the people of Racak, Kosovo, heard the familiar sound of gunfire in the hills, close to positions held by members of the KLA. A half-hour later, Serbian police surrounded the village. Everyone who was left there feared—with good reason—that they were about to be killed. People tried to flee from their houses. Here's how one survivor described the scene: "My son was running on my left side, maybe two metres from me. He had his trousers in his hands; we did not have time to dress properly. He was warning me to move aside and suddenly he fell down. The bullet hit him in the neck. In front of me my husband fell as well. He didn't move any more."

The police searched every house, looking for weapons. They rounded up the men and boys, took them out of the village and killed them. Journalists who saw the bodies the following day observed that fingernails had been torn out. Some had their throats cut; all were savagely beaten before being killed. Members of the Verification Mission for Kosovo arrived later in the day to examine the bodies. In all, forty-five people had been murdered, including two women. Some of the men were old. Some had been shot while fleeing, and others were killed execution style, a rifle shot to the head. Nine of the forty-five were members of the KLA, while the others were civilians.

It wasn't the most brutal of the massacres the people of Kosovo had experienced, nor was it a particularly large slaughter by the standards of the former Yugoslavia. But it was a rare occasion on which outsiders, including representatives of the OSCE, arrived to examine the bodies. There was also an element of cold calculation in the Racak killings that distinguished them from the random attacks and generalized terror perpetrated by the Yugoslavian army and the special police in other raids during the previous year. It's not clear when Operation Horseshoe actually began, but the nature and style of attacks like the one on Racak indicated that the armed forces in Kosovo were under new orders.

Louise Arbour was monitoring developments in Kosovo closely. ICTY staff had been busy reconstructing the murder scenes and war crimes of Bosnia and Croatia for several years—slowly building case files from events that had occurred a comparatively long time ago. But as Arbour tracked the events in Kosovo, she saw an opportunity to turn the prosecutor's office into a real-time enforcement agency. Kosovo, as part of the former Yugoslavia, was within her jurisdiction. Here was a chance to nab the perpetrators at the scene of the crime, not after they'd had a chance to hide all the evidence. If there ever was a time when Arbour could see the game—and all seventeen moves in front of her—it was now.

Two days after the Racak murders were reported, Arbour flew to Skopje, Macedonia, and drove by car towards Kosovo. At the border, a crowd had formed; the international media had heard about her trip and turned out en masse. Arbour's security advisers told her not to get out of the vehicle, to simply hand her documentation to the border guards through the car window. She had no visa for Yugoslavia, but as a UN diplomat, she had a blanket laissez-passer that legally allowed her to go anywhere she wanted. However, the border officials were under orders not to honour it. They handed the documents back to her and told Arbour she could not enter. Notwithstanding the jitters of her security detail, she got out of the car immediately and marched into the booth.

"Do you know who I am?" she asked the border guard. Of course he did. And he had specific instructions from Belgrade not to allow her into the country. According to intercepted messages between the government and its commander in charge of Kosovo, the Belgrade regime was truly concerned by all the media attention paid to Racak, and the military was under instructions to hide the evidence. Even after the Kosovo Verification Mission had seen the bodies, the police confiscated them.

Arbour had no plan for what to do next. She remembers taking down the guard's badge number, stalling for time. But finally she turned to the media scrum and made it explicitly clear who she believed was behind this obstruction — Milosevic himself.

Rejected at the border, she settled into a Skopje hotel to try to negotiate her way into Kosovo. With one assistant and a cellphone, she pulled out all the stops, calling every world leader who had promised to help her over the years. "I put lots of pressure on members of the Security Council to finally act," recalls Arbour, and many of them responded — including Richard Holbrooke and Wesley Clark. But it was the Russians who tried the hardest. She had taken a lot of flak from the Americans when she hired a full-time Russian assistant, but it finally paid off. At her behest, Moscow leaned heavily on Milosevic, but even that wasn't enough. In the end, she was denied access to the Racak crime scene. "I was so discouraged, I wrote my letter of resignation," says Arbour.

It may have been discouraging to be turned away from an obscure border crossing by an even more obscure functionary. But she'd achieved a powerful effect, and in politics, appearances are as powerful as reality. The point was not that she had to see the massacre site in Racak. The point was that the world's media had to see her *attempting* to get there — to send the message that this *was* a crime scene, and that there *was* a prosecutor in the field of international justice demanding to examine it first-hand. If Arbour wasn't allowed, the world would know that it was because Milosevic had something to hide. "Racak focused public attention on our work, on our relevance," Arbour says of the event. "In very simple two-line statements you could get the message out." Arbour's photo was suddenly on the front page of *The New York Times*, "above the fold!" exclaimed her excited office staff. The United Nations, heads of state and NGOs issued press releases demanding that Milosevic relent and allow the chief prosecutor access to her jurisdiction in Kosovo. He didn't, but it didn't matter any more. Arbour would get the evidence one way or another.

As daily reports of police brutality came out of Kosovo, weary Balkan watchers knew they were seeing a rerun of the same old movie. Here was the international community again unable to act, unable to impede the progress of the war-mongering Serbian president. How long would the UN drag its feet this time, stumbling from one set of broken promises to another? How many Albanians would have to die before the world's embarrassment would crystallize into action? There was evidence after the war in Bosnia that the Americans had known all along about atrocities in the country and had declined to act. Intelligence agencies from Bonn to London to Washington knew what was going on in Kosovo now; they were intercepting communications, taking photographs of what was happening in the Kosovo countryside from satellites, recording inflammatory radio messages. This time, would they have the political will to stop Milosevic?

Of the members of the UN Security Council, the French and the Americans were the most wary of what Arbour was doing in the field. They were in the midst of peace negotiations with the Serbian president. Holbrooke returned to public life (he had never really left it) in order to talk to his old friend, Milosevic. The ICTY had made Holbrooke's life difficult before — he believed that Richard Goldstone had almost shattered the Dayton peace process by throwing a couple of Serbs in jail. Holbrooke was sympathetic to Arbour's massive and commendable assignment, but he didn't want her getting in the way of his far more worthy efforts at international statesmanship.

In late February 1999, negotiations for a peaceful solution to the crisis in Kosovo ended at a conference in Ramboillet, France. The talks broke down over Belgrade's refusal to agree to the presence of foreign observers and armed peacekeepers in Kosovo. As the various diplomats departed Ramboillet, there was a depressing sense of déjà vu; people around the world recalled similar dismal images from past Balkan conferences. The meetings concluded with familiar threats of air strikes, but the Serbian president had heard it all before and brushed it aside as more of the same old bluster.

But perhaps Milosevic hadn't noticed some new faces in the crowd that now ran things in "the international community." This wasn't 1992. Bill Clinton was approaching the denouement of his presidency and hoping that the Dayton Peace Accords had secured his place in the history of world affairs. Tony Blair was firmly in charge of the U.K., and the weary

French president, François Mitterand, had been replaced by *le bulldozer*, Jacques Chirac. There was an eager group of new people in the U.S. State Department, led by Madeleine Albright, now secretary of state. They didn't want another Bosnia on their watch. The world had grown tired of Milosevic.

On March 24, 1999, thirteen of NATO's member states began to bomb Yugoslavia, without consulting or waiting for permission from the United Nations. Wesley Clark, the supreme allied commander of NATO forces in Europe, seemed to take a personal interest in the campaign: Milosevic was a man with whom he had negotiated often, and by whom he'd been betrayed. NATO media conferences broke records for rhetorical excess, as spokespersons characterized Milosevic as another Hitler and the Yugoslav government as a reconstruction of the crowd that ran the Third Reich. But even in these charged days of bellicose overstatement, Louise Arbour heard something she had trouble believing: officials of the NATO alliance were saying that they were eager to hand over all their evidence of crimes by Serbian security forces in Kosovo to the ICTY. She was on the telephone in a flash — "So I'm waiting! Hand it over."

It wasn't quite that easy, as Arbour had suspected. Although she had done a remarkable job at breaking down the resistance of various intelligence agencies to sharing information with the tribunal, she knew how much they hated to part with the goods (in case people figured out where and how they got it). Over the years, she had pried little bits of intelligence from their tight fists, but never entirely what she wanted. Now, with NATO on the record and the whole world watching, it was the moment to make her mark. She started with a long plane ride.

In ten days, she travelled to Bonn, London, Washington, Paris and NATO headquarters in Brussels, and she also made a call on the Dutch government in The Hague. She told them all that the time had come to arrest Radovan Karadzic, Ratko Mladic and all the other fugitives from justice on her list of war criminals. That, she told the governments of the Western world, would send the clearest message possible to those in Kosovo and Belgrade that they were not going to get away with this latest affront to civilization. "I was very persuaded that if they cleared up the arrest list, it would have a sobering effect on the Serb leadership," she says.

And she had another demand: "Now is the time to give me all the intelligence you have. The more you give me, the more you co-operate, the better." Arbour didn't tell them directly that she was planning to indict Milosevic and a number of his associates, but they certainly could have guessed that she was heading towards a showdown.

"The third thing I told them, and I'm not sure the message got across or how it was understood, was that, 'By the way, while you're bombing that country, pay attention to the Geneva Conventions.'" Just in case it hadn't occurred to them, Arbour made it clear that they were now at war in an area under her legal jurisdiction, and she would be watching. In the New World Order, nobody was above the law. Contrary to reports that Arbour suggested only after the war that NATO might be part of her investigation, she in fact made it crystal clear to all the principals even as they were dropping the bombs. "Some of the countries were surprised when I said it. It didn't go over very big. But others said, 'Yes, of course.'"

NATO leaders, and the peace negotiators, got their first hint that Arbour was playing hardball when, days after the air strikes began, she made public her sealed indictment against Zeljko Raznjatovic, better known as Arkan. She released it after learning that Arkan and his Tigers were operating in Kosovo. If the ICTY was to function as an enforcement agency, Arbour declared, then it must also try to prevent further crimes. Publicizing Arkan's indictment made travel almost impossible for him (he was sure to be arrested), and it meant he could no longer get at his offshore bank accounts. Among his many business enterprises at the time, Arkan was running a private airline offering flights from Italy to Canada. Arkan went on American TV to say what he thought of Arbour: "She's a bitch."

On the Saturday after the air strikes began, the Albanian ambassador to Holland was in Arbour's office telling her that he had reliable reports that seven thousand refugees had crossed into his country from neighbouring Kosovo that weekend. The ambassador's numbers were already a bit out-dated. By then, eighty thousand people had trekked into Albania, and as the stream of refugees turned into a flood, the humanitarian agencies, from the UNHCR to the International Red Cross, gradually lost count. By the end of March, there was a rough estimate that more than 700,000 people had been uprooted. The scramble was on to find tents, food and medicine. Authorities refused to allow the Kosovo refugees into Macedonia. An estimated seventy thousand people were stuck for days in the rain and cold, living in their own waste, while the foreign agencies negotiated their release.

Arbour was under enormous pressure from the United Nations to send investigators into the refugee camps to start collecting evidence for future indictments. She dispatched as many of her people as she could. But she thought it was a waste of time. They didn't need proof that there was an atrocity in progress. That was pretty obvious. She instead needed evidence that connected it to Operation Horseshoe, a carefully planned and deliberate attack on a civilian population.

As she travelled around the state capitals, she was also trying to negotiate her way into Kosovo. "I want to be there when you go in," she told an amused British general, Michael Jackson, as soon as she heard there might be ground troops. "When you roll into Kosovo, I want to be on your shoulder. We'll sleep in your tents. Ride in your vehicles! But I don't want anyone tampering with the evidence."

Arbour wanted evidence that would show command responsibility, starting with Slobodan Milosevic and ending with the police in Kosovo, who were rounding people up to put them on trains and summarily executing those whom they accused of supporting the KLA. Without such hard evidence, she would have just another case of de jure guilt: Milosevic was head of state, so he *should have known* crimes were being committed. Arbour wanted de facto responsibility: evidence that *he knew* what was happening and even participated in it.

Arbour was able to get some hard evidence from the intelligence agencies, but as the days wore on, the bombs fell and Milosevic hung in, there was panic growing among NATO members. The campaign was supposed to have been over quickly. NATO partners, including Canada, had started to airlift Albanian refugees out of the squalid camps. But there was no way the world could continue to accommodate the massive tide of humanity flooding into Albania and Macedonia.

On April 20, the British foreign secretary, Robin Cook, made a show of delivering to Arbour what he described as the biggest handover of British intelligence to an outside agency in history. The British government even appointed a special liaison team to work with her. Madeleine Albright and David Scheffer, the American special ambassador for war crimes, scrambled to obtain intelligence files for Arbour from U.S. sources. Even the Germans shared some of what they knew about the situation in Kosovo.

And yet, even though there was a public show of co-operation, Arbour sensed an unsettling ambivalence about her plan to indict the president of Serbia. She couldn't tell whether the governments of the alliance supported her plan or opposed it. A few influential players, including Holbrooke, were alarmed about the impact such an indictment would have. Arbour heard rumours of a possible offer of amnesty for Milosevic; there were also rumours that he was organizing his foreign bank accounts and planning a swift departure.

Human-rights groups urged Arbour to get on with it and issue the indictment before the man was able to escape. The Hague tribunal hummed into overdrive; almost daily, Arbour and her staff called governments that had offered help, asking for single bits of information or confirmation of data. Arbour knew she had to get everything she needed before the indictment. She had the momentum, the moves were laid out before her. She was getting close to her end-game.

There was one unexpected glitch from, of all places, the University of New Brunswick. In the final days leading up to the indictment, Arbour attempted to cancel a speaking engagement there without disclosing the urgent reasons. No, the school could not accept her cancellation, the UNB administration told Arbour's personal secretary. She had agreed a year earlier to be there, and they would hold her to the engagement. In the midst of the most important week of the tribunal's history, she flew to Canada to pick up yet another in a long string of honorary degrees. But she took advantage of the speech in New Brunswick to warn NATO, this time publicly, that the same laws and moral imperatives applied on both sides of the conflict in Kosovo.

On Saturday night, May 22, 1999, Arbour reviewed the final draft of the indictment. She was sure she had what she needed to show de facto responsibility for crimes against humanity. A number of people in her office urged her to hold back until her investigators could actually show proof of genocide, but if she waited any longer, Milosevic might escape. As she was about to sign the indictment, someone found a UN flag and tidied her desk for a photo of the historic moment—an officer of the court issuing the first indictment in history against a sitting head of state. The following day, a tribunal judge, David Anthony Hunt, reviewed the indictment, found it thorough and signed it. The champagne corks popped that night.

The case of the *Prosecutor of the Tribunal against Slobodan Milosevic* and four other political and military leaders runs for nearly thirty pages, citing "crimes against humanity and violations of the customs of war." In its final pages, there is a chilling list of 340 people from sixteen villages, including Racak, that the five men on the indictment are accused specifically of murdering.

On Monday morning, Arbour informed Secretary-General Kofi Annan and the governments of a few countries (presumably the United States and Britain were at least two of them, though Arbour will not name them) that she had prepared an indictment against the president of Yugoslavia. If there were direct security reasons for not releasing it, they were to speak up. Arbour gave them until noon on Thursday, the date and time scheduled for a UN investigative team, including a member of her staff, to pull out of Kosovo. For their own safety, they had to leave before the document was issued. If that wasn't possible, she would postpone. But Arbour made it clear that it would take a lot to stop her from proceeding with the charges.

"I didn't want to be in the position where I would say, 'I'm thinking of bringing down an indictment on Slobodan Milosevic. What do you think?' I put it to them that 'I have done this, and if you have not lost consciousness, in two days from now I'm going to make it public.'" Even Arbour was locked in: there was no way she could back down after the judge had signed the indictment. "That was part of the strategy. The document was dated." If she was prevented from issuing the charges because it was inconvenient to the negotiators, everyone would find that out when they saw the date on the document. "So if their problem was—as they claimed it was—that they couldn't negotiate with an indicted war criminal, they had that problem as soon as I told them.... Whether it was made public after that didn't change the moral dilemma. The moral dilemma commenced the moment I told them I had it."

For forty-eight hours, Arbour recalls, there was a kind of spooky international silence. After a decade of dithering about Milosevic, and wishing he would just go away, leaders had grown accustomed to solving their problems with Milosevic Number Two when Milosevic Number One disappeared to the locker room. After ten years, they were about to lose the despot they all loved to hate in the middle of a war with him that was proving much harder to win than they had ever imagined.

Arbour was told by her private sources that President Bill Clinton and Prime Minister Tony Blair had a ten-minute phone conversation in which they decided this was...okay. Maybe it was even good. But the German chancellor, Gerhardt Schroder, was angry: "Sometimes there are goals — such as peace in Europe — that take precedence over other considerations."

The French interior minister, Jean-Pierre Chevènement, never much of a friend to the tribunal, openly declared the indictment to be a grave mistake. But the biggest reaction came from Viktor Chernomyrdin, the Russian peace envoy, who was actually in transit to Belgrade for a crucial meeting with Milosevic. He had high hopes that he was going to end the war during that visit. Chernomyrdin says he heard about the indictment only when it was released. Arbour thinks it unlikely he didn't know it was coming. He ordered his plane to turn around and return to Moscow, where he declared grimly, "Today, we reached the finishing line in the negotiating process, but somebody needed to put obstacles on the road to a peace dialogue."

By Wednesday, the news had leaked. On Thursday, Arbour called in the whole staff to tell them what had happened. "I haven't called you here to tell you I've resigned," she declared. Moments later, she convened a press conference where she announced that the president of Yugoslavia and four of his closest advisers were charged with the murder of 340 Kosovo Albanians as well as the forced expulsion of hundreds of thousands. "Beginning in January 1999 and continuing to this date," reads the indictment, "Slobodan Milosevic, Milan Milutinovic, Nikola Sainovic, Dragoljub Ojdanic and Vlajko Stojiljkovic planned, instigated, ordered, committed or otherwise aided and abetted in a campaign of terror and violence directed at Kosovo Albanian civilians living in Kosovo and the Federal Republic of Yugoslavia."

Milosevic became an international pariah overnight. His foreign bank accounts were frozen; he was unable to travel safely, unable to meet other heads of state. "The world has become a smaller place for him," said Arbour. When asked about the chances for a negotiated settlement to the war, Madeleine Albright said curtly, "We are not negotiating." That option was now gone. The war continued and General Clark — unable to deploy ground troops because NATO members didn't want to, and unable to get Milosevic to capitulate — increased the strength of the bombing and expanded the type of targets. The electrical grid of Belgrade was wiped out, as were many of its bridges. Civilian casualties were mounting. NATO blew up the Belgrade TV building, killing sixteen civilians.

It's not clear why Milosevic finally capitulated, but three weeks after his indictment he agreed to a ceasefire. The fighting had begun without a

formal declaration of war and it ended without an unconditional surrender. In mid-June, Wesley Clark was walking down the streets of Pristina,
capital of Kosovo, still unsure if what they really had was victory.

Under the terms of the final agreement, Yugoslavia had to turn Kosovo
over to international control. Milosevic had lost yet another part of Yugoslavia, and this time, it was the mythical Serb heartland. Yugoslavia was
seriously damaged, its economy ruined, and it had an indicted criminal as
a president. The Kosovo Albanians came back to their villages and began
to rebuild their destroyed homes, while the KLA proceeded to terrorize the
Serb population and drive them out of the province.

Throughout the spring of 1999, as Arbour plotted her moves against Milosevic, she was distracted by domestic developments in Canada. She'd been
on loan to the United Nations since the summer of 1996. She had agreed
to an initial four-year appointment, and had been prepared to consider
another term.

But even before she went to work at the international criminal tribunals, Arbour was considered an heir apparent to a seat on the Supreme
Court of Canada. There had been a vacancy in early 1998. Rumours in the
Canadian legal community suggested that Arbour was actively lobbying for
the job, but that wasn't true: Arbour was enjoying her work on the international stage, and she was hardly ready to go home. But when Justice
Peter Corey indicated he would be retiring in the summer of 1999, matters were somewhat different.

Arbour was tired. She and her family had been living under heavy
security all the time, and her mother, Rose, had moved in with Arbour at
The Hague to help take care of her youngest daughter, Catherine. The two
other children, Patrick and Emilie, were at school in Canada. Larry Taman,
her partner for nearly thirty years, had left Arbour a year earlier for another
woman, whom he would eventually marry.

She had the feeling that she had achieved all she could hope for in
advancing the work of the two tribunals. In Rwanda, her staffers were becoming increasingly hostile towards her, complaining that she spent too
much time in The Hague and not enough time in Kigali and Arusha. In
reality, she suspected they'd have been happier if she'd spent all her time in
Europe. She was a demanding taskmaster.

At The Hague, Arbour believed she had expended all her political
currency and used up all her contacts first in order to get NATO to blink

on the arrests and then to get the Milosevic indictment. She had called in every favour, wrung dry every bit of goodwill. "I had played all the cards I was dealt," she says. It was time to move on. Then she got a phone call from Prime Minister Jean Chrétien. She'd known it was coming, and she knew what it was all about. Would she accept a seat on Canada's highest court, the Olympian pinnacle of her profession? It was an offer she could not refuse. She told her staff shortly after the Milosevic indictment that she was returning to Canada. Someone asked her why she would want such a job. "Because that is what I am," she said. "I'm a judge."

EPILOGUE

PORCELAIN GRAND PRIX

A gentle, soft snowfall piles up slowly in the Christmas-card landscape of an old Ottawa neighbourhood. Many of Canada's most powerful people live here; Stornoway, the official home of the leader of the opposition, is nearby. But the pretty charm of the place belies the Powertown reality. On a quiet street, there's a warm, comfortable house with a big fireplace. It's become a refuge, from literally the whole world, for the woman who lives here.

The Honourable Louise Arbour, justice of the Supreme Court of Canada, is enjoying her first year on Canada's most eminent bench. Coincidentally, in the winter of 2000, the rape shield law is back in the Supreme Court, in a revised form—still contested by those who believe it denies accused rapists a fair trial. Arbour must also deal with a legal challenge to Canada's child pornography and gun control laws. Then there's the big question that could determine the fate of Canada as a nation: Quebec's place in the federation looms ominously on the Supreme Court's horizon. For Arbour, it all has a calming effect. She's home, back in Kansas after a trip to Oz. Ottawa is the city where she started her legal career as a clerk, and now she's back as a Supreme Court justice. The Hague is far away, in memory as well as distance.

Does she miss it? Not in any way one might expect. The power and influence, the sense of creating a place in history, never really appealed to her, she insists. But the chase, the hunt for documents, the Perry Mason drama of it all was like a drug. She misses that.

The peace of sitting by a fire on a snowy Saturday afternoon is quickly shattered by a news bulletin. Arkan has just been shot dead in the lobby of the Inter-Continental Hotel in Belgrade. Arbour thinks about her former staff and all the work that went into his indictment. And now he's escaped into eternity, to face whatever justice awaits him there. But perhaps there's still a chance that Radovan Karadzic and Slobodan Milosevic will see the inside of the old Dutch prison in The Hague. She'll wait and see.

In the final months of her time as chief prosecutor, Arbour toured the Balkans—drawing crowds like a royal visitor, giving instant scrums at the sites of mass graves, grieving with widows who had lost their husbands, accepting flowers from children and holding babies. Cameras clicked and images of the compassionate prosecutor flew around the world. She made the same tour through her jurisdiction in Africa, with, of course, much less media attention and without the same blind adoration from the citizenry. None of the travel was necessary from an investigative point of view, but Arbour had become an even more effective media performer than her predecessor, the flamboyant Richard Goldstone. The reserved Quebec-born judge who once gave long-winded discourses about international law to interviewers had transformed herself into a sharp-witted master of the sound bite and a savvy media personality, someone recognized in restaurants and sought out as the perfect after-dinner speaker.

She exuded confidence. Her expressive eyes, one moment reflecting profound tragedy and the next a withering flash of disapproval over the top of her reading glasses, became familiar throughout Europe as she appeared frequently on any interview program that mattered. Her director of prosecutions in The Hague, James Stewart, noted that his boss had a remarkable way of getting state leaders to give her what she wanted, whether it was money for digging up a grave or the authority to persuade a NATO general to issue an arrest warrant. Stewart remembers how she could punish her opponents without leaving any traces: "I once saw her correct the grammar of a government minister in Paris. Imagine this Québécois woman telling a Frenchman how to speak?"

Was Arbour successful? Considering how many powerful people wanted the tribunals to die of neglect, the answer is yes. She left a strong prosecutor's office to her successor, the Swiss attorney Carla Del Ponte, with hundreds of staff to work on dozens of indictments. The sexual-assault cases that had showed so much potential for making legal history were a disappointment to many people who had worked to get them into court, but the few successful prosecutions for rape did set some precedents.

She set another precedent in the indictment of a Belgian journalist, George Ruggiu—the only known foreign interloper to play a part in the Rwandan genocide—who pled guilty and was sentenced to two consecutive terms of twelve years in jail for inciting people to kill their neighbours. Such abuse and use of the media is now a crime against humanity. The biggest fish of all, Colonel Théoneste Bagosora, awaits trial in Arusha on charges of genocide and war crimes.

Just before Arbour left The Hague, a NATO-led SWAT force arrested General Momir Talic, one of the main culprits in the massacre at Srebrenica. The unsuspecting Talic had been the subject of one of Arbour's secret indictments. Another such indictment was served on Momcilo Krajisnik, a man who by the end of the decade had become more powerful than Karadzic in Republika Srpska. SWAT force officers blew up Krajisnik's door in the early hours of the morning of February 21, 2000, and dragged him off to Holland in his pyjamas.

Following Arbour's departure, the suspects in the Foca Indictment, which she had directed, were finally in the dock—two men charged with the brutal rape of dozens of women and children. More than a hundred women testified to the horrible torture and sexual assault of themselves and their daughters, and many of them had been impregnated. Arbour's Yugoslavian prosecutors had done a model job assembling the indictment. The men's lawyers argued in court that while their clients may have got a little carried away, the rapes were hardly crimes against humanity.

But there are many disappointments. Karadzic, the poster boy for Serbian ultra-nationalism, is once again going about his business. A Bosnian newsweekly reported in May 2000 that Karadzic was out and about in the Pale area, driving through checkpoints unmolested despite a force of thirty thousand NATO peacekeepers. General Mladic comes from Serbia routinely to visit his farm in Bosnia, where he keeps bees. He still attends soccer matches and goes to the beach. The U.S. State Department recently offered US$5 million for information as to the whereabouts of the wanted men. (The U.S. Republican senator Jesse Helms quickly responded with a report about the many sightings of the indicted and a home address for Slobodan Milosevic.)

In Rwanda, defence lawyers are attempting to have all the remaining cases against their clients thrown out of court, primarily because newspaper reports in early 2000 suggested that Juvénal Habyarimana, whose death sparked the genocide, was really killed by Paul Kagame's RPF. The *National Post* in Toronto published documents that charged that Louise Arbour had evidence implicating Kagame but had deliberately scuttled the investigation.

Arbour responds that the plane crash was beyond her jurisdiction. "I would ask my prosecutors and investigators, 'What's the indictment? Show me the evidence.' And then I would say, 'You're trying to prove that the RPF shot down the plane in order to start a massacre against the Tutsi? Their own people? I hope you have a lot of proof.'" Arbour concedes that the downing of the president's plane is one of history's unsolved crimes, but it's not a war crime; it is for someone else to investigate and prosecute in another court of law. She is coy when asked why the ICTR never indicted anyone in the RPF. The problem was always the same—how could you indict people who ran the country you were working in? Locating the prosecutor's office in Rwanda had been a major problem, and ultimately, perhaps, the cause of its biggest failing.

The success for Arbour, personally, is that her "porcelain grand prix racing car" survived what might have been a demolition derby. How did she accomplish that? "First of all, you decide what is the right thing to do, the moral thing to do. You start with what you should do. But if that means you will smash your Formula One ceramics into a cement wall, you have to turn." Arbour learned to turn on a dime, to feel the obstacles long before she saw them and smashed up against them. And she survived.

Now she is home with her children, with familiar things. She has settled into her ermine-trimmed crimson robes at the Supreme Court of Canada as though she always belonged in them. "This is what I am. I'm a judge."

CONCLUSION

"BY NO MAN'S LEAVE"

Civilization asks whether law is so laggard as to be utterly helpless to deal with crimes of this magnitude by criminals of this order of importance.
It does not expect that you can make war impossible. It does expect that your jurisdiction will put the forces of International Law, its precepts, its prohibitions and, most of all, its sanctions, on the side of peace, so that men and women of good will, in all countries, may have "leave to live by no man's leave, underneath the law."
—Robert H. Jackson, opening speech for the prosecution, Nuremberg, November 21, 1945

On December 29, 1999, *The Globe and Mail* newspaper published a *fin de siècle* editorial called "The World Is Developing a Conscience." It outlined what the writer regards as evidence of this optimistic claim. First was the astonishingly bold arrest a week earlier by SFOR troops stationed in the Balkans. On a road in southwestern Bosnia, British commandos stopped a vehicle carrying the Serb general Stanislav Galic. The soldiers smashed through the car window, dragged the general out, pulled a hood over his head and immediately transported him to The Hague, where he was charged with crimes against humanity. He was another of Arbour's secret indictments.

Galic was one of the principal players in the siege of Sarajevo, the man responsible for implementing the orders of the Pale Gang. Galic is also the man who taught the French colonel Patrice Sartre what the war was all about. When Sartre advised the Serb general to move his heavy guns to another position in order to minimize civilian casualties (fifteen children had been hit that week), Sartre says Galic told him civilian casualties were his objective. There was nothing the French officer could do as a member of UNPROFOR, but as a human being, he refused to meet with the Serb general again.

According to the conditions of the airport agreement, or at least the UN's understanding of them, the Serbs were free to pursue their siege. If someone had told Sartre that before the decade was finished, Galic would be arrested by NATO-led peacekeepers in a violent raid, he probably would not have believed it. The culture that allowed such an arrest did not exist in the early 1990s. It does now.

The Globe and Mail editorial read: "Only a few years ago, a little brute like General Galic would have scuttled away untouched from the scene of his crimes, and no one would have thought of going after him.... Suddenly all of that has begun to change. Around the world people are saying: Enough.... We won't turn our heads any more. We won't let the killers hide behind the skirts of national sovereignty. Someone must pay."

That is exactly what NATO publicly declared shortly before launching its bombing campaign in the spring of 1999. Milosevic's argument that he was dealing with a domestic matter of internal security carried no weight. American and European envoys told him that the world would not stand by and allow him to unleash another round of ethnic cleansing, even if it was in a province of his own sovereign country. The United Nations never sanctioned the war that was waged by thirteen members of NATO against Yugoslavia, but NATO took the initiative anyway. "Collateral damage," the rate of civilian casualties during the NATO campaign, was high and, arguably, NATO should have done more to prevent it. But the objective was commendable: this was about not oil interests or border disputes but human rights. No claim to sovereignty, according to international law, allows a nation-state to abuse its people. And in this one instance, NATO chose to put some muscle behind that claim.

Canada was one of the five countries that contributed bomber planes to the mission and flew "a significant number" of sorties during the war, according to the secretary-general of the NATO alliance, George Lord Robertson. But soon after the campaign in Yugoslavia, Robertson chided Canada for its weak-kneed commitment to its military forces and what he considered its appallingly low level of defence spending. The average defence budget among NATO members is 2.1 per cent of GDP, but Canada spends half that. As testimony to Robertson's complaints, senior officers in the Canadian Armed Forces later published an article in which they stated that Canada's war effort in Yugoslavia was so underfunded that pilots were actually flying the sorties at personal risk. The CF-18 bombers were serviced by a skeleton crew and the planes didn't have anti-jam radios, which meant all the other countries that took part in the campaign had to conform to the Canadian system, leaving the whole mission reliant on a single, jammable, frequency. The Canadian planes also lacked the kinds of bombs that would allow the pilots to effectively hit—and destroy—their targets.

Shortly after the war in Yugoslavia, Canada had to withdraw its peacekeepers from Kosovo because it could not sustain the commitments it had made to the force known as KFOR. And this wasn't the only problem: Canada's Hercules transport planes, which had done heroic service in Rwanda, were in such a state of disrepair that some could not fly to East Timor in late 1999 when Canadian troops were part of the UN mission there. Military equipment had been failing Canadian soldiers for years. The American journalist David Rieff says, "I spent half my time in Bosnia driving past Canadian APCs broken down on the side of the road. These were vehicles that should have found themselves part of someone's military antiques collection in Texas years ago."

In 1995, the foreign affairs minister at the time, André Ouellett, championed the idea of a rapid reaction force for peacekeeping, exactly the plan Roméo Dallaire proposed before and during the war in Rwanda and at every "Lessons Learned" conference he attended afterwards. It was to Canada that Dallaire had turned, in February 1994, when he could see the horror coming, and it was Canada that had said it could not, or would not, mount such a force. Dallaire had petitioned his government in Ottawa to do what he believed it had the people and material to do: assist him in preventing the killing of civilians. Canada had failed him, and the Rwandan people.

Since 1994, the Canadian government has hacked back the defence budget so severely that the Department of National Defence has been forced to reduce the number of troops in the armed forces from seventy-five thousand to sixty thousand. Critics say Canada is prepared for neither a traditional combat role nor effective peacekeeping.

All of this would matter less if Canada had decided it was no longer an international do-gooder. But Canada has actually expanded its original commitment to peacekeeping. In the 1990s, Foreign Affairs Minister Lloyd Axworthy advanced a policy, called the Human Security Agenda, in which Canada declared it will do what is necessary to combat threats against people. The policy is a bold and direct challenge to the notion of state sovereignty, a declaration that Canada must do whatever is possible to defend the rights of all citizens of the world when their security is threatened. Ottawa's commitment to the NATO offence in Yugoslavia was not a direct product of the new policy, but it was certainly consistent with it.

As early as 1996, Canada campaigned for a worldwide ban on the production and deployment of land mines. The country has subsequently championed the rights of children and the necessity of securing their safety during conflicts, even pushing for an international protocol banning the use of child soldiers. And Canada is a leader in the drive to create a permanent international criminal court that, should it finally be ratified by the United Nations, would take up the roles of the two ad hoc war crimes tribunals and apply them universally.

Since those initiatives, the Human Security Agenda has become more sophisticated. Its creators at the Department of Foreign Affairs in Ottawa say that Canada's commitment now involves five areas, or "clusters," in the language of bureaucrats. They are: the protection of civilians in armed conflict, which means anything from the creation of civilian safety zones to military intervention (both took place in Kosovo); other forms of peace support, including promoting civilian police and peacebuilding negotiators; the development of "conflict-prevention initiatives" directed at reducing the availability of weapons and, in particular, small arms; accountability and transparency, whereby foreign powers would be required to account for their policies and face the possibility of economic, military or even criminal sanctions; and a public-safety agenda aimed at reducing the threat of international crime, terrorism and drug trafficking. If the word "ambitious" comes to mind, the policy wonks at foreign affairs would agree. If the word "expensive" surfaces, the bureaucrats would concede that as well.

Canada has declared itself to be in the business of protecting people: the last Throne Speech of the decade said that the federal government was committed to ensuring that the military had "the capacity to support Canada's role in building a more secure world." But there was no money included in that commitment from Ottawa. Newspaper headlines ring out almost monthly with new revelations that add up to the same thing: "Military May Soon Be Unfit for Combat," says the *National Post*; "Air Force Racked by Poor Gear, 'Burnout,'" says *The Globe and Mail*. Where is the commitment?

Dallaire asks a similar question, but his is not about money: How many lives is Canada willing to lose in the name of human security in a foreign country? Dallaire argues that the mission is always the priority in peacekeeping—the safety of the soldiers comes second. Lewis MacKenzie argues that the security of soldiers is a priority—the mission comes second. These are the lines of debate within the ranks of the Canadian Forces as it struggles to define its role in the Human Security Agenda. The United States has made it clear—in both its rhetoric and its policies—that it is not prepared to lose its soldiers in peacekeeping missions. Canada, which officially doesn't use the word "peacekeeping" any more but has switched to a broader term, "peace support operations," may be more willing. But how far would we go? More than 100,000 Canadians have been sent to serve in peacekeeping missions over the past five decades; more than one hundred have lost their lives. But Canada has never seen its own soldiers targeted for death the way the American Rangers in Mogadishu or the Belgian commandos in Kigali were. Many people in DND believe Canadians understand that death is a condition of conflict and are more accepting of such an atrocity. But there is nothing on which to base that belief.

In their 1998 book, *Tested Mettle: Canada's Peacekeepers at War*, Scott Taylor and Brian Nolan suggest that peacekeeping as a symbol of Canadian do-goodism may be a bit of a sham. The two Ottawa-based investigative reporters pointed out that Lester Pearson often tried to excuse Canada's poor contribution to global defence, and that the idea of a lightly armed intervention force, for which Pearson won the Nobel Prize, was in many respects a way for Canada to avoid more costly military intervention. Pearson had first proposed such a force during the Korean War, when the United States asked Canada to play a larger military role. During the Suez crisis, Canadians were dispatched to replace combat troops from France and Britain as a non-combat monitoring force with only light weapons—the cheaper model. "Thereafter," wrote Nolan and Taylor, "the Canadian army was extensively committed to the business of peacekeeping as successive Canadian governments tried to emulate Pearson's formula for getting a maximum political return on a minimal military investment."

Canadian foreign affairs policy-makers will grudgingly admit that, even now, Canada is quick with the ideas but slow with the cash (in the best tradition of Lester Pearson). The Human Security Agenda is something that Lloyd Axworthy hopes other countries will help to implement, but Canada can lead with little more than initiative. This is true—more than anywhere else—in the area of international law.

In July 1998, representatives of 148 countries met for a United Nations diplomatic conference in Rome to work out a plan for an International Criminal Court (ICC), an institution that in the future would prosecute the likes of Pol Pot and Augusto Pinochet. One hundred and twenty countries approved the plan, seven opposed and twenty-one abstained. Canada led the central committee to have the court approved, and it continued to play the key role afterwards in something with a wholly Canadian ring to it, the Like-minded Group. Made up of the nations that approve the court in principle, the Like-minded Group is helping to galvanize support for ICC ratification. Sixty countries must ratify the ICC in their legislatures before it can become law; Senegal and Trinidad and Tobago were the first to do so. For the rest, it's been a slow process. (Full international ratification is expected within the early part of this decade.)

The United States is not a part of the Like-minded Group, and in fact, Washington declared the ICC fatally flawed from its inception. What the Americans fear most is that their own soldiers, who are frequently in action overseas, and their own leaders may be dragged before the court and prosecuted. Louise Arbour actually gave the U.S. its most palpable taste of that possibility during the NATO campaign in Yugoslavia, when she told the Pentagon generals that they were operating in her theatre and they'd best look smart. Later, a group of legalists, led by the Canadian law professor Michael Mandel, filed a petition at the Yugoslavian tribunal demanding that the leaders of several NATO countries—including Bill Clinton and Jean Chrétien—be prosecuted for crimes against humanity. The Americans were apoplectic at the thought, with one U.S. representative suggesting that the entire UN building would be dismantled, brick by brick, before a single American serviceman would ever appear there. Other U.S. politicians attempted (unsuccessfully) to pass a ban on U.S. aid to any country that ratified the ICC. Carla Del Ponte, who replaced Arbour at The Hague, reviewed the petition from the Mandel group and found it had no basis in international law, but that has done little to reassure the Americans.

The U.S. State Department has tried to amend the ICC statute adopted in Rome so that it would have no jurisdiction over any country that didn't sign up. Such an amendment, argues Canada and all other supporters of the court, would render the institution meaningless. Rogue states would fail to submit to ICC jurisdiction, and fugitives from international justice could hide out in such territories. Canada and the other members of the Like-minded Group have also managed to scuttle another attempt to weaken the ICC: some countries proposed that they should be able to opt out of laws they didn't like, and that every state government should be able to select from a menu of crimes they would be willing to accept. The idea was nixed.

But Canada has yet to test its own ability to prosecute war criminals. Recent amendments to the Canadian Criminal Code, which were designed to correct the shortcomings of Canadian law so amply demonstrated by the Imre Finta case, have yet to be applied. Finta never denied committing the crimes of which he was accused but claimed he was innocently just following orders. The Canadian courts that acquitted him concluded that he legitimately thought he was defending his country from what he had been told was "the Jewish menace." Canadian justices from Louise Arbour all the way up to and including those on the Supreme Court of Canada regarded Finta's defence as legitimate.

With this amended law allowing the government to prosecute people who committed war crimes on foreign soil, perhaps Canada is better equipped to deal with such prosecutions. The RCMP is also investigating dozens of people whom it suspects committed crimes against humanity in their countries of origin in recent years. But will Canada dedicate money and resources to bring those people to trial? Such prosecutions are expensive and time-consuming, as other countries who have active modern-day war crimes legislation have discovered. Will Canada put its money where its idealistic mouth is?

The Globe and Mail proclaimed that "the world is developing a conscience," and there is a lot of evidence to support that claim. Issues of sovereignty are challenged at every turn. The defence of "just following orders" is considered hogwash in the tribunals of Rwanda and Yugoslavia, and that may soon be the case in international jurisprudence as well. The security of children in conflict is now considered a global priority.

And yet, is there even now the political will to avoid another Bosnia or Rwanda? Or would the Security Council again drag its feet? Would the Office of Peacekeeping Operations again decide not to pass on faxes that speak of a plan to exterminate a race of people? Would Canada support another arms embargo, like the one against Bosnia, that prevents a legitimate government from procuring the weapons needed to defend its civilian population? And would it continue to support that embargo long after its utter folly was clearly demonstrated? Or will the people we send out into the world to do the right thing have to rely only on their own moral compasses?

ACKNOWLEDGEMENTS

IN researching and writing *The Lion, the Fox and the Eagle*, I relied on Ernest Hemingway's difficult—but very effective—rule for writers: You can only leave out what you know. The dictum was made easier only because of the extraordinary range and number of people who helped me to know enough to write it. Since I have been gathering this material for a number of years, my debt of gratitude is extensive, so I will have to confine these acknowledgements to those who assisted with the immediate writing of the book.

The three subjects featured here, Roméo Dallaire, Lewis MacKenzie and Louise Arbour gave freely and generously of their time and were available for many hours of interviews and e-mail inquiries. I do not know what they will think of the final product (none asked to see it before publication), but I can assure them, and anyone else, that this account is true to the best of my research powers and my knowledge. I thank all three of them for their candour and insight.

I owe an immense debt of gratitude to a number of people who have taught me about the Balkans, Rwanda and the tribunals and have kept me on the right course through the year of writing. I want to thank Eno Causevic who launched my interest in this story; Aida Alibalic who has been a constant source of ideas and encouragement; the Knezevic family—Gordana, Ivo, Boris, Igor and Olga—whose integrity was my inspiration; Javor Probic who taught me more than he will ever know; Katarina Subasic who risks her personal safety each day to report on events in Yugoslavia and who helped me travel throughout the country; Yvan Patrie who used his last ounce of strength to tell the truth about Rwanda; Alison Des Forges who gives generously to everyone who calls her for help; Gerry Caplan who shared whatever he could in the interest of disseminating the story of Rwanda; William Stuebner who was never too busy to give me an hour (or two) of his time when I got hopelessly muddled; and dozens of Rwandans and Bosnians who provided their personal stories.

A number of soldiers and military officers contributed enormously to the telling of this story, and I want to thank Colonel Michel Drapeau, Lt. Colonel Dr. Bernd Horn, Major Anthony White, Lt. Colonel Barry Hamilton, Colonel Ralph Coleman, Lt. Colonel Hugh Culliton, and especially Majors Brent Beardsley and Phil Lancaster who trusted me more than all their instincts told them to. Many of these people will be embarrassed to find themselves named—since the Canadian Forces is still a secretive place despite years of attempted reform. But I can assure DND that their first loyalty is to the forces and any assistance they gave me was only in that interest. Soldiers and officers in the Belgium armed forces were very candid and honest with me, and I want to thank, in particular, Luc Marchal, Petrus Maggen and Joe Dewez. I also want to give a special thanks to Joris Van Bladel who helped me find my way around Belgium.

While journalists are usually a competitive lot, a number of them were generous with me and gave freely of their research material. I want to especially thank Brian Stewart and Carmen Merrifield. I could not have known enough to write this book if not for my talented colleagues at the CBC, who often risked their lives to tell the stories of these two wars and whose reporting I relied upon, including Anna Maria Tremonti, Nancy Durham and Susan Harada. The producers and crews I worked with in the course of my own coverage were exceptional, and I want to thank cameraman *extraordinaire* Brian Kelly plus producers Mecki Furlani and Tamar Weinstein with whom I did the difficult spade work for this book. Sheila Mandell is right about almost everything and she gave me excellent advice. Pam Clasper, Ginny Oakland, Claire Robinson and Sonja Carr are the talented researchers without whom there would have been no TV programs on these subjects.

Journalists in other countries were equally as generous with their time, their ideas and even—God forbid—their research material. I want to thank Roy Gutman and David Reiff in the United States; Gojko Beric, Hamza Baksic and Senad Pecanin in Bosnia; Heikelina Verrijn Stuart in Holland; Thierry Cruvellier at *Ubutebera* in Arusha; and Filip Reyntjens in Belgium.

People in both tribunals went beyond the call of duty to help me, and I must note the assistance of Paul Kennedy in Arusha and Paul Risley in

The Hague. Nader Hashemi, Ausma Khan and Jacques Castonguay read this manuscript and saved me from a number of embarrassing errors and oversights.

I am also grateful to Sandy McKean and Kelly Crichton who gave me time off work at the CBC to write this book and to Bob Bishop, Peter Puxley and Janet Thompson who put up with my prolonged absences.

Working with my editor, Random House Canada publisher Anne Collins, was a rare and wonderful experience. Anne had an uncanny knack for ferreting out things that were left out because I didn't know them: there was nothing I could hide from her unfaltering eye. She is now on my very short list of people who have taught me about this profession.

Pam Robertson kept me honest and on time, and I am forever in her debt. Janice Weaver politely pointed out anything that Anne Collins might have missed and made the manuscript as tight as a drum.

Special thanks to Don Sedgwick and Suzanne DePoe who launched this project and found me the best arrangement possible. They started as literary agents and became dear friends, even as they nudged me along through the long, dark winter of 1999–2000.

Sian Cansfield called one day a year ago to introduce herself and announce that she would be researching for me whether I wanted it or not. Thus began one of the most fruitful professional collaborations I have ever had. Sian has an almost clairvoyant ability to find hidden documents and deliver them with breathtaking speed, and to persuade reluctant interview subjects to tell all. I am forever in her debt.

Finally, I want to thank my husband, Linden MacIntyre. Without his assistance and encouragement you would not be reading this book.

SOURCE NOTES

The Lion, the Fox and the Eagle is based largely on original material derived from a series of interviews conducted in 1999 and 2000 involving approximately seventy-five subjects and 150 hours of recorded conversations. I also worked with an extensive amount of documentation, some of which has never been published before.

I have also drawn heavily on research and interviews conducted by me and other people I have worked with at the Canadian Broadcasting Corporation over the past five years, as well as from my own reporting from the field as a documentary reporter on the CBC's *The National Magazine*.

This book is not intended as a history or any kind of comprehensive document on the wars in Bosnia and Rwanda or the war crimes tribunals. It is, instead, an account of three individuals and how they coped with those events. There are a number of excellent and immensely detailed books on those wars and I have used them extensively in the writing of this account. I have listed the principal texts in these source notes as they pertain to each chapter. There are few books or secondary sources on the tribunals, however, and I drew from primary sources most heavily for Book Four.

BOOK ONE   THE LION

CHAPTER 1: SLOUCHING TOWARDS THE MILLENNIUM

Historical material for this chapter comes principally from Gérard Prunier's *The Rwanda Crisis: History of a Genocide* and from probably the definitive work on the Rwandan war, *Leave None to Tell the Story*, produced by Human Rights Watch and its authority on Rwanda, Alison Des Forges. Philip Gourevitch wrote the most accessible book on the war in Rwanda and its origins, called *We Wish to Inform You that Tomorrow We Will Be Killed with All Our Families*, from which I have quoted.

The role of Canadian clerics and their contribution to modern Rwandan society came from discussions with Quebec filmmaker Yvan Patrie and from his extensive research on Canada's role in the Great Lakes Region. Before he passed away in 1999, Patrie did seminal work on the religious origins of the genocide and the part played by Canadian priests. He produced a three-part documentary, *Chronicles of a Genocide Foretold*, from which some of the historical background for this section is derived.

Patrie also co-produced a documentary with CBC TV's *the fifth estate* on the death of a Canadian priest, and I have used that documentary and its supporting research material for the history of the National University of Rwanda and its Canadian connection, as well as for the biographical data on Léon Mugesera. Many of the interviews from which I derived this material were conducted by Linden MacIntyre and Anita Mielewczyk from *the fifth estate*.

CHAPTER 2: INTO AFRICA

Most of the material for this chapter comes from interviews with Roméo Dallaire and from his own archival material. General Dallaire allowed me to review his collected notes, speeches and writings from his year in Rwanda and from after the genocide when he was still in the Department of National Defence. Dallaire wrote—and spoke—extensively on the war in Rwanda and the failure of the international community. The DND eventually stopped granting him permission to do so, except for rare occasions when the benefit to the DND could be clearly demonstrated. But Dallaire continued to take part in various private, unrecorded conferences, and his speeches and notes from those events were also available to me.

The officers who served with Dallaire, foremost among them Major Brent Beardsley and Colonel Luc Marchal, provided much of the account of the pre-genocide months supplemented by the detailed accounts and supporting documents published in *Leave None to Tell the Story*. More background material and description came from interviews with Faustin Twagiramungu who now lives with his family in Belgium, as does the remains of the Kavaruganda family who also provided much information on the conditions in Rwanda leading up to—and including—the genocide.

My research assistant for this book, Sian Cansfield, also interviewed many Rwandans who had contact with Dallaire and UNAMIR before and during the genocide, including the sisters of Landoald Ndasingwa, who survived the events of 1994 (one was abroad at the time) and who recalled the happier times at Chez Lando.

Some of the documents used for this chapter are available to the public on various Web sites: the so-called genocide fax is posted with PBS's program *Frontline* and in the Human Rights Watch Report. Dr. Jacques Castonguay has one of the best collections of faxes and exchanges between UNAMIR and New York City, and he has published or quoted from many of them in his book *Les Casques Bleu au Rwanda*, along with the Security Council resolutions that formed the background of the UNAMIR mission.

Canada's unwillingness to participate any further in the UNAMIR mission is now part of the public record released under Access to Information legislation. I used a memo submitted to the Department of Foreign Affairs by Africa desk officer Yvon St. Hillaire for the account of Dallaire's request for a Canadian battalion.

The Belgian senate's mammoth report on the genocide provides much of the material on the Belgian foreign affairs minister's warnings about the precarious stability of Rwanda before the war and threats to the UNAMIR mission, though only excerpts of the report have been translated into English. The report is a scathing attack on the Belgian government's lack of preparedness for the events of 1993 and 1994.

Human Rights Watch has published the invoice records concerning the purchase of machetes, which document the sharp increase in orders for them in the year preceding the war in *Leave None to Tell the Story*. Material for the account of Iqbal Riza's reaction to Dallaire's warnings are part of the PBS *Frontline* documentary on the Rwandan genocide. Transcripts of the Riza interview are published on the PBS Web site and I used them for this account. General Maurice Baril refused all requests to be interviewed by me and every other reporter working on the Rwanda story. Baril spoke with Jacques Castonguay during his debriefing by DND after he returned to Canada from the UN.

CHAPTER 3: THE PRESIDENT IS DEAD: THE GENOCIDE BEGINS

The core of this chapter is the accounts of the genocide found in *Leave None to Tell the Story* and *The Rwanda Crisis*, as well as daily newspaper accounts from the time. The story of Dallaire and his officers comes from interviews with many of them, including the principal Belgian officers involved in these events, Luc Marchal, Joe Dewez and Petrus Maggen as well as Brent Beardsley and, of course, Dallaire. Other officers and soldiers who were interviewed — some involved in intelligence — do not want to be named.

Joseph Kavaruganda's widow, Annonciata, and her two children described the events of the night of April 6 in interviews, as did the prime minister designate, Faustin Twagiramungu.

The story of what happened to the Belgian commandos on the morning of April 7 is still incomplete, since representatives of the United Nations have not testified publicly. The most detailed account — which I relied on — was the Belgian senate report; the senate committee interviewed almost all the players and had access to government records. Senator Alain Destexhe provided me with supplementary information and gave me access to the background files, documents and transcripts that made up the Belgian report.

A very important source of first-hand information was the Africa Rights Watch publication *Death, Despair and Defiance* — more than a thousand pages of interviews and personal accounts of the genocide. It was an excellent source for me, since the material was gathered immediately after the war before people knew the extent to which they had been abandoned by the UN. The testimonies are fresh, even if they are horribly bleak.

Chapter 4: This Time We Knew

The epigraph is from a published essay by Roméo Dallaire. Most of this chapter is derived from interviews with Dallaire, Phil Lancaster and Brent Beardsley. Major Beardsley became extremely ill in May 1994 and was flown out of Kigali on a Hercules aircraft (he recovered to full health back in Canada). Major Lancaster replaced Beardsley, and between the two men — who both worked in Dallaire's operations office — I was able to piece together much of what happened in the way of communication between UNAMIR and the UN's peacekeeping office in New York. Beardsley and Lancaster were responsible for transmitting the messages to New York. Lancaster also wrote extensively and eloquently about his experiences in Rwanda, and he shared that material with me. Many of his quotes in this book are from his written work.

The American reaction to the genocide — and the State Department's almost comical efforts to avoid getting involved in Rwanda — are well documented in the *Frontline* program. The PBS Web site posts the State Department press conferences at length as well as interviews with former State Department and UN personnel. My assessment of State Department inaction also comes from testimony before the congressional committee called to investigate the U.S. response to the genocide and from interviews with former and current State Department people.

Roméo Dallaire's plan for stopping the genocide was examined in detail by a number of American military critics who took part in a conference just after the war: the Carnegie Commission on Preventing Deadly Conflict. The conference concluded that the Dallaire plan had merit and probably would have worked. Since that time, there have been a number of efforts to discredit Dallaire's ideas and to dismiss the findings of the Carnegie Commission conference. The periodical *Foreign Affairs* published an essay in February 2000 stating that the plan would not have worked and arguing that the United States and the United Nations had no way to accurately assess that there was a genocide until the war was almost over. The *Foreign Affairs* article is consistent with a wave of revisionism in recent reporting on the Rwandan war.

The minutes to the meeting held in Rwanda with Iqbal Riza, UNAMIR and the Rwandan government are from a private source and have never been published. Again, General Baril refused to comment publicly on his visit to Rwanda but apparently gave a forceful account of what he observed when he returned to New York, in which he stated his conviction that there was a genocide. Dallaire's own understanding was that Baril supported Dallaire's position and view of the war and while this is probably true, there is no documentation of this.

The description of events surrounding Operation Turquoise came from interviews with Dallaire and from *The Rwanda Crisis*. Gérard Prunier had much inside knowledge of Turquoise since the government in Paris consulted him on it. He characterized the French plan—and the thinking behind it—as confused.

My report on the death threats that Dallaire received are pieced together from a number of interviews with people who were privy to the phone calls and intelligence surrounding the incidents. My interview subjects are not entirely consistent and some actually contradict each other. As far as I am able to assess, the account in this book is accurate. There are no written reports—or at least I could find none. Ottawa's DND took the threats very seriously and ordered that Dallaire have a permanent escort.

CHAPTER 5: THE SEARCH FOR A SCAPEGOAT

Roméo Dallaire gave me a list of his close friends and colleagues and asked them to talk to me. I derived my description of Dallaire's behaviour and personality from interviews with those men and from others who knew him. Brian Stewart interviewed Roméo Dallaire for three hours as soon as the general returned from his holiday in Europe. A portion of that interview was aired, but I was able to screen it in its entirety.

Many of the leaked faxes and documents now appear on various Web sites— including *Frontline*'s—and in *Leave None to Tell the Story*. Jacques Castonguay's book *Les Casques Bleu au Rwanda* includes a number of them. Philip Gourevitch first received the UN response to the January fax. I was able to review some support material for the Belgian senate report, which provided me with more documents. But Beardsley and Dallaire say that the bulk of what passed between New York and Kigali was in the form of phone calls that were unrecorded.

Boutros Boutros-Ghali's memoir *Unvanquished: A U.S.—U.N. Saga* is a fascinating source of insight, if only because it completely exonerates the secretary-general. Boutros-Ghali wrote that he didn't even know of the famous fax until years later.

Chapter 6: The Belgian Legacy
Most of this chapter comes from a series of interviews I did in the winter of 2000 with Belgian officers. The level of post-traumatic stress among those soldiers is profound, but the Belgian military seems to be less concerned about the psychological casualties than the Canadian Forces. Material for this chapter came from the Belgian senate report and supporting documents. I also obtained the letters Dallaire wrote to his staff explaining—in great detail—the events of April 7 and his rationale for not launching a rescue operation for the Belgian commandos. I also used Dallaire's confidential written testimony submitted to the Belgian military court to write this chapter.

A number of Rwandans who live in Belgium, including Annonciata Kavaruganda and Faustin Twagiramungu, gave me interviews and support documentation for this chapter.

Epilogue: Lessons Learned
This final chapter of Book One is constructed around interviews and correspondence with Dallaire. Additional information came from Dallaire's very frank conversation with Michael Enright on CBC Radio's *This Morning* and the subsequent letter he sent to the program describing his breakdown in a park in Hull. The CBC published the letter—with Dallaire's permission—on its Web site.

BOOK TWO   THE FOX

Chapter 1: Birth of a Nation
Descriptions of post-war Bosnia are based on my numerous field trips to the country starting in January 1996. Even now, in 2000, much of Sarajevo lies in ruins, including the Sarajevo library and the *Oslobodjenje* offices. It's widely believed that these buildings haven't been repaired so as to remain visual symbols of what the war wrought, particularly to institutions of intellectual freedom. The journalists who reported this war risked their lives to do so. Before it was over, more reporters and photographers became casualties to the Bosnian war than any previous conflict. A plaque is mounted on a wall of the main street of Sarajevo to commemorate those who lost their lives covering the events.

For historical analysis I relied on Noel Malcolm's book *A Short History of*

Bosnia and on *The Death of Yugoslavia*, considered by many the definitive text on the breakup of the country. Many people swear by a book by Steven Burg and Paul Shoup, called *The War in Bosnia Herzegovina: Ethnic Conflict and International Intervention*, particularly those who share the authors' contention that all sides were responsible for the war, and that the war was essentially ethnic and not ideological.

In this chapter, I relied on many interviews with the players in these events: Warren Zimmerman and a number of people in the U.S. State Department characterized the run-up to Bosnian independence from an American point of view. Journalists who covered the war and met the political leaders contributed a great deal to my understanding of the sides in the conflict. I spoke with a number of ministers, advisors and collaborators from the Serb, Croat and Bosnian sides, including Jovan Zamatitza, who advised Radovan Karadzic, and Sabina Izetbegovic, who advised her father. I never got to meet with either Alija Izetbegovic or Radovan Karadzic. Both men remained elusive despite my repeated attempts. Documentary filmmaker Nancy Durham and I travelled throughout the former Yugoslavia in 1998, exploring all the reported hiding places of the doctor but never came across him. We turned the search effort into a kind of road movie entitled *Looking for Doctor Karadzic*, broadcast on the CBC. Though I didn't find him, I learned a great deal about his family and background, especially from an interview with his mother who lives in Montenegro. That research formed the basis of my analysis of Karadzic.

CHAPTER 2: WAR IN BOSNIA
Radovan Karadzic's speech to the Bosnian parliament in which he warns the Muslims that they have no way to defend themselves was recorded and has turned up in a number of documentaries on the origins of the war, including *The Death of Yugoslavia*, the five-part film version of the book of the same name. Milosevic's role in the Bosnian war, and his involvement in setting up the Bosnian Serb army, did not surface publicly until after the war was in progress, but Western intelligence agencies had some idea of what he was up to. Based on what they had seen in Croatia the year previously, the pattern should have been apparent.

The analysis of Canada's policy on the Yugoslavian wars is based on interviews with the former ambassador to Croatia, Graham Green, and with people in foreign affairs who do not wish to be named. Nader Hashemi of the University of Toronto has done the most comprehensive analysis of Canada's Balkan policy to date, in a yet-to-be-published work he allowed me to use. It is often suggested that Brian Mulroney's wife, Mila, of Serbian extraction, may have been a major influence on Canadian policy, but I did not find evidence of this. More likely, the old friendship with Yugoslavia and traditional support for Belgrade was behind

Ottawa's folly. Canadian policy was much too confused and ill-informed to be conspiratorial.

Much of Book Two, including Chapter Two, is derived from extensive interviews with Major General Lewis MacKenzie, conducted over the winter of 1999–2000, and also from his memoir, *Peacekeeper: The Road to Sarajevo*.

The description of the Bosnian army comes from numerous interviews and encounters with soldiers and officers over the years, but principally from conversations with Jovan Divjak, the deputy commander of the Bosnian Territorial Defence Force in Sarajevo during the war. Juka moved back into the world of crime during the war (he probably never left it) and he was later found dead. Many people believe, perhaps romantically, that he is still alive and in hiding. I was unable to find him.

The numerous descriptions of Lewis MacKenzie and his actions in Bosnia and on the world stage come from a range of books and periodicals, the best of which is Peter Maas's *Love Thy Neighbour*. The Burg and Shoup book gives the most appreciative and uncritical account of MacKenzie's activities during the war.

CHAPTER 3: THE PRESIDENT IS KIDNAPPED

The Death of Yugoslavia, both the film and the book, forms the spine of my account of May 2, supported and advanced through interviews with Colm Doyle, Sabina Izetbegovic, Ejup Ganic, Zlatko Lagumdzija, Stjepan Kljuic, soldiers with the Bosnian armed forces, Lewis MacKenzie and other personnel of UNPROFOR.

Reports on the destruction of principal buildings in Sarajevo, especially the sabotage of the post office, come from the extensive annexes of the Commission of Experts' report, which formed background research for the war crimes tribunal.

Interestingly, the Burg and Shoup book states that the president was kidnapped May 3, not May 2. No other account of the event suggests there was any confusion over the day. But the May 3 date allows the authors to theorize that the president was kidnapped only in an effort to acquire a bargaining chip in negotiations to free JNA soldiers from the Bistrik barracks and not out of any design on the part of the Serbs to stage a coup.

CHAPTER 4: DAY OF THE GENERAL

I do a disservice to Fred Cuny, author of the chapter's epigraph, by describing him as simply a Sarajevo aid worker, but it's difficult to sum up this individual in a few words. Cuny was a maverick among NGO workers, from Bosnia to Chechnya, and he earned the nickname "master of disaster." The legendary, and often mysterious, Texan disappeared in Chechnya in 1995. The American journalist Scott Anderson published Cuny's story last year in his book, *The Man Who Tried to Save the World: The Dangerous Life and Mysterious Disappearance of Fred Cuny.*

This chapter also relies on *The Death of Yugoslavia* and my own interviews, many of them not for attribution. Named subjects include: Jovan Divjak, Sabina Izetbegovic, Zlatko Lagumdzija, Ejup Ganic, Stjepan Kljuic, Lewis MacKenzie and Serb general Milutin Kukanjac, who gave a detailed interview to a Bosnian paper *Slobodna Bosna*, where he admits he had planned to kill everyone in the APC.

According to witnesses, the number of vehicles that attempted to leave the Bistrik barracks on May 3 is seventy, and that number has been reported in most independent accounts. Other witnesses I spoke with, including MacKenzie, say they don't know how large the convoy was since not all the military vehicles and private cars trying to evacuate the barracks that day were able to do so. But observers as varied as MacKenzie and Sabina Izetbegovic concur that no one, with the possible exception of General Kukanjac, had advance notice that the convoy would be so large. Extra transport vehicles had arrived at Bistrik in order to expedite the JNA departure. Kukanjac told MacKenzie as soon as he arrived that the JNA would need six or seven hours to pack. MacKenzie told Kukanjac he had only one hour. A stream of paper, files and other debris trailed out all over the street in the wake of the departing trucks since they had no time to properly pack, or destroy, all the material.

CHAPTER 5: THE BREADLINE MASSACRE

Susan Sontag and her son, David Rieff, were part of an informal group of writers who felt passionately about the Bosnian war and maintained that the world's intellectuals had a moral obligation to bear witness to those atrocities. Rieff's book, *Slaughterhouse: Bosnia and the Failure of the West*, is an eloquent rant against the United Nations and the abject failure of the Western world to intervene in the war. Rieff provides a detailed description of the odious policy of moral equivalency and its application to peacekeeping activities in Bosnia as does Norman Cigar in his book, *Genocide in Bosnia: The Policy of Ethnic Cleansing*.

Susan Sontag became a fixture in Sarajevo during the war and even directed a production of *Waiting for Godot* — a timely mockery of Bosnians waiting for help from the outside world. Despite the extreme danger citizens faced in the streets of Sarajevo during the siege, the city's cultural life flourished. Ballerinas considered it a badge of honour to cross the city under shellfire and arrive in time for rehearsal. Concerts were held in the bombed-out Sarajevo library and, with outside help, Sarajevans organized a film festival. Mirroring the black humour of the city's citizens at the time, Tarantino's *Reservoir Dogs* was one of the most popular films during the war. The clinging to a cultural life was a declared defiance of the Pale Gang—in particular, the well-known Shakespeare professor, Nicole Koljevic—who deliberately targeted cultural institutions for destruction.

Tom Gjelten reported for National Public Radio and wrote for *The New Republic*. He investigated the breadline massacre at length and included his observations in his magazine articles and his book, *Sarajevo Daily*. The book is about the *Oslobodjenje* newspaper and its not always successful struggle to remain objective during the war. The paper and its editors, Kemal Kurspahic and Gordana Knezevic, won numerous international human rights and media awards and citations during and after the war. They include the European Parliament's 1993 Sakharov Prize for fostering "freedom of spirit"; the Oscar Romero Award of 1993, presented to the paper's editors for "keeping a free press and a multi-ethnic staff during the war"; the 1993 Louis Lyons Award for "conscience and integrity in journalism." Tens of thousands of dollars in international prize money went to keep the paper running through the war.

The Burg and Shoup book suggests it is quite possible that the Bosnians were responsible for the breadline massacre. The authors cite examples of massacres of Bosnian Muslims from 1994 that the UN reported as definitely carried out by the Muslims; if the Bosnians were capable of killing their own people in 1994, the authors extrapolate, then the world can't completely dismiss the possibility that they were doing it in 1992. But the UN is not the best source on these massacres. Often it would declare that one side was responsible for a massacre and then, a few days later, change its mind (citing new evidence) and blame the other side. Tom Gjelten suggests the UN attributed atrocities to the side it needed to pressure on a particular day. UNPROFOR people I spoke with say that it was extremely difficult in most cases to figure out where any of the mortars were coming from since the warring positions were so close together.

William Fenrick and the Canadian War Crimes Investigation Team, part of the Commission of Experts, did a complete incident study of another brutal mass murder that took place during a soccer game a year after the breadline massacre. The WCIT determined that the Serbs were responsible for that incident. Fenrick said in an interview with me that he and others at the commission and later at the war crimes tribunal, found UNPROFOR far too ready to blame the Muslims for massacres than the evidence allowed. He could only conclude that UNPROFOR personnel were frustrated by their inability to stop the mass murder of civilians and it became easier if they could, to some extent, demonize the victims. Fenrick says he found no evidence that the Bosnian government was responsible for any of the massacres.

Ratko Mladic telling people in Srebrenica that they would not be harmed—just before he had at least seven thousand of them killed—was videotaped by local people and is part of an extraordinary documentary called *Srebrenica: Cry from the Grave* by Antelope Films of Great Britain.

CHAPTER 6: A TIME FOR APPEASEMENT AND A TIME FOR WAR

I could find no official record of the phase two negotiations to keep the airport open. My interview with Brigadier John Wilson is the source of the account in this book. Wilson says it may not have been officially called "phase two" but that is certainly how he and Cedric Thornberry described it to President Izetbegovic. Ejup Ganic, who was the one who kept demanding that MacKenzie force the Serbs to move the guns back twenty kilometres, says he understood at the time of the airport negotiations that moving the guns was part of the deal. He felt betrayed by the international negotiators when it failed to happen.

Biljana Plavsic is the source of the story of what happened the day she tried to move her mother. UNPROFOR soldiers involved in the event, including John Wilson, confirmed most of the details, but Plavsic is the exclusive source of the information that MacKenzie was involved in the negotiations for her release. Ejup Ganic does not recall which parties intervened, but he remembers he was under considerable pressure from UNPROFOR to let Plavsic go and that he was in telephone communication with people in Belgrade.

CHAPTER 7: THE AIRPORT IS OPEN — THE CITY IS CLOSED

The story that the Mujezinovic brothers told me is similar to many such accounts. Most people were not shot at but were simply dragged back into the city by UNPROFOR soldiers and sometimes handcuffed for a time to the fence surrounding the airport to prevent them from trying it again. Everyone I interviewed in UNPROFOR says they heard that such things happened at the airport but no one recalls them occurring on their own watch. Local people remember them quite vividly, but there are few records.

The most interesting source of such information on wartime Sarajevo is a mock guidebook of the city called *Sarajevo Survival Guide*. It was published in 1993 by a local artists and writers collective called FAMA, and bears a completely intended resemblance to a Michelin guidebook—long, slim and pocket-sized. Humour doesn't get much blacker than this publication. There are tips for "Sarajevo By Night" (don't go out) and on where to try the local "cuisine," which included such delicacies as boiled garden snails and soup made of leaves found in the park. It's no joke: people boiled and fried anything they could find for food.

They made their own cigarettes and alcohol and burned their books in makeshift (and very dangerous) apartment-sized wood stoves. In the "Going Out of Town" and "Excursions" sections of the guide, one can read about the dangerous crossing of the airport runway and learn how much it cost to bribe UNPROFOR soldiers to let you do it (between one hundred and two hundred German marks).

Most of the memos from UNPROFOR to New York published here come from MacKenzie's own files and are included in his book. My description of the Mitterand visit is a blend of the account in *Peacekeeper* and interviews with MacKenzie as well as newspaper accounts of the day.

Chapter 8: Major General Superstar

The anecdote of the lost letter comes from my interview with Sabina Izetbegovic. The president's daughter rarely gives interviews though she is considered a more reliable source of events in the Bosnian Presidency than her father, or the vice president, Ejup Ganic.

Both Lewis MacKenzie and Biljana Plavsic remember the final lunch on Jahorina mountain, but MacKenzie says it could not have been a farewell party since his departure had not yet been made public. But Bosnians and foreign journalists in Sarajevo say they knew long before the announcement that MacKenzie would be leaving. There were few secrets in Sarajevo, as MacKenzie eventually learned: if the Bosnians knew he was leaving by mid-July then the Serbs would have known as well. That's the best explanation for why Plavsic remembers the lunch as a going-away party.

MacKenzie's appearance before the congressional committee is somewhat unusual. The United Nations refused to allow Roméo Dallaire to testify before a different Washington committee a year later. Dallaire was a force commander of a peacekeeping mission and MacKenzie was only in charge of a sector of UNPRO-FOR, albeit the most controversial one. American congressional representatives bitterly complained of a double standard when Dallaire, who wanted to speak, was told not to. Clearly it was unusual for MacKenzie to appear before the committee; it required the American president to call the Canadian prime minister in order to get permission.

Lewis MacKenzie's documentary, based on his book, is called *A Soldier's Peace*. His interview with Radovan Karadzic is not part of the documentary. When Izetbegovic and the Bosnian government refused to take part in the program, the producers decided it would be unfair to feature only Karadzic. The interview has never been released.

CHAPTER 9: LIFT AND STRIKE

In 1994 and 1995, the U.S. Congress was involved in an intense debate over the issue of Bosnia's right to self defence. Public relations experts representing Bosnian interests in the U.S. argued that the arms embargo broached the country's legal right to bear arms to defend itself. But a powerful lobby that supported Serbian nationalist interests developed in the 1990s and attempted to exert influence on members of Congress (and also, to a lesser degree, in Canadian political circles). Brad Blitz, a doctoral candidate at Stanford University at the time, launched an investigation into the Serbian influence in Washington and published a number of detailed and documented essays on the lobby. Helen Bentley's group, SerbNet— according to Blitz—was the most active. SerbNet argued that any support for the Bosnian claim to self defence was designed "to promote German/Turkish influence in the Balkans and thereby, extinguish the Serbian people and the Serbian Orthodox Church." SerbNet revisionism on all events during the war was often breathtaking and is well-documented in Blitz's essay: "Serbia's War Lobby: Diaspora and Western Elites" published in *This Time We Knew: Western Responses to Genocide in Bosnia*. Blitz uses congressional records to show which congressmen and representatives received funding from Serbian groups or from Greek organizations who were supporting the Serbian nationalist position.

Revisionism plays a large role in post-war coverage and is often sophisticated enough to make Holocaust deniers look like amateurs. There has been a curious marriage between Serbian ultra-nationalists and left-wing ideologues. The most stunning offspring of this marriage was an article published by *Living Marxism* magazine that declared that the POW camps in northwest Bosnia were nothing of the kind and that Western media conspired with the Muslims to craft an elaborate hoax. According to the magazine, videotape of emaciated Muslims in camps, broadcast by ITN TV in Britain, was false and what the tape really depicted were hungry refugees in a transit camp awaiting their turn to freely depart.

In a rare move against such a small publication, the media organizations accused of this fabrication took *Living Marxism* to court and successfully sued. The magazine was forced to pay £375,000 in damages and newspapers who picked up on the erroneous story published abject apologies. The successful plaintiffs said they had pursued the magazine so aggressively because they regarded the blatant distortion in the story as patently dangerous.

Roy Gutman's exposés on UNPROFOR and MacKenzie's involvement with SerbNet are published in his book *A Witness to Genocide*. I also interviewed Gutman about his research. Lewis MacKenzie says he has lost somewhere in the area of US$100,000 in potential revenue since the Gutman article because he has turned down dozens of speaking engagements for fear of provoking similar stories. Serbian nationalist organizations all over the U.S. regularly attempt to book MacKenzie, he says, and sometimes use false names when they approach him since they know of his policy to avoid such appearances.

Chapter 10: An Officer and a Gentleman

The story of this chapter is based on interviews with Roy Gutman and his reporting, and my own interviews with prosecutor Mustafa Bisic, survivors of the Kod Sonje concentration camp, and reports on the rape camps of Bosnia. The commission of experts has an appendix devoted to sex crimes and mentions in its report that Herak saw MacKenzie at Kod Sonje.

Witness testimonies come from a book called *I Begged Them to Kill Me: Crimes against Women in Bosnia and Herzegovina* published in Bosnia by the Centre for Investigation and Documentation of the Association of Former Camp Internees of Bosnia and Herzegovina. It is not yet available in English.

BOOK THREE   THE BLASTED HEATH

Sources are interviews, on-the-ground reporting and the big picture texts and documents already mentioned in these notes.

BOOK FOUR   THE EAGLE

There are few books on the war crimes tribunals, and very little of the background story of the two courts is on the record. I relied on primary sources and background briefings not-for-attribution in this section more than in any other section of this book. In particular, the Rwandan tribunal has been dismally under-reported.

I conducted extensive interviews with people in the prosecutor's offices in both The Hague and Arusha, with defence lawyers at ICTR and ICTY, with people at the UN and the State Department; I used letters, documents and transcripts from the courts extensively.

As with all original accounts of historical events, I often found disagreement among the principal players as to how things had transpired. I have indicated in these notes where there were disputes among them over the course of events; I chose to tell the versions that seem to have the most consensus and where the information fit with other parts of the story. This is, as they say in the news business, a first draft of history. I await with enthusiasm future accounts of these extra-

ordinary events, which will add new insights and perhaps even contradict what I
have written here.

Chapter 1: In the Shadow of Nuremberg

Interviews with former State Department lawyer Michael Scharf, with Cherif
Bassiouni, chairman of the Commission of Experts, and with Bill Fenrick, former
member of the Commission of Experts and now with the prosecutor's office at
The Hague are the basis of this chapter. They are supported by interviews with
former and current State Department employees who do not wish to be named.
There is a dearth of books on the tribunals and Scharf has written one of the first,
Balkan Justice, an excellent account of the early days of the Yugoslavian tribunal
and a description of the origins of the tribunal's jurisprudence. Scharf also co-
wrote with Virginia Morris *An Insider's Guide to the Criminal Tribunal for the Former
Yugoslavia*, an exhaustive two-volume scholarly text. It's an excellent source of tribunal documents and information on laws and precedents.

Scharf was with Lawrence Eagleburger before his "naming names" speech
and Scharf says that though the speech appeared spontaneous, it was the product
of hours of planning and prepping in an effort to choose the right wording. Eagleburger was careful to say that the ten people were suspects who should be investigated and not suspects who should be immediately incarcerated.

Richard Goldstone described his hiring during my interviews with him, but
has since published his own book on the early days of the tribunals, a slim, highly
readable volume called *For Humanity: Reflections of a War Crimes Investigator*.

Documents, testimonies and the rulings on the Dusan Tadic trial run into the
thousands of pages. Critics of the ICTY say that the Tadic trial went on far too
long, but Dutch radio journalist Heikelina Stuart, one of the few people to cover
the proceedings almost daily, believes that the Tadic trial was extremely useful in
that it produced the first clear, factual and documented account of how the POW
camps worked and how the paramilitaries went about their brutal business.

Dr. Borko Djordjevic, a plastic surgeon from Montenegro, now practising in
Los Angeles (though he keeps a clinic in Montenegro), has known Karadzic for
years and stays in touch with him. Djordjevic was an excellent source of information for names and events concerning Karadzic. He arranged for Jimmy Carter to
meet with Karadzic during the war in an effort to find a way out of the prolonged
conflict. The former president and Karadzic spent a few days talking, drinking
and negotiating in Pale (Karadzic even entertained Carter by singing Montenegrin
folk songs) and Carter was subsequently able to arrange a short-lived ceasefire. Dr.
Djordjevic also helped to arrange legal counsel for his fugitive friend.

CHAPTER 2: EDUCATION OF A CONVENT GIRL

This chapter is based on material from a series of interviews with Louise Arbour starting in February 1997. Information from Arbour is supplemented by interviews with her friends and colleagues. Ambassador Bob Fowler gave first-hand accounts of what transpired between the Canadian mission to the UN and the Security Council members. Though Madeleine Albright and Boutros Boutros-Ghali declined to be interviewed, a number of State Department and UN insiders gave numerous tips and supporting information.

I took my description of the Finta and rape shield (*Seaboyer v. the Crown*) cases from court documents, newspaper accounts and interviews with representatives of the Jewish National Congress, Calgary law professor Catherine Mahoney and the Canadian Civil Liberties Association.

I spoke with three journalists who recall being told in interviews with their own sources the story of Louise Arbour's supposed affair with Richard Goldstone, though none of the journalists pursued the matter any further.

The Prison for Women Inquiry that Arbour conducted was the direct result of a report aired on *the fifth estate*, which showed the prison guards' own videotape of the strip search. The notorious Prison for Women shut its doors for good in May 2000.

There is a lively debate in Washington circles over who were the true champions of the tribunals and who prevented them from meeting an untimely death. There are those who maintain that officials in the State Department were the movers and shakers while others claim the principal force was the very vocal and well-informed NGOs, some staffed by former employees of the State Department. In my view, it was undoubtedly them both. Both camps seek to minimize the influence of Madeleine Albright, claiming that her championing of the courts was more from political expediency than from moral conviction. No matter the motivation, it seems doubtful that the ICTY and the ICTR would have survived without such a powerful supporter.

CHAPTER 3: CULTURE OF IMPUNITY

The Balkan wars of 1912 and 1913 were fought for territory ceded by the crumbling Ottoman empire. Serbia won both wars but the heightened nationalism brought on by the conflicts was a principal cause of the First World War.

I produced two documentaries for the CBC's *The National Magazine* on the Yugoslavian tribunal and was able to broadcast some of the first pictures of the inside of the court and its vault of evidence. I used that material to write parts of this chapter.

Human Rights Watch and Amnesty International are two of the many organizations that exposed both NATO's and the UN's lack of political will to make arrests. They were among a group of NGOs that attempted to shame the international community into taking action against the indicted war criminals.

Milan Kovacevic met with a number of foreign reporters, including Peter Maas and Roy Gutman, who wrote descriptions of this gatekeeper of Omarska and who reported on Kovacevic's surreal policy of forcing journalists to watch propaganda films before they could see the camps. *The New York Times Magazine* reported on Kovacevic's condition just before he was finally arrested, indicating that he was listless, moody and feeling somewhat repentant even as he enjoyed the spoils of war.

Human Rights Watch published a lengthy report on the wealth and power the warlords of Bosnia continued to enjoy long after the war was over. Travelling in Republika Srpska in 1998, I found that the warlords were still running municipal government and controlling nearly all commerce. When you buy gas, stay at a hotel or dine in a restaurant, chances are good that a former paramilitary is your host.

The Foca case is one of the most alarming and heinous examples of rape as a weapon of war, emblematic of the moral decay of the paramilitaries. Teenaged girls were not only raped but forced to run naked through the streets as part of their humiliation. Muslim women were impregnated by their Serb captors and then incarcerated for the duration of the pregnancy to prevent them from aborting. Two of the men charged with running the rape camp pleaded not guilty in an ICTY courtroom in late 1999. Their lawyers have argued that, while there may have been acts of sexual assault (dozens of women had already testified to that effect), the defendants were not guilty of war crimes.

CHAPTER 4: LE COUSIN PAUVRE

Barbara Crosette of *The New York Times* was the first to report on alleged corruption at the ICTR. Karl Paschke filed an immensely detailed account of the ICTR excesses and shortcomings with the Office of Internal Oversight at the United Nations; and most of my description of what was wrong with the tribunal is from that report. My account is supplemented by interviews with people who witnessed the excesses, though no one, including Paschke, could prove that there had been any criminal activity.

There are very few accounts of Operation Naki. This description is based on interviews with a half dozen of the people directly involved in the arrest sweep.

Of great assistance overall is the witty and colourful reporting of *Ubutebera* — the ICTR's independent newsletter, published with funding from the French company Intermedia. In addition, *Ubutebera*'s editor-in-chief, Thierry Cruvellier, helped Sian Cansfield and myself steer a course through the troubled waters of the tribunal and figure out which parts of the rumour and innuendo that swirl around the ICTR have any real significance for the proceedings.

The case of Esdres Twagirimana was somewhat complicated by the fact that the young man did not want to leave the ICTR after he had been arrested. He had no place to go and feared being shipped back to Rwanda. Amnesty International took up his case, but the controversy surrounding Twagirimana's arrest was certainly fueled by the ICTR's defence lawyers who were growing increasingly frustrated with the tribunal's registrar. They saw the young man's case as an excellent opportunity to expose the excesses of the ICTR. Why Twagirimana was given $1,500 (and by whom) is not clear. I was given various explanations. It seems to have been a kind of informal out-of-court settlement for damages.

Descriptions of the Matticks affair I took from Quebec newspaper accounts of the investigation into police malpractice and the subsequent inquiries. Some of the proceedings of the Poitras Commission are posted on the Government of Quebec's Web site. It is highly unlikely that Duclos's past would have become known to media covering the ICTR if not for the fact that Tiphaine Dickson happened to have been working there at the same time. There is no public record that Duclos was the one to conduct most of the interviews with Jean Kambanda, but those who have seen the interview tapes and transcripts say there are name references throughout that indicate it was Duclos doing interrogations.

There is no public record that Kambanda was taken to Shevenegen prison in The Hague. This comes from sources who wished not to be named.

Chapter 5: Justice Delayed
The account of the trial of Jean-Paul Akayesu comes from *Ubutebera* reports, trial transcripts and news wire stories.

Debate over the issue of rape as a crime of war is one of the most contentious within tribunal circles. Reports of rape gangs and enforced pregnancies as a method of ethnic cleansing were among the most sensational in the first years of the Bosnian war and galvanized public opinion in Western countries. Women's groups put considerable pressure on governments to take action, and it was the accounts of sexual abuse and gender crimes, perhaps more than any other issue, that forced the hand of those who resisted the war crimes tribunal. There is not a lot of literature about the rape investigations and the witnesses are under considerable pressure not to tell their stories to the media so as to keep their testimony uncorrupted. The Centre for Investigation and Documentation of the Association of Former Camp Internees of Bosnia and Herzegovina has published two volumes of testimonies, one of which is devoted to rape victims. Neither volume is yet translated into English (as of this writing) though the association says it plans to issue English versions. I had parts of the publications translated for inclusion in this book.

African Rights has collated one of the best collection of testimonies from Rwanda in its thousand-page report *Rwanda: Death, Despair and Defiance*. For particularly macabre testimonies of gender crime victims where women are also the culprits, one should read *Not So Innocent: When Women Become Killers*, also by African Rights.

Robert Gersony of the UNHCR was part of a three-person team sent to post-genocide Rwanda to investigate how refugees might be repatriated more efficiently. What Gersony discovered, according to confidential documents obtained by Human Rights Watch, was that the RPF was involved in "clearly systematic murders and persecution of the Hutu population in certain parts of the country." According to HRW, the UN suppressed this information so as not to disrupt the peace process and the UNAMIR II mission. When individuals inquired after the Gersony findings, including officials who had a right to know, the UNHCR declared that "*le Rapport Gersony n'existe pas*," according to a letter published by HRW in its book *Leave None to Tell the Story*.

The description of the Rwandan indigenous legal system is from interviews with officials in CIDA, the Canadian aid agency that helped fund the new judiciary, and with William Schabas, who played a key role in the set-up of the court system. Schabas disagrees with my characterization of the first trials as being "near hysteria"—he maintains the entire process was born in an atmosphere of calm. But news reports in *Harper's* and *The New York Times Magazine* and interviews with journalists who covered the early legal system, persuaded me that Rwandans were at first quite panicky about the justice system.

I also made use of reports and conversations with Yvan Patrie who filmed extensively in the prison system and who also investigated the reprisal killings on the part of the RPF. Patrie co-produced, with the CBC, a series of stories on the murder of a Canadian priest, presumably by the RPF. Patrie suffered from acute diabetes and risked his health each time he travelled and worked in Rwanda. Before he died last year, he urged Louise Arbour to leave, as her legacy as war crimes prosecutor, the first indictments of RPF leaders. It never happened.

Bernard Muna's comments about rape not being a priority for the ICTR came from an interview conducted by my researcher, Sian Cansfield.

CHAPTER 6: IN THE FIELD OF BLACK BIRDS

Descriptions of Kosovo and the condition of the Albanians came from my own travels in the region. For the history of Kosovo and the development of the KLA, I relied on Noel Malcolm's book *A Brief History of Kosovo*. Malcolm is also the author of *A Brief History of Bosnia* and it should be noted that neither volume is brief. Critics say Malcolm is wrong to suggest that the peoples of Yugoslavia were getting along just fine before Milosevic began his campaign for Greater Serbia. Serb ultra-nationalists claim that the ethnic tensions between the different groups were so powerful that it was historically inevitable that they would eventually come to war. Malcolm argues that such an inevitability is true of many countries but it takes leaders and instigators to turn ethnic division into armed conflict and pre-planned ethnic cleansing. Anyone who has read this book will realize that I share that view.

Other historic sources I used for background here are John Lampe's book, *Yugoslavia as History: Twice There Was a Country*, and Mark Almond's fascinating — and angry — account of Western ineptitude in regard to Yugoslavia, *Europe's Back Yard War*.

There are numerous profiles of Slobodan Milosevic and his wife, on which I relied. A good brief biography of all the players in the Yugoslav drama can be found in *The Death of Yugoslavia*.

Vojeslev Seselj's outrageous solution for the "Albanian problem" is published by the Helsinki Committee for Human Rights in Serbia. The Helsinki Committee has also reproduced, in books and pamphlets, the various news reports that were published to incite ethnic hatred throughout Yugoslavia as well as excerpts from an ultra-nationalist document by the Serbian Academy of Arts and Sciences, considered the inspiration for Greater Serbia.

Despite the brutal suppression of dissent in what's left of Yugoslavia, a number of human rights activists continue to do their work at great personal risk. I interviewed two of the most celebrated women in the struggle for human rights in Belgrade, Sonja Biserko of Helsinki Watch and Natasa Kandic of the Humanitarian Law Centre, both of whom gave me material for this chapter.

The description of how the Milosevic indictment came to pass comes from interviews with Louise Arbour, James Stewart, representatives from NATO, the American State Department and from newspaper accounts. For an excellent description of Wesley Clark's personal role in the bombing of Serbia, see Michael Ignatieff's article on Clark in *The New Yorker* magazine, August 2, 1999.

INDEX

Abbreviations

ICTR   International Criminal Tribunal for Rwanda
ICTY   International Criminal Tribunal for the former Yugoslavia
UNAMIR   United Nations Assistance Mission in Rwanda
UNPROFOR   United Nations Protection Force

PEOPLES' NAMES

and DND, 177, 195, 210
criticized by people of Dobrinja, 182
death threats against, 5, 182, 196, 199, 211
early life and military career, 137–38
and foreign media during mission, 141, 187–89, 194–95
influence on UN, 208–9
——— U.S. policy on Bosnia, 200–4, 214–17
and Izetbegovic and Muslim leadership, 157, 195–96
and Karadzic, 170–71, 186, 187, 195
and kidnapping and rescue of Izetbegovic, 150–51, 153–60
and Kod Sonje allegations, 226–34
and local media during mission, 139, 183–85, 194–95, 197–98
and media following return to Canada, 89, 193, 201–5, 210, 213–18
and bombing of Belgrade, 238
on individual peace-keepers as more important than the mission, 108
on intervention, 201–4
on NATO bombing of Serbia and Kosovo, 236, 237
on prisoner-of-war camps in Bosnia, 205–6
on Srebrenica massacre, 220
on war atrocities in Bosnia, 213–14
and Milosevic, 139, 236–38
peacekeeping mission compared to that of Dallaire in Rwanda, 238
promotes partition of former Yugoslavia, 214–15
and propaganda, 166, 207, 213, 214, 216–18, 228
publishes memoirs, 210

and removal from Bosnia, 8, 196, 198
rescues Izetbegovic, 144–45, 147–51, 216
retires early from military (1993), 210, 214
and UN, 138–39, 176–77, 181, 186, 192, 193, 196–200, 214, 225–34
Maggen, Major Petrus, 54, 106–7
Major, John, 263
Mandela, Nelson, 268, 275, 290
Mandela, Winnie, 268
Marchal, Colonel Luc
and Bagosora, 48–50
and Belgium's senate inquiry into failure of UNAMIR, 105–12
court martial of, 102–5, 107
and Dallaire, 36, 41–42, 48–50, 52–54, 56, 61–63
interviews informant Jean-Pierre, 41–42
and massacre at the École Technique Officielle, 61–63
Markovic, Mirjana, 340
Martic, Milan, 297
Medvene, Edward, 273
Milosevic, Slobodan
and Arbour, 345–46, 349–53
and Bentley and SerbNet, 214
and Dayton Peace Accords, 222, 297, 303
Eagleburger recommends investigation of for war crimes, 263–64
and ICTY, 274, 286, 309, 311, 332, 338, 339, 356, 357
indicted by ICTY, 350–53
issues press releases on atrocities, 163–64
and Karadzic, 130–31, 133, 140, 174, 208, 256, 297
and Kosovo Albanians, 237, 340–49
and MacKenzie, 139, 237
and Major government (U.K.), 263–64, 304

and Mladic, 155, 174, 256
NATO bombs strongholds of, 303
Serbs of Belgrade protest leadership of, 299
and Tudjman plan to divide Bosnia, 131
and United States, 346
vision of an ethnic Serbia, 125–26, 128, 131, 342
and Yugoslav National Army, 135–36, 140
Milutinovic, Milan, 352
Mitterand, François, 46, 73, 79, 187–90, 347
Mladic, Ana, 256
Mladic, General Ratko
Arbour pushes to arrest, 294, 310, 311–12, 347
and breadline massacre, 166, 169, 207
Clinton considers assassination of, 308–9
after Dayton accords, 256, 295
Eagleburger recommends investigation of for war crimes, 263
expects American air strikes, 192
and ICTY, 212, 270, 272, 357
and Karadzic, 169, 188, 263, 267
and MacKenzie, 168
and Milosevic, 155, 174, 256
meets Mitterand, 188–89
and partition, 222
and Srebrenica, 218–20
U.S. pushes for amnesty for, 274
Mme Agathe. See Uwilingiyimana, Agathe
Mohommad, Shaharyar Khan, 112
Moi, Daniel Arap, 319
Morillon, General Philippe, 219–20
Morrisette, Gilbert, 319
Mugesera, Léon, 16, 18, 19, 249, 330
Mujezinovic, Ejub, 179–80, 181